C. S. LEWIS

Life, Works, and Legacy

C. S. LEWIS

Life, Works, and Legacy

Volume 2: Fantasist, Mythmaker, and Poet

Edited by
Bruce L. Edwards

PRAEGER PERSPECTIVES

Westport, Connecticut
London

Library of Congress Cataloging-in-Publication Data

C.S. Lewis : life, works, and legacy / edited by Bruce L. Edwards.
    p. cm.
    Includes bibliographical references and index.
    ISBN 0–275–99116–4 (set : alk. paper)—ISBN 0–275–99117–2 (v. 1 : alk.
paper)—ISBN 0–275–99118–0 (v. 2 : alk. paper)—ISBN 0–275–99119–9 (v. 3 : alk.
paper)—ISBN 0–275–99120–2 (v. 4 : alk. paper)
    1. Lewis, C. S. (Clive Staples), 1898–1963—Criticism and interpretation.   I. Edwards,
Bruce L.
  PR6023.E926Z597   2007
  823′.912–dc22   2006100486

British Library Cataloguing in Publication Data is available.

Library of Congress Catalog Card Number: 2006100486
ISBN-10: 0–275–99116–4 (set)   ISBN-13: 978–0–275–99116–6
               0–275–99117–2 (Vol. 1)   978–0–275–99117–3
               0–275–99118–0 (Vol. 2)   978–0–275–99118–0
               0–275–99119–9 (Vol. 3)   978–0–275–99119–7
               0–275–99120–2 (Vol. 4)   978–0–275–99120–3

First published in 2007

Praeger Publishers, 88 Post Road West, Westport, CT 06881
An imprint of Greenwood Publishing Group, Inc.
www.praeger.com

Printed in the United States of America

This work is dedicated to my son,

Justin Robert Edwards.

Justin's passion for life and for the life to come,
his creativity and excellence in music and movie-making,
his faith and resilience in the face of this world's challenges,
all inspire and amaze me,
and bless everyone who knows him.

Contents

Acknowledgments

The genesis of this four-volume reference set is the kind invitation I received from Suzanne Staszak-Silva of Greenwood Publishing Group in late Spring, 2005, asking me to consider creating a reference work that would comprehensively deal with the life and work of C. S. Lewis. As it was the case that I was almost literally heading out the door to Tanzania on a Fulbright-Hays Grant, we did not get to consider the project in much detail until the end of the summer when, with the help of my literary agent, Matt Jacobson, we cheerfully exchanged ideas with Suzanne that have led to the expansive volumes you now hold in your hands. Suzanne and all the capable editors and reviewers at Greenwood have been terrific to work with, and I am once again grateful to Matt Jacobson of the Loyal Arts Literary Agency for his expertise and wise counsel.

No project of this kind can, in fact, come to fruition without the help of many hands. I want to start with the contributors to this volume and the breadth and depth of C. S. Lewis scholarship they represent. Each of them, especially those contributing more than one essay, have cheerfully met my prescribed deadlines and offered both incisive and learned commentary on the topics for which they were chosen. I want to offer special thanks to busy and illustrious Lewisian colleagues and scholars, David Downing, Diana Glyer, David Bratman, Don King, Marvin Hinten, Lyle Dorsett, Colin Duriez, Victor Reppert, Devin Brown, Wayne Martindale, and Marjorie Lamp Mead, for making and taking the time to contribute their unique vantage points to this collection. Their knowledge of the Lewis canon continues to provide us with fresh insights into his legacy. The exciting thing about this particular collection, however, is not only the opportunity to recruit the already renowned scholars listed above, but also to attract new talent and younger scholars who bring their own generational insights into the issues and contexts many of us have been sifting for years.

Walter Hooper has been unfailingly kind in his support of this project, helping me arrange access to some special collections at the Bodleian Library at Oxford University. Of course, Lewis scholars everywhere are in his debt for decades of indefatigable efforts to make the letters and papers of C. S. Lewis available to the public. Likewise, Christopher Mitchell, Director, and his staff, at the Marion C. Wade Center at Wheaton College in Wheaton, Illinois, continue to operate the most outstanding resource center on C. S. Lewis and the Inklings in North America. I treasure every moment I get to spend in the beautiful Wade Center's hallowed library.

Scott Calhoun, a longtime colleague and friend from Cedarville University, Ohio, answered my call for some late counsel on the disposition of the last several essays to be included for publication, and I will always be grateful for his graceful editorial touches. (The only thing missing in this collection is an essay that I am sure Scott wishes to compose on the influence of Lewis's work on U2's Bono. Maybe next time, Scott?)

My colleagues at Bowling Green State University, especially my immediate supervisors, continue to be generous in support of my research and lecturing on C. S. Lewis. They have provided me with the writing time one needs to produce a set of volumes of this magnitude. Dr. William K. Balzer, Dean of Continuing and Extended Education and Associate Vice-President, along with Dr. Linda Dobb, Executive Vice-President, made possible a Spring 2006 trip to the Bodleian Library, Oxford, England, and a presentation at the "C. S. Lewis, Renaissance Man" Conference at Cambridge University that significantly affected the scope and accuracy of this work. My own staff headed by Ms. Connie Molnar, Director of Distance Education at Bowling Green State University, has indirectly made possible the efforts herein reflected, since their diligence and professionalism allowed me the freedom at crucial moments during the project to travel for research or to siphon off time for its final editing.

Finally, while we were completing the last stages of this volume, my wife Joan and I were trying to finish the building of a new home. As anyone who has ever tried such a foolish and audacious thing can testify, it can make for some tense (and intense) hours. Joan has been her usual patient, kind, and thoughtful self in shouldering the burden for all sorts of decisions and contingency planning for the house, liberating me to read, write, edit, and email incessantly. In the end, her contribution to this four-volume set is equal to any I can claim. These volumes are for the "Keeping Room" shelves, Sweetie. Enjoy them!

Since I have never left them out of any book I have published, I will not become inconsistent or ungrateful now. My children, Matthew, Tracey, Mary, Casey, Justin, and Michael always inspire me to reach higher and perform at my best. Their love and encouragement make all the difference on those dark and stormy nights when you wonder whether even one more word will come forth. Each of them is an artist or creator in their own right, with plenty of books (and songs and movies) of their own on the horizon. Michael specifically enhances this text further by contributing one of the most significant essays in Volume 4; I should have turned him loose on more topics! My father, Bruce L. Edwards, Sr., has always been steadfast in his support and encouragement for my work, and I sincerely thank him for continuing to take such good care of all of us. As does God Himself.

Preface

Scholars and admirers alike have long sought a full-fledged, balanced bio-critical treatment of the life and works of C. S. Lewis. They, rightly, seek a treatise that does justice to his remarkably successful, multiple careers as a Christian apologist, science fiction and fantasy writer, literary historian, poet, cultural critic, and historian of words. Such a book will be sympathetic without being sycophantic, incisive without being sensational, and comprehensive without being copious. It will illuminate his life and times, including his interesting friendships, his composing techniques, and, of course, his personal piety.

Above all, it will also help explain his enormous impact on contemporary Christianity, particularly in America, and it will set in appropriate historical context the important contribution his scholarship makes to literary culture and social and ethical discourse in philosophy and theology. Until such a book arrives, if it ever does, this current four-volume set will represent the most lucid, most dispassionate, well-informed, up-to-date, and comprehensive treatment of Lewis's life, times, and legacy to have so far been produced, exemplifying the highest standards of historical research and employing the most responsible tools of interpretation.

It has been too typical of the variety of biographies now available on Lewis for their authors to range between two extremes: (1) works furtively focused on certain presumed negative personality traits and ambiguous relationships and incidents that obscure rather than illuminate Lewis's faith and scholarship; or (2) works so enamored of Lewis that their work borders on or exceeds hagiography and offers page after page of redundant paraphrase of his putatively unique insights. The former, despite their protestations that they operate out of an objectivity missing in other treatments, or out of a respect and a healthy admiration for Lewis's "literary accomplishments," tend to be transparently premised on a rather tendentious amateur psychoanalysis and often programmatically dismiss Lewis's readership in order to discredit his literary and theological judgments. The latter evince the effects of the worshipful homage, exhausting readers and convincing them that Lewis is readily reducible to a few doctrines, a few genres, and, perhaps, a few penchants. Even so, enough of Lewis's enumerable strengths usually emerge even from these biographies to reward the Lewisian enthusiast or skeptical inquirer hungry for more informed assessment of his achievements, and his continuing impact.

It is the case, nevertheless, that the underlying theme of recent works, and among them I include biographies written by Britain's A. N. Wilson and Australia's Michael White, have been to "rescue" Lewis from the assumed cult of his evangelical idolaters, particularly in America. It is these folks who, Wilson, for one, avers in his 1991 study of Lewis, desire to create a Lewis in their own image, one they can promote as a "virginal, Bible-toting, nonsmoking, lemonade-drinking champion for Christ." But such a stance reflects a surprising naiveté about Lewis's American readership and barely disguises its contempt for the esteem accorded Lewis's scholarship, fiction, and apologetics in many diverse circles.

One aim of this present reference work is thus to correct such stereotypes of both Lewis and his readership. To accomplish this, and many more worthy goals, one must offer a thorough-going, well-researched, yet also theologically sensitive treatment of Lewis's life and times that takes into consideration not only his tumultuous upbringing but also his mature development, his successes and failures, his blind spots and prescience, his trek into and impact on both "Jerusalem and Athens" (i.e., religion and philosophy), and, the essential perspective discerning readers need to understand the key people and relationships in his life.

Consequently, assembled for this volume are contributions from the finest C. S. Lewis scholars from North America and Europe. Their essays, one and all, have been solicited to be expansive, comprehensive, informed, and self-contained prose works that contextualize each respective topic historically and deliver expository clarity to its reader. As one considers the table of contents, he or she will realize that the essays fall into four volumes slated to emphasize four distinctive areas of Lewis's life and work.

Volume 1, *C. S. Lewis: An Examined Life*, is explicitly biographical in its orientation and scope. Lewis's early life, collegiate days, military service, friendships, achievements, and ongoing impact are set in historical context, starting from his Belfast birth in 1898 to his auspicious death on November 22, 1963, the day U.S. President John Kennedy was assassinated. New essays illuminate his relationships with J. R. R. Tolkien, Owen Barfield, and his beloved wife, Joy Davidman Gresham. Volume 2, *C. S. Lewis: Fantasist, Mythmaker, and Poet*, focuses on Lewis's imaginative writing, foregrounding his achievements in fiction and poetry as one dimension of his notoriety and popularity worldwide. The provenance of his works and their significance in his times and ours are explored and defined capably. Volume 3, *C. S. Lewis: Apologist, Philosopher, and Theologian*, draws attention to the celebrity Lewis received as a Christian thinker in his radio broadcasts and subsequent renown as a defender and translator of the Christian faith among skeptics and believers alike in postwar Britain and abroad. His well-known works such as *Mere Christianity*, *Miracles*, and *Letters to Malcolm* are given close readings and careful explication. Finally, in Volume 4, *C. S. Lewis: Scholar, Teacher, and Public Intellectual*, Lewis's lesser known vocations and publications are given careful consideration and examined for the models they may provide contemporary readers and academics for responsible scholarship. This set of essays helps assess Lewis's ongoing legacy and offers an extensive annotated bibliography of secondary sources that can guide the apprentice scholar to worthy works that will further assist him or her in extending the insights this collection presents.

Within each volume, essays fall into one of three distinct categories: (1) historical, fact-based treatment of eras, events, and personages in Lewis's life; (2) expository and literary analysis of major Lewis works of imaginative literature, literary scholarship, and apologetics; (3) global essays that seek to introduce, elucidate, and unfold the connections between and among the genres, vocations, and respective receptions elicited by Lewis in his varied career.

In my original invitation letter, each essayist was told to trust his or her instincts as a scholar, and thus to be empowered to write the essay from the unique vantage point they represent from inside their discipline. Generally speaking, each kind of essay was thus written to accomplish the following:

- The *historical essays* begin with a well-documented overview of their topic, foreshadowing the era, events, personages, etc., then proceed to a chronological treatment of the particulars, interspersed with connections, informed interpretations, contextualizations that illuminate the specific era covered as well as illuminating their relationships to other historical circumstances, publications, etc. When readers finish the essay, they should have at hand all the essential facts, accurately and chronologically marshaled, with a confident sense of the significance of this period, era, or relationship for Lewis's life and work.

- *Exposition and analysis essays* focus on single works in the Lewis canon and offer the reader a comprehensive overview of the work, including coverage of its origins and place in Lewis's life and times, its historical meaning and contemporary significance, its reception among readers, scholars, academics, critics, and a reflective judgment on its enduring influence or impact. The readers of these essays will come away with a profound grasp of the value and impact of the work in itself and the reputation it creates. In cases where there may exist a range of opinions about or competing interpretations of the meaning or value of a work, the essayist articulates the varying points of view, weighing their cogency, and offering the reader an informed perspective.

- *Global essays* provide an introductory, broad contextual sweep of coverage over the main themes of an individual volume's topic areas, one per volume, focusing on the four divisions enunciated for the project.

My general exhortation to all contributors was that they try as much as it is within their power to emulate C. S. Lewis in style and substance, practicing the kind of empathetic dialogue with the subject matter that is characteristic of his own prose and poetry—as he saw it: "Plenty of fact, reasoning as brief and clear as English sunshine . . ." No easy task! But I am pleased to say that each essay does its job well—and, in my view, Lewis would not be displeased.

I want to make the distinction as clear as possible between the four volumes published here and the typical "companion to" or "encyclopedia of" approach found in other treatments of Lewis's life and work. We have not created a set of "nominalist" texts that focus on so many particulars that the "whole" is lost in the "parts." Ours is not a "flip-through" set of texts in which "key words" drive the construction of essays and the experience of the reader—but one that features holistic essays that engross and educate earnest readers seeking an inclusive view of the essay's topic area. While we enforced some general consistency of length and depth of coverage, there is no "false objectivity" or uniformity of prose style to be imposed.

No, by contrast, these essays are meant to have "personality," and serve as "stand-alone" essays that reflect an invested, personal scholarship and whose learned opinion is based on deep acquaintance with their subject matter. As independent Lewis scholars, it is important that all were granted the freedom to interpret responsibly and offer informed judgments about value, effectiveness, and significance of components of his life, times, and works, and to follow the scholarly instincts and unique insights wherever they may have led. It may be that here and there two essays will cross boundaries, and offer a different point of view on a shared topic. This is to be expected, and is not to be discouraged. Where there are controversial topics in Lewis scholarship, the task at hand was to "referee" the debate, explain the options, and gently lead us to the conclusions, if any, that best fit the facts.

The bibliography for each essay is intended to be as current as possible as we reached our publication deadline, and should reflect the span of scholarship that has emerged since Lewis's death in 1963. But, there is a major and comprehensive bibliographic essay on Lewis scholarship included in Volume 4, and we direct the reader's attention there. As in any reference set of this scope, there will be unavoidable overlap in coverage of events, people, theme, citation of works, etc., throughout the volumes, and I humbly submit this is one of its strengths.

Our contributors were attracted to this project because they saw that it offered C. S. Lewis scholars an opportunity to disseminate their work to a broader, popular audience and, consequently, offered them the potential to shape the ongoing public understanding of C. S. Lewis for a population of readers around the world for many decades. Those readers brought to C. S. Lewis through the increased visibility and popularity of *The Chronicles of Narnia*, will be especially enthused and rewarded by their sojourn in these pages.

Our common approach in writing and editing this set is "academic" in the sense that it relies on studies/research/corroborated knowledge and reflection on assigned topics, but it is also the case that we always kept our general audience in mind, avoiding as much as possible any insider jargon or technical language that tends to exclude general readers. (Of course, any well-founded disciplinary terms necessary to explain and/or exemplify the achievement of Lewis are introduced and explained in context.)

In the end, I am proud to say that our desire to present accurate and interesting information, wearing our scholarship firmly but lightly enough to invite entrance into fascinating, timely, and relevant subject matter about Lewis has been met. These essays were designed to reach, engage, and even enthrall educated and interested readers anxious to find out more about C. S. Lewis, including those who yet may not have any formal training in literary criticism or theology or apologetics per se. Indeed, these have always been Lewis's most appreciative and attentive readers, and we are most pleased to have joined him in welcoming you here.

Bruce L. Edwards

1

"Patches of Godlight": C. S. Lewis as Imaginative Writer

Bruce L. Edwards

Writers may not become what they are by nature, but they certainly do so by nurture. Childhood and adolescence seem in large measure to determine the destiny of those who become writers, and both what and how they write. The truism that the trials and tribulations, as well as the advantages and privileges (or lack thereof), shape the formative behind-the-scenes story of countless authors, certainly includes C. S. Lewis. But his story needs no elaborate recounting here—it is told, eloquently and poignantly, by Lewis himself in his book *Surprised by Joy*, and is explained and illuminated in the first volume of this reference set by several competent contributors. It simply needs to be observed that what Lewis read, beginning as a precocious three-year-old and on through to his boarding school and wartime experiences (long before he landed in Oxford for collegiate schooling) had a profound effect not only on the man he became, but also on his concept of the vocation of authorship. As Lewis explained in *Surprised by Joy*:

My father's house was filled with books. . . . I am a product of long corridors, empty sunlit rooms, upstairs indoor silences, attics explored in solitude, distant noises of gurgling cisterns and pipes, and the noise of wind under the tile. Also, of endless books.... Nothing was forbidden me. In the seemingly endless rainy afternoons I took volume after volume from the shelves.[1]

Throughout his young life, whether immersed in children's fiction like E. Nesbit's *The Amulet*, or Beatrix Potter's *Peter Rabbit*, or in poetry like Longfellow's *Saga of King Olaf*, the voracious reader Lewis became was alert to something more than just mundane plot details or poetic imagery—an intangible, numinous feeling pointing him beyond the natural and into the eternal. Myth and fairy tale ruled his imagination early on, and mediated this subtle but real transcendent touch. In addition, his deep friendship with his brother Warnie, whose penchant for creating miniature playsets, like the toy garden he invented for their mutual pleasure, gave Lewis his first encounter with a certain elusive feeling, which he first associated with autumn, and later with the calling of heaven.

These were what his beloved romantic poet, William Wordsworth, called "intimations of immortality," or, as Lewis put it liltingly toward the end of his life, "'patches of Godlight' in the woods of our experience."[2] There were no artificial compartments in Lewis's adult world—just as there were none during his early years; what he learned, cherished, embraced, rejected, refined, and championed—these find their way into everything he eventually wrote, prose or poetry, fiction or nonfiction. Authorship included, demanded some kind of uplink to the grand or grander narratives that help explain what it means to be human—and divine, whether created by myths or discovered through revelation. In recalling his conversion, Lewis directs his audience to the nineteenth-century Christian writer, George MacDonald, whose fantastic adventure, *Phantastes*, served as a corrective work that Lewis claims, in a memorable phrasing, "baptized his imagination." It led Lewis to glimpse for the first time since his childhood a pathway into the realm of the supernatural, something he later recognizes as "holiness." His famous summary statement of his journey to faith captures well the impact of his this text and others like them:

In reading Chesterton, as in reading MacDonald, I did not know what I was letting myself in for. A young man who wishes to remain a sound Atheist cannot be too careful of his reading. There are traps everywhere—"Bibles laid open, millions of surprises," as Herbert says, "fine nets and stratagems." God is, if I may say it, very unscrupulous.[3]

It should also be noted that what held the "Inklings"—the writing community shepherded by friends C. S. Lewis and J. R. R. Tolkien—together beyond their common erudition and overlapping religious worldviews was the fact that they were superb craftsman in matters in which they were rank amateurs and infectious enthusiasts. Not a single Inkling was a trained or credentialed creative writer (if there could be such a thing as credentials for becoming a chronicler of Middle-Earth or Malacandra!) but rather had "day jobs," which meant they would need to pursue their interests in imaginative writing as a hobby. As we know, Lewis did earn degrees in philosophy, as well as medieval and renaissance literature, but he confined neither his research nor his publication to these academic fields, prolific in them though he was. Rather, Lewis simultaneously maintained an active writing and publishing vocation in Christian apologetics, poetry, fantasy, science fiction, mythmaking, allegory, and the unique territory of "dream-vision" literature (inspired by writers as diverse as the Apostle John, Dante, St. Teresa of Avila, Coleridge, John Bunyan, and, again, George MacDonald).

The adult Lewis shared an affection (some of his Oxford and Cambridge colleagues might have jadedly called it a weakness) with colleague Tolkien for popular literature and popular genres. Rather than dismissing the common reader and his or her seemingly misplaced love for lower-echelon fantastical novels about "interplanetary travel" or "swords and sorcery," they embraced them, emulating and elevating these genres but also imbuing them with a complexity and a sophistication that ennobled their original practitioners (for example, Jules Verne or H. G. Wells) and those who read them.

A case in point is Lewis's well-known interest in Scottish writer, John Buchan, the early twentieth-century creator of both the imaginative "shocker," featuring wickedness in high places, elemental spirits, mysterious curses, ghosts and demons, all exemplifying the interpenetration of the modern world by the ancient and pagan; as well as the conspiracy or espionage "thriller" that reveals the thin layer of honesty, courage, and honor that upholds civilization and the rule of law, and how one brave man or woman can tip the scales toward decency, civility, and justice. It is the Buchan hero, someone like Richard Hannay of Buchan's *The Thirty-Nine Steps,* the ordinary fellow caught up in extraordinary circumstances, who inspires Lewis's own protagonist, Edwin Ransom in *Out of the Silent Planet,* and hero of the rest of the Space trilogy. (Without Buchan, it is safe to say, there would not have been an Ian Fleming, the creator of James Bond, and certainly no John le Carré, the master of the contemporary spy novel.)

SEEING WITH THE HEART

As his literary career evolved, Lewis wrote well-received works of science fiction, wise and sprightly volumes of Christian apologetics, and many learned tomes on medieval and renaissance literature, but his heart was always centered in myth and fairy-tale. His greatest triumph and most enduring works were destined to be his Narnian tales. Indeed, the question most people want to ask C. S. Lewis after they read *The Chronicles of Narnia* is well expressed by a young reader, Meredith, who wrote to him three years before his death in 1963, asking, "What inspired your books?" Lewis replied: "Really I don't know. Does anyone know where exactly an idea comes from? With me all fiction begins with pictures in my head. But where the pictures come from I couldn't say."[4] Ah, those pictures! When he explained the origins of Narnia, Lewis always pointed to these recurring images:

All my seven Narnian books, and my three science-fiction books, began with seeing pictures in my head. At first they were not a story, just pictures. They all began with a picture of a Faun carrying an umbrella and parcels in a snowy wood. This picture had been in my mind since I was about sixteen. Then one day, when I was about forty, I said to myself: "Let's try to make a story about it." At first I had very little idea how the story would go. But then suddenly Aslan came bounding into it. I think I had been having a good many dreams of lions about that time. Apart from that, I don't know where the Lion came from or why He came. But once He was there he pulled the whole story together, and soon He pulled the other six Narnian stories in after Him."[5]

One doubts it can be put more simply or eloquently than that. Aslan pulled the stories together—and Lewis himself—into Narnia. And that is probably as good a description as any of what happens to us when we enter the wardrobe. Aslan pulls us in, and we keep seeing pictures in our head. How intriguing to witness the intrepid Lucy and the irreverent Edmund stumbling into the chill and wonder of wintry Narnia, meeting up with such contrasting Narnian characters. How interesting that it is Mr. Tumnus, the faun with the umbrella and parcels, whom Lucy first sees, and that it is the wicked white witch who is waiting to greet Edmund. How different their respective reactions are to hearing that "Aslan is on the move"!

But none of this should surprise us too much. The emphasis in Lewis's fiction (and nonfiction) is always "seeing with the heart," of apprehending images and tracing metaphors that instill faith and inspire journeys into the never-never land of the spirit. For the heart reveals our true character, and, ultimately, where our treasure is. And the perfect genre for hosting such stories and themes is the fairy-tale. Tolkien himself made explicit the connection between how fairy-tales touch the soul and how the Gospel account of the incarnation embodies "true history" in a fascinating lecture called "On Fairy-Stories":

The Gospels contain a fairy-story, or a story of a larger kind which embraces all the essence of fairy-stories. They contain many marvels—peculiarly artistic, beautiful, and moving: "mythical" in their perfect, self-contained significance; and at the same time powerfully symbolic and allegorical; and among the marvels, the greatest and most complete conceivable eucatastrophe. The Birth of Christ is the eucatastrophe of Man's history. The Resurrection is the eucatastrophe of the story of the Incarnation. This story begins and ends in joy. It has preeminently the "inner consistency of reality." There is no tale ever told that men would rather find was true, and none which so many sceptical men have accepted as true on its own merits. For the Art of it has the supremely convincing tone of Primary Art, that is, of Creation. To reject it leads either to sadness or to wrath. It is not difficult to imagine the peculiar excitement and joy, that one would feel, if any specially beautiful fairy-story were found to be "primarily" true, its narrative to be history, without thereby necessarily losing the mythical or allegorical significance that it had possessed. . . . Because this story is supreme; and it is true, Art has been verified. God is the Lord, of angels, and of men—and of elves. Legend and History have met and fused. But in God's kingdom the presence of the greatest does not depress the small. Redeemed Man is still man. Story, fantasy, still go on, and should go on. The Evangelium has not abrogated legends; it has hallowed them, especially the "happy ending." The Christian has still to work, with mind as well as body, to suffer, hope, and die; but he may now perceive that all his bents and faculties have a purpose, which can be redeemed. So great is the bounty with which he has been treated that he may now, perhaps, fairly dare to guess that in Fantasy he may actually assist in the effoliation and multiple enrichment of creation. All tales may come true; and yet, at the last, redeemed, they may be as like and as unlike the forms that we give them as Man, finally redeemed, will be like and unlike the fallen that we know.[6]

Tolkien's words—especially his neologism for the death and resurrection of Christ, the "eucatastrophe," meaning, oxymoronically, a "tragedy with a happy ending"—capture the delight he and Lewis shared in this literary form, but they also prepare us to recognize and engage the spiritual insight we may encounter in Lewis's postconversion fiction. Later Lewis himself summarized his own convictions on the topic of how "myth" works in understanding the historical fact of the incarnation, not as the relatively recent convert as he was in 1931, but now as a completely persuaded and notable apologist for Christianity:

As myth transcends thought, Incarnation transcends myth. The heart of Christianity is a myth which is also a fact. The old myth of the Dying God, *without ceasing to be myth,* comes down from the heaven of legend and imagination to the earth of history. *It happens*—at a particular date, in a particular place, followed by definable historical consequences. We pass from a Balder or Osiris, dying nobody knows when or where, to a historical Person crucified (it is all in order) *under Pontius Pilate.* By becoming fact it does not cease to be myth: that is the miracle. . . . Those who do not know that this great myth became Fact when the Virgin conceived are indeed to be pitied. But Christians also need to be reminded . . . that what became Fact was a Myth, that it carries with it into the world of Fact all the properties of a myth. God is more than a god, not less; Christ is more than Balder, not less. We must not be ashamed of the mythical radiance resting on our theology [emphasis, Lewis].[7]

The fairy-tale was perfectly suited as a vehicle for expressing transcendent truth and provided for Lewis in particular the perfect "canvas" on which to paint the "pictures in his head" that in words became the Narnian tales. What Lewis observes of Tolkien's achievement in his original review of *The*

Hobbit (published first in the October 2, 1937 edition of *The Times Literary Supplement*) could equally be said of his Space Trilogy, *The Chronicles of Narnia*, and certainly in *Till We Have Faces:*

The publishers claim that *The Hobbit*, though very unlike Alice [in Wonderland], resembles it in being the work of a professor at play. A more important truth is that both belong to a very small class of books which have nothing in common save that each admits to a world of its own—a world that seems to have been going on long before we stumbled into but which, once found by the right reader, becomes indispensable to him. To define the world of The Hobbit is, of course, impossible because it is new. You cannot anticipate it before you go there, as you cannot forget it once you have gone.[8]

The worlds Lewis created, even before he became a Christian, are inherently spiritual and betray his inclination toward the transcendent. Postconversion, Lewis deftly uses the conventions of the fairy-tale to depict for us a winsome and whimsical landscape that stirs our heart and directs our soul, mind, and strength toward the world beyond this one. To inhabit that elusive but accessible world, Lewis believed, we must be poised to receive a story grander than one we have ever been told before—but a narrative and an experience after all, and thus resonating with all the stories we have read or heard nonetheless. In so doing, we come to see that first and foremost, Glome, Perelandra, *The Great Divorce*'s heaven, Narnia, like Middle-Earth, is a world "you cannot anticipate ... before you go there, ... and cannot forget ... once you have gone."

Still, Lewis cautioned that in his fiction, he was not creating allegories requiring a one-for-one parallel with personages and events in the Gospels, but a series of "supposals," as Lewis reckoned it. What if the Son of God were incarnate in a world like Narnia—what would happen? What if we discovered an unfallen planet and fellow humans were conspiring to bring it to ruin like our own world has suffered? What if we could glimpse for a night the realities of the next world on a bus ride between heaven and hell, and see ourselves from the perspective of eternity? How would these tales unfold and how would we receive the news they bring?

ASKING THE RIGHT QUESTIONS

Lewis's poetry and fiction inevitably raise key questions for the modern consciousness he faced, as well as the contemporary one today's readers inhabit. *Why should it matter what and how one imagines, dreams, or invents? Why can't we just be logical, fact-based folk, who operate out of reason, and from reason, responsibility, and from responsibility, performance of duty. Do we really need to use anything but pure logic? Why can't we, as rules become apparent, just obey them, build community around them, and be happy? Isn't the imagination something that just gets us into trouble?*

The world of the imagination is not just the terrain inhabited by artists, musicians, scriptwriters, novelists, and quilters—it's the domain of every human being . . . and, in Lewis's understanding, it is how God made us, how we are to negotiate the world to reckon with what we euphemistically call "thought lives." What could a phrase like that mean, except that the world we envision in our hearts and minds is different from the one we "actually" inhabit? And, if so, what does that imply for how we can shape our "real world" by the potential or unrealized ones in our heads? Lewis had an answer.

The fact is, he suggested, we never fully live our lives out on the surface—we are never completely logical creatures; we are, in fact, made in the image of God, and therefore, spiritual, and because God imagines, invents, and creates the world, so, too, are we involved in an imaginative enterprise that determines whether we live lives of "quiet desperation" or meaningful engagement with the world He is redeeming, including our imagination.

Why should we care about our imagination? Doesn't it just get us into trouble? Well, Lewis, opines: Yes, the unused and undisciplined imagination does offer trouble—when it is inactive or used sparingly for, let's face it, cheap thrills, petty lusts, minor envies, when we neglect it in favor of satisfying mere bodily appetites, yes, the imagination becomes less a vital, spiritual force, and more a temporary escape from the mundane, a wasteful trek into fantasyland where we're the hero or the villain, exacting our revenge or extracting our glory.

Lewis called this "morbid, egoistic castle-building." *Morbid* because it is unproductive, noncontributory to one's growth, focused on what is dead or dying; *egoistic,* because it is merely self-gratifying, self-congratulatory, "incessant autobiography"; *castle building* because it is merely elevated daydreaming, the construction of the unattainable in pursuit of the unworthy. I'm not going to live in a castle; I am not a king, and besides the fuel bills are outrageous. The ultimate problem with such mis- and disuse of the imagination for Lewis is that he believed it was given to us for so much more. The redeemed and discipled imagination, like the redeemed and discipled intellect—intellect as reason and logic in service of extending heaven's rule on earth—is meant to enlarge our vision, encourage our hearts, and engage us in the battle for and nurture of souls. So, why, Lewis asks Socratically, did God give us this nature, this tool, this ability, one that can both enslave and liberate, enhance and debilitate? Simply this: because we are to be like God in every way, we partake of Him by exercising our imagination. If we don't feed our imagination and put it to godly use, the vacuum will be filled with something else, something that at best will merely distract or divert us, or, something that at worst may derail and divorce us from our heavenly pathway.

OUR ALTERNATE HISTORY

In his fiction, Lewis is determined to turn hearts toward this "true country," to rewrite its unknown or faded history in our hearts, by drawing attention to the "echoes" that already exist in our imagination. From Middle-earth to Narnia, from Perelandra to Cair Paravel, and on to Mordor and Malacandra, Lewis and Tolkien call upon all of us to reenchant the cosmos, keeping alive the promise and animating the search for the world beyond the world. They point us to the surprising reality of the fellowship of heaven to be glimpsed in Lewis's Space trilogy, his *Chronicles of Narnia*, or in Tolkien's *Middle-Earth*.

In engaging his fiction, Lewis would have us come to see "imagination" as the divinely given human faculty of comprehending reality through the use of images, pictures, shapes, patterns: seeing what is, seeing what was, and seeing what could be, through artistic "representation." It is the counterpart and complement to reason. We come to know what is true not only through words and propositions, but also through what is mediated beyond the words, in the heart, "groanings too deep to be uttered." It is by the imagination that we are called upon to grasp, negotiate, understand the world directly before us, and as well the world just beyond them in pictures and images that create their own reality. Lewis's conviction was that it is through our imagination that we are thereby enabled to fashion representations of and alternatives to reality, for imagination engages both creation and interaction with the cosmos, not just static gazing. Through the tools of the imagination, art imitates life and life imitates art, reality leaking through both: the products of creative imagination becoming part of the reality that is in turn engaged by that same imagination. In fact, it is our encounter with art actualized by the imagination that helps us "defamiliarize" what has become habitual and mundane in our world, and allows us to revise (or re-see) it as it is—permitting personal change and godly renewal. Great hymns, great novels, great movies, and great sermons can do this.

Now Lewis held that the *Christian imagination* at work in Narnia and Tolkien's Middle-Earth is imagination *illuminated by revelation,* by the life and light of Jesus Christ. It is, as we saw in the passage earlier, an echo of the metaphor the Apostle Paul chooses to inform his prayer for the Ephesians' illumination in chapter 1, verses 18–19, what we called earlier, "seeing with the heart":

I pray also that the eyes of your heart may be enlightened in order that you may know the hope to which he has called you, the riches of his glorious inheritance in the saints, and his incomparably great power for us who believe. (New International Version)

This is one of Paul's most arresting metaphors—one that offers an initially strange image of two essential organs sharing a vital function: how does one "see with the heart"? It is clearly the case that sometimes "the eyes of our heart" but must be further enlightened for us to understand what logic alone cannot reveal, and that we can be oblivious to something God wishes us to know but which we cannot apprehend only through the "head." For instance, it is possible for one to read the New Testament as a piece of literature or history, and thereby come to know facts about Jesus of Nazareth intellectually as a "man with a message." But if we learn to "see with the heart," Lewis would aver, He emerges as more than that; He is the Son of God, and, not only that, He is a Shepherd, the King of Kings, the Morning Star, the Way, the Truth, the Life, but, still further, He is also a Lamb, and, most certainly, a Lion. All true, but all images, all captured first in the heart, and then only with the intellect.

This set of principles is what Lewis, Tolkien, and the other Inklings took to be foundational to what they called *mythopoeia*—or the act of new myth-making. Myth for them was not defined as a legendary tale told with dubious authority; but instead it was the grand overarching narrative that created the reason to be, and to become, for members of the village, the polis, and the nation, touched by its encompassing themes, images, characters, and plot lines. Neither antihistorical, nor ahistorical, myth evokes awe, wonder, passion, and, what's more, pursuit—a culture's myth is the story that has the power to explain the origin and destiny of a people, the text that orients them in history, guides them in the present, and points them to a future in which they and their offspring will live, and move, and have their being. It places them in the presence of their Creator and Benefactor, Judge or Advocate, and answers the questions when, how, who, and why. A "true myth," has the power to explain where we came from, shape our identity and purpose, instill hope, promote justice, and sustain order.

The only reliable, encompassing world story or Grand Narrative, the one integral to Lewis's craft and motive, as well as the Inklings, is found in the Judeo-Christian Scriptures, and it has provided cultures from Asia to Africa, and Europe to South and North America, just such a frame for working out their place (and salvation) in the cosmos with fear and trembling. For the Inklings, this forms the true history of our planet, of all peoples, and the only trustworthy forecast of our destiny. But the biblical narrative has been crowded out or discarded in civilizations that have ignored its relevant witness and forgotten its historical impact. How does one go about getting recovering postmoderns to take a second or third look at its testimony?

The Inklings' answer was to create fantasies and new myths, a "Neverland," which could yet serve as an "alternate history," a winsome, redemptive, inclusive worldview that would restore personal dignity and a promised destiny to those with ears to hear, and eyes to see. *A history alternate to what?* Simply put, it is the alternative to the false history written in the rise of a dehumanizing and disenchanting naturalism that reduces men, women, children, and even whole civilizations to instincts, impulses, genetics, and the environment: "cosmic accidents" whose dreams and visions nevertheless point them to longings they cannot account for in purely "scientific" terms.

In a later review of Tolkien's *The Lord of the Rings*, Lewis defends his friend's choice of genre by explaining why the fairy-tale may be the best medium for accomplishing the heady goal of redirecting wayfarers to their real identity and homeland:

But why some ask, why if you have a serious comment to make on the real life of men, must you do it by talking about a phantasmagoric never never land of your own? Because, I take it, one of the main things the author wants to say is that the real life of men is that of mythical and heroic quality. One can see the principle at work in his characterization. Much that in a realistic work would be done by "character delineation" is here done simply by making the character an elf, a dwarf, or a hobbit. The imagined beings have their insides on the outside; they are visible souls. And man as a while, man pitted against the universe, have we seen him at all till we see that he is like a hero in a fairy tale? In the book, Eomer rashly contrasts "the green earth" with "legends," and Aragorn replies that the green earth itself is a "a mighty matter of legend."

The value of myth is that it takes all the things we know and restores to them the rich significance which been hidden by the veil of familiarity. . . . If you are tired of the real landscape, look at it in a mirror. By putting bread, gold, horse, apple, or the very roads into a myth, we do not retreat from reality: we rediscover it.[9]

"The veil of familiarity" is a telling phrase; in the realm of the fantastic, within mythic landscapes, vistas, and perspectives—anything might happen, anything might be discovered. One is not restricted by what he or she knows of the "real world," its colors, shapes, creatures, languages, and predicaments. The author of fantasy can use these but also invent still more—thus intermixing them with the familiar and the real to create a "secondary" world that envelops and surpasses both. These alternate histories rescue readers from the "veil of familiarity," ushering them into a transcendent realm unreachable by mere reason or coldhearted induction. We do not "retreat from reality," Lewis reminds, "we rediscover it."

This is certainly the case with C. S. Lewis's greatest creations: the landscapes of the Space Trilogy, the foreboding domain of Glome in *Till We Have Faces*, and, of course, the glorious kingdom of Narnia. In our mythical sojourns with his characters, Lewis indeed renews in us a longing for "the scent of a flower we have not found, the echo of a tune we have not heard, news from a country we have never yet visited."[10] Long before Willy Wonka or Harry Potter appeared on the scene, C. S. Lewis was "reenchanting a cosmos" that had been emptied of significance by those twentieth century thinknocrats who reduced the universe to mere numbers or human life to bodily appetites and genetic impulses. With a little help from his friends, Lewis has managed to establish an outpost on the edge of darkness, opening the wardrobe door to help us find the object of our longing, and the true end of our journey.

NOTES

1. C. S. Lewis, *Surprised by Joy* (New York: Harcourt, 1955), 10.
2. C. S. Lewis, *Letters to Malcolm* (New York: Harcourt, 1963), 91.
3. Lewis, *Surprised by Joy*, 189.
4. C. S. Lewis, *C. S. Lewis's Letters to Children*, ed. Lyle Dorsett and Marjorie Lamp Mead (New York: HarperCollins, 1985), 68–69.
5. C. S. Lewis, "It All Began with a Picture," in *On Stories*, ed. Walter Hooper (New York: Harcourt, 1982), 53.
6. J. R. R. Tolkien, "On Fairy Stories," ed. C. S. Lewis, *Essays Presented to Charles Williams* (Oxford: Oxford University Press, 1947), 83–84.
7. C. S. Lewis, "Myth Become Fact," *God in the Dock*, ed. Walter Hooper (Grand Rapids, MI: Eerdmans, 1967), 66–67.
8. C. S. Lewis, "Review of *The Hobbit*," in *On Stories*, 81–82.
9. C. S. Lewis, "Review of *The Lord of the Rings*," in *On Stories*, 89–90.
10. C. S. Lewis, "The Weight of Glory," in *The Weight of Glory and Other Addresses* (Grand Rapids, MI: Eerdmans, 1965), 5.

BIBLIOGRAPHY

Lewis, C. S. *Surprised by Joy.* New York: Harcourt, 1955.
———. *Letters to Malcolm.* New York: Harcourt, 1963.
———. *The Weight of Glory and Other Addresses.* Grand Rapids, MI: Eerdmans, 1965.
———. *God in the Dock.* Edited by Walter Hooper. Grand Rapids, MI: Eerdmans, 1967.
———. *On Stories.* Edited by Walter Hooper. New York: Harcourt, 1982.
———. *C. S. Lewis's Letters to Children.* Edited by Lyle Dorsett and Marjorie Lamp Mead. New York: HarperCollins, 1985.
Tolkien, J. R. R. "On Fairy Stories." Edited by C. S. Lewis, *Essays Presented to Charles Williams*. Oxford: Oxford University Press, 1947.

2

Rehabilitating H. G. Wells: C. S. Lewis's *Out of the Silent Planet*

David C. Downing

C. S. Lewis's dedication for *Out of the Silent Planet* reads: "To my brother W. H. L. / a life-long critic of the space-and-time story." This tribute to Warren Hamilton Lewis seems straightforward enough, but it contains a double entendre that his brother and the other Inklings must have enjoyed. Jack sometimes used the "space-and-time story" as a synonym for science fiction or fantasy.[1] But he also used "space-and-time" to refer to the physical universe, the only reality admitted by materialist philosophers. For Warren to be "a lifelong critic of the space-and-time story" meant that he was a seasoned reader of the sort of books Jack had written; it also identified him as one who had long suspected that the physical universe is not "the whole show." This little inside joke is a synecdoche of the entire Ransom trilogy: Lewis offers his readers some lively specimens of interplanetary fantasy. But he also means to plant in their imaginations a suggestion that there may be more things in heaven and earth than are dreamt of in their philosophies.

Critics often assume that Lewis deliberately chose fantasy literature as an imaginative instrument to express his vision of the cosmos. But the truth is just the reverse: Lewis did not simply adopt fantasy as a didactic vehicle after his conversion to Christianity; rather it was his love of fantasy, myth, and romance that led him to faith in the first place. In the trilogy he recapitulates this process for his readers: first he tries to enchant them with fantasy worlds of wonder and danger, battlefields of good and evil; then gradually he reveals a correlation between these new, absorbing, fantasies and some old doctrines whose familiarity may have bred contempt in his readers, or at least indifference. The recovery of childhood things that Lewis himself experienced is one he wants to pass on to others.

The actual writing of the trilogy began in 1937. Lewis and his good friend J. R. R. Tolkien agreed that there simply were not enough of their favorite sort of stories available, so they decided to try their own hand at it. Lewis proposed that each should write an "excursionary thriller," his a space-story and Tolkien's a time-story, both leading to the discovery of Myth.[2] Accordingly, Tolkien began a story called "The Lost Road," and Lewis, composing much more rapidly, completed a draft of *Out of the Silent Planet,* reading it in installments at weekly meetings of the Inklings. Lewis sent the manuscript first to J. M. Dent and Sons, who returned it. Then he sent it to Allen and Unwin, who had published Tolkien's *The Hobbit.* Again it was not accepted, despite a letter from Tolkien defending it against some rather woolly minded criticisms from the publisher's reader. (This letter remains one of the most perceptive brief treatments of Lewis's strengths and weaknesses as a writer.)[3] The manuscript was then accepted by a house in London called the Bodley Head, who published it in the autumn of 1938.

Out of the Silent Planet was widely reviewed, but only a few commentators noticed the theological implications of the story. The year after the first book of the trilogy was published, Lewis wrote to a friend: "You will be both grieved and amused to hear that out of about 60 reviews only 2 showed any knowledge that my idea of the fall of the Bent One was anything but an invention of my own. But if there only were someone with a richer talent and more leisure, I believe this great ignorance might be a help to the evangelisation of England: any amount of theology can now be smuggled into people's minds under cover of romance without their knowing it."[4]

Lewis's mention of only two reviews in sixty sounds hyperbolic, but a survey of *Out of the Silent Planet* reviews confirms his reckoning as essentially accurate. One reviewer, for example, confesses that he read *Out of the Silent Planet* twice and still could find no allegorical significance.[5] Another concludes that "*Out of the Silent Planet,* beautifully written as some of it is, does not seem quite to have grown from any conviction."[6]

One can hardly imagine a more inaccurate observation. *Out of the Silent Planet* is written with all of Lewis's convictions, with his whole worldview, in the background. He began the trilogy as a deliberate critique of what he called Evolutionism, a philosophy that projects Darwinism into the metaphysical sphere, speculating that humankind may eventually evolve into its own species of divinity, jumping from planet to planet and star to star. H. G. Wells was probably the most articulate and widely read proponent of this philosophy, so Lewis set out to create a Wellsian fantasy with a counter-Wellsian theme. Though one finds the idea of Evolutionism in Olaf Stapledon, G. B. Shaw, and C. H. Waddington, Lewis said that Evolutionism could, with some justice, be dubbed "Well-sianity."[7]

Lewis began the Ransom trilogy because he feared that Evolutionism was beginning to capture the popular imagination. Soon after the publication of *Out of the Silent Planet,* he wrote to Roger Lancelyn Green, later to become his biographer: "What immediately spurred me to write was Olaf Stapledon's *Last and First Men* [1930], and an essay in J. B. S. Haldane's *Possible Worlds* [1927], both of which seemed to take the idea of such travel seriously and to have the desperately immoral outlook which I try to pillory in Weston. I like the whole inter-planetary idea as a *mythology* and simply wished to conquer for my own (Christian) point of view what has hitherto been used by the opposite side."[8] The following year Lewis explained to another correspondent who had asked about the origins of *Out of the Silent Planet:* "The danger of 'Westonism' I meant to be real. What set me about writing the book was the discovery that a pupil of mine took all that dream of interplanetary colonisation quite seriously, and the realisation that thousands of people in one form or another depend on some hope of perpetuating and improving the human species for the whole meaning of the universe—that a 'scientific' hope of defeating death is a real rival to Christianity."[9]

Last and First Men (1930), the first book mentioned above, offers Stapledon's prophetic panorama of our species' future, including an invasion of earth by cloud-creatures from Mars; the laboratory development of a new, improved type of humans, all brains and hands; the colonization of Venus and Neptune; and the eventual extinction of humanity two billion years in the future. Near the end of the story, one member of the species who represents almost pure intelligence explains the transcendent purpose that has guided all humans from continent to continent, and then planet to planet: "The task that was undertaken had to be completed. For the Scattering of the Seed has come for every one of us the supreme religious duty. Even those who continually sin against it recognize this as the last office of man."[10]

For someone like Lewis, this would represent the worst of all possible worlds. The philosophy of scattering the seed as a sacred obligation could easily justify experiments on animal and human subjects, as well as extermination of other species, whether on our own planet or on others. Yet even Stapledon seems to concede that such a goal serves no ultimate purpose. In the end he seems to agree with Bertrand Russell that "only on the firm foundation of unyielding despair can the soul's edifice henceforth be built."[11]

J. B. S. Haldane, the other writer whom Lewis hoped to answer in *Out of the Silent Planet,* was a Cambridge biochemist who championed the cause of science against those in the humanities and the churches, whom he considered reactionaries. Haldane was something of a latter-day Jeremy Bentham, an un-compromising logician who tended to tackle ethical and aesthetic questions in terms of utility and efficiency. In his little book *Callinicus* (1925), for ex-ample, he offers a vigorous, if chilling, defense of chemical warfare as no more inhumane than conventional weapons. In *Possible Worlds* (1927), he argues for scientific research on animals, noting that those opposed to his laboratory experiments on rats would probably not think twice about poisoning rats that had infested the family home. (Lewis, for one, was consistent in this regard: he was an antivivisectionist and also one who never set traps for the mice in his rooms at Oxford.[12])

The essay in *Possible Worlds* that unsettled Lewis was one entitled "Man's Destiny." There Haldane rhapsodizes about "man's taking his own evolution in hand" and of the possibilities of our species literally conquering the cosmos. He surmises that humans might eventually be able to overcome all disease and disability, and that the "exceptional man" of the future will be able to think like Isaac Newton, compose like J. S. Bach, paint like the Old Masters, and live as simply and lovingly as Francis of Assisi. Haldane concludes with an almost breathless prophecy about humans conquering space and eventually, it would seem, death itself:

Men will certainly attempt to leave the earth. The first voyagers into interstellar space will die.... There is no reason why their successors should not succeed in colonising some, at least, of the other planets of our system, and ultimately the planets, if such exist, revolving around other stars than our sun. There is no theoretical limit to man's material progress but the subjection to complete conscious control of every atom and every quantum of radiation in the universe. There is, perhaps, no limit at all to his intellectual and spiritual progress.[13]

Such visions for the future, which now seem rather quixotic, appeared to Lewis as potentially very dangerous. The idea that humans may one day evolve into *Übermensch* was for Lewis the latest variant of the serpent's temptation to Eve: "Ye shall be as gods" (Gen. 3:5, KJV). A program of helping evolution do its work could also be used to justify all manner of atrocities against other species or against "inferior" members of the human species. Such a theory comes dangerously close to Hitler's dream of a "master race," a parallel that Lewis underscores in *That Hideous Strength.*

Apart from debunking Evolutionism, Lewis also hoped that taking his readers on an imaginative voyage to another world would give them a new perspective on this one. Charles Moorman has stated the underlying strategy of the trilogy most succinctly: "Lewis's main aim in the creation of the silent-planet myth is to create and maintain a metaphor that will serve to carry in fictional form the basic tenets of Christianity and present them from a non-Christian point of view, but without reference to normal Christian symbols."[14] Though his initial impulse for writing interplanetary romance may not have been quite as calculatedly didactic as Moorman suggests, Lewis does portray a cosmos ruled by a benevolent god, whose loyal subjects—angels and human—must daily battle the dark and fallen rulers of this world. In fact, Lewis's fictional representations are representations of the central doctrines of Christian myth.

COSMIC VOYAGE AS SPIRITUAL PILGRIMAGE

In the first paragraph of *Out of the Silent Planet*, the protagonist is not introduced by name but rather referred to as "the Pedestrian."[15] The term seems appropriate enough to describe a man on a walking tour, waiting out a thundershower under a chestnut tree. But the word is capitalized all three times it is used, as if referring to an allegorical character out of John Bunyan, one whose outer journey will reflect his soul's progress.

In the second paragraph the Pedestrian is identified as Ransom, a Cambridge philologist on a solitary walking tour. He is a tall, round-shouldered man, of thirty-five to forty years, with a certain shabbiness of dress that marks a university professor on holiday. At first glance, one cannot help but notice how much this description fits Lewis himself. He was in his late thirties when he wrote *Out of the Silent Planet*. He was of middle height, and was described as round-shouldered by more than one who knew him. And his shabbiness of dress was legendary. Those who first met him often thought he looked more like a gardener, a butcher, or a country farmer than a university don. Continuing in *Out of the Silent Planet*, readers soon learn that Ransom is a bachelor, an antivivisectionist, and a Christian. All of these traits remind us again of the author himself. Lewis commented that Ransom was not meant to be a self-portrait. But whatever his intentions, he created in Ransom a character whose convictions and consciousness closely resembled his own.

The opening pages of *Out of the Silent Planet* describe experiences that Lewis himself might have had on one of his walking tours. But when Ransom stops in at an isolated country house being rented by Edward Weston, a noted scientist, and Dick Devine, a former schoolmate, his adventures begin in earnest. Sensing something vaguely sinister about their intentions toward a simpleminded boy who works for them, Ransom nevertheless accepts a drink, discovering too late that he has been drugged. He loses consciousness and dreams about trying to escape from a walled garden, getting stuck with one leg outside the wall and one leg inside.

This dream marks Ransom's departure from the world of the ordinary and his entry into Other Worlds. The contents of the dream make little sense to someone reading *Out of the Silent Planet* for the first time, but later readings reveal it to be a symbolic prophecy of Ransom's adventures on Mars and Venus. The garden represents planet earth, and Ransom's straddling position suggests that from this time forth he will have a dual identity—partly a dweller of this world, partly a citizen of other worlds.

When he starts to come to, Ransom makes a feeble attempt to escape, but he is soon knocked unconscious again. Awakening the next time in an eerie metal chamber, he realizes that he is traveling in space and feels poised between "delirious terror or an ecstasy of joy" (p. 23). He fears for his own sanity as he contemplates the idea of traveling so far from earth into the dark vastness that separates the worlds. But when he looks out the window, Ransom is not appalled but rather awed by the splendid scene spread before his eyes. He sees "planets of unbelievable majesty, and constellations undreamed of," which look like "celestial sapphires, rubies, emeralds and pin-pricks of burning gold" sparkling upon the fabric of "undimensioned, enigmatic blackness" (p. 31).

As the voyage continues, Ransom feels there must be a "spiritual cause for his progressive lightening and exultation of heart." He comes to realize that the modern concept of "Space," suggesting a vast, cold, dead abyss between the planets, seems an almost blasphemous term to describe the "empyrean ocean of radiance in which they swam." Ransom concludes that "older thinkers had been wiser when they named it simply the heavens—the heavens which declared the glory" (p. 32), thus choosing the words of the psalmist (Ps 19:1) over those of the scientist.

Having awakened to a whole new set of realities, Ransom begins a long pilgrimage of purgation and illumination. Lewis called *Out of the Silent Planet* "Ransom's *enfance*,"[16] portraying Ransom as a man who, though in his middle years, is in his soul's childhood. Indeed, on the voyage to Mars, Ransom is compared to a "frightened child." Overcoming fear is the first great task that Ransom faces. Though he is a Cambridge don, a distinguished linguist, and a religious man, his attainments and beliefs are not of very great help in his present time of trouble.

On the voyage to Mars, Ransom indeed has excellent reasons to be afraid. He has been drugged, knocked over the head, kidnapped, dragged into outer space, and has overheard a conversation about his being turned over to some alien beings called "sorns". This last bit of news plays havoc with his already overcharged imagination. Having (like Lewis) grown up reading science fiction, Ransom visualizes aliens with "twitching feelers, rasping wings, slimy coils, and curling tentacles," assuming they will embody some "monstrous union of superhuman intelligence and insatiable cruelty" (p. 35).

Once Ransom and his abductors land on Mars, his first surprise is to find a landscape of surpassing beauty. Later on, he will learn that the inhabitants of Mars, who call their world Malacandra, are not at all like the nightmarish visions of his imagination. There are three rational species on the planet, very different from each other, but all benign and living in harmony. Escaping from Weston and Devine, Ransom wanders on his own for a while and then befriends human-sized otter-like creatures called "hrossa," learning some of their speech. A pious man, he begins to wonder if he should undertake to instruct them in his faith. But they have their own well-defined convictions, and it is they who marvel at his ignorance. They tell him that their world is ruled by Oyarsa, who is himself subject to Maleldil the Young, who created their world and who lives with the Old One.

After further conversations with another rational species, the sorns, and with Oyarsa, the ruler of Malacandra, Ransom comes to understand that Maleldil the Young created the Field of Arbol (the solar system) and all the beings in it. He chose an Oyarsa, or tutelary intelligence, to rule each world, served by nearly imperceptible beings called "eldila." However, on the third planet, the Oyarsa and some of his eldils rose up in rebellion against Maleldil, recognizing no authority but themselves. Led by the Bent Oyarsa, this world was now cut off from the others and thus called Thulcandra, "the Silent Planet." It remains a battleground, though there are rumors in Deep Heaven of wondrous things performed by Maleldil to reclaim his lost world.

This is certainly the stuff of science fiction. It is also orthodox Christian theology, as it might be understood in an unfallen, hierarchical world. In response to inquiries about the trilogy's symbolism, Lewis explained straightforwardly that the Old One and Maleldil the Young represent the Father and the Son of the Trinity, and that eldils represented angels, and the Bent One was Satan. Lest it seem blasphemous to add new chapters to Christian doctrine, he also explained that his stories were a form of "imagining out loud," speculations in fiction about "what God might be supposed to have done in other worlds."[17]

Despite the reassurances of the gentle hrossa, Ransom's anxiety about meeting some alien monstrosity on this planet reemerges when he first travels to meet a sorn, and later when he is called for an audience with Oyarsa. Yet as the story progresses, one can see that his nearly debilitating fears early in his adventure are becoming more and more manageable. When Ransom does eventually meet a large insect-like creature called a *pfifltrigg*, he finds it comic rather than horrific. (The name pfifltrigg is, in fact, Lewis's coinage, from two Old Icelandic words that combine to mean "safe monster.")[18]

At the end of the story, Ransom and his two fellow earthlings come before Oyarsa, the ruler of that world. Ransom serves as a translator so that Weston and Devine can try to explain themselves to Oyarsa (whom they cannot see and dismiss as a deception of some kind). Oyarsa discovers how truly depraved these fallen humans are, the one by ruthless self-love, the other by a ruthless ideology of human conquest over other worlds. In the end, the ruler of that world determines that all three should return to where they came from.

Before returning to his home planet, which will never again quite be home, Ransom receives this farewell counsel from the presiding spirit of Malacandra: "You are guilty of no evil, Ransom of Thulcandra, except a little fearfulness. For that, the journey you go on is your pain, and perhaps your cure: for you must be either mad or brave before it is ended" (p. 142). The return flight is indeed a difficult one, and Ransom does emerge largely purged of his fears. But most of his cure has came on Malacandra itself. One can see how different a person Ransom has become by comparing his terror at watching the "Earthrise" from space early in the story (pp. 22–24) to his exultant memories of watching the planet Jupiter rise from Malacandra in the closing pages of the book (pp. 159–60).

When asked about his portrayal of Oyarsa and his eldils as nearly invisible, Lewis replied that he was drawing upon the medieval idea that angels have bodies made of ether, the lighter-than-air substance that fills the space between heavenly spheres. But Lewis's quip about smuggling theology into people's minds under the cover of light fiction suggests that his portrayal of the eldils was part of a larger strategy to help readers look at old doctrines with new eyes. If eldils appeared to Ransom clad in radiant garments and announced, "Fear not," their identity would be so recognizable as to be dismissible. Lewis enjoyed subverting his readers' certainty about the barriers between the natural and the supernatural, between myth and history.

Lewis's strategy here is an ambitious one, and critics differ about how successfully he is able to blend fantasy and theology. But part of what makes his approach intriguing is the way the theological implications of Ransom's adventures emerge by "progressive revelation." As attested by the reviewers quoted above, a good many readers can finish *Out of the Silent Planet* without ever identifying Maleldil with God. Or for that matter they may finish the book without recognizing the thematic implications of the Oyarsa, the eldils, or the creatures called "hnau."

For one thing, readers may be confused by the name "Maleldil." If eldils are angels, then "Maleldil" suggests the meaning "bad angel." Obviously, this title does not fit a benevolent divinity, so critics have expended a great deal of ingenuity trying to unlock the meaning of the name. William Norwood suggests that it might stand for "male eldil," since maleness in hierarchical societies is associated with higher authority.[19] J. R. Christopher finds its roots in Anglo-Saxon *mal*, "an agreement or judgment" and *ealdor*, "lord," interpreting the name to mean "Lord of Judgment" or "Lord of the Agreement/Covenant."[20] Perhaps most convincing is Evan Gibson's speculation that "Mal" is taken from the Hebrew word for "king," so that "Maleldil" means "king of all spirits," or more familiarly, "Lord of Hosts."[21] Lewis himself said that he knew of no conscious connections between the language of Malacandra and actual languages, saying he wanted the words to have "emotional, not intellectual suggestiveness." He added that the quality in the name "Maleldil" that appealed to him was the liquidity of its sound.[22] Perhaps it is best to let the matter rest there.

Readers who do sense parallels between Maleldil and the God of Christianity may still be puzzled by the Oyarsa and his eldils. Neither of these seems to fit the usual notions of angels. Lewis explains at the end of the story that the word *Oyarses* comes from Bernardus Silvestris, a twelfth-century Platonist. The Oyarsa is the tutelary spirit of the planet, a higher order of angel responsible to rule that sphere (p. 152).

Some early readers of *Out of the Silent Planet* thought the Oyarsa was Lewis's image of God,[23] but that is a careless reading. The hrossa tell Ransom that Maleldil made and ruled their world and that the Oyarsa is subject to him (p. 68). Far from being omniscient, the Oyarsa of Malacandra wants to hear from Ransom what Maleldil has done on earth, the silent planet. He wants Ransom to confirm stories that Maleldil "has taken strange counsel and dared terrible things, wrestling with the Bent One in Thulcandra" (p. 121). And when Ransom explains the traditions he knows on the subject, the Oyarsa shows that even a majestic spirit like himself can be awed by the deeds of Maleldil: "You have shown me more wonders than are known in the whole of heaven" (p. 142).

The wonders Ransom told the Oyarsa about were the life, death, and the resurrection of Christ, which atoned for the sin of Adam and broke the power of the Bent One. To confirm that this is what Lewis has in mind, note the Oyarsa's phrasing about his wanting to hear what Maleldil has done on Thulcandra: "It is a thing we desire to look into." This is taken word for word from 1 Peter 1:12, where the suffering of Christ and the glory that followed are described as "things which angels desire to look into." Here Lewis cleverly takes theological doctrines that readers might find dull or unpalatable and reshapes them into an interplanetary battle scenario more compelling than most of the science fiction available in the pulps.

The passage from 1 Peter also confirms that the Oyarsa and his eldils are Lewis's representations of angels, although we find no harps or halos on Malacandra. In fact, they are so unlike biblical or traditional pictures of angels that one young reader asked Lewis if they were supposed to represent fairies.[24]

Lewis's portrayal of the eldila clearly illustrates his strategy of representing old doctrines in new literary forms. He well knew that angels in the Bible are never portrayed with harps and halos. He reminded one reader that angels who appear in scripture nearly always excite terror in those who see them and that the word *kherub* in Hebrew referred not to "horrid little fat baby 'cherubs'" but to a creature like the fabled Gryphon, with the body of a lion and wings of eagles.[25]

In *The Discarded Image* Lewis laments the increasingly disappointing portrayal of angels he finds in Western literature. After the "unrivalled majesty" of Dante's angels come the classicist angels of Milton, with "too much anatomy and too much armour" and behaving too much like characters out of Homer or Virgil. After Milton, Lewis finds "total degradation," ending in "the purely consolatory, and hence waterishly feminine, angels of the nineteenth century art."[26] In trying to find a model for his eldils, Lewis must have considered first what he considered to be the best portrayal of an angel in imaginative literature[27]: the heavenly messenger in the *Inferno* who strides through the fifth circle of hell on God's errand, parting the lost souls at his feet and opening the gate of Dis with just a wave of his hand (pp. 9, 76–103).

Lewis's eldils have some of the majesty and self-possession of Dante's stern messenger, but none of his overwhelming presence. In fact, the eldils on Malacandra are just on the margins of perception. If Lewis objected to the "waterishly feminine angels" of popular art, one wonders at first how it is an improvement to portray angels as hardly visible at all. People in the Bible indeed sometimes entertained angels unawares, but that is because the angels appeared as ordinary humans, not as "footsteps of light." So Lewis is attempting something here other than just trying to get back to biblical pictures of angels.

Our best clue to Lewis's narrative strategy here comes from a letter he wrote to two children who had asked about his eldils. Where most authors might offer a short reply, or none, Lewis gives his young admirers a concise lesson in angelology: "The view that angels have no bodies of any kind has not always been held among Christians. The old idea (early Middle Ages) was that they had bodies of aether as we have bodies of gross matter. The opposite view (your one) was that of the great scholastics—Albertus Magnus, Thomas Aquinas, etc. . . . Of course, I just took, for the purposes of a story, the one that seemed most imaginable. I have no scruples about this because, religiously, the question seems to me of no importance. And anyway what do we mean by 'matter'?"[28] This letter indicates that Lewis's eldils might be hard to see because they have bodies of ether, the lighter-than-air substance that, according to the medieval model, filled the spaces between the heavenly spheres.

RECOVERING THE IMAGE OF A MEDIEVAL COSMOS

To those who know Lewis's cultural criticism, it is not at all surprising that he would draw his imaginative picture of angels from medieval literature and philosophy. Lewis was a renowned medieval and Renaissance scholar who didn't believe in the Renaissance. When he was first invited to give a series of lectures on the subject at Cambridge, he thought of calling his lectures "Absence of the Renaissance." For an alternate title he considered, "What was happening while the Renaissance was not taking place."[29] To a distinguished fellow scholar, Douglas Bush of Harvard University, Lewis defined the Renaissance as "an imaginary entity responsible for anything a modern writer approves of in the fifteenth or sixteenth century."[30]

Of course, Lewis knew there was an era called the Renaissance by later generations, a time of revived interest in Greek and Latin texts, expanding scientific knowledge, and increasing secularization. But he considered the term *Renaissance*, "rebirth," a gross overstatement, as a "dead" civilization does not produce classics of Arthurian romance, a poetic genius such as Dante, or cathedrals such as those at Chartres and Canterbury.

Lewis's whole person was drawn to a time when Western civilization could, with some accuracy, be called Christendom and when a predominant literary form was an epic romance. The world of Aquinas and of King Arthur, of Boethius and Beowulf, was the world in which Lewis the scholar, the Christian, and the lover of heroic adventure could feel most at home. In books such as *The Allegory of Love* and *The Discarded Image*, Lewis devoted a great deal of his energy and expertise as a scholar to the task of rehabilitating the medieval worldview, urging his readers to recognize the intellectual and artistic achievements of writers who might otherwise have been considered mainly as forerunners. For example, he reiterated in several published works that medieval authors knew the earth to be a globe and that they thought of it as a very small point in comparison to the vastness of the universe.[31] (One of the authors whom Lewis faulted for perpetuating the myth of medieval ignorance on these matters was J. B. S. Haldane.[32])

In writing the Ransom trilogy, Lewis's task was not to argue for the intellectual vitality of the medieval worldview, but rather to show its imaginative beauty. In all three books of the Ransom trilogy, Lewis includes a wealth of details to suggest what the medieval vision of reality might have felt like from "inside." As already seen, Ransom's first journey out of our world invites readers to reenvision dark, empty "Space" as radiant, golden "Heavens." He used the fantasy genre not to depict the universe as understood in our century but to recreate imaginatively the medieval cosmology, a vast and magnificent picture that Lewis called "the greatest work of art the Middle Ages produced."[33]

Descriptive passages in all three books of the "Space Trilogy" frequently parallel Lewis's remarks about medieval cosmology in his scholarly works. For example, his essay "Imagination and Thought in the Middle Ages" is intended as an introduction to the medieval world picture but serves equally well as a gloss on *Out of the Silent Planet.* In this essay he explains that when people in the Middle Ages gazed up at a night sky, they did not think of the spaces they looked at as silent, dark, or empty.[34] He also discusses the medieval understanding of "influences"[35] and quotes a few lines from Milton's *Comus,* the same passage that Ransom recalled when he first looked out and saw the glorious of the empyrean heavens (p. 53).

In *The Discarded Image* Lewis again underscores the differences between the ancients' picture of the heavens and our perception of outer space. He quotes the Latin poet Lucan, who envisions celestial realms bathed in light: "How dark, compared with the aether, our terrestrial day is."[36] He also contrasts the medieval and the modern in language similar to the passage from *Out of the Silent Planet* quoted above: "Nothing is more deeply impressed on the cosmic imaginings of a modern than the idea that the heavenly bodies move in a pitch-black and dead-cold vacuity. It was not so in the Medieval Model."[37]

Apart from re-imagining "space" according to the medieval model, Lewis also redefines the planets that float in space. When Ransom and his abductors approach Malacandra, they experience nausea, headaches, and heart palpitations (p. 38). At first one may consider this merely Lewis's (fairly accurate) predictions about the physiological effects of moving from a weightless state back into a gravity field. But soon it becomes clear that he has something more in mind. As the spacecraft descends, Ransom again finds his former conceptions reversed. He feels as if "the lights of the Universe seemed to be turned down" and that golden splendor of the heavens are giving way to "a pallid, cheerless and pitiable grey." Their spacecraft, which had been "a chariot gliding in the fields of heaven" suddenly felt like a cramped steel box "falling out of the heaven, into a world." After that first descent, the narrator explains, Ransom ever after "saw the planets—the 'earths' he had called them in his thought—as mere holes or gaps in the living heaven—excluded and rejected wastes of heavy matter and murky air, formed not by addition to, but by subtraction from, the surrounding brightness" (pp. 39–40).

In general, Lewis presents life on Malacandra as very positive, even utopian, so many readers are puzzled to find him describing Ransom's entry into this world in such negative terms. The passage quoted above seems neither "scientific" nor thematically congruent with the rest of the book. Yet again the explanation can be found in Lewis's own discussion of medieval cosmology. In *The Discarded Image,* he explains the hierarchy of created substance developed by the fifth-century author Macrobius: ether, the purest and most limpid form, rose the highest; beneath it came air, less pure and more heavy; then came water, and finally solids. As Lewis sums up: "Finally out of the whole tumult of matter all that was irreclaimable (*vastum*) was scraped off and cleansed from the (other) elements (*ex defaecatis abrasum elementis*) and sank down and settled at the lowest point, plunged in binding and unending cold. Earth is in fact the 'offscourings of creation,' the cosmic dustbin."[38] According to this order of creation, any planet, even an "unfallen" one, cannot match the glory and splendor of the heavens themselves.

Yet if one must inhabit a world, Malacandra turns out to be a very good choice. Weston and Devine, thinking they have come to offer Ransom as a human sacrifice to the inhabitants of Malacandra, have severely misunderstood the beings they have encountered there. Once Ransom escapes his abductors and meets the three rational species on the planet—the hrossa, the seroni, and the pfifltriggi—he discovers what he had least been expecting: a utopian society. In fact, *Out of the Silent Planet* has been interpreted both as an answer to Plato's *Republic* and as an answer to Wells's utopian novels.

Writers of utopian fiction generally present societies where the author's own cherished ideals have been successfully implemented. Lewis is no exception to this rule: the Malacandrian society he portrays as so attractive is a relatively simple society of hunter/poets, shepherd/philosophers, and artisans. As Ransom comes to know the inhabitants of that world, he learns their ideas about love, art, and spirituality—ideas usually similar to Lewis's own opinions on these subjects. Malacandrian society is also hierarchical, even theocratic, as well as pre-industrial, and pre-capitalistic. In short, it approaches the medieval ideal of a well-governed Christian society.

For example, when Ransom recounts the sordid history of earth to a gathering of sorns, they interpret our planet's woes in terms of a breakdown in the Great Chain of Being: "There must be rule, yet how can creatures rule themselves? Beasts must be ruled by *hnau* and *hnau* by *eldila* and *eldila* by Maleldil" (p. 102). (This formulation may be translated to mean that beasts must be ruled by rational species, rational species by angels, and angels by God.)

In *A Preface to Paradise Lost* Lewis argues that "the Hierarchical conception" dominated Western conceptions of order—cosmic, political, and moral— from Aristotle to Milton. With God at the top of the great chain and unformed matter at the bottom, everyone and everything had a natural station, ruling over those below, obeying those above. A great many sins, according to this conception, derive from not recognizing one's station, and thus perverting the natural order. In Lewis's reading of Milton, Lucifer sins by rebelling against his natural superiors, while Adam sins by not ruling over his natural subject, Eve.

It is not hard to see that Lewis had a great deal of imaginative sympathy for this view of the cosmic order. In the Ransom trilogy, he pictures a cosmos ordered hierarchically, with only "the silent planet," earth, out of harmony with the natural order. Lewis was pragmatic enough to advocate democracy for the contemporary world, not because people are good enough to deserve it, but because they are so prone to abuse power that it needs to be spread out.[39] Nonetheless, democracy seemed to him, like so much else about the contemporary world, prosaic and utilitarian, compared to the grandeur and elegance of earlier eras.

Having woven medieval motifs into *Out of the Silent Planet,* Lewis reveals at the end of the story that his own work as a medievalist led him to discover the extraordinary adventures of Elwin Ransom on Malacandra. In chapter twenty-two, Lewis says that he will dispense with literary conventions, drop the mask, and tell his real purpose for writing the book (p. 152). In claiming to abandon the mask of fiction, Lewis thus offers his readers an even more ingenious fiction than the one they have been reading.

At this point, Lewis the author becomes a character in his own story. He explains that he learned of Ransom's voyage after writing to him about the curious word *Oyarses,* which Lewis had run across in the work of Bernardus Silvestris, a twelfth-century Platonist. Another scholar, identified only as C. J., had interpreted the term as a corruption of *ousiarches,* a ruler of a heavenly sphere, or tutelary spirit of a planet. Ransom replied to Lewis's query by inviting him to come over for the weekend, so Ransom could relate his adventures on Malacandra. He felt compelled to do so to convince Lewis that *Oyarsa* was not just a philological oddity, but an actual being, a powerful one, known to the ancients but now forgotten on "the silent planet." Ransom convinces Lewis to write up Ransom's cosmic voyage in the form of fiction, arguing that it would be more advantageous to appeal to readers' imaginations than to attack their intellectual presuppositions directly. Ransom explains to the narrator that "what we need for the moment is not so much a body of belief as a body of people familiarized with certain ideas. If we could even effect in one per cent of our readers a changeover from the conception of Space to the conception of Heaven, we should have made a start."

INFLUENCES, MODELS, AND ECHOES

As a medievalist by training, Lewis was accustomed to reading authors who were highly syncretistic, blending classical elements with contemporary, Christian with pagan, and historical with fanciful. By temperament he was also something of an intellectual jackdaw, who took whatever ideas attracted him and "Lewisified" them. In *Out of the Silent Planet,* as in all of Lewis's fiction, a simple phrase or image may become a kind of literary shorthand for a wealth of emotional associations or a body of ideas.

Lewis's discovery of "science fiction," as usually understood, came in his schoolboy years, with his reading of H. G. Wells. Though he retained a lifelong interest in Wells, his opinion of the novelist-turned-philosopher was always mixed. At the age of fifteen, for example, Lewis wrote to Arthur Greeves, "When one has set aside the rubbish that H. G. Wells always puts in, there remains a great deal of original, thoughtful, and suggestive work in it."[40] In another letter to Greeves four years later, Lewis admitted somewhat sheepishly that he had enjoyed reading Wells's novel *Marriage,* adding, "One thing you can say for the man is that he really is interested in all the big, outside questions."[41] Of Wells's transition from science fiction writer to socialist philosopher, Lewis lamented that Wells had traded his birthright for a "pot of message."[42]

Yet Lewis acknowledged his debt to Wells, and when reading *Out of the Silent Planet,* one is often struck by its similarities to *First Men in the Moon.* Both stories portray a single-minded physicist who builds a spherical spaceship in his backyard, accompanied by a younger man seeking interplanetary gold; both ships make use of an arcane antigravity device; both mention the tinkling sound of meteorites on the ship's hull and the steel shutters used to shut out the intense sunlight; both show earthlings full of fears about alien worlds who, in an audience before the ruling spirit, discover that they themselves are the ones who pose a danger to other species.[43]

Despite these structural similarities, however, *Out of the Silent Planet* is fundamentally anti-Wellsian. In *Surprised by Joy* Lewis explains that his own trilogy was less a tribute to earlier science fiction than it was an exorcism of a certain coarse fascination, tinged with eroticism, which he found in the cosmic voyage narratives he had devoured in his school years.[44] He comments as well that his reading of H. G. Wells planted firmly in his boyish imagination "the vastness and cold of space, the littleness of Man."[45] This is, of course, the materialist myth that Lewis deliberately seeks to subvert in the trilogy.

While writers like Wells, Stapledon, and Haldane provided the matter that Lewis wanted to respond to in *Out of the Silent Planet,* David Lindsay's *Voyage to Arcturus* showed him the method for writing what he called "theologised science fiction."[46] Lindsay published a series of novels in the 1920s that reached a very small audience; in fact, he would probably be all but forgotten today if Lewis had not praised him "as the real father of my planet books."[47] Lewis wrote to the American scholar Charles A. Brady that *Voyage* first gave him "the idea that the 'scientifiction' appeal could be combined with the 'supernatural' appeal."[48] He explained more fully to his friend Ruth Pitter: "From Lindsay I first learned what other planets in fiction are really good for; for *spiritual* adventures. Only they can satisfy the craving which sends our imaginations off the earth. Or putting it another way, in him I first saw the terrific results produced by the union of two kinds of fiction hitherto kept apart; the Novalis, G. MacDonald, James Stephens sort and the H. G. Wells, Jules Verne sort. My debt to him is very great."[49]

Such high praise has encouraged some readers of Lewis to turn to Lindsay's *Voyage to Arcturus,* hoping to find there the inventive and adventurous plot of Wells and Verne blended with the otherworldliness and spirituality of Morris and MacDonald. Instead they are likely to find a rather repellent and awkwardly structured tale in which the quest for truth and goodness ends only in a maze of illusions and a sense that good and evil are one and the same.

Lewis himself was not at all attracted to the theme of *Voyage to Arcturus.* In fact, he pronounced the book "on the borderline of the diabolical . . . [and] so manichean as to be almost satanic."[50] Yet Lindsay proved that the cosmic voyage could be more than just an adventure story; it could become a vehicle for serious philosophical exploration. Lewis praised the novel for its "lived dialectic," the way its twists and turns in plot reflect successive attempts to arrive at some final truth, each one to be undercut by some new development in the story.[51]

Throughout *Voyage to Arcturus,* the inner lives of the story's characters are also revealed by their outer shapes. For example, when Maskull, the protagonist, first awakens on Tormance, a planet circling Arcturus, he discovers that his body has been changed; there is a protuberance on his forehead, a lump on his neck beneath each ear, and a tentacle growing out of his chest. Soon he learns that these seeming disfigurements are actually new organs—to give him powers of telepathy, empathy, and magnanimity that he lacked on earth. Thus Lindsay uses the fantasy convention of alien creatures with exotic anatomies to depict, perhaps a bit heavy-handedly, his characters and theme. The feature of *Voyage* that made the deepest impression on Lewis was Lindsay's creation of plausible physical details that are also imbued with psychological and spiritual significance.

Another writer whose influence is most apparent in *Out of the Silent Planet* is Jonathan Swift. Ransom's encounter with the ideal community of the hrossa and his interview with the Oyarsa bear a number of similarities to Gulliver's experiences in part four of *Gulliver's Travels,* "A Voyage to the Country of the Houyhnhnms." The word *hross* is Old Norse for "horse," and the persistent initial *h* in the hrossa's speech reminds us as well of the neighing speech of Swift's creations. Jeannette Hume Lutton has best summarized the structural similarities between the two stories:

Both [protagonists] find themselves in fantastic surroundings as the result of treachery and violence at the hands of their fellow men. Both, wandering friendless and unprovisioned in a totally unknown environment, encounter rational beings whom they initially take to be beasts. Both recognize the rationality of these creatures by hearing them talk. Both go home with the creatures they have met, live for a considerable time among them, learn their language, communicate something of the cultures they represent to their hosts . . . and learn something of the host culture, grow to love and admire their hosts but eventually find themselves under the necessity of leaving them, and after further adventures, return to their own lands with changed outlook and a kind of permanent homesickness for the culture that once seemed so alien.[52]

To this overall summary one can add incidental parallels such as the surprise of the alien creatures when they discover that the protagonist's clothes are not part of his natural covering and their disgust when they hear the sorry history of our own species. In a conversation with Brian Aldiss and Kingsley Amis, Lewis agreed that a modern-day Swift would probably send his Gulliver to some other planet, a position that has encouraged readers to look for Swiftian touches in *Out of the Silent Planet*.[53]

Apart from speculating about literary sources for the first book of the Ransom trilogy, critics have also shown a great deal of interest in possible real life models for the main characters in the story. As mentioned above, the character of Ransom seems to be largely created in the image of his maker. Some scholars, though, have compared Ransom to Tolkien, whose specialty was languages. However, Tolkien did not think Ransom was modeled on himself, though he saw in Ransom some of his own ideas "Lewisified."[54] And Lewis explained that he made Ransom a philologist because the plot would require someone who could acquire new languages quickly.[55]

There has been a wealth of speculation by Lewis's critics and biographers about possible sources for the characters of Devine and Weston. J. B. S. Haldane is most often named as the model for Weston. Certainly, some of Weston's ideas in *Out of the Silent Planet* sound like Haldane's sentiments in *Possible Worlds,* especially the defense of research on animals and the vision of our species reaching out to fill the galaxy. But Haldane's books show a healthy appreciation for the arts and the humanities, which one cannot picture him dismissing, like Weston, as "unscientific foolery" (p. 13). Lewis himself said that Weston is a composite,[56] and the books of the trilogy bear him out on this. In this book and in *Perelandra,* Weston's speeches strongly echo not only Haldane but also Stapledon, Wells, Shaw, Bergson, and other proponents of Evolutionism. Note, for example, the closing words of Weston's speech to the Oyarsa: "What lies in the future, beyond our present ken, passes imagination to conceive: it is enough for me that there is a Beyond" (p. 137). This sentence reminds us of the passage quoted above from Haldane's "Man's Destiny," but the closing words are also nearly identical to those found in Shaw's *Back to Methuselah* (1921): "It is enough that there is a beyond."

Devine is probably also a composite, though he is most often associated with T. D. ("Harry") Weldon, a philosophy tutor at Lewis's college at Oxford and his nemesis. Weldon was a progressive and a free thinker, and he and

Lewis took opposite sides, not only in philosophical matters, but also in the college's political affrays. At some points their relationship became so strained that they were barely on speaking terms.[57] If Weldon really were the model for Devine, then Lewis's satire here is especially pointed; he gives Weldon's nickname, Harry, to the half-witted boy whom Devine tries to kidnap before deciding to take Ransom instead.

Critic William Empson described C. S. Lewis as the best-read man of his generation, one who read everything and remembered everything he read.[58] Several who knew Lewis recall that if they quoted a line from *Paradise Lost,* he could begin quoting the succeeding lines from memory. In conversation or in his writing, Lewis could call to mind a passage he had seen that week or something he had read in school decades earlier. Thus in *Out of the Silent Planet,* we find interwoven with the story line not only ideas and allusions from classical mythology and the Bible, but also echoes from medieval and Renaissance writers, from Icelandic myth, from science fiction, and romance, or from people and experience in Lewis's own life. Even a cursory review of Lewis's creative synthesis in *Out of the Silent Planet* reveals the kind of literary art Lewis valued most highly in other writers and underscores his own literary art in shaping such a wide variety of allusions into a coherent narrative.

NOTES

1. Donald E. Glover, *C. S. Lewis and the Art of Enchantment* (Athens, OH: Ohio University Press, 1981), 38.

2. Humphrey Carpenter, ed. *The Letters of J. R. R. Tolkien* (Boston, MA: Houghton Mifflin, 1981), 29.

3. Ibid., 32–34.

4. Walter Hooper and Warren H. Lewis. *Letters of C. S. Lewis.* Revised edition (New York: Harcourt Brace & Company, 1993), 262.

5. John S. Kennedy, "Fiction in Focus," *Sign* 23 (November 1943), 255.

6. Frank Swinnerton, "Our Planet and Others," *Observer* 27 (November 1938), 6.

7. C. S. Lewis, *Christian Reflections*, ed. Walter Hooper (Grand Rapids, MI: Eerdmans, 1973), 71.

8. Roger Lancelyn Green and Walter Hooper, *C. S. Lewis: A Biography* (New York: Harcourt Brace and World, 1965), 71.

9. Hooper and Lewis, *Letters of C. S. Lewis,* 262.

10. Olaf Stapledon, *Last and First Men* (Los Angeles, CA: Jeremy P. Tarcher, 1988), 302.

11. Quoted in *The Penguin Dictionary of Modern Quotations*, ed. J. M. Cohen and M. J. Cohen (New York: Penguin, 1980), 290.

12. C. S. Lewis, *Letters to Children*, ed. Lyle Dorsett and Marjorie Lamp Mead (New York: Macmillan, 1985), 32.

13. J. B. S. Haldane, *Possible Worlds* (New York: Hugh and Brothers, 1928), 305.

14. Charles Moorman, *The Precincts of Felicity: The Augustinian City of the Oxford Christians* (Gainesville, FL: University of Florida Press, 1966), 109.

15. C. S. Lewis, *Out of the Silent Planet* (New York: Macmillan, 1968), 7. All references hereafter will be incorporated into the text.

16. Green and Hooper, *C. S. Lewis: A Biography*, 179.

17. Hooper and Lewis, *Letters of C. S. Lewis*, 446.

18. Verlyn Flieger, "The Sound of Silence: Language and Experience in *Out of the Silent Planet*," in *Word and Story in C. S. Lewis*, ed. Peter J. Schakel and Charles A. Huttar (Columbia, MO: University of Missouri Press, 1991), 52.

19. W. D. Norwood, Jr., "The Neo-Medieval Novels of C. S. Lewis," Ph.D. Dissertation, University of Texas at Austin, 1965, 36.

20. Joe R. Christopher, *C. S. Lewis* (Boston, MA: Twayne, 1987), 93.

21. Evan K. Gibson, *C. S. Lewis: Spinner of Tales: A Guide to His Fiction* (Washington, DC: Christian University Press, 1980), 40.

22. Hooper and Lewis, *Letters of C. S. Lewis*, 476.

23. Carpenter, *The Letters of J. R. R. Tolkien*, 34.

24. C. S. Lewis, *Letters to Children*, 70.

25. C. S. Lewis, *Letters to an American Lady*, ed. Clyde S. Kilby (Grand Rapids, MI: Eerdmans, 1967), 12–13.

26. C. S. Lewis, *The Discarded Image* (Cambridge: Cambridge University Press, 1971), 75.

27. C. S. Lewis, *Studies in Medieval and Renaissance Literature,* ed. Walter Hooper (Cambridge: Cambridge University Press, 1969), 69.

28. C. S. Lewis, *Letters to Children,* 73.

29. Hooper and Lewis, *Letters of C. S. Lewis*, 246.

30. Ibid., 475.

31. C. S. Lewis, *English Literature in the Sixteenth Century Excluding Drama* (Oxford: Clarendon Press, 1954), 2; *Miracles* (New York: Macmillan, 1968), 50; *Studies in Medieval and Renaissance Literature*, 46–47.

32. Lewis, *The Discarded Image*, 97.

33. Lewis, *Studies in Medieval and Renaissance Literature*, 62.

34. Ibid., 52.

35. Ibid., 56.

36. Lewis, *The Discarded Image,* 33.

37. Ibid., 111.

38. Ibid., 62–63.

39. C. S. Lewis, *Of Other Worlds*, ed. Walter Hooper (New York: Harper, 1975), 81.

40. Walter Hooper, ed. *They Stand Together: The Letters of C. S. Lewis to Arthur Greeves (1914–1963).* (New York: Macmillan, 1979), 49.

41. Ibid., 264.

42. Green and Hooper, *C. S. Lewis: A Biography*, 164.

43. Robert E. Boenig, "Lewis's Time Machine and His Trip to the Moon," in *Mythlore* 24 (Summer 1980), 6; Mark R. Hillegas, *The Future as Nightmare: H. G. Wells and the Anti-Utopians* (New York: Oxford University Press, 1967), 135.

44. C. S. Lewis, *Surprised by Joy* (New York: Harcourt, 1955), 35–36.

45. Ibid., 65.

46. Hooper and Lewis, *Letters of C. S. Lewis*, 444.

47. Quoted. in ed. E. F. Bleiler, "C. S. Lewis," in *Supernatural Fiction Writers: Fantasy and Horror*, vol. 2 (New York: Scribner's, 1985), 542.

48. Hooper and Lewis, *Letters of C. S. Lewis*, 375.

49. George Sayer, *Jack: C. S. Lewis and His Times* (San Francisco, CA: Harper, 1988), 153

50. Ibid.

51. Lewis, *Of Other Worlds*, 12.

52. Jeannette Hume Lutton, "The Feast of Reason: Out of the Silent Planet as the Book of Hnau," in *Mythlore* 47 (Autumn 1986), 39.

53. Lewis, *Of Other Worlds*, 143.

54. Glover, *C. S. Lewis and the Art of Enchantment*, 77; Carpenter, *The Letters of J. R. R. Tolkien*, 89

55. Glover, *C. S. Lewis and the Art of Enchantment*, 77.

56. Lewis, *Of Other Worlds*, 78.

57. Colin Hardie, "A Colleague's Note on C. S. Lewis," *Inklings—Jahrbuch fur Literatur und Asthetik*, 177; Sayer, *Jack: C. S. Lewis and His Times*, 119; Griffin, *Clive Staples Lewis: A Dramatic Life*, 140; Carpenter, *The Inklings*, 198.

58. James T. Como, *C. S. Lewis at the Breakfast Table and Other Reminiscences* (New York: Macmillan, 1979), xxii.

BIBLIOGRAPHY

Bleiler, E. F., Editor. *Supernatural Fiction Writers: Fantasy and Horror*, vol. 2. New York: Scribner's, 1985.

Boenig, Robert E. "Lewis's Time Machine and His Trip to the Moon." *Mythlore* 24 (Summer 1980): 6.

Carpenter, Humphrey. *The Inklings: C. S. Lewis, J. R. R. Tolkien, Charles Williams, and their Friends*. Boston, MA: Houghton Mifflin, 1979.

———. ed. *The Letters of J. R. R. Tolkien*. Boston, MA: Houghton Mifflin, 1981.

Christopher, Joe R. *C. S. Lewis*. Boston, MA: Twayne, 1987.

Cohen J. M. and M. J. Cohen, eds. *The Penguin Dictionary of Modern Quotations*. New York: Penguin, 1980.

Como, James T. *C. S. Lewis at the Breakfast Table and Other Reminiscences.* New York: Macmillan, 1979.

Downing, David. *Planets in Peril.* Amherst, MA: University of Massachusetts Press, 1992.

Flieger, Verlyn. "The Sound of Silence: Language and Experience in *Out of the Silent Planet.*" In *Word and Story in C. S. Lewis.* Edited by by Peter J. Schakel and Charles A. Huttar. Columbia, MO: University of Missouri Press, 1991.

Gibson, Evan K. *C. S. Lewis: Spinner of Tales: A Guide to His Fiction.* Washington, DC: Christian University Press, 1980.

Glover, Donald E. *C. S. Lewis and the Art of Enchantment.* Athens, OH: Ohio University Press, 1981.

Green, Roger Lancelyn and Walter Hooper. *C. S. Lewis: A Biography.* New York: Harcourt Brace and World, 1965.

Griffin, William. *Clive Staples Lewis: A Dramatic Life.* New York: Harper and Row, 1986.

Hardie, Colin. "A Colleague's Note on C. S. Lewis." *Inklings—Jahrbuch fur Literatur und Asthetik* 3 (1985).

Hillegas, Mark R. *The Future as Nightmare: H. G. Wells and the Anti-Utopians.* New York: Oxford University Press, 1967.

Hooper, Walter and Warren H, Lewis. *Letters of C. S. Lewis.* Revised edition. New York: Harcourt Brace & Company, 1993.

———. *They Stand Together: The Letters of C. S. Lewis to Arthur Greeves (1914–1963).* New York: Macmillan, 1979.

Kennedy, John S. "Fiction in Focus," *Sign* 23 (November 1943).

Kilby, Clyde S. and Marjorie Lamp Mead, *Brothers and Friends: The Diaries of Major Warren Hamilton Lewis.* San Francisco, CA: Harper, 1982.

Lewis, C. S. *Christian Reflections.* Edited by Walter Hooper. Grand Rapids, MI: Eerdmans, 1973.

———. *C. S. Lewis's Letters to Children.* Edited by Lyle Dorsett and Marjorie Lamp Mead. New York: Macmillan, 1985.

———. *The Discarded Image.* Cambridge: Cambridge University Press, 1971.

———. *English Literature in the Sixteenth Century Excluding Drama.* Oxford: Clarendon Press, 1954

———. *Letters to an American Lady.* Edited by Clyde S. Kilby. Grand Rapids, MI: Eerdmans, 1967.

———. *Miracles.* New York: Macmillan, 1968.

———. *Of Other Worlds.* Edited by Walter Hooper. New York: Harper, 1975.

———. *Out of the Silent Planet.* New York: Macmillan, 1968.

———. *Studies in Medieval and Renaissance Literature.* Edited by Walter Hooper. Cambridge: Cambridge University Press, 1969.

———. *Surprised by Joy.* New York: Harcourt, 1955.

Lutton, Jeannette Hume. "The Feast of Reason: Out of the Silent Planet as the Book of Hnau." *Mythlore* 47 (Autumn 1986).

Moorman, Charles. *The Precincts of Felicity: The Augustinian City of the Oxford Christians.* Gainesville, FL: University of Florida Press, 1966.

Norwood, W. D., Jr. "The Neo-Medieval Novels of C. S. Lewis." Ph.D. Dissertation, University of Texas at Austin, 1965.

Samaan, Angele Botros. "C. S. Lewis: The Utopianist and His Critics." *Cairo Studies in English* (1966).

Sayer, George. *Jack: C. S. Lewis and His Times.* San Francisco, CA: Harper, 1988.

Schakel, Peter J. and Charles A. Huttar, Editors. *Word and Story in C. S. Lewis.* Columbia, MO: University of Missouri Press, 1991.

Stapledon, Olaf. *Last and First Men.* Los Angeles, CA: Jeremy P. Tarcher, 1988.

Swinnerton, Frank. "Our Planet and Others." *Observer* 27 (November 1938).

3

Perelandra: A Tale of
Paradise Retained

David C. Downing

Perelandra (1943), the second book of the Ransom trilogy, is the story of "Paradise Retained,"[1] of an Eve who is able to resist the tempter long enough for Ransom to destroy him. In fulfilling his quest, Ransom too learns a great deal about the reality of myth and how ordinary mortals may be called upon to engage in mythic labors.

Perelandra begins in much the same spirit in which *Out of the Silent Planet* ends. Again we meet Lewis himself as a character in the novel, this time trudging toward Ransom's cottage and worrying about getting involved in "inter-planetary politics."[2] "Lewis" muses that Ransom's discovery of creatures called eldils broke down one's comfortable distinction between the natural and the supernatural, exposing it as an arbitrary division used to ease "the burden of intolerable strangeness which this universe imposes on us" (p. 11).

Lewis uses a number of techniques to break down the distinction between his fictional world and our "factual" world. Most obviously, he uses his own name and those of other real people ("C. J." in *Out of the Silent Planet* and "Humphrey" in *Perelandra,* based upon his friend and personal physician, R. E. "Humphrey" Havard). He also quotes ancient authorities, such as the Bible and a medieval scholar Natvilcius, who assume the reality of angels. He even appeals to human psychology early in *Perelandra*: "Lewis" learns that the extreme anxiety he experienced in approaching Ransom's cottage was not just a case of the jitters or fear of the unknown; his mind was actually being besieged by bent eldils who wanted him to turn back. Thus the author blurs the distinction between the "psychological" and the "spiritual."

The first theological link between Lewis's created world and the real world comes in *Perelandra* when Ransom first tells "Lewis" that he has been commissioned to travel to another planet to engage in some sort of combat with dark forces. To reassure "Lewis" that he has not succumbed to megalomania, Ransom refers to a *Bible* verse about fighting "principalities and powers" (p. 23). The verse Ransom has in mind is Ephesians 6:12: "For we wrestle not against flesh and blood, but against principalities, against powers, against the rulers of the darkness of this world, against spiritual wickedness in high places" (KJV). Ransom correctly notes that the last phrase does not refer to highly placed human rulers, but rather to "hypersomatic beings at great heights" (p. 24). "Hypersomatic" here means "beyond bodily form," and "great heights" means "in the heavenly world, in the supernatural sphere." So the dark eldils that Ransom and "Lewis" have to contend with are the same demonic powers with whom the apostle Paul predicted all Christians would have to wrestle.

Lewis also blurs the distinction between fact and fiction by supplying *Perelandra* with a scholarly footnote, which turns out to yet another of Lewis's inventions. In speculating about how eldils might choose to present themselves to human eyes, "Lewis," the character in the novel who is a friend of Ransom, quotes an ancient authority, Natvilcius, writing in Latin, about how the actual, celestial bodies of angels might differ a great deal from the way in which they are perceived by human eyes (pp. 18–19). Some Lewis commentators have pored over many a reference source trying to discover the identity of this Natvilcius, apparently not realizing that this medieval theologian is another of the author's fictions.[3] Sometimes when Lewis chose to write anonymously, he used the letters "N. W." Most of his occasional poems were published with these initials, and the first edition of *A Grief Observed* appeared with "N. W. Clerk" as its author. "N. W" is short for *Nat Whilk*, Old English for "I know not whom." It is the archaic equivalent of the modern phrase "author unknown." *Natvilcius* is simply the Latinized form of "Nat Whilk." Unlike his reference to the actual author, Bernardus Silvestris, in *Out of the Silent Planet*, Lewis has created here a fictional scholar to introduce his idea that eldils exist on a celestial plane and can be perceived only imperfectly by creatures confined to three-dimensional space. Even Lewis's little hoax here is an oblique tribute to a medieval author. In his essay "What Chaucer Did to 'Il Filostrato,'" Lewis notes with seeming delight Chaucer's citation of fanciful sources to lend a greater sense of historicity to *Troilus and Cressida*.[4]

After giving instructions to his friend "Lewis," Ransom prepares himself for another interplanetary adventure, this time a mission to Venus. In his first sojourn on another world, the story told in *Out of the Silent Planet*, Ransom, the pilgrim, made a great deal of progress. But Ransom's personal pilgrimage is far from over. If the great challenge of Ransom's first journey was to overcome his fears, the great challenge of his second journey is to overcome his self-will.

Though Ransom was taken to Mars against his wishes, he voluntarily accepts a mission to Venus, traveling naked in a translucent coffin-shaped box, and carried through the heavens by the hand of an eldil. If Ransom found Malacandra to be surprisingly beautiful when he first arrived there, he is positively ravished with pleasure upon plummeting into the ocean of the second planet, called Perelandra. With warm sweet-water seas surrounding him and a golden dome of sky above, Ransom finds that even an accidental mouthful of water from a passing wave gives him "quite astonishing pleasure almost like meeting Pleasure itself for the first time" (p. 35). Even the violent squall that rises up leaves him more dazzled than frightened. The thunder is more resonant than terrestrial thunder, making a kind of tinkling sound in the distance, "the laugh, rather than the roar, of heaven" (p. 37).

Like Malacandra, with its utopian society of divergent species all living in peace, Perelandra too is an unfallen planet. It is an Edenic world of golden seas and lush tropical islands that float upon the waves. Besides these delights, Perelandra also evokes a whole other species of pleasure. When Ransom, riding on a dolphin's back at night, approaches one of the floating islands, he experiences a sense of rapture that is somehow strangely familiar, a "cord of longing," which seems to have been fastened before he ever came to Perelandra, before his earliest childhood, and before even the foundations of the world. For Ransom, this yearning, with both its pain and pleasure, seems "sharp, sweet, wild, and holy, all in one" (pp. 102–103).

In this passage we see Perelandra, not only as a garden of unearthly delights, but also as an image of Joy itself. The exotic garden—whether Eden, Hesperides, or Avalon—is one of the places that Lewis associated with Joy from early childhood on. The luxuriant islands, too, appear throughout Lewis's books, most notably in *Pilgrim's Regress*, as a picture of unreachable paradise.

But Ransom has not come to Perelandra for his own pleasure. He has been sent on a mission not yet revealed to him. This quest does not begin on a promising note, however: the Green Lady, the Eve of Perelandra, bursts into laughter at Ransom's appearance the first time she sees him. On the voyage to Venus in a translucent casket, one side of his body has been burnt a brownish-red by the sun, and the other side left a pallid white. She apologizes for her first reaction, but nonetheless she dubs him Piebald Man, not a very dignified sobriquet for a man sent to save a planet.

Ransom's two-toned body is an image of his divided self. Though he has submitted to the will of Maleldil (God), he still has within him his natural self, his own desire for control, safety, and self-reliance. Ransom's piebald state recalls his dream in *Out of the Silent Planet,* in which he found himself straddling a garden wall—half a citizen of a fallen world, half a citizen of Deep Heaven. Critics have applied a variety of psychological models to explain Ransom's dual nature.[5] But Ransom's inner discord here can best be understood in terms of the traditional Christian paradigms, the conflict between one's sanctified self and one's natural self, between the spirit of Christ within and the spirit of the "old Adam" that resists the intrusion.

In *Out of the Silent Planet* Ransom learned a great deal about goodness, especially about diverse creatures living in harmony and their accepting change and mortality as inevitable parts of the life-process. In *Perelandra* he is forced to confront the nature of evil. As he considers its origins, he comes to realize it is not only "out there," in rebel angels or demented visionaries like Edward Weston; it is also "in here," latent within himself and even in the unfallen Eve of another world. He comes to realize that evil may come into a perfect world not because there are positive evils attempting to seduce him but because he is tempted to cling to good things desired over good things given.

This truth unfolds itself gradually in Ransom's mind. Not long after arriving on the planet, he tastes the nectar from a yellow fruit and finds it inexpressibly delicious, a whole new kind of pleasure which, on earth, would lead to wars and the conquest of nations. But as he goes to take a second drink, a vague instinct within tells him not to, that partaking again would be an excess, like demanding to hear the same symphony twice in one day.

The next day Ransom finds another exquisite delight when he touches the bubble from a Perelandran bubble-tree and it bursts in his face. He feels the urge to plunge through the whole lot of bubbles to multiply the enchantment tenfold, but again he is restrained by some inner adviser. This time, though, he is able to identify the source of his restraint. He sees that this "itch to have things over again," is the source of much evil, and that one's life is not a roll of film that can be unrolled twice. He wonders if the love of money is called the root of all evil because wealth provides "a defence against chance, a security for being able to have things over again" (p. 48). This lesson, learned from a fruit tree and a bubble-tree, becomes one of the predominant themes of *Perelandra.* Humans long for a godlike sovereignty over their lives, to maximize pleasure and security, to wall out pain and uncertainty. But only when they learn to accept vicissitudes and vulnerability as inherent to the fabric of life can they truly be free.

When Ransom later explains the nature of evil to the Green Lady, the Eve of that world, he amplifies this theme. Though she inhabits a world where everything is good, she herself could become the instrument by which evil enters in. Ransom reminds her that when she first saw him from afar, she thought he was her husband, the Adam of that planet, from whom she had become separated. She had been disconcerted for a moment—only a moment—and then adjusted to the new circumstance. But, Ransom asks, what if she had clung to her old expectation, refusing to exchange her hope to find her husband for the novel experience of meeting someone from another world? The Green Lady comprehends this, thinking of times she had gone looking for one kind of fruit and finding another. She says that you would make the fruit you found taste insipid by continuing to long for the one you expected.

The Green Lady's recognition of how evil might enter into her heart applies at the cosmic level as well. Building on her understanding about taking the good that comes instead of clinging to the good one expected, Ransom identifies the Bent One as an eldil who "clung longer—who has been clinging since before the worlds were made." The Green Lady responds that the old good would cease to be good if one did that, and Ransom agrees: "Yes. It has ceased. And still he clings" (p. 83). The Bent One (Lucifer) was granted one of the greatest of all goods—to be Maleldil's viceroy over a world. Yet he would accept no sovereign over him, considering equality with Maleldil as a thing to be grasped. And the temptation to which he fell becomes the one he will tempt humans with, to become gods unto themselves.

In Genesis, the one thing forbidden to Adam and Eve was to taste fruit of the knowledge of good and evil, to try and achieve a god-like omniscience on their own. On Perelandra, the forbidden thing is to dwell on the Fixed Land, the one continent on their world that does not float upon its golden seas. Maleldil has decreed the floating islands to be the proper home of the king and queen of Perelandra, and he has forbidden them to spend even one night on the Fixed Land.

At first thought, this may seem like an odd choice of symbolic "forbidden fruit" on Lewis's part. Readers may associate a fixed land with absolutes, eternal truths, anchoring oneself in unchanging realities. And floating islands might connote the opposite—relativism, instability, being driven by the caprices of the moment. In the Epistle of James, the doubter is described as being "like a wave of the sea blown and tossed by the wind" (1:6). And in Spenser's Arthurian allegory *Faerie Queene*, one of Lewis's favorite books, the "Wandering Islands" are to be avoided by the righteous.

But for Lewis the emphasis is not upon stability versus instability but upon demanding control versus relinquishing it. Throughout *Perelandra*, the recurring themes are accepting the fruit one is given, riding the wave instead of fighting the current, living on floating islands instead of a stable continent. These images gain added poignancy when we find them again in Lewis's memoir, *Surprised by Joy:* "With my mother's death all settled happiness, all that was tranquil and reliable, disappeared from my life. There was to be much fun, many pleasures, many stabs of Joy; but no more of the old security.

It was sea and islands now; the great continent had sunk like Atlantis."[6] One rather suspects that Lewis's doctrine of learning to be carried on the wave rather than craving the fixed land may have been derived in part from his learning to accept the untimely loss of his mother.

The Green Lady learns a great deal from her discussions with Ransom, discovering, as she puts it, "I thought I was carried in the will of Him I love, but now I see that I walk in it" (p. 69). In her unfallen state, she has an added advantage. As Lewis had envisioned Adam and Eve before their disobedience, the Green Lady is able to receive new understanding directly from Maleldil into her mind. Even though she has never traveled outside her world, she says she has received mental images of the furry hrossa and gawky sorns of Malacandra, and wishes she could see them with her "outward eyes." She also knows about the Incarnation on "the silent planet," earth.

When Ransom asks how she could know such things, she answers that Maleldil has told her, or even that he is telling her as she speaks to Ransom. She is a kind of natural mystic, and when she says she is in the presence of Maleldil, even Ransom notices something different about the landscape around them, a sense of fullness in the air, almost a pressure resting on his shoulders. His great task on Malacandra was to overcome his habitual fearfulness; his great task on this planet will be to overcome his habitual willfulness, to acknowledge this pressure as a Presence and to submit to a will greater than his own.

When the queen of Perelandra departs, Ransom discovers this sense of Presence is even more overpowering, seeming to squeeze out his very selfhood. Whenever he tries to assert his independence, the very air seems too full to breathe. But as he learns to surrender himself, he discovers it is not really a burden at all, but rather "a sort of splendour as of eatable, drinkable, breathable gold, which fed and carried you and not only poured into you but out from you as well" (p. 72). As his adventure on Perelandra continues, Ransom alternates between these two moods. When he tries to assert his own will, it seems almost suffocating. But when he gives himself up, it seems a glorious fullness, which makes earthly life, by comparison, seem barren and empty.

Evil does not come to Perelandra from either Ransom or the Green Lady. Rather, it arrives from outside, from the fallen planet, in the person of Weston. With the arrival of Weston, the serpent in this Eden, the contest over the Green Lady—and the fate of the planet—greatly intensifies Ransom's inner strife. Weston's philosophy has changed somewhat since his misadventures on Malacandra. Rather than the interplanetary imperialism he espoused in *Out of the Silent Planet,* he now admits of spiritual forces and sees himself as the instrument of some Universal Life Force. Though Ransom tries to warn him— "There are spirits and spirits you know"—Weston arrogantly claims that he is both the God and the Devil of Christian mythology, declaring grandiosely, "I call that Force into me completely . . . " The darkest of all spirits obliges him, causing Weston to lose his selfhood, probably also his life. His body becomes a demonized corpse: the man becomes Un-man (pp. 93, 96).

Weston, later the Un-man, plies the Green Lady with arguments for disobeying Maleldil far more subtle than anything the Eve of Genesis had to face. His recurring theme is that staying on the Fixed Land would be only superficially disobedient to Maleldil, and that in asserting a self-will, making herself a "little Maleldil," she would actually be pleasing him. Try as he might to refute the Un-man's devious arguments, Ransom fears that he is not up-to-the-job and that the Green Lady will eventually succumb.

With the Green Lady and her planet nearing a crisis, Ransom becomes physically and emotionally exhausted. After many long days and nearly sleepless nights (the Un-man doesn't sleep), he reaches the end of his resources, sitting alone in the dark, in a state very near despair. "This can't go on," he thinks to himself repeatedly, as he enters into an internal debate every bit as fierce, protracted, and theologically subtle as any of his contests with the Un-man (p. 130). This dialogue touches upon fundamental questions of Christian theology—free will versus determinism; the seeming absence of God; how a good God could allow evil and suffering in his creation.

Throughout this inner debate, one side of Ransom demands some reasonable explanation for this sorry state of affairs, and the other side is willing to trust Maleldil even in the face of seeming failure. His "voluble self" asks why Maleldil sends no miracle to save this world, why is he absent at such a critical juncture. As an answer, he suddenly senses, "as if the solid darkness about him had spoken with articulate voice," and that Maleldil is not absent, and that "the darkness was packed quite full." At that moment one side of Ransom is "prostrated in a hush of fear and love that resembled a kind of death." But Lewis's narrator comments that such "inner silence" is difficult to achieve for humans, and that there is an earthbound part of the self that continues to "chatter on even in the holiest of places" (pp. 140–141).

When one side of Ransom, listening to the "silence and the darkness," realizes that he himself is the miracle, the other side replies that it is all nonsense, and that he, "with his ridiculous piebald body and his ten times defeated arguments—what sort of miracle was that?" Why allow the fate of a world to hinge upon the decisions of this "man of straw?" (pp. 141–142).

Eventually, it occurs to Ransom that his mission might not be to out-argue Weston, but to destroy the "managed corpse" being animated by a devil (p. 122). At first he considers it ridiculous to "degrade spiritual warfare to the condition of mere mythology" (p. 143). But then he recognizes that the earthly distinction between myth and fact is a result of the Fall, and that the

Incarnation brought the two together again, a historical event which enacted the great myth of the Dying God who lays down his life to redeem his people. Ransom's "voluble self" revolts at the idea of physical combat with the Un-man and continues offering up one objection after another. But "the terrible silence" around him begins to seem more and more like a face, the sad face of one waiting for him to exhaust his complaints and evasions. Once his inner rebel is silenced, Ransom assumes he will probably be killed doing battle with a "mechanized corpse" (p. 129). Then he hears a "Voice in the night," which tells him it, "It is not for nothing you are named Ransom," adding, "My name also is Ransom" (pp. 147–148). Once he is truly willing to give up his life in obedience, Ransom can hear a Voice, directing and comforting him, where earlier there had only been a fullness in the air, and then a Presence in the darkness, and finally a kind of face.

In determining to silence the Un-man once and for all, Ransom is casting his whole force of will toward the side of his divided personality who trusts in Maleldil. Once this decision is made, Ransom finds a peace he had not yet known on this planet. On the morning he awakens resolved to do battle with the Un-man, he discovers that the piebaldness of his body has largely faded away. In the end Ransom succeeds in overcoming both his fears and his inner divisions. As he approaches physical combat with the Un-man, Ransom does not expect Maleldil to forestall this encounter or to supply him with supernatural powers to overcome his diabolic enemy. He has simply resolved to do his best in the battle and has no assurance of the outcome. In fact, in the middle of their combat, Ransom shouts a line from the *Battle of Maldon.* We know from more than one source what Lewis's favorite line was from this Old English poem about heroic defeat at the hands of the Danes (a sort of Anglo-Saxon version of the Battle of the Alamo). This is assuredly the line Ransom cries in the middle of this battle to the death: "Purpose shall be the firmer, heart the keener, courage shall be the more, as our might lessens."[7]

This is quite stirring and heroic—and quite unlike Ransom. Earlier in the trilogy, his temperamental habit in times of stress has been to feel betrayed by those who should have helped him. But Ransom has found a strange new courage. When he first confronts the Un-man, offering to do physical battle, the demon corpse taunts him, playing upon his worst fears, conjuring up images of martyrs "screaming recantations too late in the middle of the fire, mouldering in concentration camps, writhing under saws, jibbering in mad-houses, or nailed on to crosses" (p. 153).

The Ransom we have seen earlier in the trilogy might have been paralyzed by so many appalling images of annihilation and abandonment. But he stands firm in the fray and fights with unfaltering determination. Perhaps the secret of his steely resolution lies in his hearing again, quoted from memory by one who had been there, those words from the cross: *Eloi, Eloi, lama sabachthani,* "My God, my God, why hast thou forsaken me?" (p. 153). In his letters, Lewis used Christ's sense of abandonment on the cross as an illustration to those who felt abandoned: "The Father was not *really* absent from the Son when He said 'Why hast thou forsaken me?' You see God Himself, as man, submitted to man's sense of being abandoned."[8] In his battle with the Un-man, Ransom imitates Christ's passion, setting aside fears and feelings of abandonment to complete the task given to him.

The Un-Man proves to be no stronger than an ordinary human of Weston's size and build; but it is seemingly a good deal harder to kill. After several vicious rounds of boxing, wrestling, and clawing on one of the floating islands, there is a long sea chase and a descent into a subterranean cave. The two become separated in the dark and Ransom climbs up a sheer rockface, until he discovers a fiery underground cavern. There the Un-man accosts him one last time, filling Ransom with sudden fear. Wondering if somehow the Un-man is able to manipulate his thoughts, Ransom cries in a rage, "Get out of my brain. It isn't yours, I tell you!" (p. 181). Then, invoking the Trinity, he hurls a stone at the Un-man and does away with him once and for all. After this long-sought victory, Ransom climbs some more until he finds a passage to the surface, reemerging on top of a high mountain, a place of brilliant flowers and singing voices in the air. There he rests beside a pool for several days, trying to regain his strength and recover from his wounds. His back is shredded as if he has been scourged, but his most serious wound is on his heel.

The culminating fight scene is quite a bit more prolonged than most readers expect, taking up almost a fifth of the novel. Obviously, Lewis has more in mind than just dispatching the villain of his story. As the story reaches its climax, it seems less about external combat and more about divisions in the inner world of Ransom's consciousness. In this section, Weston, or what is left of him, seems a kind of anti-self of Ransom, a projection of Ransom's own doubts and misgivings. Several times a pathetic Weston-esque voice emanates from the Un-man, not at all the pompous, unfeeling scientist, but a frightened, petulant whine uttering gibberish about fears and petty grievances stretching back to boyhood.

Ransom never knows if this is a diabolical trick from the one who absorbed Weston's personhood or if it is the actual residue of Weston's decaying psyche. But the fearful, egocentric babblings of the Weston-voice seem uncommonly like a demented version of the complaints Ransom has been hearing from his own "voluble self"—the demand for an explanation, the self-pity, the tireless ego asserting its rights.

Thus the protracted fight scene is less about hand-to-hand combat than it is about Ransom's ultimate conquest of Self. In destroying the Un-man,

Ransom is defeating as well that side of himself that might have prevented him from accomplishing his mission on Perelandra. The fact that this last confrontation occurs in a maze of underground caverns certainly reinforces one's sense that the conflict is to be seen, at one level, as a battle within the deeper reaches of the mind.

THE MEDIEVAL CHRISTIAN BACKDROP OF *PERELANDRA*

Though Lewis supplies his protagonist with depth-psychology in the second novel of the Ransom trilogy, his exploration of the human mind is not drawn from modern or post-Freudian sources; rather he reaches back to medieval cosmology and spiritual allegory. Readers familiar with Dante, for example, will recognize frequent parallels between the final cantos of the *Purgatorio* and the fight scene in *Perelandra*. At the age of eighteen, long before he became a Christian, the young Lewis pronounced the final quarter of the *Purgatorio* to be the "heart of the whole book."[9] And this is the section Lewis would later draw upon so freely in the final quarter of *Perelandra*.

In the culminating scenes of Dante's book, the narrator climbs a steep slope, fearfully crosses through a wall of fire, and emerges outside upon the Garden of Earthly Delights, an unspoiled Eden. There he hears angelic voices, regales his eyes in dazzling flowers, and bathes in the waters of healing and forgetfulness. Only after that final stage of purification on what he calls the Holy Mountain ("santo monte") is Dante ready to move on to his vision of Paradise. In Dante's understanding, Purgatory is not a place of punishment, but of cleansing. Lewis's frequent borrowings from Dante, in this and the following scene, certainly underscore the idea that the last quarter of the novel is less about Weston's defeat than about Ransom's progress in his soul-journey.

Of course, Ransom's wounded heel and the Un-man's crushed head remind us also of the Bible, the redeemer promised in Genesis 3:15 who will atone for Adam's sin by crushing the serpent's head after being wounded by him. Indeed, Ransom's adventure on Perelandra offers a number of parallels with Christ's mission on earth. He enters a world in order to fulfill God's purpose for it; he is tempted to give up his mission; he undergoes a kind of Gethsemane of anxiety and loneliness the night before he must suffer; he experiences a symbolic death and rebirth in being dragged below the surface and spending three days there; he reemerges to have his mission celebrated by others; and finally he returns to his former sphere. To a reader who asked if Ransom was meant as an allegorical representation of Christ, Lewis replied that Ransom played the role of Christ on that world, not in an allegorical sense, but because in fact all Christians must in their calling play the role of Christ.

The final section of *Perelandra* is even more symbolic than the fight scene, and the closing pages of the book contain a mystical vision as vivid and compelling as anything in Dante. Impelled by some inner guide, Ransom descends from the mountain and climbs an even steeper one, called the Holy Mountain. He sees an angel with a flaming sword, like the one who guarded Eden, but knows he is not meant to turn back. He feels by then that climbing has become "not a process, but a state, and in that state of life he was content." He feels no weariness in his ascent, and wonders if he might be on some "trans-mortal journey" (p. 192). Finally, he reaches the summit and meets the archangels of Malacandra and Perelandra, who take the form of darting pillars filled with eyes, then great slow-rolling wheels, and finally gigantic human forms, like the gods Mars and Venus. Next Ransom witnesses the coronation of the King and Queen of that planet, and hears an angelic litany on the wondrous and ineffable qualities of Maleldil. Eventually, the sounds turn to sights, and he sees the Great Dance of the cosmos as a kaleidoscopic circle of incandescent images (much like the Inviolate Rose in Dante's *Paradiso*.) Finally, his mission accomplished, Ransom bids farewell to the newly enthroned King and Queen and begins his journey through the Heavens back to earth.

The culminating scene of the novel contains a great deal of mystical theology expressed in poetic language and imagery. The Holy Mountain, the angel with a flaming sword, and the seraphim—all eyes and wheels—may all be found in the *Purgatorio*. (Both Dante and Lewis acknowledged that their descriptions of seraphim drew directly upon the book of Ezekiel.[10])

Lewis's visionary creations resemble Dante's not only in their theology, but also in their social order. Like the unfallen society on Malacandra, ruled by Oyarsa, Perelandra is a hierarchical world, ruled by a single king and queen. Though these are the first pair, the Adam and Eve of that world as yet without descendants, they rule the animals and will eventually have authority over the Oyarsa of this world as well. Ransom is confused by this seeming reversal of the cosmic order, but the queen explains to him that their world was created after Maleldil the Younger had taken human form. As unfallen humans, the king and queen need have no authorities between themselves and Maleldil.

Though it might seem grievous for eldils to serve those whom they once ruled, the queen explains that it is "their glory and their joy" to nurture creatures before whom they would later bow (pp. 82–83). Later the Oyarsa of Perelandra confirms this, saying that her relationship with the royal pair is like that of two Perelandran creatures, the dumb dam who suckles the singing beast: "The [singing beasts] have no milk and always what they bring forth is suckled by the she-beast of another kind. She is great and beautiful and dumb, and till the young singing beast is weaned it is among her whelps and is subject to her. But when it is grown it becomes the most delicate and glorious of all beasts and goes from her. And she wonders at its song" (p. 196). In this passage Lewis suggests that a hierarchical social order entails more complex relationships than usually understood in our era, when the only political models we are familiar with are democratic, autocratic, or totalitarian.

Lewis often referred to the metaphor of the dance, both as an image of harmonic social order and as a picture of the cosmic order. In *Miracles* he explains that hierarchy itself is more like a dance than a pyramid, with the highest sometimes bowing low and the lowest often raised up. Lewis calls the principle of descent and reascent "the very formula of reality."[11] God had to descend into human form in order to redeem humanity; Christ had to descend into earth and then reascend three days later in order to complete his atoning work; humans must likewise descend into earth before they are raised up again on some final day. In this context, it is interesting to recall that Ransom is carried to Perelandra in a casket, which descends and then reascends upon plunging into the seas of Perelandra (p. 34). Later, when he is dragged downward to the ocean's depths by the Un-man, the language describing his descent (pp. 171–172) is intriguingly similar to the language Lewis uses in *Miracles,* in which he compares the Incarnation to the descent and reascent of a deep-sea diver.[12]

Behind Lewis's principle of ascent and reascent and his metaphors taken from dancing is the medieval commonplace of the Great Dance. Though we have become accustomed since Newton's time to think of the universe as essentially a mechanism, the medieval picture was much more festive. Lewis noted in one of his lectures on medieval cosmologists that their symbol for the primum mobile was a young girl dancing and playing a tambourine. He explains that the orderly movements of the heavenly spheres in the medieval picture "are to be conceived not as those of a machine or even an army, but rather as a dance, a festival, a symphony, a ritual, a carnival, or all of these in one."[13]

The Great Dance in the closing pages of *Perelandra* summarizes a great deal of theology in poetic form, as well as imaginatively recapturing some of the medieval sense of festival, symphony, ritual, and carnival, an intricate equipoise of freedom and order. In the dance, beasts, humans, and spirits all find their place; fallen worlds and unfallen ones, ancient ones and new ones, each participate in the pageant. The dance also serves as a kind of liturgical answer to the angst produced by positivism, the sense that humans inhabit a vast, dead universe that mocks all philosophy, all desire for justice, all yearning for some larger meaning. As Ransom chased the Weston/Un-man overseemingly illimitable seas, he became overwhelmed by "mere bigness and loneliness" and felt that those vast solitudes were haunted, not by some god, but by "the wholly inscrutable to which man and his life remained eternally irrelevant" (p. 164). Thinking of the even vaster solitudes of space, Ransom was oppressed by what he calls the Empirical Bogey, "the great myth of our century with its gases and galaxies, its light years and evolutions, its nightmare perspectives of simple arithmetic in which everything that can possibly hold significance for the mind becomes the mere byproduct of essential disorder" (p. 164). Once Ransom caught up with the Un-man, the Weston-voice echoed many of Ransom's own anxieties about some fundamental meaninglessness at the core of things (pp. 167–169). At the time Ransom had nothing to recommend except to repent and offer a child's prayer.

But the Great Dance offers a whole different cosmic picture. One speaker in the ritual affirms that Maleldil's greatness does not reside in "years to years in lumpish aggregations, or miles to miles and galaxies to galaxies"; for all of him dwells in the seed of the smallest flower and is not cramped, yet "Deep Heaven is inside Him who is inside the seed and does not distend Him" (pp. 214–215). Another voice explains that in the Great Dance all is at the center, whether the dust or beasts or hnau species or gods, for "where Maleldil is, there is the center" (p. 216). A third voice, most directly addressing the Empirical Bogey, proclaims, "All that is made seems planless to the darkened mind, because there are more plans than it looked for. . . . There seems no plan because it is all plan: there seems no centre because it is all centre" (p. 218).

The exclamations heard during the Great Dance frequently echo declarations by mystical writers whom Lewis knew well. Bonaventure (1217–1274) maintained that "God is in all, and all is in God. His center is everywhere, and his circumference nowhere." Jacob Boehme (1575–1604) wrote that if you conceive a circle "as small as a grain of mustard seed, yet the heart of God is wholly and perfectly therein." And for those born in God, he said, "the whole Heart of God is undivided." And John Ruysbroek (1293–1381) spoke of the "unplumbed Abyss of God."[14]

If the Great Dance tableau of *Perelandra* is mystical, so is Ransom's response to it. As he watches, everything in the cosmos, from a momentary spark to the lifespan of a star, shines out as a circle of swirling ribbons of interwoven light. The vision becomes three-dimensional, then four-dimensional, and continues adding dimension upon dimension, until "the part of him which could reason and remember dropped farther and farther behind the part of him which saw." Finally Ransom's vision reaches a "zenith of complexity" that melds into an utter "simplicity beyond all comprehension," which draws him "with cords of infinite desire into its own stillness." At the end of his vision Ransom is caught up into "a quietness, a privacy, and a freshness" that stands "farthest from our ordinary mode of being" (pp. 219–222).

Feeling utterly free of encumbrances and contradictions, Ransom suddenly has a sensation of awakening. He wonders if it is still morning, but discovers he has actually been enraptured for one whole year on Venus, time enough for the planet to complete its circle around the sun and stand again where it stood when his vision began. After such an enthralling vision, there is little more to be said. As Ransom lies down in his coffin-shaped spacecraft, he receives a fitting benediction from the newly crowned king of Perelandra: "The splendour, the love, and the strength be upon you" (p. 222).

LITERARY ECHOES IN *PERELANDRA*

Besides the book of Genesis and Dante's *Divine Comedy*, *Perelandra* also draws upon John Milton, Edmund Spenser, and several more recent writers. Lewis probably first got the idea for *Perelandra* while working on his *Preface to Paradise Lost* (1942). Margaret P. Hannay has shown that Lewis retained in *Perelandra* the elements of *Paradise Lost* that he most admired, while altering the elements he found fault with in Milton. Lewis considered Milton's Satan to be too impressive in the early books, so he made the tempter of the Green Lady entirely contemptible; he thought that Milton was mistaken in trying to portray God directly, so that Maleldil is only an elusive but powerful presence on Perelandra; he thought that Milton erred in trying to show human sexuality before the Fall, so he keeps the king and queen apart for most of the story; finally he rewrites the ending so that a second Fall may be averted.[15]

Apart from its broad narrative outlines, *Perelandra* is indebted to *Paradise Lost* for a great many details of characterization and setting. For instance, Lewis approved of the regal demeanor with which Milton invested the first pair,[16] and he heightens this element in his Eden story. Also, the Green Lady's momentary disappointment when she sees Ransom and recognizes that it is not her husband (p. 68) parallels Eve's initial disappointment when she first sees Adam and does not consider him as fair as her own reflection in a pool.[17] And when the Un-man scorns Ransom and boasts that he is of a much higher order of creation than the human (p. 119), he echoes the fallen Satan contemptuously telling the angels who guard Eve that once they were no peers of his.[18]

The other masterpiece of English poetry whose influence is most apparent in *Perelandra* is Spenser's *Faerie Queene*. The descriptions of the floating islands as paradisal gardens recall the Garden of Adonis (bk. 3), and Lewis's depiction of the dragon and tree with golden apples closely resembles Spenser's Hesperides. As noted above, however, Lewis's floating islands reverse the moral valence of Spenser's Wandering Islands (bk. 3), which are unsafe places where true knights should not dally. *The Faerie Queene* may also have provided Lewis with the idea of having people travel through oceans on the backs of dolphins, though that tradition is older than Spenser.

In Lewis's lectures on *The Faerie Queene,* he points out several motifs in the poem that reappear in his own *Perelandra.* He mentions, for example, medieval and Renaissance speculations that "aquatic elemental spirits" may actually exist, then adds cryptically, "and who knows, perhaps in this as in so many things the ancients knew more than we."[19] Whether or not mermen and mermaids exist in the earth's oceans, they do in Perelandra's (pp. 161–162). Lewis also mentions the Renaissance love of literary pageants as found in Spenser,[20] and then he presents a splendid modern specimen in the Great Dance sequence at the end of *Perelandra.* Lastly, it is interesting to note that Lewis interprets the episode in which Florimell is held captive in a dark cave (bk. 3) as "very like an allegory of the descent of the soul into material embodiment."[21] As mentioned above, Lewis's description of Ransom's descent into the subterranean cavern in *Perelandra* is intriguingly similar to his comparison of the Incarnation to a deep-sea diver in *Miracles.* Lewis's reading of Florimell's captivity suggests that the image in both books is derived from Spenser.

Lewis's borrowing from more recent writers cannot be demonstrated with any certainty. Lewis's biographers Roger Lancelyn Green and Walter Hooper suggest that the idea of floating islands on Venus may have come from a phrase in Olaf Stapledon's *First and Last Men* about "great floating islands of vegetable matter." Donald Glover speculates that the contest between Ransom and Weston over the will of the Green Lady may be rooted in another scene in *First and Last Men* in which an American emissary and a Chinese emissary compete over a naked native woman from another planet. C. N. Manlove, in his turn, asserts that "without a doubt" Lewis got his image of the island paradise from a little book called *Melmoth the Wanderer* published in 1820.[22] But there are so many pictures of an island paradise for Lewis to draw upon— Hesperides, Avalon, Tirnanog, and others—that readers need not assume his imagination was fed by only one spring.

In *Out of the Silent Planet* (1938), Lewis adapted the general plot outline from H. G. Wells's *First Men in the Moon* in order to tell an essentially anti-Wellsian tale. In *Perelandra,* Lewis pays a similar backhanded compliment to the man he admired as a speculative writer, but not as a philosopher. The broad narrative structure of *Perelandra* resembles another novel by H. G. Wells, *The Time Machine* (1895). In both stories, the protagonist enlists the help of a friend, vanishes to no one knows where, returns wounded and exhausted with an otherworldly flower, and recounts his adventures to the friend who had helped send him on his voyage. In Wells's novel, this narrative outline provides the basis of a quasi-Marxist fable about effete bourgeoisie and surly proletariat. In Lewis's hands, a similar story structure tells a very different tale, one in which the ultimate battles are not economic and political, but rather cosmic and spiritual.

NOTES

1. The term "paradise retained" comes from Victor M. Hamm, "Mr. Lewis in Perelandra," *Thought* 20 (June 1945), 271.

2. C. S. Lewis, *Perelandra* (New York: Macmillan, 1968), 10. References to *Perelandra* are hereafter incorporated into the text.

3. Jocelyn Gibb, ed. *Light on C. S. Lewis* (New York: Harcourt, Brace, and World, 1965), 92; Nancy-Lou Patterson, "Anti-Babels: the Images of the Divine Centre in *That Hideous Strength*," in *Mythcon II Proceedings*, ed. Glen GoodKnight (Los Angeles, CA: Mythopoeic Society, 1972), 11.

4. C. S. Lewis, *Selected Literary Essays*, ed. Walter Hooper (Cambridge: Cambridge University Press, 1966), 30.

5. See Corbin Scott Carnell, "Ransom in C. S. Lewis' *Perelandra* as Hero in Transformation: Notes toward a Jungian Reading of the Novel," *Studies in the Literary Imagination* 14(2) (Fall 1981), 67–71; Lee D. Rossi, *The Politics of Fantasy: C. S. Lewis and J. R. R. Tolkien* (Ann Arbor, MI: UMI Research Press, 1984), 39.

6. C. S. Lewis, *Surprised by Joy* (New York: Harcourt, 1955), 21.

7. Gibb, *Light on C. S. Lewis*, 54.

8. C. S. Lewis, *Letters to an American Lady*, ed. Clyde S. Kilby (Grand Rapids, MI: Eerdmans, 1967), 36–37.

9. Walter Hooper, ed. *Collected Letters of C. S. Lewis*, vol. 1 (London: Harper-Collins, 2000), 560.

10. "Descriptions of Seraphim: Dante," *Purgatorio*, canto 29; C. S. Lewis, *Letters to an American Lady*, ed. Clyde S. Kilby (Grand Rapids, MI: Eerdmans, 1967), 12.

11. C. S. Lewis, *Miracles* (New York: Macmillan, 1968), 128–129.

12. Ibid., 116.

13. C. S. Lewis, *Studies in Medieval and Renaissance Literature*, ed. Walter Hooper (Cambridge: Cambridge University Press, 1969), 13.

14. "Bonaventure: William R. Inge," in *Christian Mysticism* (New York: Charles Scribner's Sons, 1902), 28; "Boehme, Ruysbroek: Evelyn Underhill," in *Mysticism* (London: Methuen, 1911), 100, 229.

15. Peter J. Schakel, ed. *The Longing for a Form: Essays on the Fiction of C. S. Lewis* (Kent, OH: Kent State University Press, 1977), 73.

16. C. S. Lewis, *A Preface to Paradise Lost* (Oxford: Oxford University Press, 1970), 119.

17. John Milton, *Paradise Lost*, 4, 477–491.

18. Ibid., 4, 27–34.

19. C. S. Lewis, *Spenser's Images of Life*, ed., Alistair Fowler (Cambridge: Cambridge University Press, 1967), 129.

20. Ibid., 127.

21. Ibid., 126.

22. Roger Lancelyn Green and Walter Hooper, *C. S. Lewis: A Biography* (New York: Harcourt, Brace Jovanovich, 1974), 174; Donald E. Glover, *C. S. Lewis and the*

Art of Enchantment (Athens, OH: Ohio University Press, 1981), 77; C. N. Manlove, *Modern Fantasy: Five Studies* (Cambridge: Cambridge University Press, 1975), 119.

BIBLIOGRAPHY

Carnell, Corbin Scott. "Ransom in C. S. Lewis' *Perelandra* as Hero in Transformation: Notes toward a Jungian Reading of the Novel." *Studies in the Literary Imagination* 14(2) (Fall 1981).

Downing, David. *Planets in Peril*. Amherst, MA: University of Massachusetts Press, 1992.

Gibb, Jocelyn, Editor. *Light on C. S. Lewis*. New York: Harcourt, Brace, and World, 1965.

Glover, Donald E. *C. S. Lewis and the Art of Enchantment*. Athens, OH: Ohio University Press, 1981.

GoodKnight. Glen. *Mythcon II Proceedings*. Los Angeles, CA: Mythopoeic Society, 1972.

Green Roger Lancelyn and Walter Hooper. *C. S. Lewis: A Biography*. New York: Harcourt, Brace Jovanovich, 1974.

Hamm, Victor M. "Mr. Lewis in Perelandra." *Thought* 20 (June 1945).

Hooper, Walter, Editor. *Collected Letters of C. S. Lewis*, vol. 1. London: HarperCollins, 2000.

Inge, William R. *Christian Mysticism* (New York: Charles Scribner's Sons, 1902).

Lewis, C. S. *Letters to an American Lady*. Edited by Clyde S. Kilby. Grand Rapids, MI: Eerdmans, 1967.

———. *Miracles*. New York: Macmillan, 1968.

———. *Perelandra*. New York: Macmillan, 1968

———. *A Preface to Paradise Lost* (Oxford: Oxford University Press, 1970), 119.

———. *Selected Literary Essays*. Edited by Walter Hooper. Cambridge: Cambridge University Press, 1966.

———. *Spenser's Images of Life*. Edited by Alistair Fowler. Cambridge: Cambridge University Press, 1967.

———. *Studies in Medieval and Renaissance Literature,* Edited by Walter Hooper. Cambridge: Cambridge University Press, 1969.

———. *Surprised by Joy*. New York: Harcourt, 1955.

Patterson, Nancy-Lou. "Anti-Babels: the Images of the Divine Centre in *That Hideous Strength*." In *Mythcon II Proceedings*. Edited by Glen GoodKnight. Los Angeles, CA: Mythopoeic Society, 1972.

Rossi, Leo D. *The Politics of Fantasy: C. S. Lewis and J. R. R. Tolkien*. Ann Arbor, MI: UMI Research Press, 1984.

Schakel, Peter J., Editor. *The Longing for a Form: Essays on the Fiction of C. S. Lewis*. Kent, OH: Kent State University Press, 1977.

Underhill, Evelyn. *Mysticism*. London: Methuen, 1911.

4

That Hideous Strength: Spiritual Wickedness in High Places

David C. Downing

In *Perelandra* Ransom explained to his friend "Lewis" that a biblical reference to "spiritual wickedness in high places" did not refer to corrupt human rulers, but rather to malign transhuman powers.[1] In *That Hideous Strength*, Ransom and his small company at St. Anne's are called upon to fight "wickedness in high places" in both senses of the term. They must stop a conspiracy by the totalitarian technocrats at the National Institute of Coordinated Experiments (N.I.C.E.) at Belbury. But they must always thwart an attempt by bent eldils to take control of planet earth.

The third book of the Ransom trilogy represents the culmination of what might be termed the "Infernal Period" in Lewis's writings. In four consecutive books Lewis introduces hellish characters and hellish settings (imaginatively recast for modern readers) in order to explore the psychology of faith and doubt, of temptation and spiritual trial. In 1942 *The Screwtape Letters* appeared, featuring advice from a senior devil in the "lowerarchy" to a junior tempter. In 1943 came *Perelandra,* where Ransom spends half the story contending with a demonized corpse. In 1945 *That Hideous Strength* appeared, as well as *The Great Divorce,* a fantasy about denizens of hell who take an excursion to the outskirts of heaven, most finding reasons to prefer their nether abode.

Rooted as he was in traditional Christian doctrine and convinced of the theological soundness of much of the medieval worldview, Lewis believed in the reality of malevolent spirits opposed to God. But in the books mentioned above, the literal existence of the diabolical beings is secondary to their usefulness as metaphors of human vice and folly. Lewis believed that every moral choice humans make moves them one step closer to heaven or to hell; in fact, hell and heaven did not represent for him God's judgment so much as God's acknowledgment of the pattern of choices people make throughout their lifetimes. Lewis summed up his position best in *The Great Divorce:* "There are only two kinds of people in the end: those who say to God, 'Thy will be done,' and those to whom God says, in the end, '*Thy* will be done.' All that are in Hell, choose it."[2]

The villains in Lewis's fantasies are not hard to find; they do not, as St. Paul warned, cloak themselves as angels of light. Lewis's bad characters range from the merely pompous to the outright demonic, but they share a few common traits: they set aside ordinary morality in favor of utility or in favor of some lofty, abstract goals for humanity; they disregard the sanctity of life, whether human or animal; they are "progressive" and find little value in history, tradition, or the classics; they prefer the scientific, artificial, and industrial over the simple and natural; they use language to conceal and distort reality, rather than to reveal it.

In his preface to *That Hideous Strength,* Lewis calls it "'a tall story' about deviltry," adding that it "has behind it a serious 'point' which I have tried to make in *The Abolition of Man.*"[3] Lewis goes on to explain that he created the tale partly in response to some disturbing notions he had encountered in talking to a scientific colleague and later in the works of Olaf Stapledon.

Olaf Stapledon's *Last and First Men* (1930), with its doctrine of humanity's sacred obligation to scatter its seed among other worlds, provided the impetus for Lewis to start writing the Ransom trilogy in the first place. In *That Hideous Strength* Lewis goes beyond *Out of the Silent Planet* in trying to expose the fallacies and dangers in the philosophy of what he called "Westonism." By the time Lewis composed the third book of the trilogy, he had read Stapledon's other well-known novel, *Star Maker* (1937), which surveys the entire history of the cosmos and suggests that some sort of god, or creative principle, is evolving amid the galaxies. Writing to Arthur C. Clarke in 1943, Lewis described the ending of Stapledon's novel as "sheer devil worship."[4]

The protagonists of *That Hideous Strength* are Mark and Jane Studdock, a pair of anchorless modern intellectuals in an unfulfilling marriage, who undergo diametrically opposite pilgrimages as the story unfolds. As Mark works his way through the "wheels within wheels" at the National Institute of Coordinated Experiments (N.I.C.E.), readers find there too a progression from scientific pragmatism, to evolutionism, to "sheer devil worship." At the lowest level are functionaries like Busby and Curry, who think the purpose of

N.I.C.E. is to provide centralized organization for scientific research. Busby calls N.I.C.E. "the first attempt to take applied science seriously from the national point of view" (p. 37), while Curry burbles about putting "science itself on a scientific basis" (p. 38). Lord Feverstone (Devine) laughs at these simpleminded marionettes and explains the goals of N.I.C.E. to Mark in Westonesque terms: to continue interplanetary expansion; to rid the planet of species that compete with humans for resources; and to purify the human species itself, through "sterilization of the unfit [and] liquidation of backward races" (p. 42). (The parallels between the animating ideas of N.I.C.E. and those of Nazism would certainly not be lost on the novel's original readers in 1945.)

Even more radical than Feverstone are those at N.I.C.E., like Filostrato, who want to dispense with organic life altogether, retaining only Mind (p. 173), and Straik, who offers Mark "the unspeakable glory of being present at the creation of God Almighty" (p. 179). Readers who think that Lewis is resorting to caricature tactics here will find similar ideas in J. B. S. Haldane, Olaf Stapledon, and G .B. Shaw and in more recent writers like Ray Bradbury and Arthur C. Clarke.

To explain the intellectual climate in which such diverse, and sometimes outré, notions could come together, the narrator probes the thoughts of Ransom, who leads the opposition against N. I. C. E.: "The physical sciences, good and innocent in themselves, had ... begun to be warped, had been subtly maneuvered in a certain direction. Despair of objective truth had been increasingly insinuated into the scientists; indifference to it, and a concentration upon mere power, had been the result.... Dreams of the far future destiny of man were dragging up from its shallow and unquiet grave the old dream of Man as God" (p. 203). The narrator continues, perhaps with an excess of exposition, explaining why positivists should not be shocked by where their ideas are leading: "What should they find incredible, since they no longer believed in a rational universe? What should they regard as too obscene, since they held that all morality was a mere subjective by-product of the physical and economic situations of men?" (p. 203).

Looking back after nearly a half century, it seems ironic that Lewis's apprehensions would be more fully realized in his own discipline, in the study of literary texts, than in the sciences. The work of Thomas Kuhn and others concerning the subjectivity of the scientific paradigms seems to have been more warmly received by scholars in the humanities than by scientists themselves. Perhaps the trait that most unites poststructuralist approaches to literature is a "despair of objective truth" and a "concentration upon mere power."

As Lewis himself explained, the ideas touched upon in *That Hideous Strength* are more fully developed in his book-length essay *The Abolition of Man*. There he makes the case for objective moral values and objective aesthetic values. Lewis begins by taking to task the writers of an elementary textbook who teach that when one calls a waterfall sublime, one is actually saying, "This waterfall induces sublime feelings in me." Sublimity, according to them, is a label for an emotional state; it is not anything in nature but something imputed by human minds upon the environment. Lewis argues that such an approach reduces all value judgments to mere expressions of emotion, largely irrelevant in serious discussion.[5]

Against this climate of relativism and imputed value, Lewis harkens back to the traditional model: "Until quite modern times all teachers and even all men believed the universe to be such that certain emotional reactions on our part could be either congruous or incongruous to it-believed, in fact, that objects did not merely receive, but could *merit,* our approval or disapproval, our reverence, or our contempt."[6] Lewis quotes Plato, Aristotle, Confucius, Augustine, and others to show that traditionally moral education has been defined as a process of learning to conform one's sentiments to the acknowledged pattern of the universe. Though this pattern is assumed by all religious traditions, according to Lewis, he borrows the concept of "the Way," which he calls the "reality beyond all predicates," something that exists in itself apart from all subjective human perceptions or interpretations.[7]

Such analysis is unabashedly essentialist. Depending upon one's own response to the contemporary climate of postmodernism, *The Abolition of Man* may seem woefully naive and obsolete, or else it may seem a prescient forewarning of trends that would become much more radical after Lewis's time. If Lewis could hear current discussions that assume that not only values but also meanings are radically indeterminate, he might sigh, "Après moi, le deluge."

In *The Abolition of Man* Lewis makes a compelling case that one cannot arrive at value judgments using reason alone. In-between the head (reason) and the belly (the appetites) must come the chest—the seat of magnanimity, of "Sentiment," of "emotions organized by trained habits into stable sentiments."[8] Lewis calls these "the indispensable liaison officers between cerebral man and visceral man." In fact, he says, these may be the defining trait of humans, for by intellect they are mere spirit and by appetites they are mere animals. Those who deny the reality of sentiment, of objective values, are—in Lewis's term—"men without chests."[9]

In *That Hideous Strength* virtually all of the technocrats at N.I.C.E. would qualify as people "without chests." In their disregard for traditional moral norms, for natural beauty, for the suffering of animals and of other humans, they reduce all questions of value to matters of rationality, utility, or self-interest. They dismiss any ethical qualms about what they are doing with grandiose abstractions about the advancement of the species (p. 258), or else they dismiss such qualms as meaningless biochemical events (p. 296).

In Lewis's mind, such attitudes can lead ultimately to destruction, of the innocent, of the environment, and ultimately of themselves.

MARK STUDDOCK'S DANTESQUE DESCENT

Elwin Ransom's encounters with evil in the first two books of the trilogy provide the context for understanding the people at N.I.C.E. in *That Hideous Strength*. N.I.C.E. represents the values of Edward Weston and Dick Devine writ large. Weston is revered at N.I.C.E. as a great scientist murdered on one of his interplanetary travels, and Devine reappears as Lord Feverstone (a rather infernal title). The dreamer and the schemer have spawned at N.I.C.E. a whole academy of dreamers and schemers.

In his homily "The Inner Ring," Lewis speaks about people who become scoundrels by degrees, making increasingly serious compromises of their integrity and values in order to make their way into an exclusive circle, then the circle-within-the-circle. Mark Studdock is quite clearly a victim of the inner-ring syndrome as he tries to gain acceptance at N.I.C.E. He is willing to put up with pompous bureaucrats like Busby and Curry just for the pleasure of being an insider in the Progressive Element. Then he is liberated to see Feverstone baiting these two boors and inviting him to join a more elite set of insiders. As he gets more enmeshed in the machinations at N.I.C.E., Mark finds it harder and harder to tell who really is on the inside and who is just a "mascot." Even Filostrato, who dismisses almost everyone else at Belbury as *canaglia* (plebians), is not a true insider; he knows about the living head at N.I.C.E., but he does not know—until too late—that it is not his science that keeps the head alive. In "The Inner Ring" Lewis warns that trying to penetrate all the inner circles is like peeling an onion.[10] In the center there is nothing.

Mark's attempted ascent up the organizational ladder is actually a descent into hell. The many references to the inner rings, inner circles, and wheels-within-wheels make plain Mark's inner-ring syndrome. However, these allusions also reveal a less obvious subtext: Mark's experiences at N.I.C.E. closely parallel Dante's trek through the *Inferno*.

The Divine Comedy was never very far from Lewis's mind. He first read the poem, in Dante's medieval Italian, during his midteens, while studying with Kirkpatrick. He read and reread Dante's masterwork for the rest of his life, often praising it in his letters. According to George Sayer, Lewis considered Dante the most sublime of all poets and judged the "Paradiso" to be the greatest poetic achievement in European literature.[11] Lewis borrowed freely from the "Purgatorio" and the "Paradiso" in the closing chapters of *Perelandra;* in *That Hideous Strength*, he drew just as heavily on the "*Inferno*."

Throughout the third novel of the Ransom trilogy, the conversation of the people at N.I.C.E. is peppered with hellish rhetoric. In the sections of *That Hideous Strength* devoted to Bracton and Belbury, there are nearly eighty phrases such as "raise hell," "the devil of a stink," "I'm damned," "these infernal college politics," "what in the blazes," and so forth. These sections also contain more specific Dantean echoes. In describing Wither, the deputy director of N.I.C.E., as one of those "souls who have lost the intellectual good" (p. 213), Lewis is translating from "*The Inferno*": "c'hanno perduto il ben delFintelletto" (pp. 3, 18).[12] Later when Wither impassively looks upon his own death and perdition (p. 353), the narrator comments, "So full of sleep are they at the time when they leave the right way," taken directly from canto i, lines 11–12.

In general, there is a close correlation between Mark's increasing entanglement in the affairs of N.I.C.E. and Dante's journey through the circles of hell, guided by the poet Virgil. The narrator of "*The Inferno*" (designated here as Dante, for convenience) begins his passage at the vestibule of hell, where he sees the opportunists, those who served neither good nor evil, but only themselves. The first person from Bracton College who appears in *That Hideous Strength* is Curry, the officious subwarden. Feverstone describes Curry as "a man who loves business and wire-pulling for their own sake and doesn't really ask what it's all about" (p. 40). Curry is not necessarily evil; he is just someone who thrives on college politics. Accordingly, when the great conflagration comes to Belbury at the end of the story, Curry is the only one associated with N.I.C.E. who survives.

The first circle of the inferno is Limbo, the abode of virtuous pagans. There Dante meets the great poets and philosophers who lived before the time of Christ and so could not benefit from his atoning work. Curry mentions to Mark early on that there will be resistance to the plans of N.I.C.E. from the likes of Hingest (a true research scientist), Glossop (a classics scholar), and Jewel (the college canon). These men are not directly allied with Ransom and the followers of Maleldil, but neither will they be any part of N.I.C.E. When Jewel tries to argue at the faculty meeting against the sale of Bragdon Wood, he is so feeble and so upset that his voice is barely audible, and Feverstone mocks him into silence (p. 28). This may allude to the virtuous pagans in circle one who speak with muted voices (pp. 4, 114).

In the second circle, Dante encounters those who sinned through carnal desire. In the next section of *That Hideous Strength,* after the one in which Jewel is humiliated, Jane is asked by Mrs. Dimble about her sex life and then bursts into tears (p. 30). We have already learned from the opening pages of the novel that Mark pays little attention to Jane; when he comes to bed, he has little to say to her, and only one thing can keep him awake—and that not for long (p. 14). Later, when Mark gradually comes to see the emptiness and squalor of his life, he feels that somehow he has violated his wife, made her the object of his lust, not his companion in love (pp. 247, 381). It would seem that Mark himself best exemplifies the carnal sinner.

In the third circle are the gluttons, those who overindulge in food and drink. In the next section of *That Hideous Strength,* Mark has dinner with Feverstone and Busby in the Curry's rooms. Busby is described as "busily engaged in eating" during the conversation, and he has to wipe his beard before speaking up (p. 36). Busby is also described as having a third glass of wine, which loosens his tongue and makes him easy prey for the glib Feverstone (p. 37). Mark also enjoys the excellent port being served, and he is "not perfectly sober" when he returns home to Jane that evening (p. 46). Throughout the rest of the story, Lewis emphasizes all the heavy drinking that goes on at N.I.C.E., including Mark's increased reliance on alcohol.

In the fourth circle, Dante witnesses a battle between the avaricious and the prodigals, those who cling too much to material things and those who waste material things. The same kind of conflict arises when Feverstone, the spendthrift, mocks the aspirations of Busby and Curry. Busby, enraptured by the program of N.I.C.E., exclaims upon "the buildings alone, the apparatus alone! . . . Fifteen department directors at fifteen thousand a year each!" (p. 37) When Feverstone offers a mocking reply about "careers for our sons," Curry takes Busby's side and rhapsodizes about the Pragmatometer, a device to coordinate all the research activities that will cost half a million (p. 38). Feverstone dismisses all this to Mark as drivel. He is the same Dick Devine he was in *Out of the Silent Planet;* his only real concern is how he personally can benefit from all this. And we assume he is benefiting when we see him in the next scene driving recklessly in a flashy, big car, taking Mark to N.I.C.E.

In the fifth circle of hell are the wrathful and the sullen. And when Mark arrives at Belbury, he is assigned to work with Steele and Cosser, who are both wrathful and sullen. Steele is "a tall, unsmiling man," who complains that Mark has been unloaded on his department without anyone consulting him (pp. 58–59). At their first meeting, Cosser and Steele talk about Mark as if he is not even there, but later Cosser confides to Mark, while picking his nose, that he hopes to get rid of Steele and take over his position (pp. 85–86).

As he continues at N.I.C.E., Mark encounters more and more sinister colleagues. The repulsively obese Professor Filostrato, the sadistic Fairy Hardcastle, and "Mad Parson" Straik make self-important functionaries like Curry and Busby seem almost likable. Straik's rambling diatribes are loaded with biblical phrases and motifs, but his ideas sound like those of an anti-Christ. He ludicrously misapplies verse after verse from Scripture to advocate violence, coercive collectivism, and extermination of any who resist (pp. 78–80). He certainly parallels those whom Dante finds in the sixth circle of hell—the heretics.

This pattern continues until the final judgment of everyone at N.I.C.E. In the seventh circle of the inferno are the violent, those who do violence to nature and violence to others. And succeeding pages in *That Hideous Strength* describe what sounds like a murder outside the Common Room of Bracton (p. 93), Fairy Hardcastle's arousal when inflicting pain (p. 96), and the noise of animals being tortured in the name of science (p. 102).

In the eighth circle are the fraudulent. And in the next section of the novel, Mark discovers that his position at Bracton has been fraudulently taken away from him (pp. 105–106), and Feverstone fraudulently denies any responsibility (p. 111). Mark himself joins in the fraud, writing newspaper editorials that blame Jews, lawyers, and other resisting elements for riots that were engineered by the secret police at N.I.C.E. (pp. 131–134).

The ninth circle of hell is reserved for the worst of offenders, those who betray kindred, country, and their faith. Mark has been carnal, gluttonous, greedy, prodigal, and fraudulent. But he stops short of the most serious crimes he might commit in the service of N.I.C.E. The whole reason that Mark was recruited in the first place was not for his work as a sociologist but so that Frost and Wither could get their hands on his wife, to make use of her power of second sight. Not realizing its significance at first, Mark balks at the whole idea of bringing Jane to Belbury: "Her mere presence would have made all the laughter of the Inner Ring sound metallic, unreal; and what he now regarded as common prudence would seem to her, and through her to himself, mere flattery, back-biting and toad-eating" (p. 171). As Wither and the others put increasing pressure on Mark to turn her over to them, his resistance too increases: "For almost the first time in his life a gleam of something like disinterested love came into his mind; he wished he had never married her, never dragged her into this whole outfit of horrors which was, apparently, to be his life" (pp. 185–186). Besides his refusal to betray his wife, Mark also refuses to trample on a cross. It would seem that in the last circle of his own descent, he finally discovers the moral core within himself, which will allow for his escape.

The sinners in "The Inferno" are already suffering, but the sinners at N.I.C.E. will receive their punishment all at once. In the closing chapters of *That Hideous Strength* especially, images from the final cantos of "The Inferno" predominate. When Frost and Wither, the leaders of N.I.C.E. and the two most depraved characters in the story, lock into a bizarre embrace and fall onto the floor, seeming to wrestle without moving (p. 243), they recall the two brothers in "The Inferno" who had quarreled all their lives and are frozen together for eternity in a sheet of ice (pp. 32, 40–60). When Filostrato and Straik are both decapitated as a sacrifice to the dark eldils (pp. 354–355), their fate echoes the beheadings and dismemberments of the schismatics and heretics in the ninth circle (canto 38).

Mark, who found his moral bearings just in time, is spared from the carnage at the end of *That Hideous Strength*. Yet his part in the story is also related with Dantean images and phrasing. When Mark sees an elephant join in with the other animals venting their rage on their tormentors at the banquet, the elephant is described as standing with "its ears standing stiffly out like the devil's wings on each side of its head" (p. 349). This image comes directly from "The Inferno"; at the very center of hell sits Satan, frozen in ice, with batlike wings fluttering at the sides of his head (pp. 34, 38–54). As he watches the elephant carelessly trampling people and glorying in the destruction, Mark calls him "the King of the world" (p. 350); this phrase seems less odd when one compares it to Dante's description of Satan as "the emperor of his sad world" (pp. 34, 28). Mark loses consciousness briefly, but he is told by Merlin to "get up," to make good his escape (p. 352). The words "get up" are used to translate Virgil's words—*Levati su*—when he stirs Dante to shake off his stupor and escape the lowest circle of the inferno (pp. 34, 94).

One of the most unforgettably grotesque images in "*The Inferno*" is that of Lucifer gnawing on the skulls of Brutus and Cassius, betrayers of Caesar, and Judas, betrayer of Christ. The idea that Satan devours the condemned is taken literally—and whimsically—by Lewis in "Screwtape Proposes a Toast," where Screwtape is the after-dinner speaker at a banquet of devils feasting on human souls. Used more obliquely in the trilogy, the Dantean image suggests two more traits shared by Lewis's evil characters: abuse of intellect and self-destruction.[13]

Dante's phrase rendered by Lewis as "souls who lose the intellectual good" may be interpreted to mean those who lose the good of intellect or those who do not use intellect for good. Weston and Devine are pronounced only "half hnau" on Malacandra[14] because they have their rational faculties but no moral sense. Their science is not tempered by conscience. In the same way, the major figures at N.I.C.E. all abuse their intellects and deny their moral instincts. Wither habitually uses evasive, circumlocutory speech to disguise his true aims and to manipulate others. Frost convinces himself that all moral responses are mere by-products of biochemical processes. Straik takes biblical phrases wildly out of context in order to make them seem to support his violent radicalism and blasphemous deification of humans.

All of these who habitually abuse language have their powers of speech taken from them. The epigraph of *That Hideous Strength* explains that the title of the book is taken from a poem by Sir David Lyndsay describing the tower of Babel. N.I.C.E. is a new Babel, another attempt to marshal human resources to clamber up to heaven, or to bring heaven to earth by main force. In the end, these new Nimrods experience another confusion of tongues and achieve only their own destruction.

Like Weston in *Perelandra,* the leaders of N.I.C.E. are destroyed by the forces that they themselves have set into motion. Weston called a force into himself that did indeed come in and take over. Filostrato and Straik would sacrifice human lives so that they may rule as gods, but they end up themselves as human sacrifices. Feverstone, who hopes to subdue the earth, is swallowed up by the earth. Frost, who denies the reality of the passions, is consumed in flames that he ignites himself. The others, who have been destroying animals for trivial causes, are destroyed by liberated animals. In the end, the banquet at Belbury is another devils' banquet.

TWO OPPOSITE PATHS TO REDEMPTION

In his supposed organizational ascent that was actually a spiritual descent, Mark Studdock finds himself continually suppressing his natural instincts and his better judgment. He moves from the merely vulgar to the unethical and then to the criminal, but he stops short of sacrificing his wife to the ambitions of his superiors. Placed in the "Objective Room," a chamber whose proportions and furnishings are designed to subvert his sense of normality, Mark's instincts carry him in the opposite direction: "That idea of the Straight or the Normal which had occurred to him during his first visit to this room, grew stronger and more solid in his mind till it had become a kind of mountain. He had never before known what an Idea meant: he had always thought till now that they were things inside one's own head. But now, when his head was continually attacked and often completely filled with the clinging corruption of the training, this Idea towered up above him—something which obviously existed quite independently of himself" (p. 310). Though the narrator declares that Mark's modern education had provided him with "hardly one rag of noble thought, either Christian or Pagan" (p. 185), he still has an inborn sense of some reality towering above all the reductionistic rhetoric at N.I.C.E.

Later, when he is commanded to trample a crucifix, Mark recognizes that he is in mortal danger, but some instinct deeper than self-preservation arises within him. He decides that even if Christianity is a fable and the universe without ultimate meaning, he will side with the Normal over the Perverse, the Straight over the Crooked. Mark refuses to trample on the cross, the first courageous thing he has ever done in his life. This is the beginning of his recovery. Stripped of all other supports and defenses, Mark's regeneration begins when he discovers that he has nothing left but the Way.

Like her husband, Jane Studdock will also be "shaken out of the modest little outfit of contemporary ideas which had hitherto made her portion of wisdom" (p. 150). Mark discovers the Straight by the *via negativa,* by almost losing himself to the Crooked, the Perverse, and the Bent. Jane moves in the opposite direction as she is drawn closer to Ransom's community at St. Anne's.

Several critics have noted the structural symmetries in *That Hideous Strength* by which the Studdocks' opposite pilgrimages are marked. Jane begins with a malaise and lack of commitment, either to her marriage or to her scholarship; Mark begins with a reckless commitment, a headlong plunge to fulfill his ambitions by the shortest route possible. Jane dreams realities and thinks they are illusions; Mark is deluded about the actual workings of Bracton and N.I.C.E., just when he thinks he knows what is really going on. Jane takes a slow train to St. Anne's, while Mark rushes to Belbury in a big, flashy car driven by the reckless Feverstone. Jane is invited to join St. Anne's, while Mark is coerced into joining N.I.C.E. The fresh garden at St. Anne's fills Jane with images of paradise, while the garden at N.I.C.E. is artificial and sterile, like "a municipal cemetery" (p. 101). Jane is filled with ineffable joy when she first meets the head of St. Anne's—the regal and mystical Ransom, returned from Perelandra. Mark is filled with unspeakable horror and revulsion when he meets the "head" of N.I.C.E—a decapitated head supposedly kept alive by scientific apparatus but actually animated by dark eldils.[15]

Like Ransom in *Out of the Silent Planet,* revelations come to Jane bit by bit. First she learns that she is not a neurotic but a clairvoyant, one with the power to dream realities (pp. 64–65). Then she learns, begrudgingly, that she has contributed to her failing marriage as much as her husband (p. 147). Then she discovers that Arthurian legends are truer than she ever could have imagined (p. 176). Eventually, she undergoes a complete paradigm shift. On Malacandra Ransom had gradually come to realize that Maleldil was the same person as the God he already believed in. In *That Hideous Strength* Jane makes the even more startling discovery that Maleldil is the God she had not believed in, and that the "religion" she had set aside in her youth actually pointed to "alarming and operative realities" (p. 234).

MEDIEVALISM ASSOCIATED WITH RANSOM AND HIS COMPANY AT ST. ANNE'S

In the first two books of the trilogy, Ransom traveled to other worlds to discover the truth of myth and to find a cosmos more similar to medieval models than to modern ones. In *That Hideous Strength* Arthurian legends and other medieval traditions prove their relevance, and reality, on twentieth-century earth.

The most prominent Arthurian element in the third novel of the trilogy is the return of Merlin. Bragdon Wood, the ancient garden owned by Bracton College, is the site of Merlin's Well, the reputed resting place of Arthur's wizard. The leaders at N. I. C. E, those who know its real goals, would like to unearth Merlin and awaken him from his enchanted slumber in order to combine his powers with their own.

It might seem highly incongruous to have modern technocrats trying to use magic, but in *The Abolition of Man* Lewis argues that science and magic spring from the same impulse.

There was very little magic in the Middle Ages: the sixteenth and seventeenth centuries are the high noon of magic. The serious magical endeavour and the serious scientific endeavour are twins: one was sickly and died, the other strong and throve. . . . There is something which unites magic and applied science while separating both from the "wisdom" of earlier ages. For the wise men of old the cardinal problem had been how to conform the soul to reality, and the solution had been knowledge, self-discipline, and virtue. For magic and applied science alike the problem is how to subdue reality to the wishes of men.[16]

Since Lewis identifies magic not with the Middle Ages but with the humanists who came afterward, one can see why the words *magic* and *magician* usually have negative connotations in his writings. Magicians in Lewis's fiction (see *The Magician's Nephew)* and his nonfiction are generally depicted as those who abrogate moral laws in order to gain illicit power over nature and over others. Even in *That Hideous Strength* Lewis takes pains to distinguish Merlin's kind of magic, which originated in Atlantis, from Renaissance magic (p. 201).

Once Merlin is awakened from fifteen centuries of sleep, he does not unite his powers with N.I.C.E. but joins the humble company at St. Anne's. Eventually he becomes the instrument by which the conspirators at N.I.C.E. are exterminated. This resolution to the story has troubled some critics. Chad Walsh, for example, complains that Merlin's role in the story comes close to being a deus ex machina, and that the victory of Ransom and his followers is based upon the lucky circumstance that they found Merlin before the others did.[17] But this objection overlooks several key elements in the narrative. First, Merlin does not simply stumble into the hands of the good side. Once he awakens, he is guided by some preternatural means, and he rides directly to St. Anne's and Ransom. Second, Merlin does not offer his services to whoever asks. He subjects Ransom to three arcane questions that no one at N.I.C.E. could have possibly answered (pp. 272–274). Ransom can speak to these occult matters because he has traveled to other worlds and continues to have contact with lords of other planets. In their conversation, Ransom learns that Merlin, despite his rather druidic appearance, is a Christian—another reason Merlin would never have allied himself with N.I.C.E. Finally, it should be noted that Merlin does not destroy Belbury using his own weapons alone.

Ransom arranges to have the powers of the Oyarsas channeled into Merlin (p. 317), powers that the leaders of N.I.C.E. could not have drawn upon.

Merlin submits to Ransom's authority, not only because Ransom can answer Merlin's questions, but also because Ransom is the pendragon. In Arthurian tradition, the pendragon is the head of all the armies in times of war. Though Arthur was only one of many kings in his time, he inherited the title of pendragon from his father, Uther, so he was the chief commander in the wars against the Anglo-Saxons. (Pendragon is from Celtic "head of a dragon," taken from the dragon's head pictured on the standard of the one who held the title.) Lewis imagines that the title has been passed down secretly from generation to generation and that it now rests upon the one appointed to lead the battle against a new type of invasion. As pendragon, Ransom is also the head of Logres. From the Welsh word for "England," Logres traditionally represents the Britain of King Arthur, whose royal court was at Camelot. Though Logres is mentioned in Spenser and Milton with about the same connotations as the word "Camelot," Lewis's friend Charles Williams gave the term a more specialized meaning. In his Arthurian books, Williams used Logres to represent the spiritual side of England, the combination of Christian and Celtic ideals, a force that stands against the tides of worldliness and corruption. Lewis's use of the term "Logres" in *That Hideous Strength* clearly follows the precedent established by Williams.

Besides his title of pendragon, Ransom is also called Mr. Fisher-King. Lewis offers a rather contrived explanation for this, noting that Ransom received a large inheritance from his sister, Mrs. Fisher-King, on the condition that he takes her name (p. 114). Despite this unconvincing detail, the name does add another Arthurian dimension to the story and to Ransom's role in it. In the matter of Britain, the fisher-king is the keeper of the grail, a fisherman and king wounded in the thighs who holds court at his castle, Carbonek. The knight-errant Percival (or Parsifal) visits the grail castle and finds the fisher-king in pain, reclining on a couch in front of a fire. During dinner Percival sees a bleeding lance and a radiant golden cup but does not ask about them. The next morning he learns that his fateful silence has serious consequences: the fisher-king cannot be healed, and all his lands will be devastated. This is the beginning of Percival's quest to recover the grail. There are different versions of what happens to Percival. Some versions end happily, some not so. But all present the fisher-king as a wounded godlike figure who is keeper of the grail.

Critic Ellen Rawson has shown that Jane Studdock is a new Percival in *That Hideous Strength*. When Jane first visits Ransom, his chamber seems to her like a throne room, and she finds him reclining in front of a fire with a painful wound, just as the fisher-king appeared to Percival.[18] Ransom reminds her of King Arthur and of Solomon, and for the first time since childhood she could "taste the word *King* itself with all linked associations of battle, marriage, priesthood, mercy, and power" (p. 143). Percival became a Christian because of his encounter with the fisher-king, who is a Christ-figure in most versions of the grail legend. Jane too discovers spiritual realities at St. Anne's, coming to suspect that Maleldil is indeed God (p. 234) and finally surrendering her will to Maleldil (pp. 318–319).

Besides his roles as pendragon and fisher-king, Ransom embodies other Arthurian elements as well. In answer to one of Merlin's questions, Ransom explains that King Arthur is not dead but sits in the House of Kings in the land of Abhalljin on Perelandra (p. 274). Later it is revealed that Ransom will be taken to Perelandra to be with Arthur once his work on earth is done. Abhalljin (spelled "Aphallin" later in the text) is taken from the Welsh term *Afallon,* the abode of dead heroes, and the Celtic version of Elysium. In Arthurian legend this appears as "Avalon," the mystic isle where Arthur was taken to be healed of his wounds. Since the trilogy suggests that Perelandra was the true source of all myths of paradise, it is only fitting that Avalon should be found there and that Ransom should be healed on the world where he was wounded.

At the end of *That Hideous Strength* Venus herself (the Oyarsa of Perelandra) descends to earth not only to carry Ransom back to her world but also to unite with the other Oyeresu in defeating the dark powers that have gathered at N. I. C. E. Ransom had discovered the reality of planetary "influences" when he traveled through the heavens to Malacandra, though astrology plays only an incidental role in *Out of the Silent Planet.* But in *That Hideous Strength,* all of the planetary intelligences meet with Ransom and Merlin, their very proximity making the rest of the company at St. Anne's successively mercurial, amorous, martial, saturnine, and jovial. This chapter, "The Descent of the Gods," is a brilliant prose-poem on how planetary influence might be supposed to affect human psyches, but it also sets up the turning point in the story: the passing of their powers into Merlin for the purpose of eradicating N. I. C. E.

Astrology is associated with St. Anne's just as clearly as magic is associated with Belbury. Since Lewis did not approve of magic, one supposes at first that he would not have any imaginative attraction for astrology either. But Lewis explains in his volume of the *Oxford History of English Literature* that magic and astrology were never allied. While the first occult science sought power over nature, the second assumed nature's power over humans.[19] Lewis also noted that medieval astrologers did not believe that the planets compelled human behavior, only influenced it. The usual view in the Middle Ages, he says, was that a person, assisted by grace, could overcome a bad horoscope just as he or she could overcome a naturally bad temper.[20]

Apart from Arthurian and astrological elements, another medieval motif that figures prominently in *That Hideous Strength* is the image of the enclosed garden. In the Song of Solomon and other books of the Old Testament, the walled garden is a protected place, associated most often with a woman's virginity. In the Middle Ages, the walled garden symbol accrued multiple associations. As Lewis explains in *The Allegory of Love,* the enclosed garden is associated with youth and youthful love in early writers like Andreas Capellanus and Claudius; in Guillaume de Lorris, it includes also the life of the court, the arena for games of love; in later writers it represents allegorically the heart of a woman and the many emotions that reside there. "Deeper than these," concludes Lewis, "lies the world-wide dream of the happy garden—the island of the Hesperides, the earthly paradise, Tirnanog."[21]

This summation is perfectly sound scholarship, but it also reveals the man behind the literary historian. The Garden of the Hesperides is the image of Joy, or *Sehnsucht,* which Lewis used most often-in *Surprised by Joy,* in *Perelandra,* and in his poetry. The phrase "the earthly paradise" is the title of a romance by William Morris, much beloved and often read by Lewis, which cleverly interweaves classical and medieval motifs. Tirnanog, "land of the young ones," is the Irish equivalent of Avalon. Lewis most likely first heard of Tirnanog from his childhood nurse, Lizzie Endicott, who was full of Irish lore and song. So when Lewis speaks of the deeper meanings of garden imagery, he not only is casting light on the medieval mind but also is revealing his own.

In *That Hideous Strength* the sequestered garden first appears in the narrator's description of Bragdon Wood, the ancient copse owned by Bracton College and coveted by N. I. C. E. Indulging a bit too much in elaborate description and historical allusion, Lewis conjures up all the rich traditions of the place, going back to British-Roman times (that is, the era of King Arthur). The narrator has a sense that he is penetrating a place holy of holies as he enters Bragdon Wood (p. 20), and this indeed will turn out to be a kind of sacred ground. After this elaborate spell of history and legend has been woven around Bragdon Wood by the narrator, readers cannot miss the irony when in the very next section of the novel, the bureaucrats at Bracton College treat this hallowed ground merely as a pink rectangle on a map, land to put up for sale.

While Mark Studdock and his colleagues are discussing what to do with Bragdon Wood, his wife, Jane, encounters another walled garden when she goes to visit Ransom and his little community at St. Anne's. As she is led toward the house, Jane passes by a vegetable garden and a line of rosebushes that fill her with wistful thoughts about *Peter Rabbit, Alice in Wonderland,* and *The Romance of the Rose.* The walled garden at St. Anne's evokes in Jane all those images of earthly paradise—from children's stories to medieval romances. The gardens of *Peter Rabbit* and *Alice's Adventures in Wonderland* are well known. *The Romance of the Rose* is an allegorical love poem begun in thirteenth-century France by Guillaume de Lorris and continued by Jean de Meung. It is discussed at length by Lewis in *The Allegory of Love*; indeed, Lewis's monumental work did a great deal to revive interest in the poem. All of these are enchanted gardens that evoke a sense of paradise, suggesting that Jane herself is on the verge of discovering the spiritual home she has been seeking all her life.

Jane's husband, Mark, is transformed by the opposite process, not by approaching the outskirts of heaven, but by losing himself in Dantesque circles of hell. In the closing pages of the novel, once Mark has recovered himself and realized how weary, flat, stale, and unprofitable all his ambitions have been, he discovers also that he really does love his estranged wife. At the same time Mark realizes that his lifelong obsession to be an insider has led him only to "the dry and choking places"; he thinks of Jane as one who has within her "deep wells and knee-deep meadows of happiness, rivers of freshness, enchanted gardens of leisure, which he could not enter but could have spoiled" (p. 247).

At the end of the story, Mark contemplates his failure as a husband and lover, and again he conjures up the image of the walled garden and the cloistered rose. He feels he had been a "lout and clown and clod-hopper" treading on sacred ground "where great lovers, knights and poets, would have feared to tread." He sees himself as someone who trampled over the protecting hedge and plucked the rose "with hot, thumb-like, greedy fingers" (pp. 380–381). Though Mark's mind is full of self-loathing here, he is actually gaining the humility and self-recognition needed to redeem him from moral failure. In using so many medieval motifs to describe Mark's self-condemning thoughts, Lewis suggests that Studdock is developing more humane patterns of thought and feeling.

Fortunately for Mark, one of the things that Jane has learned in her time at St. Anne's is forgiveness. So when Mark and Jane are reunited in a kind of honeymoon cottage, we feel assured that their marriage will be renewed. In a suitably medieval ending, it is Venus herself who bids Mark to go in to his wife and who blesses their marriage bed.

NOTES

1. C. S. Lewis, *Perelandra* (New York: Macmillan, 1968), 2.

2. C. S. Lewis, *The Great Divorce* (New York: Fontana, 1972), 72.

3. C. S. Lewis, *That Hideous Strength* (New York: Macmillan, 1968), 7. Further references to this work are incorporated in the text.

4. Quoted in Donald E. Glover, *C. S. Lewis and the Art of Enchantment* (Athens, OH: Ohio University Press, 1981), 76.

5. C. S. Lewis, *The Abolition of Man* (New York: Macmillan, 1973), 15.

6. Ibid., 25.

7. Ibid., 28.

8. Ibid., 34.

9. Ibid.

10. C. S. Lewis, *The Weight of Glory and Other Addresses.* 1949. Reprint (Grand Rapids, MI: Eerdmans, 1965), 64.

11. George Sayer, *Jack: C. S. Lewis and His Times* (San Francisco, CA: Harper and Row, 1988), 63.

12. Cf. Dante Aligheri, *The Inferno.* New York: Signet Classics, 2001, trans., John Ciardi. All line references to *The Inferno* in the text are keyed to this edition.

13. C. S. Lewis, "Screwtape Proposes a Toast," in *The World's Last Night* (New York: Harcourt, Brace, Jovanovich, 1964).

14. C. S. Lewis, *Out of the Silent Planet* (New York: Macmillan, 1968), 81.

15. See Richard Purtill, "*That Hideous Strength:* A Double Story," in *The Longing for a Form: Essays on the Fiction of C. S. Lewis,* ed. Peter J. Schakel (Kent, OH: Kent State University Press, 1977), 91–98; Margaret P. Hannay, "A Preface to *Perelandra*" in ed. Peter J. Schakel *The Longing for a Form: Essays on the Fiction of C. S. Lewis* (Kent, OH: Kent State University Press, 1977), 103; Evan K. Gibson, *C. S. Lewis: Spinner of Tales: A Guide to His Fiction* (Washington, D C: Christian University Press, 1980), 72–73.

16. Lewis, *The Abolition of Man,* 86–88.

17. Chad Walsh, *The Literary Legacy of C. S. Lewis* (New York: Harcourt Brace Jovanovich, 1979), 119.

18. Ellen Rawson, "The Fisher King in That Hideous Strength*,*" *in Mythlore* 34 (Winter 1983), 30–33.

19. C. S. Lewis, *English Literature in the 16th Century Excluding Drama* (Oxford: Clarendon Press, 1954), 6

20. C. S. Lewis, *Studies in Medieval and Renaissance Literature,* ed. Walter Hooper (Cambridge: Cambridge University Press, 1969), 55.

21. C. S. Lewis, *The Allegory of Love* (Oxford: Oxford University Press, 1973), 119–120.

BIBLIOGRAPHY

Alighieri, Dante. *The Inferno.* Translated by John Ciardi. New York: Signet Classics, 2001.

Downing, David. *Planets in Peril.* Amherst, MA: University of Massachusetts Press, 1992.

Gibson, Evan K. *C. S. Lewis: Spinner of Tales: A Guide to His Fiction.* Washington, D C: Christian University Press, 1980.

Glover, Donald E. *C. S. Lewis and the Art of Enchantment.* Athens, OH: Ohio University Press, 1981.

Hannay, Margaret P. "A Preface to *Perelandra.*" In *The Longing for a Form: Essays on the Fiction of C. S. Lewis.* Edited by Peter J. Schakel, Kent OH: Kent State University Press, 1977, 91–98.

Lewis, C. S. *The Abolition of Man.*1943. New York: Macmillan, 1973.

————. *The Allegory of Love.* 1936. Reprint. Oxford: Oxford University Press, 1973.

————. *English Literature in the 16th Century Excluding Drama.* Oxford: Clarendon Press, 1954.

————. *The Great Divorce.* 1946. Reprint. New York: Fontana, 1972.

————. *Perelandra.* 1943. Reprint. New York: Macmillan, 1968.

————. "Screwtape Proposes a Toast." In *The World's Last Night.* New York: Harcourt, Brace, Jovanovich, 1964.

————. *Studies in Medieval and Renaissance Literature.* Edited by Walter Hooper. Cambridge: Cambridge University Press, 1969.

————. *That Hideous Strength.* 1945. Reprint. New York: Macmillan, 1968.

————. *The Weight of Glory and Other Addresses.* 1949. Reprint. Grand Rapids, MI: Eerdmans, 1965.

Purtill, Richard. "*That Hideous Strength:* A Double Story." In *The Longing for a Form: Essays on the Fiction of C. S. Lewis.* Edited by Peter J. Schakel. Kent OH: Kent State University Press, 1977, 91–98.

Rawson, Ellen. "The Fisher King in *That Hideous Strength.*" *Mythlore* 34 (Winter 1983): 30–33.

Sayer, George. *Jack: C. S. Lewis and His Times.* San Francisco, CA: Harper and Row, 1988.

Schakel, Peter J., Editor. *The Longing for a Form: Essays on the Fiction of C. S. Lewis.* Kent OH: Kent State University Press, 1977.

Stapledon, Olaf. *Last and First Men.* Los Angeles, CA: Jeremy P. Tarcher, 1988.

Walsh, Chad. *The Literary Legacy of C. S. Lewis.* New York: Harcourt Brace Jovanovich, 1979.

5

The World of Narnia: Medieval Magic and Morality

Marvin D. Hinten

THE VIRTUES OF ANIMALS AND INDEPENDENT CHILDREN

The best-loved children's books of all time tend to be part of a series: *The Hardy Boys; Nancy Drew; The Three Investigators; The Bobbsey Twins; Little House on the Prairie; Harry Potter*; and, of course, *The Chronicles of Narnia*.

When C. S. Lewis began writing what eventually turned into *The Lion, the Witch and the Wardrobe*, however, he had no idea he was working on a series. He simply wanted to write a book with talking animals in it, of the kind he had loved as a child. Lewis grew up with the characters of Beatrix Potter, such as Squirrel Nutkin and (most famous today) Peter Rabbit; he also (later on in life) loved the animal figures in Kenneth Grahame's *The Wind in the Willows*: Rat, Mole, and Toad.

Talking animals allow an author the rights of adulthood without requiring corresponding responsibilities to be shown. In talking animal books, animals own homes, drive cars (if the time frame permits), and fight battles, but one doesn't see them serve on school boards, punch a time clock, pay taxes, or carry a briefcase.

The other successful character element in a children's book is, of course, children; but child characters work best when they are on their own. *The Bobbsey Twins*, for instance, repeatedly go on trips (*The Bobbsey Twins in the Country, The Bobbsey Twins at the Seashore*, etc.) to prevent them from having to check in constantly with their careful parents. Alice goes through a looking glass and into a wonderland to allow her a chance for individualized adventuring. And the Pevensie children are doubly separated from their parents. Most obviously, the world of Narnia is generally disconnected from our own, so the children need have no concern about whether to phone or telegraph (in our times, e-mail or text message) the folks. But even in our world, the children are separated from their parents in every book. It is noteworthy that Mr. and Mrs. Pevensie do not say a single word in the entire series. Thus the children need not worry about what would doubtless happen in our planet to kids who seriously claimed to have been to another world—being fussed over as sick or hallucinating (in Lewis's day) or being sent to counseling (in our own time).

THE HALTING BEGINNING OF NARNIA

Lewis began *The Lion, the Witch and the Wardrobe* in the late 1930s but gave it up, apparently because he couldn't figure out what to do with it. It would be more accurate to say Lewis began "the book" rather than *The Lion*, because there was no lion; coming up with the idea of Aslan as a Christ-figure was one of the keys in helping Lewis decide what the series would be. Aslan is the only character to appear in every book, and at least three of the books would not have a plot without his involvement.

When the novel was finally completed in the late 1940s Lewis, as was his custom, solicited responses to *Lion* from his friends, especially those in the Inklings, his weekly reading and conversation group. The responses ran the gamut from delighted, through tepid, to appalled—the last reaction being that of Lewis's close friend and fellow-writer, J. R. R. Tolkien. Tolkien disliked the book almost entirely, but he particularly abhorred the mixing of images—the blending of mythology, history, Bible, and literature that is a prime feature of Lewis's style. The greatest target of Tolkien's wrath was the appearance of Father Christmas (Santa Claus) in a book featuring a Christ-figure. Had most of his friends reacted in the same way as Tolkien, Lewis might well have never sent the book out for possible publication, and the world of children's literature would be notably poorer. Fortunately, leveler heads prevailed, and Lewis decided to send the book forth.

His publisher suggested making *Lion* the opening book in a series, and Lewis readily agreed. He decided to stop with seven, despite the fact that many children (and adults) wanted him to continue, for a typically Lewisian reason: seven is the biblical number of completion, so that number of books should complete the series.

READING ORDER: THE FIRST SHALL BE—SECOND?

The original publication order, with date of publication after each title, is as follows:

Book 1: *The Lion, the Witch and the Wardrobe* (1950)
Book 2: *Prince Caspian* (1951)
Book 3: *The Voyage of the "Dawn Treader"* (1952)
Book 4: *The Silver Chair* (1953)
Book 5: *The Horse and His Boy* (1954)
Book 6: *The Magician's Nephew* (1955)
Book 7: *The Last Battle* (1956)

When the series was taken over by HarperCollins in America in 1994, they changed the order of the books as follows:

Book 1: *The Magician's Nephew* (hereafter "*Nephew*")
Book 2: *The Lion, the Witch and the Wardrobe* (hereafter "*Lion*")
Book 3: *The Horse and His Boy* (hereafter "*Horse*")
Book 4: *Prince Caspian* (hereafter "*Prince*")
Book 5: *The Voyage of the "Dawn Treader"* (hereafter "*Treader*")
Book 6: *The Silver Chair* (hereafter "*Chair*")
Book 7: *The Last Battle* (hereafter "*Battle*")

Is one order "better" for reading through the series than the other? It probably doesn't make much difference how a reader familiar with the series goes through them, and even for a first-time reader the books pretty much each stand on their own (unlike, say, Tolkien's *Lord of the Rings* trilogy, which is more a novel in three volumes than a trilogy). Once having entered Narnia, one is always a Narnian, as the novels suggest. But which is the preferable way to enter Narnia: through *Lion* or through *Nephew*? I think there are sound literary, intellectual, and theological reasons for a person's first acquaintance with Narnia to come through *Lion*.

Literarily, if we read *Nephew* first, we fail to appreciate the predicament Lewis found himself in upon completing *Lion*. Lewis, recall, had no original plan of writing a series. When the publisher asked if he could produce more books like *Lion*, Lewis's first thought, naturally enough, was to tell how Narnia got started. But he couldn't tell it—because he didn't know! Why was there a gas lamppost, an object not invented until the nineteenth century, in the medieval world of Narnia? Why was the wardrobe magical? Why did the land have some animals that talked and some that didn't? This is why *Nephew* appeared so late in the original publication order; Lewis wrote other books while he tried to solve the mysteries of Narnia, and it was not until finishing up the series with *Battle* that he was able to have all the pieces of Narnia's creation in place.

Intellectually, reading *Nephew* first causes the professor's emphasis on logic in *Lion* ("what do they teach them in the schools these days?") to seem a cheap stunt. The professor doesn't need to use logic to determine that Lucy could be telling the truth about visiting a magical world: he's been to one himself! Suppose one of my students were to ask how many sites I thought would come up if they Googled C. S. Lewis, and I answered, "Use logic. There are about 500,000,000 native speakers of English in the world, and there would probably be about one site for every hundred speakers, so you can estimate 5,000,000." The student's amazement at my powers of logic would be great—unless she discovered that I had already checked on the number of sites earlier in the week!

Theologically, reading *Nephew* first gives us a very indirect approach to Aslan's importance in the history of Narnia. As Dr. Bruce Edwards sagely notes in the preface to *Further Up and Further In*,[1] his study of *Lion*, where is a more logical place to begin a potential convert and new reader of the Bible: Genesis or the Gospels? Just as one would not ordinarily take a potential new Christian through Genesis before introducing them to the sacrifice of Christ, it would seem a new Narnian needs to see the love of Aslan before witnessing his creativity. For all of these reasons, *Lion* is the place to first meet with Aslan.

THE THEMES OF NARNIA

The Narnian books are clearly part of a series, in that they all take place in the same world, and one character in that world (Aslan) appears in each of the books. (Trivia question for Narnia buffs: Aslan aside, who is the only character to appear in five of the seven books? To give you a chance to ponder, the answer will be found later in this chapter.) Although the books make up a series, each one is self-contained, with its own underlying thematic emphasis. Those themes can be presented as follows:

BOOK	THEME
The Lion, the Witch and the Wardrobe	Death and Resurrection
Prince Caspian	Faith
The Voyage of the "Dawn Treader"	Renewal
The Silver Chair	Scripture

The Horse and His Boy	Humility
The Magician's Nephew	Creation
The Last Battle	End Times

It will be seen that this displays a fairly full picture of spiritual life. I do not suggest at all that Lewis determined, "I'm going to write a book emphasizing the importance of holding onto faith." Instead, this chart indicates that Lewis undergirded his children's adventure series with Christian meaning and that each book has a particular aspect of Christianity that runs through the book as an underlying motif. With that in mind, this section covers the themes that are brought forth in each of the novels.

Death and Resurrection in *Lion*

If the key element of Christianity is the death and resurrection of Christ, then *Lion* is the key to understanding the *Chronicles*, as I have noted above. Aslan doesn't just die; he is sacrificed on behalf of Edmund as a redemptive act, just as Christ was sacrificed on behalf of the sins of humanity in our world. And Aslan undergoes a bodily resurrection just as Christ did. We should not push these parallels too far; unlike Christ, Aslan sacrifices himself on behalf of one person alone, and unlike Christ, Aslan comes back to life within twenty-four hours of his murder. These sorts of disparities may be part of what Lewis meant when he repeatedly argued that his stories are not allegories; we should not expect to find every detail a match. On the other hand, lack of matching details should not dissuade us from recognizing clear spiritual parallels. Aslan is clearly intended to be like Christ in another world; in fact, Lewis would go further and say Aslan *is* Christ in another world.

But Aslan's is not the only death and resurrection portrayed in *Lion*. The witch turns numerous creatures to stone in the book, and they are in effect dead until rescued by the breath of Aslan, when they return to the land of the living. (I have called Aslan a Christ-figure, and he is; but the repeated references to his breath in the series show that in some ways Aslan resembles the Holy Spirit as well, since the Greek word *pneuma* refers to both breath and spirit.) Edmund's spiritual death, while less overt than the physical death undergone by the others, is also followed by a renewing spiritual resurrection.

Faith in *Caspian*

In my edition of *Lion*,[2] the children first meet Aslan on page 122. From that point until the end of the book, Aslan is present in fifty-two pages out of sixty-five, or 80 percent of the work. Although the children are warned by

Mr. Beaver that Aslan comes and goes, certainly the reader has no sense of that in the opening work of the series. The years without Aslan, while the children rule Narnia, slip by in a few pages; and in reality, we actually don't know that those years are without Aslan. Perhaps he reappears from time to time without any authorial comment. But *Caspian* is a different story, thematically as well as literally. In my edition of *Caspian*, the children spend 212 pages in Narnia, but Aslan appears on only forty-two of those pages, or a bit under 20 percent. It's a sharp contrast; once the children meet Aslan, they have 80 percent of the *Lion* pages with him, but only 20 percent of the *Caspian* pages. Even more disconcerting, on the pages where Aslan does appear, not everyone can see or hear him.

So the children have to have faith in their memories of previous experiences with Aslan, and they have to have faith in an Aslan who seems to have changed his method of operation. II Corinthians 5:7 says that Christians "walk by faith, not by sight" (all biblical references: King James Version), and in their nighttime journey through the forest the children have to do this literally.

But it's not just Aslan that the children have to exhibit faith in; they also need faith in Lucy. In deciding which way to go, Edmund points out that Lucy was trustworthy in the past; therefore "[W]ouldn't it be fair to believe her this time?"[3] Faith is "the evidence of things not seen," as Hebrews 11:1 observes, but it is still evidence; the past is not seen, but it still can serve as evidence, just as the Bible does for Christians in our world.

Finally, Caspian, the title character of the book, has to exhibit faith in order to initiate the entire process; without his faith in the old stories leading him to blow Susan's horn, he can receive no help for Narnia. If Susan's horn represents a prayerful call for help, faith is the impetus that causes one to use it.

Renewal in *Treader*

Treader is the most sacramental of the *Chronicles*, with clear references to both baptism and communion. The baptism scene, in which Eustace is "undragoned," is justly famous, filled with spiritual insight. II Corinthians 5:17 says that becoming a Christian makes a person a "new creature," and here Eustace literally becomes a different creature. But it's not entirely a new creature; he has been a boy before, and now his boyhood is renewed. Yet at the same time he is new in nature, so both newness and renewal operate together, here and throughout the book. On the island of the Duffers, for instance, becoming visible again renews their former state; yet being given the new name of Dufflepuds symbolizes their new condition of happiness, discovering how they can use the water for recreation and transportation.

The other sacrament, communion (Eucharist) appears near the end of the book at the island of the three sleepers. The place where they have fallen asleep is called Aslan's Table, or as we would call it in our world, the Lord's Table, where the Lord's Supper is observed. As Ramandu's daughter notes, the food there is "renewed, every day."[4]

Scripture in *Chair*

Just as Edmund Pevensie (answer to earlier trivia question) is a unique character by appearing in five *Chronicles* (*Lion, Caspian, Treader, Horse,* and *Battle*), Jill Pole is unique in being the only person from our world for whom Aslan is the first character she sees upon her entrance to Narnia. (For some characters, Aslan may be the first Narnian they see, but they are accompanied by other people from our world whom they see first.) Aslan gives Jill four Signs to remember and believe, indicating that the ease of her mission will depend upon her ability to use and recognize them, just as the words of Scripture are repeatedly proclaimed as a lamp to the believer's feet and a light to his path, to use the language of Psalm 119:105.

Reaffirming the importance of these instructions, Aslan says to her about the Signs, "Say them to yourself when you wake in the morning and when you lie down at night, and when you wake in the middle of the night."[5] For biblically literate readers this is reminiscent of Deuteronomy 6:7, where the Israelites are told to "talk of them [God's words] . . . when thou liest down, and when thou risest up." Aslan's emphasis on memorizing the Signs parallels the previous verse in Deuteronomy, where the Jewish people are told to have God's words "in thine heart."

Humility in *Horse*

Lewis, like most traditional Christian writers, considered pride the chief sin to war against. Dante's *Inferno,* for example, is arranged by order of how wicked each of the Seven Deadly Sins is, and pride is found at the very bottom. The list of characters in *Horse* needing to learn humility is long. Even minor characters, such as Lasaraleen, are filled with pride; her assertions that the Tisroc is "dear" and "kind" to her and that he invites Lasaraleen and her family to his palace "almost every day"[6] are belied by her later terror at the nearness of the Tisroc. Aravis takes offense at Bree's initial conversations with Hwin and has to be told that horses are as important as people among Narnians. Rabadash learns humility by being turned into a donkey, in an episode reminiscent of the humiliation of Nebuchadnezzar in the biblical book of Daniel.

But the chief character needing baptism in humility is the magnificently portrayed warhorse Bree. Lewis brilliantly shows his insecurities and pride to be bound up together, as his assertions of superiority and expressions of contempt keep mixing in with requests for reassurance. (Upon learning that rolling in the grass looks funny, he wants to know whether he has acted improperly from Shasta, who is of all people least likely to know.) His peak of arrogance is reached when he tells Hwin ("crushingly," according to Lewis) that "I know a little more about campaigns and forced marches and what a horse can stand than you do."[7] But at the end, having lost his conceit, Bree becomes, in the Hermit's words, a "very decent sort of Horse."[8]

Creation in *Nephew*

Creation is clearly the main motif in *Nephew*, as it is the book about how Narnia was created. We also find out along the way that numerous other worlds exist, which presumably also have been created by Aslan, and we see the beginnings of knowledge and evil as well. Because *Nephew* is, in effect, a creation myth, Lewis brings in elements of Greek, Norse, and Hebrew creation accounts. In addition, since this book contains a fall, he makes full use of *Paradise Lost* in showing how temptation begins its work. *Nephew* is the most allusive of all the *Chronicles*.

End Times in *Battle*

The very first paragraph of *Battle* says it is a book about the "last days" of Narnia, and of course that is a phrase used repeatedly in the New Testament to signify end times, as in II Peter 3:3 and James 5:3. Perhaps particularly apropos is II Timothy 3:1, which indicates that "in the last days perilous times shall come." Certainly that is the case for Narnia. Lewis, very aware of medieval numerology, felt that once a series of books goes past a trilogy, for symbolic fitness the series needs to end with either a ninth book (Trinity times three, as in the nine orders of angels) or, most fittingly, a seventh book, the biblical number of completion.

CHARACTERISTICS OF LEWIS'S STYLE

All authors have a style, a collection of characteristics that distinguishes their writing from other writers of their era, and Lewis's style is more distinguishable than most. Some of the chief elements of his style are presented and exemplified in this section.

Biography

(EXAMPLE) When they had measured the attic they had to get a pencil and do a sum. They both got different answers to it at first, and even when they agreed I am not sure they got it right.[9]

Most authors permit their personal characteristics and values to show through their works, and this is certainly true of Lewis. Despite his mother holding a college degree in mathematics, Lewis himself always struggled with figures, even with simple addition and subtraction, so while his nine- and ten-year-old characters display a precocious knowledge of Milton and Bronte, they wrestle with basic arithmetic.

Authorial Intrusions

(EXAMPLE) Bree was not in the least trying to leave Shasta out of things, though Shasta sometimes nearly thought he was. People who know a lot of the same things can hardly help talking about them, and if you're there you can hardly help feeling that you're out of it.[10]

Twentieth-century authors often try to stand aside and let the novel proceed on its own, but this was not the case for eighteenth- and nineteenth-century British authors, who generally provide commentary on the action. The ancient Roman writer Horace, in *Ars Poetica*, had said that good writing should both delight and instruct, and older authors followed his dictum faithfully, with the plot being the primary vehicle for delight, and the commentary providing part of the instruction. In any split between modernists and traditionalists, Lewis always favors tradition, so it's no surprise that in the *Chronicles* he works in avuncular insights from time to time, even to the extent of repeatedly noting in *Lion* that the reader should be careful about wardrobe doors!

Humor

(EXAMPLE) "I tell you it is an animal," said the Bulldog. "Smell it for yourself."
"Smelling isn't everything," said the Elephant.
"Why," said the Bulldog, "if a fellow can't trust his nose what is he to trust?"
"Well, his brains perhaps," she replied mildly.
"I object to that remark very strongly," said the Bulldog.[11]

Lewis is exceptionally clever in matching animals with their supposed characteristics in folklore; the elephant who "never forgets" elevates brainpower, while the bulldog tenaciously defends the power of smell. Somehow a dispute between a bulldog and an elephant is funnier than the same dispute between humans; to sense this, I will show you what the dialogue above would lose if it were presented as being between two people, with "see" substituted for "smell" and "eyes" substituted for "nose."

> "I tell you it is an animal," said Bill. "See it for yourself."
> "Seeing isn't everything," said Elizabeth.
> "Why," said Bill, "if a fellow can't trust his eyes what is he to trust?"
> "Well, his brains perhaps," Elizabeth replied mildly.
> "I object to that remark very strongly," said Bill.

Notice how much the exchange loses if the same conversation is engaged in by people rather than animals. When people are asked why they read *The Chronicles of Narnia*, they often forget to mention the wit. I have heard two of the *Chronicles* read aloud in groups of a dozen or so adults and was surprised by how frequently people laughed audibly at touches of Lewisian humor.

Pro-Maturity, and Anti-"Grownupness"

(EXAMPLE) "Oh Susan!" said Jill, "she's interested in nothing now-a-days except nylons and lipstick and invitations. She always was a jolly sight too keen on being grownup."[12]

Every religious book Lewis ever wrote was designed to encourage spiritual and emotional maturity, but he always distinguished maturity from acting "grownup." For Lewis, the difference appears to have meant being unable to appreciate the interests of others—children, animals, and other types of people. He had no patience with men who could talk only about "manly" subjects—engines and sports—or women who could talk only of fashion and cosmetics. Similarly, he felt that a person should never "outgrow" children's books, but should simply add an appreciation for good adult literature to an appreciation for good children's literature. For Lewis, "growing up" involved shrinking interests and awareness; maturity involved expansion.

Fascination with Language

(EXAMPLE) Prince Caspian lived with . . . his aunt, who had red hair and was called Queen Prunaprismia.[13]

Lewis loved words—their origins, meanings, alterations, and sounds. One of his books, *Studies in Words*, focuses entirely on how selected words began, changed, and expanded. In keeping with this interest, the *Chronicles* have numerous examples of rare and coined words, and particularly Lewis liked to play with names. "Prunaprismia" is a coined name designed to guide the reader toward an instant dislike of the character. The name is a blended combination of "prunes" (a food Lewis loathed) and "prissy," meaning overly feminized. As noted above, Lewis had no respect for prissy women. In addition, the combination is meant to remind literary readers of Dickens's novel *Little Dorrit,* in which young ladies are taught to repeat the words "prunes" and "prism" as a way of developing well-rounded lips; in fact, the forty-third chapter of the book is entitled "Prunes and Prisms." It is entirely characteristic of Lewis to combine linguistics, literature, and autobiography in creating a character's name.

Intriguing Characters

(EXAMPLE) "I'm trying to catch a few eels to make an eel stew for our dinner," said Puddleglum. "Though I shouldn't wonder if I didn't get any. And you won't like them much if I do."[14]

We read novels for many reasons—plot, theme, and style—but certainly one reason is character; if an author can create characters that we care about and find interesting, we are more likely to read to the end and to search out other books by that author. Many readers fall in love with Lewis's Narnian characters, especially the nonhuman ones. In my own case, for example, our family hamster was affectionately named Reepiceep after the valiant mouse of the series. People generally do not want to live in the real world with a constant pessimist, one who finds the dark cloud behind every silver lining, but we like to read about them (note the similarity of Puddleglum to Eeyore in the Pooh books), particularly when at bottom they are good-hearted and loyal.

Moral Teaching

(EXAMPLE) "Rotten?" said Uncle Andrew with a puzzled look. "Oh, I see. You mean that little boys ought to keep their promises. Very true. But of course you must understand that rules of that sort can't possibly be expected to apply to great thinkers and sages. No, Digory. Men like me are freed from common rules."
As he said this he looked so grave and noble that for a second Digory really thought he was saying something rather fine. But all at once he saw through Uncle Andrew's grand words. "All it means," he said to himself, "is that he thinks he can do anything he likes to get anything he wants."[15]

As with his adult books, Lewis in his children's books perpetually wants to inculcate wisdom and goodness into his readers. Honesty, courage, humility, and service are repeatedly held up in the series as characteristics to pursue and acquire. And when Lewis fears children may not get the point, as in this excerpt, he makes quite clear what is wrong in the thinking being presented. Teaching is such an important part of Lewis's writing that I shall devote a complete section to this topic later in this chapter, under the heading "What Lewis Has to Teach Us."

ALLUSIONS

Walter Hooper, who lived with Lewis for a few months near the end of his life as a secretary and personal assistant, wanted to make sure he fit himself properly into Lewis's schedule, so he one day asked, "Do you take a nap in the afternoons?" Lewis responded with a smile, "No—but sometimes a nap takes me!" I remember when I first heard that story admiring Lewis's wit, how quickly he could come up with an apt, clever answer.

A few years later I read an unabridged edition of Boswell's *Life of Johnson* for the first time. James Boswell, getting to know the much older and more famous Samuel Johnson (somewhat the eighteenth-century equivalent of C. S. Lewis), found himself in much the same position as the later Hooper. Early in their acquaintance Johnson made the witty (and to my knowledge original) remark, "I never take a nap after dinner but when I have had a bad night; and then the nap takes me."[16] I remember roaring when I read that, "What? Lewis stole that from Johnson!" But of course it wasn't stealing; Lewis probably expected Hooper, as a man of letters, to recognize the quotation and to admire how splendidly it fit their current situation.

C. S. Lewis was the most allusive popular writer of the twentieth century; he read voraciously, he remembered incredibly, and he included his memories in his works voluminously. Allusion, from Latin *allusio* ("a playing with") involves making direct or indirect references to people, sayings, events, and literary works—well, almost anything. Almost everyone uses allusions to some extent; when someone refers to the patience of Job they are making a biblical allusion, and saying someone has the strength of Hercules is a mythological allusion. But writers use more allusions than most people, and certainly more allusions to literary works. When John Steinbeck named his novel *Of Mice and Men*, for instance, he was clearly alluding to Robert Burns' poem "To a Mouse," in which Burns comments on the plans "o' mice and men." But no other popular writer incorporates as many allusions as Lewis, and because it was such a distinctive feature of his writing, I shall devote a few pages to it. (In the interests of full disclosure, I will note that these examples come from my book *The Keys to the Chronicles: Unlocking the Symbols of C. S. Lewis's Narnia*,[17] published by Broadman and Holman in 2005. It is the most complete and accurate study of Lewis's Narnian allusions to date.)

Sample Allusion from *Lion*: The Stone Table

The Stone Table represents the Old Testament Law, specifically the Ten Commandments; thus it has ancient writing on the side of it, in keeping with Exodus 32:16: "And the tables were the work of God, and the writing was the writing of God graven upon the tables." According to the Old Testament, the Ten Commandments were given on Mount Sinai, which partially explains why the Stone Table in Lion is found on a hillside. (In addition, Calvary, the place of Jesus' crucifixion, was a hill, and since Aslan is killed on the Stone Table, the hilltop location fits that aspect of the story as well.) A pavilion (tent) is located beside the Stone Table, representing the tabernacle of the Jewish religion in the Old Testament.

Sample Allusion from *Caspian*: The Wer-Wolf

The typical spelling is werewolf, but Lewis spells the word this way to draw attention to its linguistic origins: "wer" is the Anglo-Saxon word for man, so a wer-wolf is literally a man-wolf. Indeed, the creature is in the process of changing from man to wolf as it is killed. Significantly, at the time of death its head has already turned into a wolf while its body is still human. Lewis, as a teacher of medieval and Renaissance literature, was quite familiar with the duel between Reason and Passion, mentioned repeatedly in the literature of the period. Writers noted that we humans are a mix of rationality and emotions, which is fine; that's part of what it means to be human. The danger comes when we let our emotions be in charge of our decision-making; emotions are intended as support troops, while reason is to be in charge. Since the wer-wolf has the animal head on top and the human part underneath, it is being governed by the bestial side, which leads to bad decision-making; a being split between human and animal should have the rational part on top to be good. Thus in *Lion* mixed beings with the human part on top (fauns, centaurs) support the side of Aslan, while mixed beings with the animal part on top (such as the Minotaur, a creature from Greek myth with a bull's head on a human body) support the Witch.

Sample Allusion from *Treader*: Aslan's Table

As noted earlier, Aslan's Table represents the Lord's Table, also known as Communion or Eucharist. Communion is a time to remember the death of

Christ; thus we find the cross-like Knife of Stone, which killed Aslan, lying on the Table. The three lords of Narnia who get to the Table fail to recognize its significance, and in fact, one of them grabs the Knife to fight the others, whereupon they all fall asleep. This parallels the statement of I Corinthians 11:29-30, in which people approach the Lord's Table "not discerning the Lord's body. For this cause many are weak and sickly among you, and many sleep." The metaphorical sleep of I Corinthians 11 transposes into literal sleep in the allusion.

Sample Allusion from *Chair*: Jill's School

Chair is the most autobiographical of the *Chronicles*, which helps explain why it is one of the less popular books in the series. On the first page Lewis comments on Jill's school at length, working in his own thoughts on contemporary education. There were two problems with Jill's school, Lewis notes in his authorial commentary: coeducation and bullying. The second of those problems Lewis had experienced himself as a precocious and somewhat arrogant youngster; in *Surprised by Joy* he called himself a "marked man" when it came to bullying,[18] and the experience was repeated and painful enough to leave scars on his psyche years later. The first "weakness" in Jill's school, Lewis thought, was that they tried to educate boys and girls together, which Lewis during most of his life feared would weaken the amount of knowledge gained by boys. This viewpoint does not endear Lewis to modern readers.

Sample Allusion from *Horse*: The Sofa/Divan

In the seventh chapter of *Horse*, Lewis engages in a piece of impressive linguistic place-setting. Unlike the other books of the series, *Horse* takes place primarily in Calormen, a dry, hot (*calor* is Latin and Spanish for hot) country with a Middle Eastern feel. A few pages into the chapter "Aravis in Tashbaan," Aravis and Lasaraleen have to hide behind a couch. Significantly, however, Lewis does not call it a couch; he calls it a sofa. In fact, he repeatedly refers to it as a sofa while the girls are alone in the room, a total of four times. But then when the Tisroc, Rabadash, and Ahoshta enter the room, Lewis begins calling that item of furniture a divan, and he refers to it as a divan throughout the next chapter until the Calormen trio has left. Why?

Let us consider the five most common options Lewis had for labeling the piece of furniture: couch, davenport, settee, sofa, and divan. *Couch* comes from French; *davenport* comes from the British maker's name; *settee* comes from Anglo-Saxon; *sofa* and *divan* come from Turkish. Since this scene has a Middle Eastern setting, Lewis avoids the word choices from a Western

European background and uses the two words of Middle Eastern derivation. That's impressive.

But there's more. In English, *sofa* means only the piece of furniture. But *divan*, though we think of it today as having only one meaning, actually had two standard meanings in Renaissance English. The first, of course, is the article of furniture. But the other meaning is, in the words of one of my dictionaries, "a private political conference, particularly in Renaissance-era Turkey."

So Lewis uses the word *sofa* when there's no conference in the room, and the word *divan* when there is. And this is no accident. Actually, according to the *Oxford English Dictionary*, the political conference meaning entered the English language before the furniture meaning did. And if Lewis had found the meaning in no other place, he certainly would have known it from his beloved *Paradise Lost*. In Book 10, line 457, when Satan returns from having led humanity into the fall, he interrupts a conference of his colleagues; as Milton puts it, they "[R]aised from their dark divan."[19] So even in what would seem insignificant word choices, Lewis engages in linguistic subtlety that only his fellow-scholars could appreciate.

Sample Allusion from *Nephew*: Digory Kirke

In *Nephew*, we find out the last name of the professor from *Lion*; he is Professor Kirke. And that is significant in numerous ways. First, *kirk* is the Middle English (and Scottish) word for church. It was used allegorically by Edmund Spenser in one of Lewis's favorite Renaissance works, *The Faerie Queene*, and in fact Lewis had already used *kirk* for church in one of his earliest books, *Pilgrim's Regress*. Presumably Lewis named the professor in this way because it is through his house that the children come into contact with Aslan; in other words, it is through the church (*kirk*) that they get to meet Christ. Besides these linguistic and literary allusions, Lewis also picks the name to honor his high-school tutor, William Kirkpatrick, known as "Kirk" to the Lewis family. Thus the name "Kirke" allows Lewis his usual method of allusion-blending.

Sample Allusion from *Battle*: Shift the Ape and *Animal Farm*

C. S. Lewis loved George Orwell's novel *Animal Farm*, and in fact in 1955 published an article telling how much he preferred that book to Orwell's more famous work *1984*. The article (entitled "George Orwell") was written in 1954, perhaps within a year of Lewis's completing *Battle*. Shift in *Battle* displays a remarkable similarity to Napoleon, the leading animal (a pig) in

Animal Farm. Possibly some similarities between the two are a natural outcome of any animal rising in status, but the extent of the similarities (and Lewis's acknowledged fondness for Orwell's novel) certainly suggests that some of the ideas for Shift's behavior come from Napoleon's behavior in *Animal Farm.* Here are some of the ways Shift parallels Napoleon:

- Wearing clothes
- Walking on two legs
- Making other animals serve him
- Wearing weapons
- Finding new work continually for the other animals to do
- Being less frequently seen as time passes
- Taking up drinking
- Telling the other animals that he is doing these things for their own good

More correspondences could be listed, but even this list seems to indicate that Lewis borrowed some concepts from Orwell regarding how an ascendant animal would act.

WHAT LEWIS HAS TO TEACH US

I was a nineteen-year-old college junior when I first read Bree's response to Hwin in *Horse* about whether the two of them could continue traveling when they were bone weary: "I think, Ma'am," said Bree very crushingly, "that I know a little more about campaigns and forced marches and what a horse can stand than you do."[20]

When I read that sentence I had four thoughts instantly follow one another through my mind: (1) He's not very nice; (2) That's the way I sound when I put down people; (3) Maybe I'm not very nice; and (4) I've just learned something about myself from reading a children's story about a horse; I need to read more of this author and see what else he can help me learn.

And that has been the experience of numerous Lewis readers. Young and old, believing and nonbelieving, they find they gain intellectual understanding, spiritual insight, and character awareness from this children's series. Rather than providing examples of moral and social teaching from each book, as was done with the allusions above, I would like to use one book as an example of how Lewis provides character education in the series. Thus, what are some values Lewis teaches in *The Lion, the Witch and the Wardrobe?*

Chapter 5: "Why Don't They Teach Logic at These Schools?"[21]

Principle: Be Open to Something That Seems Wrong to You at First

My first experience with Mr. Lewis was a violent one; I threw *Mere Christianity* across the room, bouncing it off my dorm wall, because it had theology that differed from what I already believed. One of the things Lewis wants to teach people, whatever their age or theological position, is to be willing to carefully consider opposing viewpoints. Peter and Susan automatically assume Lucy is wrong about saying she has been in a magic world, partly because there are no magic worlds (they think) and partly because she has not been gone from our world long enough for that to occur. The professor points out that there are other factors to consider. One of those is Lucy's truthfulness level; another is that if Lucy were making the story up, she would be incredibly stupid not to hide longer, and Lucy does not seem incredibly stupid. Ever the moral philosopher and Christian teacher, Lewis does not want his readers (even for adult nonfiction) to reject miracles and the supernatural out-of-hand, so he begins logical preparation for that here.

Chapter 6: "I Apologise"[22]

Principle: Apologize Quickly and Properly

The novel says Peter turned "at once"[23] to Lucy. Lewis's point is that a person who has wronged someone should apologize as quickly as possible, and this particularly applies to Peter as the leader of the group; he serves as a role model of humility and correct behavior. It's interesting to note that Susan does not apologize to Lucy here; perhaps that is one way of Lewis displaying Peter's greater character and maturity.

Chapter 6: "We Shan't Take Them Even out of the Wardrobe"[24]

Principle: Think Through the Implications of Your Actions

Lewis is always keenly aware that he is writing for children, some of whom will be influenced in thought and behavior by the models he presents. Elsewhere in *Lion*, for instance, Lewis repeatedly warns children against shutting doors behind themselves when they explore a wardrobe. Here, he doesn't want children reading his books to think it's OK to steal, so he carefully points out that since the coats are staying in the closet, they're not being stolen. The same conflict appears in *Horse*, where Shasta has concerns about taking items they need for their flight, but Bree reassures him that in a wartime situation morality has a bit more flexibility regarding using the enemy's things. That way of looking at it may be rather disingenuous, depending on the reader's personal code of ethics, but the point is that Lewis is always concerned about the impact of his books upon children, and whenever characters appear to be doing wrong he has them fail or be punished (if in his judgment they really are doing wrong), or he explains why what looks wrong is actually OK in this particular case.

Chapter 12: "Never Forget to Wipe Your Sword"[25]

Principle: Take Care of Your Belongings

Every parent of a grade-schooler has experienced having a child neglecting to take care of personal belongings—leaving a bike in the rain, forgetting a basketball at the playground, failing to put away a toy and having it stepped on. Lewis knew this characteristic of children and has Aslan indicate to Peter that part of maturing is taking proper care of belongings. When we consider how many people drive around on underinflated tires or forget to change their furnace filters regularly, we realize that, as usual, Lewis has a message for adults as well as for children!

Chapter 17: "It Was All Edmund's Doing"[26]

Principle: Compliment People Who Do Well

Children have to be trained to look beyond themselves and speak a word of encouragement to those who struggle or compliment to those who do well. With Peter making this remark about Edmund, perhaps part of Lewis's point is that children particularly need to do this for their siblings!

PREDICTING THE FUTURE FOR *THE CHRONICLES OF NARNIA*

The Chronicles of Narnia sold briskly from their first appearance in the 1950s and continue to do so today. There is no way to know for sure how many books have been sold nor how many readers the *Chronicles* have had, because of the variety of publishers and editions, the number of languages the books have been translated into, and the way the series tends to be passed along from one family member to another. Estimates are rough and vary widely, but they are always well up in the millions, and like the number of hamburgers sold by McDonald's restaurants when they used to keep track on their front signage, the numbers increase by a significant amount every year.

As I write this paragraph, the completed series has been out for fifty years. What will the next fifty years bring? Will parents, and children, and scholars still be enjoying and perusing the *Chronicles* in 2056? I believe the *Chronicles* will easily maintain both their popularity and their critical attention for decades to come.

Three main factors will keep the *Chronicles* popular. First, in the field of children's literature, fantasy works have a longer "shelf life" than books of contemporary realism. I teach a course at my university entitled "Young Adult Literature and Writing," and it is amazing how quickly the books become dated. The oldest book I currently use is *The Pigman* by Paul Zindel, published in 1968. My students are always flabbergasted that one of the (urban) characters has never heard of a credit card and has to have its use explained to him. A nontraditional student in her thirties commented this year, regarding a part of the plot where a character fixes a telephone dial so it won't turn, that middle school students will need to have the concept of a telephone with a rotary dial explained to them. As I glanced around the room, some of the twenty-year-olds looked like they were a bit fuzzy about the use of rotary dials themselves!

Realism in itself does not rapidly date a book, if it is historical realism, such as the works of Laura Ingalls Wilder and Mark Twain; rather, it is the author trying to be "up-to-date" who will become dated most rapidly. With medieval fantasy, however, readers expect the language and adventures to be somewhat old-fashioned.

A second factor to keep the *Chronicles* popular is the theological content of the books. Many adults remember certain books from their childhood fondly—*Pokey Little Puppy, Little Women, Green Eggs and Ham, Little House on the Prairie*—but they are unlikely to go back and reread those classics unless they are reading them to their own children. This is not the case with the *Chronicles*, however. I have repeatedly met adults who have read and even reread the series while well past their childhood years, and usually it's because they value the books for theology as well as plot and character. I belong to a Sunday School class that does book studies by authors such as Dietrich Bonhoeffer and A. W. Tozer, and two of the books the class has studied are *The Lion, the Witch and the Wardrobe* and *Prince Caspian*.

A final factor that appears destined to keep the *Chronicles* alive and well for at least the next decade is the success of motion pictures based on the series. After the success of movies based on J. K. Rowling's *Harry Potter* books and J. R. R. Tolkien's *Lord of the Rings* trilogy, Hollywood decided a similar fantasy would do similarly well, and that reasoning was correct. The *Lion* movie had a budget of $180 million, and by the end of April 2006, the movie had grossed an astonishing $740 million worldwide, with over $290 million of that coming in the United States. Those are figures to spawn sequels, and the *Caspian* movie is thus due out in 2008.

These statistics clearly show that few people were disappointed in the movie, despite the fact that no movie of reasonable length can contain all the elements and dialogue of even a children's novel. People familiar with *Lion* would have noticed alterations and omissions. When my wife and I saw the movie, for instance, she was surprised and disappointed that Father Christmas gave gifts only to the children; she leaned over to me and whispered, "What happened to Mrs. Beaver's sewing machine?" I noticed how many of the teaching elements were left out. As a teacher, I have always found Aslan's inclusion of the other lion in chapter 16 with "us lions"[27] to be impressive. Usually we think of humility as a person lowering himself or herself, but here we see Aslan raising another being to his level. The line, as well as the lion, was omitted from the movie, perhaps because it would confuse children. (And Lewis seems to have had second thoughts about the wisdom of a second lion himself, since no other living lions besides Aslan appear in the later books of the series.) For most viewers, however, these omissions were more than made up for by the spectacular special effects and high-quality production values.

What sorts of things happen when a children's book becomes a blockbuster movie? Here are some of the occurrences I saw around the time of the movie's release, from late 2005 to early 2006:

• Churches ran many Narnian events for their children's programs. At one church I read about, a featured game was Narnian freeze tag, where the Witch froze players with a wand and the person playing Aslan would breathe on them to free them.

• Churches promoted Narnia in numerous other ways. Many had Lewis workshops; some had sermon series based on Narnia; many bought blocks of movie tickets. I heard of one showing where the entire theater was sold out to a pair of church groups.

• Reading groups—some secular, some religious—chose *Lion* for a book-of-the-month selection.

• Media attention went wild; Narnia was talked about in magazines, newspapers, radio, and television.

• Bookstores promoted the series heavily. One bookstore near my home put in large letters on their marquee, "YOUR NARNIA HEADQUARTERS." The words were accurate. I entered and was stunned to find a huge four-sided display, complete with wardrobe on loan from a furniture store, covered with books, calendars, music, figurines, and other assorted apparatus. When I expressed my amazement to an employee, she said, "Did you see our other display?" The store had another huge four-sided display with more Narnian artifacts! I have on my desk an Aslan "snow globe" that one shakes to make glitter swirl around his mane; behind me is an Aslan from a fast-food meal, both gifts from friends of Narnia.

With this sort of promotion and attention stretching out for the next decade, awareness of Narnia among popular audiences can only increase. Among critical audiences I also see continuing attention given to the *Chronicles*, probably more so than for any other series of children's books. Two main factors will contribute to this. First is the variety of places in a college curriculum where the books might appear. A typical children's series, such as the Mrs. Piggle-Wiggle books by Betty MacDonald, can only be studied in a children's literature course. *The Chronicles of Narnia*, in contrast, can be found in any number of courses in higher education: children's literature, fantasy literature, religious literature, C. S. Lewis, and the Inklings. Unlike other children's literature, which can only be found in English or Education departments, the *Chronicles* are used in Religion departments as well. For books to receive scholarly attention, they must be read by scholars, and this will continue to be the case for the *Chronicles*.

More importantly, the *Chronicles* will continue to generate scholarly articles because they have so much greater depth and complexity than the average children's book series. Virtually everything that can be written about another children's book (plot, character, theme, and teachability, etc.) can be written about the *Chronicles* as well, plus the layering of allusions, noted above, provides a dimension of study for this series lacking in other books.

When people are asked which C. S. Lewis book has most influenced them spiritually, the most common answer is *Mere Christianity*. But if people were asked which C. S. Lewis book they have enjoyed the most, I suspect the most common answer would be, "*The Chronicles of Narnia*."

NOTES

1. Bruce L. Edwards, *Further Up and Further In: Understanding C. S. Lewis's The Lion, the Witch and the Wardrobe* (Nashville, TN: Broadman and Holman, 2005).

2. C. S. Lewis, *The Lion, the Witch and the Wardrobe* (New York: Macmillan, 1950).

3. C. S. Lewis, *Prince Caspian* (New York: Macmillan, 1951), 123.

4. C. S. Lewis, *The Voyage of the "Dawn Treader"* (New York: Macmillan, 1952), 174.

5. C. S. Lewis, *The Silver Chair* (New York: Macmillan, 1953), 21.

6. C. S. Lewis, *The Horse and His Boy* (New York: Macmillan, 1954), 98.

7. Ibid., 131.

8. Ibid., 146.

9. C. S. Lewis, *The Magician's Nephew* (New York: Macmillan, 1955), 8.

10. Lewis, *The Horse and His Boy*, 41.

11. Lewis, *The Magician's Nephew*, 132.

12. C. S. Lewis, *The Last Battle* (New York: Macmillan, 1956), 135.

13. Lewis, *Prince Caspian*, 37.

14. Lewis, *The Silver Chair*, 59.

15. Lewis, *The Magician's Nephew*, 18.

16. James Boswell, *The Life of Samuel Johnson* (Garden City, NY: Doubleday, 1946), 327.

17. Marvin D. Hinten, *The Keys to the Chronicles: Unlocking the Symbols of C. S. Lewis's Narnia* (Nashville, TN: Broadman and Holman, 2005).

18. C. S. Lewis, *Surprised by Joy* (New York: Harcourt Brace Jovanovich, 1956), 94.

19. John Milton, *Complete Poems and Major Prose*, ed. Merritt Y. Hughes (Indianapolis, IN: Bobbs-Merrill, 1957), 417.

20. Lewis, *The Horse and His Boy*, 131.

21. Lewis, *The Lion, the Witch and the Wardrobe*, 45.

22. Ibid., 51.

23. Ibid.

24. Ibid., 52.

25. Ibid., 129.

26. Ibid., 175.

27. Ibid., 171.

BIBLIOGRAPHY

Boswell, James, *The Life of Samuel Johnson*. Garden City, NY: Doubleday, 1946.

Edwards, Bruce L., *Further Up and Further In: Understanding C. S. Lewis's The Lion, the Witch and the Wardrobe*. Nashville, TN: Broadman and Holman, 2005.

Hinten, Marvin D., *The Keys to the Chronicles: Unlocking the Symbols of C. S. Lewis's Narnia*. Nashville, TN: Broadman and Holman, 2005.

Lewis, C. S., *The Horse and His Boy*. New York: Macmillan, 1954, 98.

———. *The Last Battle*. New York: Macmillan, 1956, 135.

———. *The Lion, the Witch and the Wardrobe*. New York: Macmillan, 1950.

———. *The Magician's Nephew*. New York: Macmillan, 1955, 8.

———. *Prince Caspian*. New York: Macmillan, 1951, 123.

———. *The Silver Chair*. New York: Macmillan, 1953, 21.

———. *Surprised by Joy*. New York: Harcourt Brace Jovanovich, 1956, 94.

———. *The Voyage of the "Dawn Treader."* New York: Macmillan, 1952, 174.

Milton, John, *Complete Poems and Major Prose*. Edited by Merritt Y. Hughes Indianapolis, IN: Bobbs-Merrill, 1957, 417.

6

Sons of Adam, Daughters of Eve, and Children of Aslan: An Environmentalist Perspective on *The Chronicles of Narnia*

Margarita Carretero-González

Whereas the reader of C. S. Lewis's academic writings may easily ignore the activism as Christian apologist, which made him so famous and once led J. R .R. Tolkien to refer to him as "Everyman's Theologian,"[1] this is something impossible to do when one approaches his fictional works. Indeed, it would be unwise, for instance, to try to ignore the religious component in *The Chronicles of Narnia*, since the seven-volume set was precisely one of Lewis's ways "to say something about Christianity to children"[2] even if, as he admitted, at first there was nothing Christian about the images that triggered the stories. The Christian element that informs *The Chronicles of Narnia* or *The Cosmic Trilogy* is in consonance with the worldview Lewis considered to be the correct one. His opinions about authority, obedience, or the relationship between the genders—to name a few of the issues that have stirred more controversy— permeate the pages of his fictional works and may certainly take aback the readers who have grown up questioning the whole issue of authority. There are, however, other matters in which Lewis seems to be ahead of his time, especially as concerns his respect for the natural environment.

An environmentally conscious reader who decides to open the pages of *Prince Caspian*, for instance, will certainly take pleasure in the way Lewis constructs the relationship between human and nonhuman forms of existence, presenting as a desirable world order one that respects lives outside the human species. If he/she decides to start the series in internal chronological order, that is, according to the chronology of events in Narnia itself, the reader will then see that the world of Narnia was created on the principle of equality among the animals—that is, the Talking Beasts, one is forced to specify—and that, after Digory, a Son of Adam, brought evil into Narnia, it was his task to join the Narnians and struggle against the forces threatening that balance. This makes the series consistent with both ecological thought (in one of its lighter shades, however, since it displays a somewhat patronizing attitude toward the nonhuman)—and with Lewis's own Christian values. Nevertheless, it is my contention that, since the Christian component takes precedence over any type of environmental worry, some of Lewis's tenets—such as human superiority over the rest of the nonhuman world—are not very palatable to ecologists in general and of modern ecotheologians in particular. Before further exploring this issue, it will be useful to pay attention to the views Lewis held on nonhuman animals as he expressed them when dealing with animal suffering in *The Problem of Pain*.

LEWIS ON ANIMAL PAIN

Lewis's brief and insightful excursion on the issue of animal pain raises some very interesting questions concerning the relationship between human and nonhuman animals, which is nowadays at the core of important debates in ecological thinking.[3] When discussing animal rights, for instance, it is always advisable to approach the subject from a nonanthropocentric position; that is, we must tale not to judge everything in terms of what is good or bad for our species, lest we be accused of what Mary Midgley calls "human chauvinism."[4] In dealing with animal pain, Lewis is fully aware of these dangers. However, he seems to hold the view that anthropocentrism may be a first good step to raise awareness. After all, acknowledging that a nonhuman animal may suffer like a human may eventually lead to a respect for that suffering and reluctance to inflict it.

For Lewis, animal pain is "appalling" since the Christian explanations of human pain he has given in the previous chapters of *The Problem of Pain* cannot be extended to nonhuman animals: "So far as we know beasts are incapable either of sin or virtue: therefore they can neither deserve pain nor be improved by it."[5] It is good that Lewis admits that most of his statements are based on guesswork, since they can be thoughtfully challenged. One might argue, for instance, why he finds it necessary to establish a difference between the way human and nonhuman animals experience pain. For him, it is incorrect to utter the statement "This animal feels pain," when one should instead say "Pain is taking place in this animal,"[6] thus rendering the nonhuman animal as a mere recipient of an event—in fact, even a location where the particular event unfolds—rather than an experiencer. Trying hard not to privilege anthropocentrism, Lewis warns the reader that an inappropriate behavior for one species does not equate with the same behavior in another, and may indeed not be wrong for another. Thus, "[a] forest in which half the trees are killing the other half may be a perfectly 'good' forest: *for its goodness consists in its utility and beauty* and it does not feel [italics added]."[7]

However, no matter how hard Lewis tries to avoid anthropocentrism, the conclusion of this statement betrays the fact that he judges the goodness of this particular forest depending on the service it renders to the human beholder, as the italicized words indicate. In the same way, while he admits that certain animals may have "in some degree, a self, or a soul which connects experiences and gives rise to rudimentary individuality,"[8] Lewis negates any possibility of their reaching immortality unless it is through human intervention: "certain animals may have an immortality, not in themselves, but in the immortality of their masters."[9] Denying the existence of an immortal soul in the animal, unless provided by its relationship to a human, runs close to negating any intrinsic value in the animal itself. In fact, Lewis goes as far as to say that a tame animal is "in the deepest sense, the only 'natural' animal—the only one we see occupying the place *it was made to occupy* [italics added],"[10] and that this tame animal owes its real self or personality "almost entirely to its master."[11]

In drawing this conclusion concerning not only animal pain but also animal immortality, Lewis does not depart from the biblical account of the relationship established by God between humans and beasts, but he makes clear that the superior position given to humans entails a high degree of responsibility toward those who are inferior: "Man was appointed by God to have dominion over the beasts, and everything a man does to an animal is either a lawful exercise, or a sacrilegious abuse, of an authority by Divine right."[12] Although this assertion is helpful in raising awareness about our duty to respect all forms of life, it is extremely condescending and difficult to make it coexist with ecological ethics, since, as said above, it just values an animal depending on the relationship established with humans, thus providing an instance of human chauvinism: "The error we must avoid is that of considering them [higher animals] in themselves. Man is to be understood only in his relation to God. The beasts are to be understood only in their relation to man, and through man, to God."[13]

Eventually, Lewis believes wholeheartedly in the human capacity to restore peace into the nonhuman animal world, "and if he had not joined the enemy he might have succeeded in doing so to an extent now hardly imaginable."[14] To admit that humans can contribute to the lessening of pain in the animal world is perfectly legitimate—after all, much of this pain is inflicted by us— but to believe that humans can run close to eradicate it is, again, an exercise in anthropocentrism. There are patterns of nonhuman animal behavior that humans are not expected to and should not try to control, no matter how disagreeable they may appear to us as a species. As Nathan Kowalsky puts it, "to expect coyotes not to kill and eat rodents, or adult male lions not to kill lion cubs of another sire, means we expect nonhuman nature to act like a good human being even outside its interaction with us. These expectations are bizarre—unless, of course, we think human beings really are the centre of the universe."[15] That is precisely the issue at stake here; Lewis had complete faith in the dogma that humans had been appointed by God to be the center of the universe and this assertion can hardly be reconciled with deep ecological ethics.

LEWIS AND AQUINAS

Lewis's own respect for nature and animals is consonant with St. Thomas Aquinas's philosophical considerations about the physical reality of the universe and the role of humans in it. According to John Haught, in basing much of his philosophy on Aristotelian realism, Aquinas's impregnated the Christian mind with a respect for nature, which was not very common at the time in Christian discourses.[16] In his hierarchical organization of the universe, Aquinas establishes an "ontological link between the spiritual and the material, a hierarchical structure which," in Mark Muldoon's words, "gives a foundation for reverence of other creatures as brothers and sisters sharing the relationship of divine recognition and dependence."[17] Both Lewis and Aquinas concur that, in order to achieve ultimate union with God, human beings need to transcend the material world, because nature is imperfect. It is this idea of "ordered discontinuity" where the rub resides to make both Lewis's and Aquinas's tenets difficult to be completely appropriated by environmental ethicists. A closer look at some of Aquinas's views in the *Compendium of Theology* or the *Summa Theologicae* will show where both he and Lewis rub shoulders.

In his *Compendium of Theology*, Aquinas states that "although all creatures are ordained to the divine goodness as their end . . . 'some are closer to the end than others, and so participate in the divine goodness more abundantly.' "[18] Further on, he argues that lesser creatures, having a smaller share in their divine goodness, "are in some way subordinated to higher beings as to their ends;" thus, "lower beings realize their last end chiefly by their subordination to higher beings; . . . lifeless beings exist for living beings, plants for animals, and the latter for man; . . . the whole of the material nature is subordinate to intellectual nature . . . the whole of material nature exists for man."[19] Likewise, in *Summa Theologicae*, Aquinas asserts that "'the less perfect fall to the use of the more perfect' such as the life of animals and plants is preserved not for themselves but for humankind."[20]

This series of examples serves to illustrate the problems arising when trying to use Lewis's and Aquinas's views of the nonhuman world for environmental awareness: they offer a good step in that they invite the reader to respect forms of life outside humanity, but fall short of being completely acceptable for environmental ethics since they are terribly anthropocentric, confusing the use a human being can make of a nonhuman animal with the role that the animal has to perform in life. A meat-eating human, for instance, may use a lamb to obtain nourishment from it, but that is not necessarily what the lamb was made for. The lamb's intrinsic value resides in its mere existence, its needs to eat, breathe, drink, and reproduce. Thus, although the interests of a lamb—or even those of a tree, for that matter—may differ from ours, they still have to be acknowledged as legitimate interests for the lamb and the tree.

In reviewing what makes Lewis's views on animal suffering not fully compatible with current animal ethics, my desire is not to critique his argumentation; on the contrary, even if I cannot embrace his views, they are perfectly in consonance with the religious creed that informs them; the same that runs in the pages of *The Chronicles of Narnia*. To his credit, Lewis created a secondary world where the nonhuman animals could achieve a sort of agency and employ self-motivated action, thereby rendering the reader more aware of the intrinsic value of animals. A closer analysis of the seven books reveals, nevertheless, that Narnia is ultimately built upon the same account of human superiority and responsible stewardship model depicted in Genesis.

ANIMALS IN NARNIA

The happy land of Narnia—Narnia of the heathery mountains and the thymy downs, Narnia of the many rivers, the plashing glens, the mossy caverns and the deep forests ringing with the hammers of the Dwarfs. Oh the sweet air of Narnia! An hour's life there is better than a thousand years in Calormen.[21]

After reading evocations or descriptions of Narnia like the one above, it is tempting to try to envision Lewis's imaginary world as a sort of utopian realm, an idyllic paradise where life is led with no worries. Truly, like the horse

Bree and many other Narnians, the narrator very frequently praises Narnia for its natural resources. In a way, it seems as if Lewis, lamenting the way humans have become separated from both God and nature after the Fall, had attempted to create a secondary world where this breach was less evident. In contrast to merry England whence the Pevensie children come, nature in Narnia is always perceived as richer and brighter. Thus, for instance, the blaze of sunshine that greets Jill Pole on her first entering Narnia makes "the drops of water on the grass glitter like beads"; the turf is "smoother and brighter than Jill had ever seen before," and the things she observes darting to and fro in the blue sky are "so bright that they might have been jewels or huge butterflies."[22]

Indeed, passages of great beauty abound whenever the Narnian landscape is described, especially when, at the end of *The Last Battle*, the characters reach the Real Narnia, which is, truly, a reenactment of Paradise. In contrast to this Real Narnia, the one the children travel to and from before the railway accident, has experienced the presence of evil from the beginning of its existence. Narnia is, like ours, a fallen world.

From the very first moment Narnia entered his imagination, Lewis conceived the breach with nature as an external symptom of the loss of innocence, much in the same way as it is narrated in Genesis. Here God quarantined the first humans from the original paradaisal earth, their fall displacing the earlier harmonious bond between human and nonhuman nature with an antagonistic relationship. This is the germ of the story that would later become realized in *The Magician's Nephew*; preserved in "The Lefay Fragment," it tells the story of Digory, a child who loses his ability to speak with the animals and the trees after he is persuaded by an Eve-like Polly to cut a limb off the big Oak in his garden in order to make a raft.[23] In the definitive version, it is also his thirst for knowledge that moves Digory to give in to temptation and ring the bell that awakens Jadis, thus starting a chain of events that will lead to the arrival of evil in Narnia. On this occasion, however, Polly acts not as a temptress, but as the voice of conscience that Digory chooses to ignore.

Granted that Narnia is no earthly paradise, it is however true that Lewis created a world that could be more appealing to the 1950s reader than the industrialized England the children—and the reader himself/herself—came from. Even if a fallen world, Narnia is still a place where the importance of keeping a harmonious relationship between the human and the nonhuman is more easily perceived; the characters are rewarded or punished depending not only on how they related to each other, but also on the way they treat other species. As María José de la Torre-Moreno has pointed out, beneath the religious intentions and references in *The Chronicles of Narnia*, "there surfaces a series of social and political implications underscoring the tenor of the moral indoctrination pervasive in the tales: the observation of the principle of authority," a cult of authority that also permeates Lewis's "approach to literary criticism and his vision of literature itself."[24] Indeed, from the very beginning, Narnia is hierarchically structured and the triumph of good over evil always depends on the success in keeping the *status quo*.

HIERARCHY IN NARNIA

Immediately after he has awakened them, Aslan establishes a hierarchical organization of the world and the creatures he has originated. Pacing to and fro among the animals, the pairs the lion selects automatically leave their kind, follow him, and form a wide circle around him. These become the Talking Beasts that are hierarchically superior to the Dumb Beasts who wander away and get lost in the distance. Before this first division takes place, the narrative seems to imply that certain species of animals are not eligible to be given the capacity of speech, since Aslan passes over them altogether.[25] The chosen ones, in contrast, are literally given the rest of Narnia and the other creatures:

"Creatures, I give you yourselves," said the strong, happy voice of Aslan. "I give to you forever this land of Narnia. I give you the woods, the fruits, the rivers. I give you the stars and I give you myself. The Dumb Beasts whom I have not chosen are yours also. Treat them gently and cherish them but do not go back to their ways lest you cease to be Talking Beasts. For out of them you were taken and into them you can return. Do not so."[26]

The above quotation illustrates Meredith Veldman's contention that the work of C. S. Lewis, embedded in "the romantic tradition of protest," reveals a romantic worldview that calls the human being "to an awareness and an appreciation of the nonhuman realms."[27] In the tradition of children's classics such as *The Wind in the Willows*, *Black Beauty*, or the tales of Beatrix Potter, Lewis's use of talking animals certainly makes it easier for the child reader to come closer to their concerns. Furthermore, granting speech—and, therefore a conscience, and even a soul—to nonhuman animals does not contradict the Christian doctrine Lewis was trying to put across to young readers. As he explained in his *Letters to Children*, the world of Narnia entered Lewis's mind with a picture and a supposition: "Let us *suppose* that there were a land like Narnia and that the Son of God, as He became a Man in our world, became a lion there, and then imagine what would have happened."[28] It follows, then, that "since Narnia is a world of Talking Beats . . . He would become a Talking Beast there, as He became a man here."[29] In this secondary world of Narnia, the talking beasts are given the same position as humans in our primary world. However, Lewis needed to make clear his belief in the superiority of human over nonhuman animals and so, as Trufflehunter puts it, "Narnia was never right except when a son of Adam was king. . . . It's not Men's country . . . but it is a country for a man to be king of."[30] Narnia certainly is a multicultural, multiracial, world inhabited by all sorts of species and mythological creatures: "It is the country of Aslan, the country of the Waking Trees and Visible Naiads, of Fauns and Satyrs, of Dwarfs and Giants, of the gods and the Centaurs, of Talking Beasts."[31] Therefore, even if, as Veldman contends, the roads leading to Narnia "cut through the quads and common rooms of this elite university [Oxford]," and the resulting fantasy world, "like Oxford in the middle of the twentieth century, [is] male dominated, hierarchical, and communal,"[32] it displays a more holistic conception of life in the way the narrative deals with the interrelation between the human and the nonhuman, and the need to respect every single form of life that works, so as to keep the established order.

RULING RIGHTS IN NARNIA

Not every human being, however, is entitled to rule over Narnia. In fact, Lewis seems to be harsher in the way the narrative deals with those humans who try to break the hierarchy established by Aslan than he is with any of the other nonhuman characters. Accordingly, the human races of the Calormenes and the Telmarines share an eagerness to impose their own order and control the natural world. In contrast, from the first king, the cabby Frank, any rightful king of Narnia must show a respect for human and nonhuman forms of existence.

In this manner, Lewis uses the relationship humans establish with the nonhuman world as a characterization tool from the very beginning: the good characters bear respect to other species and their environment, whereas the wicked—ranging from the real evil to the plain nasty—fail to establish a dialogical relationship with any manifestation of the nonhuman. For them, the natural environment is just something to control, destroy, or simply profit from. In *The Magician's Nephew*, for instance, the Faustian character of Uncle Andrew dismisses Digory's complaints about the magician's use of guinea pigs for his experiments in the following terms: "That's what the creatures were for. I'd bought them myself."[33] The wicked uncle only regrets that the guinea pigs cannot communicate with humans and are therefore rendered useless for him. In contrast, Digory appreciates the creatures' intrinsic value, irrespective of their usefulness for humans. His adoption of the guinea pigs' perspective when imagining their disorientation in a world they do not know is ridiculed by Digory's uncle, who retorts that he is looking at the whole issue "from the wrong point of view."[34] Applying Lewis's stance on animal suffering in *The*

Problem of Pain, Digory might be charged with "the 'pathetic fallacy' of reading into the beasts a self for which there is no real evidence"[35] —after all, it later turns out that Polly and Digory find that the guinea pig is perfectly happy in the Wood between the Worlds, away from mad scientific experimentation— but Digory is just acting responsibly toward this nonhuman form of life in a way Uncle Andrew cannot even understand.

The same arrogant attitude toward any manifestation of the other—human or nonhuman—is displayed by Jadis when Polly accuses her of having killed all "the ordinary people . . . who'd never done [her] any harm. And the women, and the children, and the animals,"[36] following her uttering the Deplorable Word in the battle with her sister. "I was the Queen," Jadis refutes, "They were all *my* people. What else were they there for but to do my will?"[37] Any type of supremacy, whether biologically or socially conferred, entails in Lewis's worldview a greater degree of responsibility toward those who are inferior. Jadis's dictatorial ruling can only bring forth death, as seen in the dying world of Charn or in the perpetual winter that envelops Narnia during her illegitimate reign. Her pale face and red mouth, a symbol of femininity, purity, and potential sexual appeal in the traditional tale of Snow White is here subverted and transformed into sterile beauty. Jadis is certainly beautiful, but also "proud and cold and stern,"[38] more similar to Andersen's villainous Snow Queen than to the Grimm Brothers' heroine.[39] The changes in the natural landscape following the children's arrival in Narnia and the return of Aslan, herald the witch's eventual defeat and the restoration of natural balance. The first bird they see—a robin, a symbol of fertility—announces the return of the natural cycles to the previously wintry landscape.

What is also common to such wicked characters is that they pose a threat to the harmonious order, and refuse to develop the willingness to communicate and cooperate with the surrounding world. Hence, while Polly, Digory, and the cabby stand as if mesmerized, enjoying the natural wonders displayed as the world of Narnia takes shape, Uncle Andrew and Jadis are incapable of appreciating the beauty of the moment. While Polly shows no fear of Aslan and is the first to comprehend clearly the connection between the lion's song and the created world, Uncle Andrew fails to understand anything, and Jadis simply hates the music. The magician can only value the commercial possibilities the place offers if properly exploited. In consonance with his imperialistic mentality, it is imperative "to get that brute [Aslan] shot,"[40] to remove any possible threat. The narrator informs the reader that all witches, "are not interested in things or people unless they can use them; they are terribly practical."[41] This assertion, as we will see, is not exclusive to the White Witch, but is a characteristic shared by all the evil characters in the seven *Chronicles*. Already before the journey to Narnia, a clear differentiation is established between Jadis and the future King Frank. While she mercilessly flogs the horse, the cabby risks his own safety just to calm him down. Once in Narnia, his closeness to the earth—he sings a "harvest thanks-giving hymn"[42] that neither Jadis nor Uncle Andrew join—discloses him as the perfect candidate to occupy the throne of Narnia.

Frequently, the redemption of a wicked character is externally manifested in his ability to establish a dialogical relationship with the Other, once all prejudices have been removed and its intrinsic value appreciated. The character of Eustace Scrubb undergoes this type of change. When he makes his first appearance in *The Voyage of the Dawn Treader*, the Pevensie children's cousin is presented as a disagreeable creature, only fond of animals "especially beetles, if they were dead and pinned on a card,"[43] and terribly egocentric. In contrast with Lucy, who acknowledges Reepicheep's otherness and refrains from cuddling the mouse—no matter how much she wants to—because she knows he would find it offensive, Eustace shows no such respect and constantly mocks him. His early attraction for the name Calormene is a clear indicator of his twisted nature and urgent need of redemption. For that to take place, Eustace will literally have to get in the skin of one manifestation of the Other he so much detests—a dragon on this occasion—until he learns to see the world outside his old Self. Ironically, in the process of the renovation undergone by Eustace, Reepicheep plays no small part. The mouse not only intercedes for him, but also comforts the dragon in his lonely nights. The narrator underlines the signs of improvement discernible in the character even before he goes back to his human form, by describing the dragon as "a very humane killer too, for he could dispatch a beast with one blow of his tail so that it didn't know (and presumably still doesn't know) it had been killed."[44]

Unlike Eustace (or even Edmund, in *The Lion, the Witch and the Wardrobe*), Uncle Andrew does not learn to appreciate the intrinsic value of other forms of life outside his own, thus remaining unredeemed. The redemption process begins by learning that each individual is "part of a whole system in which every constituent plays an important role,"[45] and act accordingly. After years of cruel experiments with animals, Uncle Andrew is afraid of them when he is in a disadvantageous position in Narnia. Incapable of bridging the gap that separates him from them (the Self from the Other), he simply cannot understand that they mean no harm. As Aslan explains to Digory, "he has made himself unable to hear my voice."[46] In vain does the lion try to comfort him; Uncle Andrew can only hear a roar whenever Aslan addresses him. Similarly, in *The Last Battle*, Lucy and Aslan attempt to open the dwarves' eyes to the world surrounding them, which they perceive as a dark stable. Unable to enjoy the sights, the smells, or the flavor of the delicacies offered to them, the dwarves remain trapped in a prison that, according to Aslan "is only in their own minds."[47] They rest isolated from the community they have betrayed, true to their constantly repeated motto "The Dwarfs are for the Dwarfs."

LEWIS'S PORTRAYAL OF NONHUMAN PERSPECTIVES

Having a children's audience in mind, Lewis likes to play with different points of view in order to make an incursion into the nonhuman perspective. The narrative enables the child to perceive herself from the viewpoint of the Other. He does this most brilliantly when Lucy first encounters Mr. Tumnus. One can just imagine the young reader sharing Lucy's astonishment at getting a sight of a Faun. Suddenly, she realizes that the Faun shares the same astonishment: "You are in fact Human?"[48] Lucy, understandably, fails to see the meaning of the question at first—what else could she be? She later has the opportunity to perceive her Self as Other while having a look at the Faun's library, holding titles such as *Men, Monks and Gamekeepers; a Study in Popular Legend*, or, more revealingly: *Is Man a Myth?* In this alternative world, humans are the Other. Later, Edmund undergoes a similar experience when, trapped in his own individuality, he fails to understand the question the White Witch has to repeat up to three times: "What are you?" When Jadis, for the fourth time insists, "But what *are* you?" she finally succeeds in eliciting from him the appropriate answer. Edmund is one of the feared humans.[49]

Nowhere in *The Chronicles of Narnia* is this shift in perspective more clearly expressed than in the title *The Horse and His Boy*, in which the inversion of the traditional relationship between the possessor and the possessed draws attention to the leading role of the horse. Although the association between Shasta and Bree develops on equal grounds (they both need each other to reach the north) it is the horse that acts as a guide away from Calormen and toward Narnia. Bree not only teaches Shasta to ride—obviously without reins or stirrups—but he also educates Aravis in the way she should now relate to both Hwin and himself. That Aravis sees herself superior to Shasta and any of the horses is evident when she automatically accuses the boy of having stolen Bree. "[I]f there's been any stealing," the horse rebukes, "you might just as well say I stole *him*."[50] Later, Bree reminds the Calormene girl that the idea of her owning Hwin is just an illusion: "Hwin isn't *your* horse any longer. One might just as well say you're *her* human."[51] Hwin, on her part, is less self-assured than Bree, and progressively becomes more outspoken, siding with the member of her own species when Aravis instructs her to tell Bree to mind his own business: " 'No, I won't,' said the mare putting her ears back, 'This is my escape just as much as yours.' "[52]

On other occasions, the reader is reminded of her condition of Other for the nonhuman animals by some funny comments on their part. Thus, feeling that he has been too hard on the young boy, Bree tries to comfort Shasta: "Poor little beast. . . . I forget you are only a foal."[53] In *The Last Battle*, the narrator ends Emeth's account of his religious experience with Aslan in a comic note, when the good Calormene uses the term "dog" in a way that clearly indicates he perceives them as inferior creatures:

"[. . .] And this is the marvel of marvels, that he [Aslan] called me Beloved, me who am but as a dog—"

"Eh? What's that?" said one of the Dogs.

"Sir," said Emeth. "It's but a fashion of speech which we have in Calormen."

"Well, I can't say it's one I like very much," said the Dog.

"He doesn't mean any harm," said an older Dog. "After all, *we* call our puppies *Boys* when they don't behave properly."

"So we do," said the first Dog. "Or *girls*."

"S-s-sh!" said the Old Dog. "That's not a nice word to use. Remember where you are."[54]

Together with the detailed account of their cruel actions, Lewis uses language as a powerful tool for characterizing the Calormenes, offering the reader many instances of what Bree identifies as "Calormene talk."[55] Prince Rabadash shares with other villains, such as Jadis and Uncle Andrew, a lack of care for and a will to get rid of anything that is not profitable: "[W]hy should we think twice about punishing Narnia any more than about hanging an idle slave or sending a worn-out horse to be made into dog's meat?"[56] This arrogant attitude, which contrasts with the reverence Narnians hold for their environment, reaches its highest note in *The Last Battle*. Knowing that the Calormenes are murdering the trees, the sight of one of them mistreating a talking horse is enough to enrage King Tirian and, with the unicorn Jewel, instantly kill the offender. This action, which Tirian comes to regret because it was dishonorable, is however symptomatic of the monarch's high regard for the creatures in his kingdom, a common trait shared by all the legitimate rulers of Narnia.

Lewis and Monarchy

C. S. Lewis was a clear supporter of the concept of the British monarchy. Defending this form of government, he deplored, in his essay "Equality," that "envious sort of mind which hates all superiority" suggesting "[t]hat mind . . . is the special disease of democracy," whilst describing as a "prosaic barbarian" the man "who cannot conceive a joyful and loyal obedience on the one hand, nor an unembarrassed and noble acceptance of that obedience in the other, the man who has never wanted to kneel or to bow."[57] After defending the benefits of the British monarchy, he finally celebrates its contribution to satisfy "the craving for inequality."[58] One must necessarily agree with Walter Hooper's observation that "[t]he books in which Lewis most rejoiced in Monarchy and Inequality are, of course, the *Chronicles of Narnia*."[59]

Indeed, in Narnia, a responsible monarchy is the best answer to all evils. In fact, those who fight on Aslan's side do so to keep the order he established, an order which is decidedly hierarchical and patriarchal, as Aslan's first salute to the Pevensie children clearly indicates: "Welcome, Peter, Son of Adam [. . .]. Welcome Susan and Lucy, Daughters of Eve. Welcome He-Beaver and She-Beaver."[60] In the lion's address, humans take precedence over nonhumans and males over females. As has been repeated, in Lewis's view, precedence also implies higher responsibility toward those below, not the abuses of authority displayed by all who misunderstand the nature of power.

The climax in *The Magician's Nephew* comes when Aslan asks Frank, as the first King of Narnia, to "rule and name all these creatures, and do justice among them, and protect them from their enemies when enemies arise" whilst treating them "kindly and fairly, remembering that they are not slaves like the dumb beasts of the world you were born in, but Talking Beasts and free subjects."[61] Here is the concept of responsible stewardship of the land of Narnia and its inhabitants that follows in all the books, something that becomes the main theme in *Prince Caspian*. Thus, the reign of the Pevensie children is always remembered as the Golden Age of Narnia, a time when "they made good laws and kept the peace and saved good trees from being unnecessarily cut down."[62] Likewise, the rule of King Tirian, the last King of Narnia, is emblematic of this harmony, specially displayed in his relationship with "his dearest friend, Jewel the Unicorn. They loved each other like brothers and each had saved the other's life in the wars."[63] In *Prince Caspian*, the young protagonist becomes the Arthurian figure that has to restore the order broken by his own people, the Telmarines. Longing to believe in the existence of a variety of nonhuman entities, relegated to the realm of myth and legend by his ancestors and the present king in an attempt to obliterate the past, Caspian learns the true history from his tutor, Doctor Cornelius, a half-dwarf who explains to the Prince that Narnia does not belong to Men and that his people are, in fact, a bunch of usurpers:

All you have heard about Old Narnia is true. It is not the land of Men. It is the country of Aslan, the country of the Waking Trees and Visible Naiads, of Fauns and Satyrs, of Dwarfs and Giants, of the gods and the Centaurs, of Talking Beasts. It was against these that the first Caspian fought. It is you Telmarines who silenced the beasts and the trees and the fountains, and who killed and drove away the Dwarfs and Fauns, and are now trying to cover up even the memory of them. The King does not allow them to be spoken of.[64]

In this sense, the Telmarines are not very different from the Calormenes. Like Jadis before them, the Telmarines have imposed an order that challenges Aslan's conception of Narnia, an order that is maintained—as in any dictatorship—by keeping the subjects in ignorance and fear. Nature is now perceived as an enemy, and a thick wood is allowed to grow between the land and the sea, in order to hinder access to it. The sea, as the place where Aslan comes from, acquires the connotations of the enlightenment the inhabitants of Narnia are barred from. Given the damage they have caused to the trees, the Telmarines are afraid of the wood, a fear Caspian has naturally inherited: "He remembered that he was, after all, a Telmarine, one of the race who cut down trees wherever they could and were at war with all wild things; and though he himself might be unlike other Telmarines, the trees could be not expected to know this."[65] The dynasty of the Telmarines views monarchy as an enactment of tyranny rather than responsible stewardship, clearly far from the pledge taken by King Frank when his reign started. From that body of rotten rulers who have silenced the multiplicity of voices that could previously be heard in Narnia, Caspian is the one chosen to "try to find a way of awaking the trees once more."[66]

If those who are higher up in the social or biological scale have their duty toward those who are below, an irresponsible action usually entails a demotion while, in some cases, a good action entails a promotion, such as the mice acquiring the faculty of speech for showing respect and cutting Aslan's cords after his sacrifice. Degradation after a dishonorable action seems to be in tune with Lewis's views on the consequences for humans after the Fall. Hence, "one result of man's fall was that his animality fell back from the humanity into which it had been taken up but which could no longer rule it."[67] In a similar line, Aslan warns the Talking Beasts of the possibility of their becoming dumb if they err in their conduct. Such is, in fact, the case of the cat, Ginger in *The Last Battle*, who loses the faculty of speech and, it must be inferred, the possibility to have a soul. Likewise, in *Prince Caspian*, when the festive revelers who parade along the countryside celebrating their victory come across a man beating a boy, the forces of nature respond by making the stick "burst into flower in the man's hand," thus transforming an instrument of aggression into a traditional offering of love. When the man rejects the flower and tries to drop it, he simply cannot and suffers an involution: "His arm became a branch, his body the trunk of a tree, his feet took root,"[68] while, in a like manner, the schoolchildren who mock their teacher are transformed into pigs.

The punishment awarded for the degree of evil committed varies not only according to the crime itself but also depending on the species that has committed it. Hence, at times Lewis seems to be harsher with the humans than with the nonhumans, since those are supposed to know better and act accordingly. As argued earlier, the Calormenes are on the top of the evil scale, since they commit the most terrible crime: mistreating and killing talking animals and waking trees.[69] The Telmarines' fondness for hunting animals for sport, even if they are dumb, is also frowned upon. Meat-eating, however, is a legitimate practice for humans, but, as the incident of the bear in *Prince Caspian* reveals, perceived as evil in nonhuman animals. In "Animal Pain," Lewis saw carnivorousness as a consequence of the Satanic Fall, and, consequently, a source of evil. Living in a fallen world—be it Narnia or our own—we have to learn to live with the fact that some animals are carnivores and cause a lot of suffering. We should imagine that the standards are equally applicable to human carnivores and nonhuman carnivores. Yet, they do not seem to be for Lewis. When the narrator affirms that "[b]ear that has lived too much on other animals is not very nice, but bear that has had plenty of honey and fruit is excellent, and this turned out to be that sort of bear. It was a truly glorious meal,"[70] he is clearly using double standards to judge carnivorousness. Whereas it seems to be wrong for the bear to eat other animals, a bear that does it is "not very nice"—it is perfectly acceptable for the children to eat this almost vegetarian bear. In this case, humans get away with what Lewis considers a source of evil—they cannot help it because it is a consequence of living in a fallen world—even though humans can choose vegetarianism in a way a nonhuman animal cannot. This episode helps to prove that their superior state exempts humans from certain moral judgments cast on nonhuman animals.

Harmony and Justice in Narnia

In broad terms, Barry Commoner's first law of ecology, which states that everything is connected and that nature is always wiser,[71] truly operates in Narnia; nature certainly knows how to reward those who respect her and punish the abusers. In *Prince Caspian*, the Awakened Trees join the battle in order to help Peter, driving the Telmarines away among desperate cries of: "The Wood! The Wood! The End of the world!"[72] In contrast, the reward for those who respect nature is bountiful. A somewhat orgiastic excess is displayed in the feast and dance of plenty started by Bacchus, Silenus, and the Maenads, with all sort of delicacies lavished on the Old Narnians, where even trees can enjoy a several-course meal prepared by the moles. The classical pagan deities and acolytes seem to work as instruments of nature's generosity, since the feast comes into existence the moment they touch hands:

sides of roasted meat that filled the grove with delicious smell, and wheaten cakes and oaten cakes, honey and many-coloured sugars and cream as thick as porridge and as smooth as still water, peaches, nectarines, pomegranates, pears, grapes, strawberries, raspberries—pyramids and cataracts of fruit. Then, in great wooden cups and bowls and mazers, wreathed with ivy, came the wines; dark, thick ones like syrups of mulberry juice, and clear red ones like red jellies liquefied, and yellow wines and green wines and yellow-green and greenish-yellow.[73]

The feast is just the final stage of a carnivalesque parade that has been marching around the countryside in festive celebration of the renewal of the harmonious order desired by Aslan. The revelers, led by the lion, liberate everyone and everything from real or metaphorical chains forged by any sort of oppression, leaving a trail of ivy wherever they go. This joyous renovation affects both humans and nonhumans. Not only the children are freed from the fake history lessons, thus opening their eyes to the reality of what they had always believed was mere legend, but also the river is freed from the chains provided by the Bridge of Beruna, while the girl Gwendolene is helped by the Maenads to "take off some of the unnecessary and uncomfortable clothes that she was wearing" and "[s]ad old donkeys who had never known joy grew suddenly young again; chained dogs broke their chains; horses kicked their carts to pieces and came trotting along with them."[74] It is important to notice that, in all cases, the reward comes hand in hand with a celebration of community life, where humans and nonhumans gather in celebration, as a communal representation of the healthy body in which every limb plays a decisive role. In Lewis's worldview, respecting the hierarchy is good for the community.

Instances to illustrate this abound in *Prince Caspian*, with Pauline Bayne's drawings becoming "more than illustrations . . . a collateral theme."[75] Thus, the illustration of this scene in the edition I am working with acts as a commentary on the prospective return to the harmony between human and nonhuman forms of life under Caspian's rule. Prince Caspian, the badger Trufflehunter, and the dwarf Trumpkin engage with the fauns in a festive dance from which only Nikabrik excludes himself. Five pages later, Caspian holds council surrounded by fauns, rabbits, centaurs, dwarfs, giants, and all sorts of other animals. Finally, a later Baynes illustration offers an interesting contrast between the monolithic worldview imposed by the Telmarines who support King Miraz, and the diversity displayed by the Narnians who stick up for Peter in his fight against the king. All the Telmarines wear the same uniform and have assumed a similar posture, whereas the same variety of forms that gathered in the council around Caspian is perceived on the group supporting Peter. One of them, which appears to be a polecat, even looks at the reader as if asking her to join the group.

The respect for hierarchy translates into a harmony that everyone enjoys equally, irrespective of their position in society. At the end of *Prince Caspian*, the renewed Telmarines are no longer afraid of the water, the wood, or the animals. They have joined the Narnians in a joyous celebration that ends in a happy circle, where no one takes predominance, after everyone has fallen asleep "with feet towards the fire and good friends on either side till at last there was silence all round the circle, and the chattering of water over stone at the Ford of Beruna could be heard once more."[76]

While the revelers celebrate and rest, the narrator tells us that "all night Aslan and the Moon gazed upon each other with joyful and unblinking eyes."[77] One cannot fail to read in this suggestive image, a pleasant fusion of the masculine and feminine principles: the white goddess and the sun looking intently at each other. Indeed, Aslan is very frequently associated with the sun: his golden mane, his golden voice or, more explicitly, the light that emanates from him: "A golden light fell on them from the left. He [Shasta] thought it was the Sun. . . . It was from the Lion that the light came. No one ever saw anything more terrible or beautiful."[78]

Human and nonhuman forms of life, both pagan and Christian versions, all interact to give the world of Narnia the particular flavor that, despite common accusations that Narnia is a very conservative ecology of life, still makes it appealing to children—as the success of the latest film adaptation proves. One may note traces of Lewis's alleged sexism and occasional patronizing attitude, but it would be a mistake to judge a writer without taking into account the times and place in which he had to live. In focusing too much on the negative aspects of the Narnian world, we may lose the benefit of seeing the environmentalist perspective Lewis does entertain, and there is certainly much in this regard within *The Chronicles of Narnia* to celebrate and enjoy.

NOTES

1. Humphrey Carpenter, *J. R. R. Tolkien. A Biography* (London: Grafton, 1992), 155.

2. C. S. Lewis, "Sometimes Fairy Stories May Say Best What's to be Said," in *Of This and Other Worlds*, ed. Walter Hooper (London: Fount Paperbacks, 1984), 72.

3. The Great Ape project, for instance, following their motto "equality beyond humanity" can be seen as a first step to make other forms of life susceptible to

receive the same legal and moral protection that only humans seem to be entitled to (Cf. "Great Ape Project," http://www.greatapeproject.org). From what he expressed in his chapter on "Animal Pain" Lewis seems to share the same concern for nonhuman great apes: "Clearly in some ways the ape and man are much more like each other than either is like the worm." (C. S. Lewis, *The Problem of Pain* [London: Fount, 1990], 108). To know how far down the evolutionary scale Lewis would have considered appropriate to go is a debatable question.

4. Mary Midgely, "The End of Anthropocentrism?" in *Philosophy and the Natural Environment*, Royal Institute of Philosophy Supplement 36, ed. Robin Attfield and Andrew Belsey (Cambridge: Cambridge University Press, 1994), 111. Quoted in Nathan Kowalsky, "Anthropocentrism and Natural Suffering," in *The Ranges of Evil. Multidisciplinary Studies of Human Wickedness*, ed. William Myers (Oxford: Interdisciplinary Press, 2006), 64.

5. Lewis, *The Problem of Pain*, 106.

6. Ibid., 109.

7. Ibid., 107.

8. Ibid., 110.

9. Ibid., 115.

10. Ibid., 114.

11. Ibid., 115.

12. Ibid., 114.

13. Ibid., 114.

14. Ibid., 112.

15. Kowalsky, *The Range of Evil*, 66.

16. John Haught, *The Promise of Nature, Ecological and Cosmic Purpose* (New York: Paulist Press, 1993), 81. Quoted in Mark Muldoon, "Environmental Decline and Christian Contemplation," *Interdisciplinary Studies in Literature and Environment* 10(2) (2003), 82.

17. Muldoon, *Interdisciplinary Studies*, 83.

18. Thomas Aquinas, *Compendium of Theology*, trans. Cyril Vollert (London: B. Herder Book Co., 1958), 157. Quoted in Muldoon, *Interdisciplinary Studies*, 85.

19. Ibid., 158. Quoted in Muldoon, *Interdisciplinary Studies*, 85.

20. Thomas Aquinas, *Summa Theologicae*, trans. Thomas Gilby (London: Eyre & Spottliswoode and McGraw-Hill Book Co., 1963), Ia.96.1. Quoted in Muldoon, *Interdisciplinary Studies*, 85.

21. C. S. Lewis, *The Horse and His Boy* (London: Lions, 1990), 17.

22. C. S. Lewis, *The Silver Chair* (London: Lions, 1990), 16.

23. Cf. Walter Hooper, *C. S. Lewis. A Companion and Guide* (London: Fount, 1996), 403.

24. María José de la Torre-Moreno, "Beyond Empowerment through Faith: Inversions and Contradictions in Narnia," in *Behind the Veil of Familiarity: C. S. Lewis*

(1898–1998), ed. Margarita Carretero-González and Encarnación Hidalgo-Tenorio (Bern [Switzerland] and New York: Peter Lang, 2001), 251–252.

25. C. S. Lewis, *The Magician's Nephew* (London: Lions, 1990), 106–107.

26. Ibid., 109.

27. Meredith Veldman, *Fantasy, the Bomb, and the Greening of Britain. Romantic Protest, 1945–1980* (Cambridge: Cambridge University Press, 1994), 3.

28. Hooper, *C. S. Lewis. A Companion and Guide*, 425.

29. Ibid., 426.

30. C. S. Lewis, *Prince Caspian* (London: Lions, 1990), 64–65.

31. Ibid., 50.

32. Veldman, *Fantasy, the Bomb*, 45.

33. Lewis, *The Magician's Nephew*, 26.

34. Ibid., 26.

35. Lewis, *The Problem of Pain*, 110.

36. Lewis, *The Magician's Nephew*, 61.

37. Ibid.

38. C. S. Lewis, *The Lion, the Witch and the Wardrobe* (London: Lions, 1990), 33.

39. In the Grimm Brothers' account of the tale, Snow White is described as having "a skin as white as snow, lips as red as blood, and hair as black as ebony." (J. L. C. Grimm and W. C. Grimm, "Snow White," in *Grimm's Fairy Tales* (Ware, Hertfordshire: Wordsworth Editions Ltd., 1993), 215. Like Edmund in *The Lion, the Witch and the Wardrobe*, in Hans Christian Andersen's *The Snow Queen*, Kay is carried off by the "a woman, dressed in the finest white gauze, which appeared to be made of millions of starry flakes. She was delicately lovely, but all ice, glittering, dazzling ice" (Hans Christian Andersen, "The Snow Queen," in *Andersen's Fairy Tales* (Ware, Hertfordshire, England: Wordsworth Editions Ltd., 1993), 185. The Snow Queen travels on a sledge and wraps the boy in her furs, as Jadis does with Edmund.

40. Lewis, *The Magician's Nephew*, 103.

41. Ibid., 71.

42. Ibid., 92.

43. C. S. Lewis, *The Voyage of the Dawn Treader* (London: Lions, 1990), 7.

44. Ibid., 80.

45. Margarita Carretero-González, "Into the Wardrobe and Out of a Hobbit-hole: An Ecocritical Approach to C. S. Lewis and J. R. R. Tolkien," *Studii de limbi și literaturi moderne* 1 (1999): 200.

46. Lewis, *The Magician's Nephew*, 158.

47. C.S. Lewis, *The Last Battle* (London: Lions, 1990), 140.

48. Lewis, *The Lion, the Witch and the Wardrobe*, 16.

49. Ibid., 33–35.

50. Lewis, *The Horse and His Boy*, 31.

51. Ibid., 33.

52. Ibid., 32.

53. Ibid., 19.

54. Lewis, *The Last Battle*, 155–156.

55. Lewis, *The Horse and His Boy*, 33.

56. Ibid., 91.

57. Quoted in Hooper, *C. S. Lewis. A Companion and Guide*, 579.

58. Ibid., 579.

59. Ibid., 580.

60. Lewis, *The Lion, the Witch and the Wardrobe*, 117.

61. Lewis, *The Magician's Nephew*, 129.

62. Lewis, *The Lion, the Witch and the Wardrobe*, 166.

63. Lewis, *The Last Battle*, 17.

64. Lewis, *Prince Caspian*, 50. It is tempting to establish a connection between the first Telmarine that invaded Narnia, Caspian the Conqueror, and the Duke of Normandy who, after defeating the Anglo-Saxons, became William the Conqueror, King of England, and imposed a new order on his territory. The defeated people were the remnants of those northern invaders whose culture so much fascinated C. S. Lewis and his friend J. R. R. Tolkien.

65. Lewis, *Prince Caspian*, 60.

66. Ibid., 52.

67. Lewis, *The Problem of Pain*, 111.

68. Lewis, *Prince Caspian*, 171.

69. The reverence that Narnians hold for talking animals is clearly seen in the different ways in which Jill, Eustace, and Puddleglum reacted when they became aware that they have eaten a talking stag. For Jill Pole, this was her first visit to Narnia, so she just felt "sorry for the poor stag and thought it rotten of the giants to have killed him." Eustace, who had previously visited Narnia, felt "horrified" and compared it to murder, whereas Puddleglum "who was Narnian born, was sick and faint, and felt as you would feel if you found out you had eaten a baby" (Lewis, *The Silver Chair*, 104–105).

70. Lewis, *Prince Caspian*, 120.

71. Quoted in John Button, *¡Háztelo verde!*, trans. Jimmy Clark and Begoña Oliver (Barcelona, Spain: Círculo de Lectores, 1990), 242.

72. Lewis, *Prince Caspian*, 167.

73. Ibid., 180.

74. Ibid., 171.

75. From a letter written by J. R. R. Tolkien to his publishers on March 16, 1949 regarding the illustrations Miss Baynes had provided for his *Father Giles of Ham*. Quoted in Hooper, *C. S. Lewis. A Companion and Guide*, 406.

76. Lewis, *Prince Caspian*, 181.

77. Ibid., 181–182.

78. Lewis, *The Horse and His Boy*, 130–131.

BIBLIOGRAPHY

Andersen, Hans Christian. "The Snow Queen." In *Andersen's Fairy Tales.* Ware, Hertfordshire, England: Wordsworth Editions Ltd., 1993, 183–212.

Button, John. *¡Háztelo Verde!.* Translated by Jimmy Clark and Begoña Orive. Barcelona, Spain: Círculo de Lectores, 1990.

Carpenter, Humphrey, *J.R.R. Tolkien. A Biography.* London: Grafton, 1992.

Carretero-González, Margarita "Into the Wardrobe and Out of a Hobbit-hole: An Ecocritical Approach to C. S. Lewis and J. R. R. Tolkien." *Studii de limbi și literaturi moderne* 1 (1999), 200–207.

de la Torre-Moreno, María José. "Beyond Empowerment through Faith: Inversions and Contradictions in Narnia." In *Behind the Veil of Familiarity: C. S. Lewis (1898–1998).* Edited by Margarita Carretero-González and Encarnación Hidalgo-Tenorio Bern and New York: Peter Lang, 2001, 251–272.

"Great Ape Project." http://www.greatapeproject.org.

Grimm, Jacob Ludwig Carl and Wilhelm Carl Grimm. "Snow White." In *Grimm's Fairy Tales.* Ware, Hertfordshire, England: Wordsworth Editions Ltd., 1993, 215–224.

Hooper, Walter. *C. S. Lewis. A Companion and Guide.* London: Fount, 1996.

Kowalsky, Nathan. "Anthropocentrism and Natural Suffering." In *The Range of Evil. Multidisciplinary Studies on Human Wickedness.* Edited by William Myers. Oxford: Interdisciplinary Press, 2006, 63–74. (At http://www.inter-disciplinary.net/publishing/idp/eBooks/roeindex.html.)

Lewis, Clive Staples. *The Horse and His Boy.* London: Lions, 1990.

———. *The Last Battle.* London: Lions, 1990.

———. *The Lion, the Witch and the Wardrobe.* London: Lions, 1990.

———. *The Magician's Nephew.* London: Lions, 1990.

———. *Prince Caspian.* London: Lions, 1990.

———. *The Problem of Pain.* London: Fount, 1998.

———. *The Silver Chair.* London: Lions, 1990.

———. "Sometimes Fairy Stories May Say Best What's to be Said." In *Of This and Other Worlds.* Edited by Walter Hooper. London: Fount, 1984, 71–75.

———. *The Voyage of the Dawn Treader.* London: Lions, 1990.

Muldoon, Mark. "Environmental Decline and Christian Contemplation." *Interdisciplinary Studies in Literature and Environment* 10(2) (2003), 75–96.

Veldman, Meredith. *Fantasy, the Bomb, and the Greening of Britain. Romantic Protest, 1945–1980.* Cambridge: Cambridge University Press, 1994.

7

Cartography and Fantasy: Hidden Treasures in the Maps of *The Chronicles of Narnia*

Marta García de la Puerta

The concept of a geographical context, minutely detailed, achieved not just through description, but by means of pictures and maps like those employed by C. S. Lewis in his *Chronicles of Narnia*, is what makes fantastical works stand out from others, where the physical context of the story is usually either quite abstract or much less convincing than those that Lewis typically gives us. Therefore, the richly realized secondary world of Narnia is reinforced by the maps found in the seven Narnian Chronicles. Incorporating these maps into one's work is one of the writer's resources to add verisimilitude to his or her tales, to convince the reader of the "reality" of the place where the "extraordinary" events narrated take place. As Geoff King states, "maps have been used widely by writers of fiction to make their worlds more real."[1]

It is true that, on one level, including maps and rich layeredness of these spaces undoubtedly makes the narrative more believable, while at the same time it adds the coherence necessary to elicit the reader's voluntary suspension of disbelief. According to J. R. R. Tolkien's theory of subcreation (also shared by Lewis), the writer or subcreator should have the literary capacity required to create a secondary world which the reader may enter into as if under a spell. As Tolkien states, "Inside it what he relates is 'true' ... The moment disbelief arises the spell is broken and the magic has failed."[2] This secondary world must be perfectly coherent not only with its own laws, myths, and cosmogony, but also with its geography and cartography.

However, there is another no less important function, that of creating a geography of symbols for the reader to reinterpret. By this I mean how particular settings are visually organized, not simply as mere geographical features included in maps, but the clues provided that yield a much deeper meaning. According to Federica Domínguez Colavita, "on this second level . . . fantasy spaces are the result of a symbolic-descriptive creation by the narrator which is completed by the reader."[3] From this viewpoint, each symbol, each setting, and each map image represents a set of information, which may be more or less explicit, provided by the author for the reader about a particular place, and the reader may use this information to reconstruct and reinterpret this space. There is thus a deeper level of interpretation elicited, a symbolic reading of the maps drawn of the secondary worlds the writer introduces. Thus, when we study the spaces and the maps belonging to *The Chronicles of Narnia*, we should not restrict ourselves to their descriptive value alone. Instead we should also study them as a means of expressing a triple reality: ideological, graphical, and geographical, in the same way that cartography was used in Ancient times, the Middle Ages, and the Renaissance.

This was not the first time that Lewis had illustrated his stories with maps and pictures. As a child Lewis had played at making up stories and some of the maps of those faraway lands were already there. These stories were given the generic title "Animal Land," and some maps of far-off lands appear sketched on them: "from history it was only a step to geography. There was soon a map of Animal Land—several maps, all tolerably consistent."[4] However, Lewis was a "doodler," not a skilled artist, and his drawings could only provide suggestive models for a more proficient artist. Indeed, in his desire to create a world in physical detail with its particular geography, Lewis drew a map of Narnia that was never to appear in his texts. It was a very general map of Narnia and the lands that bordered it, and from it we can see that it was not finely sketched. Two types of shading may be seen, which are explained in the caption of the illustration. In one way this reveals Lewis's inadequacies in drawing, which he was ready to admit himself: "what drove me to write was the extreme manual clumsiness from which I have always suffered."[5]

His desire to evoke through map-making a detailed physical world, with a precision in its geography, instead required a professional artist to put the adventures of Narnia on paper; he chose the illustrator Pauline D. Baynes for this task. Baynes had already been entrusted the task of illustrating a fantasy tale by Tolkien, *Farmer Giles of Ham* (1949).[6] It was Tolkien's praise of the artist that decided Lewis to trust the maps and drawings for his Narnia books, under strict supervision, to the same person.[7]

We should point out, however, that the cartographic illustrations of Narnia do not correspond to what we would regard as directional "maps" in the modern sense. Rather, the maps Lewis directed to be included in his fantasies resemble ancient, especially medieval maps. In Lewis's own words: "My idea was that the map should be more like a medieval map than an Ordnance Survey—mountains and castles drawn—perhaps winds blowing at the corners—and a few heraldic-looking ships, whales and dolphins in a sea."[8] The maps imagined by Lewis, following medieval cartography, do not have any geometric precision or scientific representation. They are more like graphic illustrations and geographical metaphors. Indeed neither aim at reflecting reality exhaustively, and they are instead a symbolic portrayal whereby the artist deliberately highlights those features he is interested in, and leaving the rest sketchy.

It must also be remembered that until the Renaissance we cannot talk about a clear distinction between painting and cartography.[9] According to King: "Map-making and landscape painting were often the work of the same artists."[10] In the well-known Hereford world map, dating from the thirteenth century, one can see a *mappaemundi* featuring numerous rivers and several mountain ranges, and buildings span the surface; and at the top under *Oriens*, the Earthly Paradise can be seen with Adam and Eve at that critical moment of endangering everything for an apple.[11] As Lewis explains in *The Discarded Image: An Introduction to Medieval and Renaissance Literature*,

a glance at the Hereford *mappemounde* . . . suggests that . . . a map of the whole hemisphere on so small scale could never have been intended to have any practical use. The cartographer wished to make a rich jewel embodying the noble art of cosmography, with the Earthly Paradise marked as an island at the extreme Eastern edge. . . . Sailors themselves may have looked at it with admiration and delight. They were not going to steer by it.[12]

In Baynes's Narnia maps, as in the medieval world maps Lewis used as models, there are no numeric references for longitude or latitude. In fact, we could probably extend King's description of medieval maps to Lewis's when he says that they "tended toward what we might now describe as an impressionistic depiction of features such as settlements and hills rather than claiming to be mathematically objective."[13]

In medieval cartography it was typical to trace orography and hydrography, and this is a feature that Lewis recovers in his maps. The mountain ranges, hills, forests, rivers, deserts, gorges, swamps, islands, and even seabeds are clearly drawn; and in the forests we can even make out quite clearly different tree species, some with round tops and some elongated. But in addition to this, as Carlos Sanz points out in his compelling studies of antique world maps, in many medieval and Renaissance maps, there are buildings, funeral monuments, bridges, or ships on the seas that surround the coasts.[14]

Throughout the twelfth through fifteenth centuries, the world of the marvelous gained in importance, to the extent that it became an integral part of the view of the world. What was important to Europeans of the time was not to distinguish between the real and unreal (in the way they detected the sacred through that which was marvelous—since the essence of "discovery" was not in finding "new things"), but recognizing in reality what the imagination and tradition already held as true. The alleged existence of a continent in the unknown southern hemisphere posed the matter of its theoretical inhabitants, the antipodeans. According to Lewis, "the other hemisphere of the Earth was . . . wholly inaccessible. You could write science-fiction about it."[15] The variety of imaginary monsters (cyclops, unicorns, sciapodes, dragons, and griffons, etc.) was perceived as a normal "anomaly." We can thus understand, as Kappler points out, the real and unreal consistency of the mythical creatures that appear on ancient maps.[16]

Having said that, it would be unfair to think that ancient map-making gave a simplistic vision of the world and universe. Some of the main cartography images were anything but an innocent view of the reality of the time, and the ideas derived from them were indispensable elements in order to interpret geographical reality by people centuries before. As David Woodward states,

Medieval *mappaemundi* carry levels of meaning that have been widely misunderstood. Their compilers have been judged on their ability to show geographical reality structured according to a coordinate system, but the primary function of these maps was to provide illustrated histories or moralized, didactic displays in a geographical setting. . . . We need to evaluate the achievements of the Middle Ages on their own terms and in the context of their purpose.[17]

Maps were a universal model of expressing and conceiving the reality of a moment (both on a physical and human plane). This is why almost all societies had used them as a useful tool to represent the known world (and sometimes also the imagined world) and to create an ordered and institutionalized vision of the human surroundings (normally specific and real, at times distant and presumed).

On the other hand, since geographical knowledge was limited at that time, the prospect of forming an image of the planet was a riskier enterprise than it would later become after circumnavigation of the earth. The process of broadening horizons encouraged the growth of a curious joining of fantasy and reality. Tales of sea voyages were evidence of the fact that mythical islands, monstrous races, and wonderful creatures really did exist. We must not forget that as time passed, the first to risk the dangerous sea journey to the Indies by the west, traversing the mysterious Atlantic Ocean, were driven by the hope to find the fabulous treasures, dreams, and marvels that were located on Far Eastern shores according to the long story-telling tradition. One only has to think of Marco Polo's *Travels* (1295) or the book by John Mandeville, *Marvels of the World* (1356). And finally, the writers of the time, although not map makers, continued to contribute to a wealth of mental maps with religious visions, literary references, and true news of travelers and traders. During the Middle Ages, there was such credulity that fables, legends, and superstitions were fed and multiplied. According to Carlos García Gual, "this fantasy literature was thought up in a universe of dreams in the Middle Ages, which was credulous and anxious for fantasy and received gems and other extraordinary objects from the East that held ancient tales of marvels and exotic creatures."[18]

When we study different samples of medieval and Renaissance maps, one frequently finds imaginary beasts and monstrous creatures, like those thought to have lived in the furthermost parts of the world: extraordinary beasts like dragons and whales, creatures with only one leg and foot, or one eye, or with no mouth, mermaids, the mythological Poseidon, and other anthropomorphic creatures. Indeed as Lewis himself says, a great deal of ancient geography is pure fantasy.[19]

In Abraham Ortelius's map from 1595,[20] for instance, there are images of fantastic creatures that remained in the imagination at that time.[21] If we bear in mind Lewis's fascination for this age, it is not surprising that he includes several mythical creatures taken directly from medieval and Renaissance cartography. If the shores of the Indian Ocean were home to all types of exotic fauna, monsters, and natural treasures for the medieval and Renaissance mentality, then the Great Eastern Ocean, with its enigmatic islands in the maps in *The Chronicles of Narnia* is the perfect dwelling for all type of wonders, including a large number of fantastic creatures.

In the map drawn for *The Voyage of the "Dawn Treader"*, for instance, the reader can see not only the islands where King Caspian's boat traveled (Galma, Terebinthia, the Seven Islands, and the Lonely Islands), but also drawings of a wide variety of fantastic creatures. Most of these beings were taken from popular imagination and mythology, like the mythological Poseidon with his famous trident, a mermaid, three dwarves who live in the depths of the earth, the giants and gnomes drawn on the map in *The Silver Chair*, or the winged dragon drawn on a map in *Prince Caspian*. This great variety of creatures taken from diverse mythologies reflects Lewis's interest in bringing together elements of different origin, which was common in the medieval mentality. This is what King explains in his brilliant study on map-making: "What might seem a strange combination of the geographical, the biblical and the pagan . . . is in fact a revealing chart of the heady mixture underlying medieval belief."[22] A constant preoccupation of travel writers during the Age of Discovery was that of making "marvels" from the lands they traveled known to the public. This is quite a normal attitude in the framework of any travel book text, be it real or fictional, from the *Odyssey* to the present day.

Travel literature holds a special position in that there is a large body of *mirabilia* that has been built upon and extended since Ancient times, and as such was an authority to be borne in mind: either by quoting as an eyewitness, or including it in maps as we have pointed out. In the case of real travels, it was common for the travelers who decided to narrate their experiences to take elements of old traditions, and even decorate their journeys with a wide variety of marvels, natural portents, and diverse curiosities to strengthen the fabulous aspect of the places visited. Also, in order to highlight how incredible the *mirabilia* were to arouse the public curiosity and awe, travel writers use explicit textual markers that show the reality of the source of the writer's amazement. One of the most frequent markers of subjective admiration is the use of the noun "marvel," and its derivatives ("marvelous," "to marvel"). Take for instance Christopher Columbus's first impression on encountering the New World: "It is a very green and flat island . . . the greatest wonder in the world . . . the fish here are so different from ours it is marvelous . . . and with such fine colors, that no man alive can but marvel."[23] At times the adjective "strange" is used or on another level the cliché of being indescribable ("it just cannot be described"). This may be applied to countries and regions, landscape, cities and buildings, customs, animals, climate, natural adversity, objects, and so on.

Likewise, Lewis uses some of these textual markers in *The Voyage of the Dawn Treader,* a sea journey across The Great Eastern Ocean: "the Wonders of the Last Sea,"[24] . . . "Then they could hear the voices of the party in the boat . . . talking in a shrill and surprised way,"[25] . . . "Then up came the sun, and at its first rising they saw it through the wall and it turned into wonderful rainbow of colors."[26] The "unusual" is also brought to the fore when the main characters witness the "marvels" that astound them: "The faces of the ladies were filled with astonishment,"[27] . . . "The whiteness did not get any less mysterious as they approached to it. If it was a land it must be a very strange land, for it seemed just as smooth as the water and on the same level with it."[28]

A constant point of interest in the geography in medieval travel writing and which was to be recorded both in medieval and Lewis's cartography is how particular privileged spaces are described, this being an essential aspect of what Olschi called ideological geography: spaces that belong to wonder, represented by fabulous islands at the end of the earth, an Earthly Paradise and in general any geographically marginal, and therefore, unknown area.[29] According to Anca Crivat-Vasile, this "terra incognita" was organized around certain recurring coordinates: plentiful vegetation, fabulous riches in gold and gems, monsters and fantastic animals, lands of a scatological kind (an Earthly Paradise or, quite the opposite, spaces structured like Hell).[30] On several occasions, these marvelous places were characterized by geographical features establishing the line between the land that had been explored and the unknown: a mountain or high range of mountains, a large rock, a desert, a chasm, thick forests, etc. Sometimes these lands were located near the sea or surrounded by it; perhaps this is why since Ancient times oceans and seas became the limit *par excellence* between the known and unknown world.

A mysterious place that must be mentioned although it is not included in Narnia's geographical borders is the "World's End," as it also marks the frontier between the known and unknown. Little is to be said about this place and it is one of the most enigmatic parts of *The Chronicles of Narnia*. Some locate it beyond the seas, where the known area supposedly ends and the real Narnia begins—that place Far East where death does not exist and spring and youth are eternal. Caspian missed no chance of questioning all the oldest sea captains whom he could find in Narrohaven to learn if they had any knowledge or even any rumors of land further east: " . . . But those who seemed the most truthful could tell of no lands beyond the Lone Islands, and many thought that if you sailed too far east you would come into the surges of a sea without lands that swirled perpetually round the rim of the world."[31] Seen from the World's End, Aslan's World seems to consist of incredibly high mountains, which are always free of snow and covered by plants and forests as far as the eye can see. In *The Last Battle*, the last in the series of Narnia books, the idea of ascending to Aslan's World is continually insisted on— accompanied by phrases like: "Narnia and the north!" and "Further up and further in!"

Kappler explains that in the Middle Ages paradise on earth was also called a high point on earth: "to get there, one must ascend."[32] Taking the Middle Ages again as a source of inspiration to create an imaginary landscape, Lewis seems to have used this idea when he takes Aslan's World as the highest point, and at its peak, for those who are able to reach it, is the most wonderful garden[33]: "And soon they found themselves all walking together . . . up toward mountains higher than you could see. . . . But there was no snow on those mountains; there were forests and green slopes and sweet orchards and flashing waterfalls, one above the other, going up forever."[34]

The image of Aslan's World as a wonderful garden, like Eden—the closest thing to an Earthly Paradise in the Middle Ages—also entails Mircea Eliade's mythical theme called "nostalgia for Paradise."[35] This nostalgia is present recurrently in art and human imagination: in Milton's *Paradise Lost*, in the Garden of Hesperides, and also in the signs of Paradise that travelers like Marco Polo or Columbus discover:

So these lands which he had now discovered were . . . the end of the East. . . . These grasses so green they seemed like river grasses. . . . the holy theologians and wise philosophers were right when they said that Earthly Paradise was at the end of the East, for it is a quite temperate place. . . . These are great signs of the Earthly Paradise, for this place are just as the holy, sacred theologians said. . . . Never have I heard nor read that such an amount of fresh water could be within and alongside salt water. . . . And if this is not from Heaven, it must be an even greater wonder.[36]

Another landscape feature that often appears in medieval and Renaissance travel writing, and which Lewis introduces in his work as pointed out below, is that of islands as a privileged land of marvels.

Island motifs, for Europeans in the Middle Ages, were those territorial and geographical bastions, which offered one to be physically removed to a whole world of prodigious and fantastic creatures. Sailors in the sixteenth century believed in the existence of islands full of marvels and treasures such as The Island of the Seven Cities, Saint Brendan's Island, or the Antilles, the fantastic island mentioned by Aristotle, which appeared in world maps as the furthest east of the lands of the Indies in the fourteenth century. This marvelous space, therefore, which has an ancient literary tradition, is revealed as one of the long preferred imaginary territories by humanity. We must only remember the islands inhabited by fantastic creatures in the *Odyssey*, the platonic Atlantis, with its great wealth of plant life and mines of precious metals, the island of Avalon in Celtic mythology, the marvelous islands of Saint Isidoro or the Hesiod's Islands of the Blessed with their fertile soil that produces flowers and fruit three times a year. It is difficult to resist the temptation to give an exhaustive list of even the most important centers of tradition from before the Middle Ages in this regard, which has been significantly increased with cartography. In fact, medieval maps record the existence of unknown islands that were sought out from the end of the fifteenth century and during the sixteenth century in successive explorations. Cartography has, therefore, contributed quite a lot to encourage that "island romance" mentioned by Olschki, and his travel books echo this obsession with the dream of wealth combining that of the monstrous.

This tradition of fabled islands with marvelous spaces, prodigious features, surprising creatures, and fantastical beasts also appears in the maps included in the *Chronicles of Narnia*. Like the sailors of olden times, the crew of the "Dawn Treader," the vessel that sailed The Great Eastern Ocean in *The Voyage of the "Dawn Treader,"* were eager to discover unexplored territory and islands, places full of marvels and fantastic creatures recorded in Narnian tales: "wild stories of islands inhabited by headless men, floating islands, waterspouts, and a fire that burned along the water."[37] Islands that had been long yearned for, from what we can make out from the words of a sailor on the "Dawn Treader" when he glimpsed The Dark Island: "That's the island I've been looking for this long time."[38] Islands inhabited by fantastic creatures such as the "sciapodes," one- footed creatures that Lewis brought into his work, more than likely due to his knowledge of medieval literature. In his work, Kappler employs a quotation by Mandeville to describe these creatures as individuals with only one leg and one foot, which is so big that when they sit on the ground, they use it to protect them from the sun.[39] As we can see, Lewis's monopods are not very different from those described by Manderville or the one included in the map of the world by Beato del Burgo de Osma, which describes a fourth continent, unknown territory, as a place of extreme heat where the sciapode lives—a naked creature with long hair and a leg ending in a large foot.[40]

There are other analogies with ancient maps that cannot go unnoticed in *The Chronicles of Narnia*. As far as medieval maps are concerned, the intention was not to include all geographical knowledge, but as Kappler explains, "to propose a selection of places to make up a painting."[41] This is why a lot of old maps show particular aspects and scenes from social and political life in the Middle Ages. Therefore, what might now seem anachronistic represents a social, economic, political, and religious organization, which reigned for more than ten centuries after the fall of Rome. To quote Woodward, "the *mappaemundi* show that maps may also consist of historical aggregations or cumulative inventories of events in addition to representing objects that exist cosynchronously in space."[42]

To take one example, the Catalan Atlas, attributed to Abraham de Cresques, shows a myriad of people, animals, walled cities, and characteristic objects from these places that aimed to show what the people who lived in that region were like.[43] If we compare this map dating from 1375 with Lewis's map for *The Horse and His Boy*, we can see the intention was to reflect very specific aspects of life in the kingdom of Calormen. There, human and beasts work in slavery under the control of the Taarkans, the masters in whose hands the administrative power of the kingdom lies. We also notice the presence of lords and ladies of Tashbaan, who are carried on stretchers.

In the Middle Ages, meanwhile, if we study the typical iconography and symbolism, we see that maps and images of the Cosmos are full of images that aim to transmit abstract truths symbolically. Geometric and nongeometric shapes, spatial fields, colors, predominant axes, and other enigmatic figures and images provide us with a very particular vision of the world:

> they were efficient vehicles for the transmission of certain world-views. They were accurate charts of the beliefs of their time.... The cartographic image became a multivalent symbol capable of expressing a host of different moral and religious meanings.[44]

When compared with medieval maps it becomes clear that Lewis had this iconography in mind when making his own. His maps, like medieval maps, were not meant to be mathematically objective or aseptic. They are more a mixture of geographical enclaves and symbolism: there are iconographic elements, symbols, and images reflecting a deeper conceptual line of thought. According to Mallarmé, the world is conceived as something to end up in a beautiful book, or, in my opinion, to be turned into a map marked out by evocative symbols.

It should thus be noted that the Narnia maps have a symbolic image (that of the quaternary), which not only shows the four cardinal points, but also reflects the double structuring of the medieval spirit, as in the circular shape included in the map drawn for *The Silver Chair*. It is circular and vertical at the same time, an image that represents the spiritual (a circle, sphere, and a rose window) and the material or manifest (the cross). Gerard Champeaux and Dom Sterckx, in their study on medieval art symbols, describe the quaternary circle as a cross inside a circular border, from which we can make out a type of radiation from the four cardinal points. The quaternary may be subdivided in eight, twelve, sixteen, etc. thus forming a compass. According to these authors, this process announces and carries out the passing from the transcendent beyond to the imminent down here.[45] This symbolism is a geometric representation of the close interdependence that exists between the two worlds, the transcendental and the supratemporal (the Land of Aslan) and the earthly, contingent, and limited (Narnia). The heavenly and supratemporal (the circle) becomes a whole with the earthly, plotting the landscape where life of the Narnia creatures goes on (vertical and horizontal lines), as in the circular shape included in *The Voyage of the "Dawn Treader."*

According to Juan Eduardo Cirlot, however, the cross is a dramatic derivation, like an inversion of the tree in paradise in medieval iconography. This is why, in his opinion, the cross is often seen as a knotted tree, even with branches, sometimes Y-shaped, and sometimes thorny. This is what happens in the Tree of Life, the cross is the "axis of the world." It is situated in the mystical center of the cosmos, and is the bridge or stairs whereby souls go up to God."[46] It is interesting if we look carefully at the circular shape in the map Lewis made for *The Silver Chair*; there are Y-shaped branches of what could be the Tree of Life inside the vertical and horizontal axes of the cross. In other words, the tree of paradise planted at the beginning of time and remaining till the end of time: the Yggdrasil or Tree of Ashes from Scandinavian peoples, which Lewis himself mentions in the American edition of *The Lion, the Witch and the Wardrobe*.[47] Therefore, the cross as axis of the world establishes the primary relationship between two worlds: the material, and the spiritual.

There is another image that allows us to see more similarities between ancient maps and those in *The Chronicles of Narnia*. This is the graphic image of the cyclical passing of time, using figures like the Moon and the Sun. These are drawn at either side of the axis of the world on the top left edge of the map in this same illustration, and symbolize the counting of time, as in medieval maps, as each one rises and sets. As the sun rises and sets each day, bringing with it the changes in light and darkness, heat and cold, it has a far-reaching effect on the world of Narnia. The circle turns into a wheel, which rotates producing cycles, repetitions, and renewals.

Another motif often appearing in ancient maps and which Lewis undoubtedly brings into his is the image of the four elements of nature. A detailed study of the left side of the map in *Prince Caspian* reveals this: earth on the inside, drops of water and flames flank the outside, and a symbol for air in the anthropomorphic figure of the wind. Cirlot believes there is a relation between the elements and those called "elemental." These correspond, according to this author, as follows: air (sylphs and giants); fire (the salamander); water (nymphs or mermaids); earth (gnomes or dwarves)."[48] In Lewis's fantasy literature, the presence of elemental beings on three maps (giants, dwarves, a mermaid, and a dragon) may reflect his intention to represent the four elements (earth, air, water, and fire). In the maps drawn for *The Chronicles of Narnia*, we can also observe Renaissance influence. As Lewis states:

For the Renaissance thinker, not less but more than for the schoolman, the universe was packed and tingling with anthropomorphic life; its true picture is to be found in the elaborate title pages of old folios where wind blows at the corners and at the bottom dolphins spout.[49]

In fact we can find several details mentioned above in all the maps. In the map drawn for *Prince Caspian*, for example, we can see several dolphins and the anthropomorphic image of the wind as a head blowing. The other maps also include, as already stated, a wide variety of fantastic animals and anthropomorphic creatures like those seen in many maps of the time. In addition, maps from the fifteenth and sixteenth centuries were usually highly decorated with ships, sea creatures, figures, and rose compasses with a lily pointing north, and these elements are plentiful in almost all the maps in *The Chronicles of Narnia*.[50] As regards ornamentation, the name of the maps of this time (and this custom was maintained until much later) was usually decorated, surrounded by mythological figures, anthropomorphic creatures, or floral motifs.

Lewis also adopts this in some of his maps, such as the anthropomorphic figure of the wind that surrounds the map in *Prince Caspian*, the mermaid at the top of the map in *The Voyage of the Dawn Treader*, the giants that hold up the name of the map in *The Silver Chair*, or the compass rose that appears in the maps in *The Chronicles of Narnia*. The wind rose or compass rose has appeared on charts and maps since the 1300s when the portolan charts first made their appearance to help orient readers.[51] Originally, this device was used to indicate the main directions according to the most important winds: the eight major winds, the eight half-winds, and the sixteen quarter-winds. North has traditionally been indicated with a "fleur de lys" symbol. In portolan charts the directions, made by lengthening the angles of a central rose, crossed with those of another surrounding it, made up a dense network of thirty-two directions. These direction lines linked ports of arrival with ports of departure. Albino Canepa's portolan chart is a magnificent example excellently outlining the Mediterranean Basin and providing notable information on the Atlantic, showing the islands (Azores, Madeira, and the Canaries) as well as some fantasy islands, of which Antilia is worthy of note (situated to the west of Azores).[52] This same technique is observed in some of the maps for *The Chronicles of Narnia*, which outlines the coast quite accurately and gives information about some lands and inland settlements. The approach is quite eclectic, so traditions from fantasy are used as well as "data" from observations.

Looking carefully at the two maps drawn for *The Voyage of the "Dawn Treader"* and *Prince Caspian*, a network of straight lines can be seen which are the result of prolonging the directions of a rose compass, sixteen and thirty-two rhumb lines respectively. The three maps introduce, as in ancient portolan charts, all their traditional ornamentation, such as the "fleur de lis" symbol pointing north, ships, coastal names, and numerous hydrographic and topographic references. The two maps drawn for *The Voyage of the "Dawn Treader"* also show the rhumb lines that indicate the point of arrival and departure of the vessels, some coastal features, the places where sailors would shelter, and, in one of the maps, the distances are also recorded—all of these being characteristic features of portolan charts.

Taking all this into account, we cannot overlook another function of the maps in Lewis's fantasy literature and which coincides, to a great degree, with some Italian Renaissance painters: the use of a landscape background to support a moral allegory. As James Hall explains, the "moralized" scenery of some Renaissance paintings "may show a clear sky in half the painting in contrast to the black clouds in the other half: both Good and Evil are reflected close up."[53] The landscape in the maps of Narnia, as well as the creatures and some objects, also seem to have taken a moral standing. We might say that these secondary worlds reflected on the maps are a huge chessboard where the struggle between Good and Evil is played out. The scenery does indeed reflect to a point the ethics of the creatures that live there. When we study the maps in Lewis's work, we see that the lands inhabited by the good creatures have abundant vegetation and forests. The areas inhabited by malignant creatures are the complete opposite. There all kinds of evil creatures dwell and they are described as arid places, with hardly any rivers, and usually freeze. This is all in consonance with the text.

Narnia, unlike Archenland or Calormen, is characterized by its plentiful forests, valleys, and rivers that run throughout the land. The green spaces are a symbol of life and wealth, and a place where its inhabitants dwell and take refuge. During what was known as the "Golden Age of Narnia," this natural environment represented a space for happiness for its inhabitants—allies of Good: "all the animals could talk, and there were nice people who lived in the streams and the trees. Naiads and Dryads they were called. And there were Dwarfs: And there were lovely little Fauns in all the woods."[54]

The Kingdom of Narnia could even evoke the mythical gardens of Eden. Far from being a hostile environment, nature here appears to be close to the creatures, and even beats to the same life rhythm. It is a refuge for creatures of peace, a stage for celebrations and "cosmic" dances, and a place of hushed conversation. The forests, valleys, and rivers of Narnia in some way turned into a prolongation of the character of its owners and thus take on the most diverse shapes, ranging from Baco's "laughing" games and his court of fauns and satyrs in times of peace and happiness, to the endless winter that covered the forests of Narnia in snow for a hundred long years, reflecting the perturbed mind of the White Witch.

In this natural environment with open spaces, places are described where the vegetation looks like it has been tamed neither directly nor indirectly by human intervention. This is why it becomes a threatening reality for the Telmarines or "New Narnians," the people who after conquering Narnia in 1998—that is, according to Narnian chronology[55]—set themselves the first measure of cutting down the highest number of trees possible in order to control these spaces, silence the beasts, and rid themselves of a presence they felt was threatening.[56] What Lewis suggests is, undoubtedly, a new relationship between man and his environment—that of reason and nature joined. The image that perhaps best reflects this idea is that of the hamadryad or nymph of the trees, whose spirit dies when the tree she dwells in is cut down.

In contrast to the idealized image of nature presented in its purest state in Ancient Narnia, Calormen appears as an extremely arid and clearly domesticated land. While Narnia is characterized by its plentiful open natural spaces, Tashbaan, the capital of Calormen is described as a city surrounded by an extremely high wall permanently guarded by soldiers. Even the gardens are subject to geometrical reason and discipline between the walls. Inside the city walls a hill covered in buildings stretches out to the top. The population gathers in the markets and trips over huge piles of rubbish all over the streets. While in Narnia there are hardly any buildings, Tashbaan surprises us with its great number of palaces, narrow streets, and slums where the people are crowded. Here, the two blocks of spaces we see are divided into natural and artificial, and are irreconcilably separate. The city of Tashbaan is an artificial place that also has clearly negative connotations both for the neighbors in Archenland and the inhabitants of Narnia, as historically it was an aggressive country that had always tried to conquer the free lands in the north.

Quite the opposite to Narnia, and also with negative connotations, is the land occupied by the giants of Harfang, to the north of Narnia. In *The Silver Chair*, Jill Pole, Eustace Scrubb, and Puddleglum could clearly see the contrast between the two spaces before leaving for the Wild Lands of the North to search for Prince Rilian: "They found a place where they could scramble up, and in about ten minutes stood panting at the top. They cast a longing look back at the valley-land of Narnia and then turned their faces to the North. The vast, lonely moor stretched on and up as far as they could see. On their left was rockier ground.... As they got deeper the moor, the loneliness increased."[57] Moreover, if we look carefully at the map in *Prince Caspian*, this feeling, and with it the negative connotation, grows as we move north, where the cliffs and permanently frozen landscape that is battered by the north winds, turn the land of the giants into a space that is bare of vegetation and progressively more dangerous and threatening.

Lewis thus organizes spaces around two different atmospheres: a natural one, on the one hand, and, on the other, the tamed or artificial (that is, towns or cities). In *The Chronicles of Narnia* we may consider this a gross simplification of dividing spaces into hostile and protecting, and the positive or negative connotations of each space vary according to the characters that occupy them. But Lewis does not just use words, as we have already seen; he also uses maps to show this.

Fernando Savater's words on Tolkien's fantasy literature also come to mind, and may be extended to include Lewis, when he says that the ethical condition pervades everything and "all physical laws submit to the supreme Law of moral courage."[58] This tendency to endow every space, every landscape with great meaning is in subtle but powerful contrast to the apparently naturalistic descriptive approach in the narration, transforming "realism" into something that is essentially magic. But this is the very reason why the leap from the ordinary to the extraordinary is made in the fantasy literature of Lewis without even startling us.

To conclude, we might say that to create a detailed geographical context, Lewis relies not only on words, but he also uses drawings and maps like those included in his fantasy work, which is another of his resources that contributes to the internal coherence of his work and to greater credibility, essential requirements when creating secondary worlds. Including maps or, that is, graphically showing the place where the events narrated occur, is one of the writer's resources to add veracity to a story.

One of the points we have highlighted here, however, is that the maps in *The Chronicles of Narnia* do not correspond to what we would normally understand by modern-day cartography. The maps that appear in editions of the series are much closer to medieval or Renaissance charts. In fact, if we compare the maps of Narnia with older cartography, it is clear that there are several elements from medieval and Renaissance imagination, such as marvels and treasures, beasts and monsters, mythical creatures, and other fabled creatures. The most typical imagery in medieval maps, in particular, is a clearly visible influence in Lewis when designing maps for the series of works on Narnia. These maps, like the world maps and medieval charts, were not conceived with scientific or objective rigor, but rather the graphic representation of a constellation of ideas. So it is that the images, symbols, and other elements in these maps, instead of being merely decorative, have meaning and symbolize something—something specific or something profound to a greater or lesser degree.

There remains no doubt, then, that Lewis had the medieval and Renaissance very much in mind when he imagined and developed the maps to be included in some of his fantasy books. He was fascinated by the time when the great Thule, the furthermost region according to the classics, was still believed in and he introduced symbols, images, and fantastic creatures just like the map makers of the time. His maps might be considered, among other things, a tribute to medieval and Renaissance cartography.

NOTES

1. Geoff King, *Mapping Reality: An Exploration of Cultural Cartographies* (London: Macmillan Press, 1996), 21.

2. J. R. R. Tolkien, *Tree and Leaf* (London: Grafton, 1992), 36.

3. Federica Domínguez Colavita, *Teoría del cuento infantil* (Buenos Aires, Argentina: Plus Ultra, 1990), 135.

4. C. S. Lewis, *Surprised by Joy* (San Diego, CA: Harcourt Brace & Company, 1955), 17. For more details, see Walter Hooper, *Boxen: The Imaginary World of the Young C. S. Lewis* (San Diego, CA: Harcourt Brace Jovanovich, 1985).

5. Lewis, *Surprised by Joy*, 17.

6. Years later Pauline D. Baynes would also illustrate for this author *The Adventures of Tom Bombadil* (1962) and *Smith of Wooton Major* (1967).

7. Walter Hooper, ed. *C. S. Lewis. A Companion and Guide* (London: Harper-Collins, 1996), 624–625. The maps that illustrate the text *The Chronicles of Narnia* only appear in *Prince Caspian, The Voyage of the "Dawn Treader," The Silver Chair*, and *The Horse and His Boy*. The first of these maps is of Narnia and the surrounding lands and it includes part of the Wild Lands to the North and Archenland to the South. The map that appears in *The Voyage of the "Dawn Treader"* shows the first part of the Great Ocean of the East, including the Seven Islands, the Lonely Islands, and the Great Eastern Islands. In *The Silver Chair* there is a map of the Wild Lands of the North, and in *The Horse and His Boy* Archenland and the desert that joins it to the warm lands of Calormen is portrayed.

8. Ibid., 625.

9. The transition from the Middle Ages to the Renaissance was reflected in a significant change in cartography. The development of mathematics coincided with that of cartography.

10. King, *Mapping Reality*, 23.

11. Cf. http://www.herefordwebpages.co.uk/mapmundi.shtml (Last accessed August 20, 2006)

12. C. S. Lewis, *The Discarded Image: An Introduction to Medieval and Renaissance Literature* (Cambridge: Cambridge University Press, 1995), 143–144.

13. King, *Mapping Reality*, 44.

14. Cf. Carlos Sanz, *Mapas antiguos del mundo (siglos XV-XVI)* (Madrid, Spain: Gráficas Yagüe, 1961).

15. C. S. Lewis, *The Discarded Image: An Introduction to Medieval and Renaissance Literature* (Cambridge: Cambridge University Press, 1995), 142.

16. Claude Kappler, *Monstruos, demonios y maravillas a fines de la Edad Media* (Madrid, Spain: Akal, 1986), 42.

17. David Woodward, "Reality, Symbolism, Time, and Space in Medieval World Maps," in *Annals of the Association of American Geographers* 75 (1985), 510.

18. Carlos García Gual, "Imagen mítica del Nuevo Mundo," in *Siglo XV* (Sevilla, Spain: Sociedad Estatal para la Exposición Universal, 1992), 155.

19. C. S. Lewis, *An Experiment in Criticism* (Cambridge: Cambridge University Press, 1995), 77.

20. Abraham Ortelius, *Theatrum Orbis Terraru,* facsimile edn, no. 560 (Firenze, Italy: Giunti, 1991).

21. Annalisa Battini, "Gli del cinquecento mercatore e la cartografía moderna," in *Alla Scoperta del Mondo,* ed. E. Milano, (Modena, Italy: Il Bulino, 2001), 191.

22. King, *Mapping Reality*, 32.

23. Luis Arranz, ed., *Cristobal Colón: Diario de abordo* (Madrid, Spain: Historia 16, 1991), 99. Christopher Columbus was accompanied by the young Fray Bartolomé de Las Casas, who would later provide partial transcripts of Columbus's logs.

24. C. S. Lewis, *The Voyage of the "Dawn Treader."* Illustrated by Pauline Baynes (New York: Harper Trophy, 1994), 218.

25. Ibid., 235.

26. Ibid., 242.

27. Ibid., 225.

28. Ibid., 234.

29. Leonardo Olschki, *Storia letteraria delle scoperte geografiche: Studi e ricerche* (Firenze, Italy: 1937), 147.

30. Anca Crivat-Vasile, "Mirabilis Oriens: fuentes y transmisión," in *Revista de Filología Románica*, 11–12. (1994–1995), 471.

31. Lewis, *The Voyage of the "Dawn Treader*," 64.

32. Claude Kappler, *Monstruos, demonios y maravillas a fines de la Edad Media*, 23.

33. The Holy Mountain in *Perelandra*, like the peak of the mountain in Aslan's World in *The Last Battle*, is also associated to the idea of spiritual elevation. According to Olivier Beigbeder "the throne of divinity is sometimes found at the peak of a cosmic mountain; . . . the mountain is the link between heaven and earth." [Olivier Beigbeder, *La simbología* (Barcelona, Spain: Oikos-tan, 1971), 42.] The hill, therefore, might be said to give up its earthly or material character becoming an image of an idea which seems to have become fact in the work of Lewis ("myth became fact").

34. C. S. Lewis, *The Last Battle*. Illustrated by Pauline Baynes (New York: HarperTrophy, 1994), 209.

35. Mircea Eliade, *Mito y realidad,* 2nd ed. (Barcelona, Spain: Labor, 1994), 181.

36. Luis Arranz, ed. *Cristobal Colón: Diario de abordo* (Madrid, Spain: Historia 16, 1991), 53–54.

37. Lewis, *The Voyage of the "Dawn Treader,"* 64–65.

38. Ibid., 183.

39. Claude Kappler, *Monstruos, demonios y maravillas a fines de la Edad Media*, 1986, 143.

40. Cf. http://www.henry-davis.com/MAPS/EMwebpages/207H.html (Last accessed August 20, 2006).

41. Kappler, *Monstruos, demonios y maravillas a fines de la Edad Media*, 88.

42. Woodward, "Reality, Symbolism, Time, and Space in Medieval World Maps," 510.

43 . Cf. http://www.henry-davis.com/MAPS/LMwebpages/246B.html (Last accessed August 20, 2006)

44. King, *Mapping Reality*, 31–32.

45. Gerard Champeaux and Dom Sébastien Sterckx, *Introducción a los símbolos*, 3rd ed. (Madrid, Spain: Encuentro, 1992), 40.

46. Juan Eduardo Cirlot, *Diccionario de Símbolos*, 2nd ed. (Madrid, Spain: Siruela, 1997), 157.

47. C. S. Lewis, *The Lion, the Witch and the Wardrobe,* Illustrated by Pauline Baynes (New York: Harper Trophy, 1994), 138. In the *Edda* by Sorri Sturluson, the great tree Yggdrasil or tree of ashes symbolizes the unchanging cosmos. As an expression of the cosmos, it is at the same time, the center of life, and the center of everything.

48. Juan Eduardo Cirlot, *Diccionario de Símbolos*, 2nd ed. (Madrid, Spain: Siruela, 1997), 162.

49. C. S. Lewis, *A Preface to Paradise Lost* (Oxford: Oxford University Press, 1961), 75.

50. José Luis Casado Soto, "El descubrimiento del mundo 1500–1630," in *La Imagen del Mundo: 500 Años de Cartografía*, Madrid, Spain: Instituto Geográfico Nacional, 1992, 56–116, 105.

51. The portolan chart is a hand-drawn navigational chart made in Mediterranean ports and used by Mediterranean sailors from the thirteenth century to the seventeenth century and characterized by a grid of intersecting rhumb lines (or loxodromes) and scalloped coastlines with the names of ports of landmarks and ports written at right angles to the coast.

52. Cf. http://www.bell.lib.umn.edu/map/PORTO/CAN/index89.html (Last accessed August 20, 2006).

53. James Hall, *Diccionario de temas y símbolos artísticos* (Madrid, Spain: Alianza Editorial, 1987), 243.

54. C. S. Lewis, *Prince Caspian*, Illustrated by Pauline Baynes (New York: Harper Trophy, 1994), 42.

55. Walter Hooper, ed. *Past Watchful Dragons. A Guide to C. S. Lewis's Chronicles of Narnia* (London: Fount Paperbacks, 1980), 82.

56. Lewis, 51.

57. Lewis, *The Silver Chair*, Illlustrated by Pauline Baynes (New York: HarperTrophy, 1994), 79.

58. Fernando Savater, *La infancia recuperada* (Madrid, Spain: Taurus, 1986), 141.

BIBLIOGRAPHY

Arranz, Luis, Editor. *Cristobal Colón. Diario de abordo.* Madrid, Spain: Historia 16, 1991.

Battini, Annalisa. "Gli del cinquecento mercatore e la cartografía moderna". In *Alla Scoperta del Mondo. Modena.* Edited by E. Milano. Modena, Italy: Il Bulino, 2001, 171–239.

Beigbeder, Olivier. *La simbología*. Barcelona, Spain: Oikos-tan, 1971.

Carretero González, Margarita and Encarnación Hidalgo Tenorio, Editors. *Behind the Veil of Familiarity: C. S. Lewis (1898–1998)*. Bern, Switzerland: Peter Lang, 2001.

Casado Soto, José Luis. "El descubrimiento del mundo, 1500–1630." In *La Imagen del Mundo: 500 Años de Cartografía,*. Madrid, Spain: Instituto Geográfico Nacional, 1992, 56–116

Champeaux Gerard and Dom Sébastien Sterckx. *Introducción a los símbolos*. 3rd ed. Madrid, Spain: Encuentro, 1992.

Cirlot, Juan Eduardo. *Diccionario de Símbolos*. 2nd ed. Madrid, Spain: Siruela, 1997.

Crivat-Vasile, Anca. "Mirabilis Oriens: fuentes y transmisión." *Revista de Filología Románica* (1994–1995): 471–479, 11–12

De cresques, Abraham. *Mapamundi del Año 1375*. Barcelona, Argentina: Ebrisa, 1983.

Domínguez Colavita, Federica. *Teoría del cuento infantil*. Buenos Aires, Argentina: Plus Ultra, 1990.

Eliade, Mirecea. *Mito y realidad*. 2nd. ed. Barcelona, Argentina: Labor, 1994.

García Gual, Carlos. "Imagen mítica del Nuevo Mundo." In *Siglo XV* Sevilla: Sociedad Estatal para la Exposición Universal, 1992, 152–161.

Hall, James. *Diccionario de temas y símbolos artísticos*. Madrid, Spain: Alianza Editorial, 1987.

Hooper, Walter. *C. S. Lewis. A Companion and Guide*. London: HarperCollins, 1996.

———. *Past Watchful Dragons. A Guide to C. S. Lewis's Chronicles of Narnia*. London: Fount Paperbacks, 1980.

———. ed. *Boxen. The Imaginary World of the Young C. S. Lewis*. San Diego, CA: Harcourt Brace Jovanovich, 1985.

Kappler, Claude. *Monstruos, demonios y maravillas a fines de la Edad Media*. Madrid, Spain: Akal, 1986.

Kilby, Clyde S. *Images of Salvation in the Fiction of C. S. Lewis*. Wheaton, IL: Harold Shaw Publishers, 1978.

King, Geoff. *Mapping Reality. An Exploration of Cultural Cartographies*. London: Macmillan Press, 1996.

Lewis, Clive Staples. *An Experiment in Criticism*. Cambridge: Cambridge University Press, 1995.

———. *The Cosmic Trilogy: Out of the Silent Planet, Perelandra and That Hideous Strength*. Great Britain: Pan Books, 1989.

———. *The Discarded Image. An Introduction to Medieval and Renaissance Literature*. Cambridge: Cambridge University Press, 1995.

———. *The Horse and His Boy*. Illustrated by Pauline Baynes. New York: Harper Trophy, 1994.

———. *The Lion, the Witch and the Wardrobe. A Story for Children*. Illustrated by Pauline Baynes. New York: Harper Trophy, 1994.

———. *A Preface to Paradise Lost*. Oxford: Oxford University Press, 1961.

———. *Prince Caspian. The Return to Narnia*. Illustrated by Pauline Baynes. New York: Harper Trophy, 1994.

———. *The Silver Chair*. Illustrated by Pauline Baynes. New York: Harper Trophy, 1994.

———. *The Voyage of the "Dawn Treader."* Illustrated by Pauline Baynes. New York: Harper Trophy, 1994.

Martín Meras, M. Luisa. "De los portulanos al padrón de Indias." In *La imagen del mundo. 5OO Años de Cartografía*. Madrid, Spain: Instituto Geográfico Nacional, 1992, 13–54.

Olschki, Leonardo. *Storia letteraria delle scoperte geografiche. Studi e ricerche*. Italy: Firenze, 1937.

Ortelius, Abraham. *Theatrum Orbis Terrarum*. Firenze, Italy: Giunti, (Facsimile edn, no. 560), 1991.

Sanz, Carlos. *Mapas antiguos del mundo (siglos XV–XVI)*. Madrid, Spain: Gráficas Yagüe, 1961.

Savater, Fernando. *La infancia recuperada*. Madrid, Spain: Taurus, 1986.

Tolkien, J. R. R. *Tree and Leaf*. London: Grafton, 1992.

Woodward, David. "Reality, Symbolism, Time, and Space in Medieval World Maps." In *Annals of the Association of American Geographers* 75 (1985), 510–521.

8

Till We Have Faces: A Study of the Soul and the Self

Karen Rowe

Each reader may be able to come up with a unique reading of C. S. Lewis's last novel, *Till We Have Faces*, but there are, nevertheless, certain themes which can serve as instructional starting points for someone reading this work for the first—or fifth—time. One thing, at least, is certain: the more one reads Lewis's complex novel, the more one finds rewards for doing so.

Placing the work in the context of Lewis's life and other works helps one see it as the culmination of his literary mythmaking and his lifelong search for joy and God. Chronologically speaking, *Till We Have Faces* follows his autobiography, *Surprised by Joy*, and has the distinction of being Lewis's last novel. Walter Hooper states that the work was begun in the spring of 1955 while *Surprised by Joy* was still presumably in production. Joy Davidman Gresham, Lewis's fan, friend, and soon-to-be wife, was making regular visits to him that year. Apparently the two worked on ideas for a story: a letter by Joy on March 23 records that their conversation that day bore fruit for the novel, which was then well underway by the end of April. Hooper records that a further letter to Bill Gresham has Joy remarking that "he [Lewis] finds my advice indispensable."[1] The influence of the future Mrs. Lewis was remarkable in many ways, not the least of which was an intellect and love of argument and learning comparable to Lewis's.

But in fact, Lewis had actually started the novel much earlier in life. In the initial British publication of the novel, Lewis writes:

This re-interpretation of an old story has lived in the author's mind, thickening and hardening with the years, ever since he was an undergraduate. That way, he could be said to have worked at it most of his life. Recently, what seemed to be the right form presented itself and themes suddenly interlocked: the straight tale of barbarism, the mind of an ugly woman, dark idolatry and pale enlightenment at war with each other and with vision, and the havoc which a vocation, or even a faith, works on human life.[2]

Lewis records this initial consideration of the idea on November 23, 1922: "After lunch I went out for a walk up Shotover, thinking how to make a masque or play of Psyche and Caspian."[3] He records nearly a year later, on September 9, 1923: "My head was very full of my old idea of a poem on my own version of the Cupid and Psyche story in which Psyche's sister would not be jealous, but unable to see anything but moors when Psyche showed her the Palace. I have tried it twice before, once in couplet and once in ballad form."[4] Hooper records these fragmentary versions, copied out by Lewis's brother, in *C. S. Lewis: Companion & Guide*.[5] These efforts, as well as the changes already intended in the retelling of the myth (both using Caspian rather than Orual and changing the motivation of the sister), reveal that Lewis had in mind the fundamental alteration that would make the novel more mythic than the original telling, for it is the introduction of the aspect of belief that allows the numinous quality of true myth to emerge.

That the novel comes on the heels of *Surprised by Joy* is perhaps no accident, for in that autobiographical work, Lewis addresses the lifelong search for what he calls "Joy," or *Sehnsucht* a nameless longing for something nearly inexplicable, a dream that dissipates as soon as one imagines he has grasped it, the almost tangible expression of an emotion, an encounter with the eternal likened always in his works to a "stab," sharp and painful in its brevity and intensity. This longing for something which he first associates with natural beauty, then with the Norse legends, and then in scattered moments throughout his life is actually the thing itself which he longs for; the "wanting," not the having, is the "Joy." He learns that the more he pursues the Stab, the less he can encounter it, but the more he turns his attention to other things, the more likely it is that he will experience the sharp longing again. This indirect way of obtaining what one desires above all else is what the main character of *Till We Have Faces* comes to experience in the culmination of both her journey of self-discovery (much like Lewis's) and her transformation. The closer she binds those she loves to her, the less love she feels.

Lewis wrote *The Four Loves* after *Till We Have Faces*. In essence, *The Four Loves* can be read as a commentary on the novel, as it is a study of the nature of

Love in its four manifestations—Affection, Friendship, Eros, and Charity—and offers an indirect analysis of the failure of the novel's main character to love properly those she is surrounded by. Lewis's grist for the analytical mill, which is *The Four Loves,* undoubtedly arose from not only a lifetime of personal interactions demanding various types of love from him (and encountering many wrong loves for him), but also from the extended analogy on love which *Till We Have Faces* can be considered. Working backward from fiction to analysis is not unheard of. In this case showing precedes telling.

In *The Four Loves,* Lewis first addresses the two distinct natures of Love: Need-love and Gift-love. Need-love, of course, is the love that looks at others always in relation to the interests of the lover. Here is the obsessive love of a mother for a child; the self-centered love of a husband for a wife, who becomes his cook, maid, and mate; the fulfilling love of a spinster teacher for her pupils. Here is the possessive love of a wife demanding all her husband's time, the alienating love of a grieving parent at the expense of a living child, the controlling love of a pastor over his flock. These examples of Need-love all reveal a love conditioned by the needs of the lover, not the needs of the loved one. On the other hand is Gift-love, which considers the needs of the loved one even at the expense of the lover.

Lewis experienced both of these loves in his life. His father, unable to bear the death of his wife, found it nearly impossible to have a relationship with his sons. Lewis, on the other hand, because of his father's overbearing manner, found it nearly impossible to build a relationship with his father. The mother of his wartime friend, Paddy Moore, to whom Lewis pledged he would care for after her son's death, showed Lewis the agonies of a possessive love that controls not just the object of love, but all those surrounding it. Lewis demonstrated Gift-love in the thirty-year sacrifice of time, money, leisure, and emotion toward Mrs. Moore as well as in a lifetime of care for Warnie, his brother. In his love for Joy Gresham, Lewis experienced his friend Charles Williams' idea of substitutionary suffering as he himself lost bone mass to osteoporosis while Joy gained bone mass in her leg. Thus, Lewis's portrayal in *Till We Have Faces* of Orual's slow realization of her overwhelming Need-love for all those around her and the damage it does evidences an understanding from personal experience.

A reader familiar with other works of Lewis's will detect similarities between them and his *Till We Have Faces.* There are elements of Narnia in the novel, most recognizably in the vision sequence where Orual walks into the vision through a picture, just as Lucy and Eustace Clarence Scrubb enter Narnia through the painting of the ship in *Prince Caspian.* And some might see in the unveiling of Orual at the judgment bar of the gods a similarity to the tearing off of Scrubb's dragon skin, acquired because of the dragon-longings in his heart. Orual, too, has longings that evidence themselves in her outer form, though she takes the veil voluntarily.

Additionally, the description of the god's valley in *Till We Have Faces* reads very much like the description of the true Narnia in *The Last Battle*. Certainly the influence of the Great Knock, Lewis' tutor, who marshaled his abilities in reason, is clearly present in the logic of both *The Lion, the Witch and the Wardrobe*, in which Peter and Susan worry over Lucy's mental state, and *Till We Have Faces*, in which Orual seeks an explanation for Psyche's condition. This logic—whether Psyche, like Lucy, is known for lying—fails to govern Orual's attempts both to fathom who Psyche's lover is and then to win Psyche's obedience. As a result of this failure, the well-known "trichotomy" options presented by Lewis in *Mere Christianity* that Christ is either a liar, a lunatic, or the Son of God, are much like the choices Orual considers for the identity of Psyche's husband: he is either a robber, a murderer, or a god. Since Orual is unwilling to accept Psyche as truthful, it is completely unthinkable for Psyche to remain with either a robber or a murderer. In another reference, we have the words of the Ungit priest in *Till We Have Faces* about the nature of "holy wisdom ... not clear and thin like water, but thick and dark like blood"[6] echoing Lewis's description of kinds of religion [as being "thick" and "clear"] in his essay "Christian Apologetics."[7] Kelli Brew notes the similarities in the figurative masking of the characters in *That Hideous Strength* with Orual's literal veiling of herself as a power play in *Till We Have Faces*.[8] In these limited ways, and in others, *Till We Have Faces* draws together many threads of Lewis's ideas and beliefs more explicitly stated in other works. In the novel, however, he weaves them naturally into the story, not as individual ideas, but as ideas in action. One is encouraged then to see the ideas as a natural part of humanity's thinking, rather like vocabulary words linked together into literature. The reader's attention is drawn to few of these ideas in isolation, but an awareness of their presence in other works is richly rewarded.

THE MYTH AND C. S. LEWIS

Throughout *Surprised by Joy*, Lewis returns repeatedly to the role that myths played in his life, which were tied to his love of literature, music, and ultimately of God, for it was through myth that he first felt the stab of Joy, which he found had its source in God. Lewis explains in his autobiography that he "desired with almost sickening intensity something never to be described ... and then ... [I] found myself at the very same moment already falling out of that desire and wishing I were back in it."[9] He also recounts the effects an encounter with "northernness" and Teutonic myth had on him in *Surprised by Joy*:

the memory of Joy itself, the knowledge that I had once had what I now lacked for years, that I was returning at last from exile and desert lands to my own country; and the distance of the Twilight of the Gods and the distance of my own past Joy, both unattainable, flowed together into a single, unendurable sense of desire and loss. . . . And at once I knew (with fatal knowledge) that to 'have it again' was the supreme and only important object of desire.[10]

For Lewis, he felt an ecstasy in which there "were moments when you were too happy to speak, when the gods and heroes rioted through your head, when satyrs danced and Maenads roared on the mountains, when Brynhild and Sieglinde, Deirdre, Maeve and Helen were all about you, till sometimes you felt that it might break you with mere richness."[11] Lewis's own words communicate the power that myth had over him, and so it is no surprise that he would see myth as a powerful vehicle for his own fiction. It was in myth that Lewis found the signpost to Christianity, seeing in the pagan stories the shadow of the true myth of Christianity, or as Lewis says, "The real clue had been put into my hand by that hard-boiled Atheist when he said, 'Rum thing, all that about the Dying God. Seems to have really happened once.'"[12] A deep and moving love of the "copy" had made him consider it worthwhile to seek out the "original."

This lifelong love of myth was the perfect impetus for Lewis's own fiction. While many people consider a myth to be merely a grown-up fairy tale, Lewis was careful in *An Experiment in Criticism* to define the genre. Some of the characteristics of myth, Lewis said, are these: (1) it is greater than the vehicle that tells it; (2) it has little reliance on the common literary elements tools such as suspense or surprise; (3) it usually does not absorb the reader into its world—the reader is more likely to feel "sorry for all men rather than vividly sympathetic with" the character in question; (4) it is always fantasy with reliance on the "preternatural"; (5) myth is always sobering, never comic in the sense of amusing; (6) and true myth is always captivating and "awe-inspiring," with a "numinous" quality.[13] The power of myth is such that the quality of the vehicle, whether in verse or prose, rarely matters. The subject is the overarching concern of the reader. And it is this power that Lewis unleashes on the reader in the novel *Till We Have Faces*.

THE MYTH: THEN AND NOW

The changes in the myth of Cupid and Psyche that Lewis made make *Till We Have Faces* even more attractive. In the original version by Apuleius, a royal couple find themselves in conflict with the gods because the people have chosen to worship their beautiful daughter Psyche rather than Aphrodite.

The Greek and Roman gods were notoriously fickle and vindictive, so Apollo commands that Psyche be sacrificed to a dragon. Her father obeys. However, the scorned Aphrodite has already decided on a worse punishment for Psyche: making her fall madly in love with the worst man possible. Her son Cupid is given the assignment. But, Cupid falls in love with Psyche himself and has her carried off to his secret valley where he lives with her as husband but prohibits her seeing his face. Lonely for her family, Psyche asks that her sisters be allowed to visit her. Against his better judgment, Cupid agrees. Overcome by jealousy, the two sisters plot to ruin Psyche by enticing her to disobey her husband and see his face. Psyche agrees to their plan, wakes Cupid accidentally, and is punished for her disobedience by being exiled. Psyche is prevented from committing suicide and then falls into the clutches of Aphrodite, who gives her impossible jobs to do, a common event in Greek myth. However, through the help of animals and even other gods, Psyche fulfills all the tasks save one. Here the myth overlaps that of Pandora, for Psyche cannot resist the urge to look into the box containing Persephone's beauty. Cupid intercedes on Psyche's behalf with Zeus, who agrees to their marriage and makes Psyche into the goddess men had already taken her for. They do indeed live happily ever after and bear a child called Pleasure. So goes the original myth.

Lewis however, objected to one key element in the story—the fact that Psyche's sisters could see her palace. Considering Apuleius to be a relater of the tale, not the author, Lewis could see no reason that he could not change the story to suit his purposes. So, Lewis created a myth in which only one of the sisters confronts Psyche about her situation. And that confrontation takes place based on belief, not sight. Orual must choose to believe both Psyche and her physical appearance or to consider her mad or deceived. Thus, Lewis complicates the original myth by adding the theme of belief to the already-present themes of jealousy and obedience.

In addition, Lewis adds another twist to the tale: the storyteller is the protagonist or main character and relates the tale in first person. It would seem then, that the narrator could be trusted by the reader. After all, who better to know the narrator than the narrator herself? However, Orual faces the same challenge of King Oedipus to know thyself, and her narrative begins with one knowledge of herself and ends with quite another.

THE MYTH RETOLD

Lewis changed the bones of the original myth in significant ways. Thus, his subtitle "*A Myth Retold*," is a significant signal about what the reader can expect. The novel is not a mere repetition of the myth, but a retelling, an amended version which Lewis thought brought it much closer to meeting the characteristics of true myth. In this revision, Lewis adds characters, changes motives, and fleshes out the setting in order to deepen the truth of the story and to make the novel more realistic for his tastes. There are attributes of the mythic in the novel, such as the Westwind's ability to carry off Psyche without unlocking her chains, but there are common human elements in the story, such as the frictions of an ordinary household, which would not have been a part of Greek myth. By foregrounding the mortals in their interactions with the gods rather than the gods' interactions with the mortals, Lewis creates a realistic portrayal that resonates more closely with his readers than traditional myth does. After all, how many of us can relate better to a jealous sibling than to the labors of Hercules?

The Characters, Or Who Do They Think They Are?

The story opens with the tirade of an angry queen, the author of a complaint against the gods. She vows to set down her case against them and to demand an answer from them. Orual is the eldest daughter of King Trom of Glome, a small kingdom in dire need of royal sons. Orual and her sister, Redival, are having their heads shaved because their mother has died. Through the comments of the servants, the reader learns of Orual's ugliness; this misfortune will cloud all of her actions and color her behavior in ways she cannot imagine. Upon the King's remarriage, Orual gains the love of her life, a beautiful half-sister named Psyche, so beautiful that the people will consider her a goddess and wreak havoc in the kingdom. Her mother dies in childbirth and Psyche becomes the especial charge of Orual, who invests every ounce of herself into the child, lavishing upon her the Need-love generated in large part by the abuse heaped on her by her selfish father who is not above adding physical harm to emotional harm. The birth of yet another daughter thwarts Trom's plans for the kingdom and sets the stage for civil unrest and religious tragedy. Alienated by Orual's obsession with Psyche, Redival falls under the influence of Batta, a self-serving opportunistic nurse who tells tales to the king and creates crises in the palace.

Against the backdrop of this dysfunctional family, Lewis sets the Fox, a captured Greek slave brought to the palace as a tutor for the king's daughters. The Fox introduces the learning and rational thinking of the Greeks into a kingdom wrapped in traditional worship of the fertility goddess, Ungit. Bardia is another positive addition to the novel, serving as a bridge between the world of men and Orual's world. Sympathetic to the plight of Psyche, Bardia risks his life to allow the sisters a chance of farewell and then offers Orual an outlet for her overwhelming sorrow in teaching her swordsmanship. He also serves as a foil to the Fox upon the discovery of Psyche in her valley, instantly according the unusual circumstances to her divinity rather than rationalizing them away as the Fox does. Through the "Grandfather" Fox and the "Ally" Bardia, Orual is given not only opposing beliefs to choose from but also the emotional support she needs.

Though Orual is the main character, the narrator, and perhaps the mirror of the reader, she would be nothing without Psyche. For Psyche is Orual's foil—beautiful, not ugly, and willing to accept the work of the gods in her life, even in her death. Psyche's self-sacrificing actions, her Gift-love on behalf of the people, during a plague contrast with Orual's consuming Need-love. The remedy to this imbalance is the ultimate focus of the novel. And it is portraying the transformation of Orual into Psyche, which is a way of showing a myth turning into a reality, which is Lewis's purpose.

CHARACTERS OF MYTHIC PROPORTIONS

The Greeks and the Romans held the same general panoply of gods; they merely called them by different names. Other cultures also had similar gods, but with different names. What follows is a brief explanation of the similar names of gods and goddesses Lewis used in his novel, with some relevant details of their mythic identities.

Figures from Myth

The Roman Cupid/Greek Eros is the son of Venus/Aphrodite and Mercury, the lad of love who falls in love with Psyche and condemns Orual's unbelief. Psyche is the Greek word for "breath or soul." Venus/Aphrodite is the goddess of love and beauty and the mother of Cupid/Eros, who assigns Psyche her tasks while in exile. Zephyr or Westwind is the son of Aeolus and Aurora, a soft and gentle wind and the rescuer of Psyche.

Figures from Legend

Iphigenia is the daughter of Agamemnon and Clytemnestra. To placate Artemis (Diana, goddess of the hunt), Agamemnon agrees to sacrifice the most beautiful thing to come into his life in a year. Unfortunately this thing is his infant daughter. He puts off the sacrifice as long as possible, but as the fleet leaves for the Trojan War, he prepares to sacrifice her. Artemis sweeps Iphegenia away just in time, substituting a deer in her place. Here is Psyche's transformation from sacrificed to saved.

Antigone is the daughter of Oedipus and his mother, Jocasta. Upon Oedipus' exile, Creon takes the throne of Thebes. When Oedipus's sons rebel against the wicked king, they are killed, and Creon declares they must remain unburied. Antigone defies Creon's edict and buries her brothers. She is caught by Creon and walled up in a cave to die. Orual's dilemma arises because of her resentment at being unable to replace her sister as Iphegenia. Instead, she is left with the role of Antigone, rescuing the bones of her sister and giving them a decent burial. And, like Antigone, Orual finds herself in a pillar-room of death, learning that her own death as well as Psyche's is also demanded.

THE CONFLICT IN LEWIS'S RETOLD MYTH

A story without conflict would be only a series of events and not very compelling reading. Lewis presents many conflicts in *Till We Have Faces*, some abstract and some concrete. It is these varied oppositions that make the novel worth rereading, for nuances of meaning emerge upon each repetition. Critics have spent vast amounts of space detailing and discussing these conflicts. Peter Schakel writes a book-length analysis of the conflict between reason and imagination.[14] The influence of the Greek emphasis on rational analysis is present most directly in the character of the Fox, named for his wily ability to manage people as well as philosophy. But undoubtedly, the Great Knock loomed large over Lewis's shoulder as he penned the novel. Himself a student of reason, especially in matters of religion, Lewis pits the Fox against the Priest of the House of Ungit both philosophically as well as actually. When attempting to save Psyche's life, the Fox argues eloquently against the mysticism of the worship of Ungit, especially the inconsistency of the explanation of who exactly Ungit and her son the Shadowbrute are, and how the Accursed can be so titled and yet be mandated to be a perfect sacrifice. But words are powerless against the priest who parries each of the Fox's rational thrusts with an exposition on the nature of religious belief. And indeed, the close of the novel sides with the priest: compared to an actual experience with divinity all else is "only words, words; to be led out to battle against other words."[15]

The Fox loses this battle and the priest sways the king's will to sacrifice his daughter (he is not-so-secretly relieved that he himself is spared). Orual finds herself in a similar conflict of religious devotion. Rather than prevailing upon Psyche to despair at her sentence, Orual is crushed to find that her sister is at peace, anticipating the fulfillment of her lifelong *Sehnsucht:* "The colour and the smell, and looking across at the Grey Mountain. . . . And because it was so beautiful, it set me longing, always longing. Somewhere else there must be more of it. Everything seemed to be saying, 'Psyche come!'"[16] Here is Orual's rationalism, even though based on mysticism, pitted against imagination and a realization that there is more to this life, as Lewis writes in *Mere Christianity,*

"If I find in myself a desire which no experience in this world can satisfy; the most probable explanation is that I was made for another world."[17] Psyche has that ability to meet death serenely, even eagerly, because she is convinced of another dimension to herself and this world. To find any peace in her own life, Orual must come to the same conclusion.

Then there is the conflict of Need-love versus Gift-Love. Orual's grasping, devouring, need for the unreserved affection of those around her drives all of her actions. Suffering a lack of natural affection in her life, Orual latches, one could almost say "leeches," onto Psyche wishing a connection to the child that encompasses all the ones possible. Psyche's refusal to stay bound by Orual's need for her, and her attempt to convince Orual of the rightness of the sacrifice, set Orual's journey of self-discovery into motion. Fueled by rejection by the object of her love, Orual is utterly unable to accept the reality of Psyche's marriage. Determined that she knows best, Orual plots to restore Psyche to her rightful affection for Orual, if not to her right mind. Contrasted with this destructive Need-love is the Gift-love of Psyche who recognizes her obligations to her husband, but willingly pays the price of disobedience in order to prevent Orual's threatened suicide. Considering the cost to Orual greater than the cost to herself, Psyche suffers exile from all she loves. Without a recognition of her selfish Need-love, Orual is condemned to wander herself, always farther from those she loves though she has them near at hand.

At the heart of Orual's journey and Lewis's alteration of the myth is another conflict: that of faith and sight. Educated by the Stoic Fox, whose philosophy relies on experience, Orual lacks the recognition of the divine nature of life. Psyche's willingness to experience that divine aspect saves her life and ultimately makes real the divinity assigned to her by the Glomish populace. Presented with the fact of Psyche's continued existence and even good health, Orual must choose whether to believe her sister's reality or be deceived by her own senses. Food and water outweigh radiant body and soul, and Orual rejects the evidence in front of her. Psyche's ragged clothes cannot cover her joyful being, but they can and do cover Orual's ability to see the alternate reality of Psyche's experience. Betraying that vision as well as their relationship, Orual threatens to destroy herself rather than see Psyche continue to thrive. But that alternate reality cannot be completely denied, and Orual is given a glimpse of the god's palace. Now she must reject her own senses as well as that of her sister. Without the dynamic of faith in her life, Orual blames the gods, the authors of that other reality that she herself is too willingly blind to see. Clinging to her reason, Orual spends years further cementing the scales of unbelief on her eyes. Her assumption of the veil is only the physical manifestation of her unwillingness to face the truth. Ironically, manipulating the senses of her subjects gives her the power she is unwilling to grant to the gods.

THE RESOLUTION IN LEWIS'S RETOLD MYTH

Resolving conflict often is a lengthy process that depends on the willingness of the parties to recognize their faults and readjust their positions. Orual's conflict with those she loves and the gods is no exception. Working through the issues is not only the substance of the novel: it is Orual's lifelong journey from self-knowledge, to renunciation, to transformation. These stages are emphasized below by key statements in the novel.

Self-Knowledge: "You, Woman, Shall Know Yourself and Your Work. You Also Shall Be Psyche"[18]

Here is the god's response to Orual after instigating Psyche's disobedience, and the words act as a sentence of judgment upon her. Borne out over the many years of Part One of the novel and culminating in Part Two, Orual learns first to know herself. Drawing upon the Greek mantra to "know yourself," Lewis's novel is set up as the self-discovery of the main character. Though Orual herself sets the book up as a complaint before the gods, she nevertheless structures it as an autobiography; introducing it is "I am old now," but beginning the account in the past with "the day my mother died and they cut off my hair, as the custom is."[19] Thus, as she writes, she records the historical details of her life and of her family and of the kingdom of Glome, but in the recording of these details, she is constantly looking for evidence against the gods. However, as Peter Schakel notes, in the final reading of her complaint before the judge, Orual judges herself, and finds that the complaint is itself the answer to itself.[20] So in this effort to muster evidence against the gods, Orual discovers instead evidence against herself and warns the reader that doing so, "the very writing itself," began her process of learning "much more than I did about the woman who wrote it [Part One]."[21]

Along the way Orual identifies herself in two significant ways: as Queen and as Ungit. As Queen, Orual gains power over her dying father and finds compensation for her ugliness both behind the veil and through the ruling of her people. She profits from the upbringing and continued advice of the Fox and improves Glome's economy, political standing, and infrastructure. But as Queen, Orual also finds additional means to subvert the process of learning to know herself. Throwing herself into her work in order to avoid the thought of Psyche and her own encounter with the god, Orual does wrong to others through her own lack of understanding the proper characteristics of agape love. Queenship power gives her not only the opportunity but also the right to order the lives of those around her, and the consuming love evidenced first with Psyche multiplies itself.

But Orual also learns to know her work. She certainly learns to know the futility of Queenship. Though she initially believes that being ruler will bring her fulfillment, she soon discovers that in spite of her military prowess, she is not "one of the boys"; indeed their behavior often disgusts her. She finds herself set apart by sex as well as by position. As Queen, she judges between the people of Glome, negotiates with neighboring lands, and tries to squelch the memory of days gone by. She sends Redival away in a political matchmaking effort, which though successful, still leaves Orual alone of her family still in Glome. She expends considerable effort to remove the memory of Psyche, alienating herself further from the past. She keeps the Fox near her, but the secret of Psyche and her palace remains a breach in their relationship. Bardia is a futile effort to create a pseudo-family, for though she can command his allegiance, she cannot command his affection, and at the end of the day, as long a day as possible, Bardia returns to his home, leaving Orual isolated in the palace. Power is not the answer to a misunderstood love; it merely compounds the effects.

As Ungit, a recognition made late in Orual's life and in the story, Orual devours those devoted to her. Orual consumes those around her, much like she consumed Psyche. The freed Fox is subtly pressured to remain in Glome, his life constrained by service to the Queen. She appropriates the Fox's wisdom for her own, refusing to recognize that she has the power to end his captivity in reality, not just in words. Though she grants him his freedom, she binds him to her in ways more unbreakable than shackles had ever been. Though he continues the filial love toward Orual, which was developed from the beginning, she does not see that her demands upon him exhaust him physically and her deception over Psyche denies him a true relationship with her emotionally. Her father may have threatened to send the Fox to the mines, but Orual is the one who truly enslaves him.

Bardia is another case illustrating the devouring nature of Ungit. Hidden behind her veil, Orual sees Bardia in another light. She consumes him physically, keeping him at the palace and on military endeavors for extended periods of time unnecessarily. Jealous of his wife, she binds Bardia to her through manly activities and patriotic fervor. In doing so she denies him the sanctuary of his home, replacing it with a false one of her royal presence. Though Ungit demands sacrifices of the Glomish people, she does so in order to preserve society and maintain order, as evidenced by the need to sacrifice Psyche in order to return the land to economic plenty. Orual, on the other hand, deprives Bardia and Ansit of the home life that Ungit blessed. In doing so, Orual manifests a greater measure of devouring than evidenced in even her relationship with Psyche. Of course, the recognition of Ungit behavior, which is crucial to Orual's reformation, is her obsessive love for Psyche. The last comfort taken from Orual even after she despises herself as Ungit is that she did not love Psyche truly. The first chronological evidence of her lack of understanding of love is the last evidence in the lifelong case against her. As Ungit, Orual reveals herself to be more than ugly and faceless; she cannot hide the consuming nature that her improper understanding of love generates. The reader is presented with one woman's journey toward self-knowledge and is invited to think of the process as being active in the reader's life as well.

And that case is also Orual's work. Her complaint is her work, the work of her hands as well as her life. It is a record of her labors, corresponding to that of Psyche in exile, the separating of word and action, the keeping of truth and dismissal of lies. But Orual does not achieve any more success with her bookwork than she does with her work as Queen. Yes, she sets down a record accurately, as far as she can tell. But without self-knowledge, it is an impossible task, as impossible a task as that of Psyche's sifting of seeds without help from the ants. This failure is acknowledged by Orual, finally, after she reads her complaint before the judge. The facts she set down do not turn out to be the truth. Self-deception is a fruit of selfish love, and when Orual confronts the deception, she is ready to face the false love. Ironically, it is in the world of "seeings" that Orual recognizes reality, the reality that her efforts as Queen and as writer have functioned to fulfill what Carnell calls her "vocation."[22] Orual's fanatical determination to recover Psyche's body from the tree of sacrifice works itself out as destruction, not salvation, both of Psyche and Orual herself. But that same destruction is the vehicle for Orual to aid Psyche in fulfilling her tasks, which in turn lead to the transformation of Orual into Psyche, just as the god ordained. This circular pattern, seen in the spiritual terms which "vocation" rather than "work" indicates, is the central truth of Lewis's work.

Renunciation: "Die Before You Die. There's No Chance After"[23]

Orual is told in her despairing attempt to rectify her faults by her own hand. Having just come from the House of Ungit and witnessed for yet another time the birth of the new year, Orual confronts the other end of life: death. In yet another "seeing" she is accosted by her father, told to leave off her veil, and taken to the Pillar Room. Here Orual is told to dig up the floor. When the hole is large enough, her father tells her to fling herself down; unwilling, she is forced to jump when he takes her hand. In yet another Pillar Room, of dirt this time, she is forced to dig again and to jump again. Each level of falling leads her into a deeper and deeper tomblike hole. The third and final Pillar Room is made of rock and actually closes in upon them. Here her father asks her, "Who is Ungit?" and leads her to the very mirror she dreaded in life.[24] Her reply, "I am Ungit," is the ending of the vision and the beginning of the re-vision.[25] Recognizing the devouring nature of her being, Orual seeks to destroy the ugliness she was previously content to veil by killing herself. Indeed, she wears no veil whatsoever as she makes her way to the Shennit. This barefaced action corresponds to the first true vision she has of herself. However, at the river she is prevented from suicide by the voice of the god. In answer to the command, she asks, "Lord, who are you?"[26] That, of course, is not the issue. And she gets no answer; instead she is told that Ungit is in the Deadlands as well and there is no escape in destroying her body.

Her reply, "Lord, I am Ungit,"[27] is, however, a step in the right direction, for it shows that she is willing to admit to a higher power her true nature. But admission is as powerless as mere self-knowledge in bringing about change. To change she must "die before [she] die[s]."[28] As a result of this second encounter with the god, Orual seeks to reform her nature; she determines to be the best ruler and person possible. But self-reformation is as impossible as committing suicide had been. Both are equally inaccessible to her. As with the admission of her true nature, Orual is accurate in her assessment of the necessary course of action; she does need a changed self. But her efforts to change must come about through the renunciation of her deceptive comfort that at least she had loved Psyche well. Until she properly understands the scope of her faulty and damaging love, in effect recognizing it for the death, not life, it brought to those in its path, Orual is left with an empty life and nothing to gain by death.

Transformation: "You Also Are Psyche"[29]

Orual's efforts to rid herself of the memory of the broken relationship with Psyche range from the physical walling up of the castle well to the enshrinement of Psyche's belongings. More importantly, she seeks refuge from memory in her work as Queen. But here, unknown to her, is the first stage of her transformation, for she fulfills aspects of the tasks assigned to Psyche and provides for Psyche's success, which in turn bring about the ultimate success of Orual herself. Only upon recognition of her role in Psyche's punishment is Orual finally able to understand her Ungit-like treatment of this beloved sister. And only through that understanding is the transformation possible. And it is this transformation—Orual into Psyche—that comes true, foretold by the god in the moment of Orual's greatest failing. It is the changing of blindness into sight, for Orual, when transformed into Psyche, has perfect vision of the god's palace and a true recognition of Psyche's position and worth. When Orual is prepared to admit Psyche's god nature and the lack of it in herself, she is able to accept Psyche's gift of beauty, which results in her transformation.

But Orual is also transformed from faceless Ungit, ugly and veiled from men's sight, consuming those nearest to her, into one with a face, finally capable of facing the truth about herself and the reality of the gods and their dealings with her. In the lowest Pillar Room, Orual's mirror reveals more than her ugliness. It confronts her with reality without which she can never hope to change. She moves from self-deception to self-knowledge. She becomes Psyche, not just does the tasks of Psyche, the work of Psyche, but becomes the essence of Psyche who is already joined unto the god, loved by him, and known by him. And when that transformation takes place, Orual's work is finished. She has little time left to add to her book, that work which culminates with a true recognition of the reality of God, the one who is "yourself the answer."[30] Ultimately, her own transformation coincides with the transformation of her view of the gods and their works in her life. She moves from the accusation in Part One that the gods give no answer in to a recognition in Part Two that they are the answer. Through this experience she becomes the essence of her epitaph: "The most wise, just, valiant, fortunate and merciful of all the princes known in our parts of the world."[31] You also shall be Psyche is now fulfilled. The prophecy comes true; Orual is Psyche in body and soul as well as in her people's opinions. A remarkable transformation indeed.

THE MYTH DEMYSTIFIED

Lewis considered *Till We Have Faces* to be his best work, though few others, now or then, have shared his judgment. But a significant and growing body of criticism now exists offering a range of comments on this last novel of Lewis's. A brief survey of these critiques reveals that Lewis drew upon all his knowledge and well-honed skills to fashion his book. Philosophically, the idea of Orual's ugliness is more than a mere plot detail. Carla Arnell argues that it is more than a mere representation of the state of her soul. Instead, the physical differences between Orual and Psyche and even between Orual and Redival point up the more important idea of justice; people do not experience life in the same circumstances.[32] Orual's sense of justice, perhaps accounted for by the terrible treatment at her father's hands, a topic thoroughly discussed by Georgiana L. Williams, nevertheless manifests itself in her treatment of others, Bardia in particular.[33] Priding herself on her work as judge of her people, she violates the very sense of right behavior toward her devoted subject, depriving him of his rest and family. In her transformation from Orual to Psyche, Orual takes upon herself the queenship of Glome, a minor triumph over her father, which is undermined by his appearance in one of her "seeings." Michael Anastasi develops the idea that Lewis is presenting a model for the Christian who is also undergoing a transformation into a "whole" person by becoming like

Christ.[34] For Orual to become the ruler of a prosperous kingdom at rest, she must arrive at that state within herself. And as Ralph Wood notes, Orual is unable to be at peace herself until her "love life" is properly ordered.[35] Orual declares herself that her love for Psyche is not undone, but that she now loves Psyche properly, unlike the devouring love of their earlier lives. And it is at that point that Orual finds herself transformed into Psyche and thus into the same relationship with the god. Augustine's idea that lesser goods must be loved less than greater goods holds true in Orual's life, a fact that Thomas Watson more fully develops in his discussion of the Fox's odd remark that even Psyche was born into the house of Ungit.[36] The identification of both sisters with Ungit and then their identification with the god finds its roots in Augustine as well.

This idea of a hierarchy of love is present in Gwyneth Hood's work as she addresses the relationship between loving and hating in the novel, a relationship that clouds the mind and perception of Orual.[37] The priest's words that "nothing that is said clearly can be said truly about them [the gods]"[38] point up the fact that human nature is naturally deficient in understanding the divine, but those who surrender themselves to improper emotions create an almost insurmountable barrier to true understanding, one that will take divine intervention to tear down. Nancy-Lou Patterson develops the idea of the distance between the human and the divine through a discussion of the physical characteristics of Ungit, her house, and the rituals associated with the goddess.[39]

And Ungit should be a matter of discussion, for if there were a power behind the throne, it would be the superstitious reality of Ungit, the ugly fertility goddess that demands human sacrifice. Though the physical description of Ungit is a shapeless, faceless stone, the living essence of her is the priest who links the human with the divine. David Landrum explores the three priests who perform this function as well as instruct the reader about the nature of the divine, mysterious, and holy—the old priest who is unafraid of King Trom; the priest Arnom who though influenced by the Greek ways of Orual even to the extent of erecting a beautiful statue of Ungit nevertheless guides the people in the old ways; and the priest of Essur whose story of Psyche is the catalyst for Orual's writing of the complaint.[40] Though Arnom seems to have changed the way of Ungit, he yet serves to unite Orual and the divine as her recognition of herself as Ungit occurs in a "seeing," which happens on the heels of the rite of the Year's birth. This crucial recognition of her devouring nature is the first step in her transformation. Kathryn Lindskoog offers some practical understanding of Ungit by exploring the historical nature of fertility goddesses as well as the meaning of the name. She also offers insight into the reason for the excavation of the Pillar Room, which leads to Orual's identification of herself as Ungit.[41]

Those interested in the narrative underpinnings of the novel will find several excellent discussions of the structure of the novel. Mara E. Donaldson's article details the significance of the storytelling phenomenon in the novel itself as well as in Lewis's own retelling of the myth.[42] Will and Mimosa Stephenson follow suit and add an inquiry into the significance of Part II as a vehicle for reader introspection concerning the very struggle Orual is undergoing in regard to her affections.[43] Doris T. Myers approaches the novel's details by way of the books which Orual collects during her reign and the accompanying insight that she should have gained based on a reading of them,[44] as well as offers a book-length study looking at the novel from various angles.[45] Ake Bergvall expounds the nature of myth both outside and inside the novel, seeing the characters themselves as living the lives that would become the myth as Lewis retells it.[46]

Though nearly all conceivable topics have been addressed, little has been done with the epigraph: "Love is too young to know what conscience is." This quotation, from Shakespeare's Sonnet 151, appears on the title page underneath the book title and, given Lewis's obvious intention to draw the reader's attention to it, it deserves a closer look. With the book *The Four Loves* following on the heels of *Till We Have Faces,* it seems reasonable to see in the epigraph a glimmer of the analytical approach to love that the treatise makes and which the novel illustrates. In Lewis's *Studies in Words*, he elaborates on the differences between *conscience* and *conscious.* In light of that discussion, it seems to me that the epigraph couples nicely with the god's injunction to Orual: "You, woman, shall know yourself and your work." The root problem in Orual's life is the flawed love that she demonstrates toward those in her life; so much has been established. Combining this flawed love with conscience is a necessary step in Orual's life, since the epigraph states that the love in the novel is not mature and thus is flawed. Lewis's discussion of conscience details two aspects, both of which apply: one is the idea of being aware of one's actions, and the other is the more familiar idea of a moral guide. It is because our conscience knows our actions that we feel guilt or approval about those actions. So the epigraph charges Love with being too young to know both what it is doing and whether what it is doing is good or evil. The god's "sentence" on Orual is to become aware of her actions and then to respond properly to them, a thing she eventually does. Thus, Lewis presents the reader with the fundamental truth of the novel on the title page: Orual possesses a flawed love that offers evidence to condemn her by her own conscience when she matures enough to recognize the truth of herself and her work.

THE MYTH ENDURES

As the fruit of nearly all of Lewis's lifetime of learning and writing, *Till We Have Faces* is a challenging but rewarding novel to read and reread. Lewis wrote in the British edition of the book that one of its themes was "the havoc which a vocation, or even a faith, works on human life."[47] The consequences of both Psyche's devotion to the god of the mountain at the expense of her relationship with Orual, and of Orual's devotion to herself at the expense of her relationship with everyone else, is a sobering warning to contemporary readers who are prone to having such devotions. Balance and proportion in relationships is a struggle common to every reader, and it is that common ground that makes the novel powerful as an indictment against not only Orual but also the reader.

The novel also remains worthwhile reading for its portrayal of a woman with various roles and societal pressures forced upon her. Finding her path through education and self-assertion, Orual could be read as Lewis's offering of a role model. However, it is significant to note that Lewis creates a character who finds that even the ultimate power of queenship is insufficient to bring her fulfillment and peace. Orual bitterly regrets her lack of personal relationships and finds her advancement cuts her off from those who remain after Psyche's departure. Lewis seems to indicate the only true solution to finding rest in a restless world is when Orual and Psyche are made one with each other and with the god.

MYTH AND REALITY

Orual ends the first part of her tale with the charge that the gods will condemn themselves in the minds of the people by not answering her accusation. It little matters to Orual what punishment they use on her; her goal is to discredit them. She accuses them of setting her a riddle by letting her see the glimpse of the palace and then withdrawing that sight and the accompanying ability to perceive other realities. Like Oedipus, Orual accuses the gods of trapping her in circumstances beyond her control, then judging her unfairly for her reactions. Like Oedipus, she must come to a knowledge of herself before she can unravel the circumstances of her life and loves. But unlike Oedipus, she comes to see that the answer is not in her power as Queen or even as a god-figure, Ungit.

Orual's answer lies in the god, which she mistrusted and caused others to betray. The answer to Orual's struggle to have a proper love is in the author of love, the figure of Cupid and Psyche's sacred lover in the novel. It is he who prophesies her transformation and ultimate reconciliation with Psyche by being made Psyche herself. And it is he who pronounces the truth: Orual is Psyche but more than being merely physically Psyche, Orual is granted the relationship which Psyche has with the god himself. Orual's veiled face is in stark contrast to the bare face of the god before whom no answer is necessary, no question is appropriate. She meets that power face to face only when she lays aside her own veil, the veil of self-deception and refuge from the truth. The lasting power of Lewis's novel lies perhaps not in its skillful telling and complex thematic material, but in its illustration of pure and selfless relationships with family and divinity as offering the answers to the most central questions of life.

NOTES

1. Walter Hooper, *C. S. Lewis: Companion & Guide* (San Francisco, CA: Harper, 1996), 77.

2. Ibid., 243–244.

3. C. S. Lewis, *All My Road Before Me*, ed. Walter Hooper (San Diego, CA: Harcourt, 1991), 142.

4. Ibid., 266.

5. Hooper, *Companion & Guide*, 246–247.

6. C. S. Lewis, *Till We Have Faces* (Orlando, FL: Harcourt, 1984), 50.

7. C. S. Lewis, "Christian Apologetics," in *God in the Dock*, ed. Walter Hooper (Grand Rapids, MI: Eerdmans, 1970), 102.

8. Kelli Brew, "Facing the Truth on the Road to Salvation: An Analysis of *That Hideous Strength* and *Till We Have Faces*," *The Lamp-Post of the Southern California C. S. Lewis Society* 22(1) (1998), 10–12.

9. C. S. Lewis, *Surprised by Joy: The Shape of My Early Life* (New York: Harcourt, 1955), 17.

10. Ibid., 73.

11. Ibid., 118.

12. Ibid., 235.

13. C. S. Lewis, *An Experiment in Criticism* (Cambridge: Cambridge University Press, 1969), 43–44.

14. Peter Schakel, *Reason and Imagination in C. S. Lewis: A Study of Till We Have Faces* (Grand Rapids, MI Eerdmans, 1984), http://www.hope.edu/academic/English/schakel/tillwehavefaces.html/.

15. Lewis, *Till We Have Faces*, 308.

16. Ibid., 74.

17. C. S. Lewis, *Mere Christianity* (Westwood, NJ: Barbour, 1952), 115.

18. Lewis, *Till We Have Faces*, 174.

19. Ibid., 4.

20. Schakel, *Reason and Imagination* (1984).

21. Lewis, *Till We Have Faces*, 253.

22. Corbin Scott Carnell, *Bright Shadow of Reality: Spiritual Longing in C. S. Lewis* (Grand Rapids, MI: Eerdmans, 1974), 111.

23. Lewis, *Till We Have Faces*, 279.

24. Ibid., 276.

25. Ibid.

26. Ibid., 279.

27. Ibid.

28. Ibid.

29. Ibid., 308

30. Ibid.

31. Ibid.

32. Carla Arnell, "On Beauty, Justice, and the Sublime in C. S. Lewis's *Till We Have Faces*," *Christianity and Literature* 52(1) (2002), 23–33.

33. Georgiana L. Williams, "Till We Have Faces: A Journey of Recovery," *The Lamp-Post of the Southern California C. S. Lewis Society* 18(4) (1994), 5–15.

34. Michael J. Anastasi, "King of Glome: Pater Rex," *The Lamp-Post of the Southern California C. S. Lewis Society* 19(1) (1995), 13–19.

35. Ralph C. Wood, "The Baptized Imagination: C. S. Lewis's Fictional Apologetics," *Christian Century* (August 30) (1995), 812–819.

36. Thomas Ramey Watson, "Enlarging Augustinian Systems: C. S. Lewis' *The Great Divorce* and *Till We Have Faces*," *Renascence* 46(3) (1994), 163–175.

37. Gwyneth Hood, "Husbands and Gods as Shadowbrutes: 'Beauty and the Beast' from Apuleius to C. S. Lewis," *Mythlore* 15(2) (1988), 33–43.

38. Lewis, *Till We Have Faces*, 50.

39. Nancy-Lou Patterson, "The Holy House of Ungit," *Mythlore* 21(4) (1997), 4–15.

40. David Landrum, "Three Bridge-Builders: Priest-Craft in *Till We Have Faces*," *Mythlore* 22(4) (2000), 59–67.

41. Kathryn Lindskoog, "Ungit and Orual: Facts, Mysteries, and Epiphanies," *CSL: The New York C. S. Lewis Society Bulletin* (2000), http://www.lindentree.org/ungit.html.

42. Mara E. Donaldson, "Orual's Story and the Art of Retelling: A Study of *Till We Have Faces*," in *Word and Story in C. S. Lewis*, ed. Peter J. Schakel and Charles A. Huttar (Columbia, MO: University of Missouri Press, 1991), 157–170.

43. Will and Mimosa Stephenson, "Structure and Audience: C. S. Lewis's *Till We Have Faces*," *The Lamp-Post of the Southern California C. S. Lewis Society* 21(1) (1997), 4–10.

44. Doris. T. Myers, "Browsing the Glome Library," *SEVEN: An Anglo-American Literary Review* 19 (2002), 63–76.

45. Cf. Doris T. Myers, *Bareface: A Guide to C. S. Lewis's Last Novel* (Columbia, MO: University of Missouri Press, 2004).

46. Ake Bergvall, "A Myth Retold: C. S. Lewis' *Till We Have Faces*," *Mythlore* (Summer 1984), 5–12, 22.

47. Hooper, *C. S. Lewis: Companion and Guide*, 244.

BIBLIOGRAPHY

Anastasi, Michael, J. "King of Glome: Pater Rex." *The Lamp-Post of the Southern California C. S. Lewis Society* 19(1) (1995), 13–19.

Arnell, Carla. "On Beauty, Justice, and the Sublime in C. S. Lewis's *Till We Have Faces*." *Christianity and Literature* 52(1)(2002), 23–35.

Bartlett, Sally A. "Humanistic Psychology in C. S. Lewis's *Till We Have Faces*: A Feminist Critique." *Studies in the Literary Imagination* 22(2) (1989), 185–198.

Bergvall, Ake. "A Myth Retold: C. S. Lewis' *Till We Have Faces*." *Mythlore* (Summer 1984), 5–12, 22.

Brew, Kelli. "Facing the Truth on the Road to Salvation: An Analysis of *That Hideous Strength* and *Till We Have Faces*." *The Lamp-Post of the Southern California C. S. Lewis Society* 22(1) (1998), 10–12.

Carnell, Corbin Scott. *Bright Shadow of Reality: Spiritual Longing in C. S. Lewis*. Grand Rapids, MI: Eerdmans, 1974.

Donaldson, Mara E. "Orual's Story and the Art of Retelling: A Study of *Till We Have Faces*." In *Word and Story in C. S. Lewis*. Edited by Peter J. Schakel and Charles A. Huttar. Columbia, MO: Univ. of Missouri Press, 1991, 157–170.

Hood, Gwyneth. "Husbands and Gods as Shadowbrutes: 'Beauty and the Beast' from Apuleius to C. S. Lewis." *Mythlore* 15(2) (1988), 33–43.

Hooper, Walter. *C. S. Lewis: Companion & Guide*. San Francisco, CA: Harper, 1996.

Landrum, David. "Three Bridge-Builders: Priest-Craft in *Till We Have Faces*." *Mythlore* 22(4) (2000), 59–67.

Lesfloris, H., and I. C. Storey, Compilers. "An Annotated Bibliography to C. S. Lewis: *Till We Have Faces: A Myth Retold*." At http://www.ivory.trentu.ca/www/cl/Lewis-bib.html.

Lewis. C. S. *All My Road Before Me*. Edited by Walter Hooper. San Diego, CA: Harcourt, 1991.

———. "Christian Apologetics." In *God in the Dock*. Edited by Walter Hooper. Grand Rapids, MI: Eerdmans, 1970, 89–103.

———. *An Experiment in Criticism*. Cambridge: Cambridge University Press, 1969.

———. *Mere Christianity*. Westwood, NJ: Barbour, 1952.

———. *Surprised by Joy: The Shape of My Early Life*. New York: Harcourt, 1955.

———. *Till We Have Faces: A Myth Retold*. Orlando, FL: Harcourt, 1984.

Lindskoog, Kathryn. "Ungit and Orual: Facts, Mysteries, and Epiphanies." *CSL: The New York C. S. Lewis Society Bulletin* (2000). At http://www.lindentree.org/ungit.html.

Myers, Doris T. *Bareface: A Guide to C. S. Lewis's Last Novel.* Columbia, MO: University of Missouri Press, 2004.

———. "Browsing the Glome Library." *An Anglo-American Literary Review* 19 (2002), 63–76.

Patterson, Nancy-Lou. "The Holy House of Ungit." *Mythlore* 21(4) (1997): 4–15.

Schakel, Peter J. *Reason and Imagination in C. S. Lewis: A Study of Till We Have Faces.* Grand Rapids, MI: Eerdmans, 1984.

———. "Seeing and Knowing: The Epistemology of C. S. Lewis's *Till We Have Faces.*" *Seven: An Anglo-American Literary Review* 4 (1983), 84–97.

Smallwood, Julie. *Out From Exile: C. S. Lewis and the Journey to Joy.* A Comparative Study of *Surprised by Joy* and *Till We Have Faces.* M.A. Thesis. Bowling Green State University, Bowling Green, OH. Unpublished. 1999.

Stephenson, Will and Mimosa. "Structure and Audience: C. S. Lewis's *Till We Have Faces.*" *The Lamp-Post of the Southern California C. S. Lewis Society* 21(1) (1998), 4–10.

Watson, Thomas Ramey. "Enlarging Augustinian Systems: C. S. Lewis' *The Great Divorce* and *Till We Have Faces.*" *Renascence* 46(3) (1994), 163–175.

Williams, Georgiana L. "Till We Have Faces: A Journey of Recovery." *The Lamp-Post of the Southern California C.S. Lewis Society* 18(4) (1994), 5–15.

Wood, Ralph C. "The Baptized Imagination: C. S. Lewis' Fictional Apologetics." *Christian Century* (August 30) (1995), 812–819.

9

C. S. Lewis's Short Fiction and Unpublished Works

Katherine Harper

Given C. S. Lewis's stellar reputation in the fields of the essay, literary criticism, poetry, and the novel, readers may find it surprising how seldom he is recognized for his short fiction. Still more surprising is how little he did of this type of work. In fact, Lewis published only two short stories within his lifetime, and those in a minor magazine outside his own country. Several other short tales and fragmentary novels have been published posthumously, and between two and four more previously unpublished works exist within the author's personal papers. Brought to light, these will be welcome additions to the canon.

This is no guarantee, however, that the "new" works will be as compelling as the author's pre-1964 writings. The short stories credited to Lewis to date fall below his usual standard. Without the flexibility to develop settings and personalities gradually over the course of chapters, their author sometimes traded characterization for caricature, and subtle persuasion for sermonizing. The logic for which Lewis was justly famous is not always put to use. Certainly these fictions have their moments, and some of those moments are excellent, but a reader cannot be faulted for expecting better overall from an author of this stature.

Lewis's short stories and posthumous works have a few more-or-less common threads. Yet in their reception by readers, at least, they have proven to be anything but common works.

FORMS OF THINGS KNOWN: TWO STORIES

"The Shoddy Lands" and "Ministering Angels," the only short stories published during Lewis's lifetime, first appeared in the mid-1950s in a digest-sized American pulp, *The Magazine of Fantasy and Science Fiction.* Both were subsequently anthologized in the magazine's annual "Best Of" collections and later in *Of Other Worlds* (1966) and *The Dark Tower and Other Stories* (1977).

Where some authors concentrate their descriptive powers on the appearances and personalities of their human characters, Lewis's particular knack was creating multidimensional other worlds. Narnia is such a place; however, because the books that feature it are intended for children, he handles his delineation in almost entirely visual style. In the works for adults, Lewis's descriptions turn sensuous, incorporating flavors, scents, music, and physical sensations outside the realm of human knowledge. When Ransom first begins to explore the floating islands of Perelandra—a deep-space Eden in formative state—he is dazzled by that planet's unfamiliar colors, the textures and luscious tastes of its newly invented fruits, and its masses of flowers whose intoxicating perfume has the ability to transport. Such gorgeous description must have had special poignancy in the shabby, bomb-scarred, and oleomargarine-and-saccharine world of wartime Great Britain. Lewis would limn these lunar cityscapes with equal care in the apologetic, *The Great Divorce* (1945).

Had the plot called for it, "The Shoddy Lands" (*F&SF,* February 1956) might have depicted an equally Lewisian locale. Instead, its narrator finds himself thrust unexpectedly into a world something like a bad impressionist painting, one that frustrates and puzzles him by its lack of detail. The people he encounters there are blurry and featureless. The grass is a fuzzy mass lacking individual blades. However, articles of women's apparel in the shop windows are clearly defined, and these to an unnatural extent. The only identifiable human in this strange world is a too-ideal young woman—one "exactly like the girl in all the advertisements"[1] —but of massive size. The narrator recognizes her as Peggy, the fiancée of the former student with whom he was chatting at the time of his transport. Then he realizes where he must be: inside Peggy's simple mind, where she and the fripperies she longs for are of primary importance and her lack of interest renders everything else indistinct.

This story's setting is only partially a C. S. Lewis creation. He based it on his friend Charles Williams's depiction of the afterlife in *All Hallows' Eve* (1945), in which the victims of a freak airplane crash wander about a spectral London where nothing and no one is distinct. The scene in which Lewis's narrator is surprised to see hats and jewelry with crystal clarity mirrors one midway through the novel where the heroine catches sight of a kitchen item she had longed to buy in life. To her, the item is even more detailed than she remembered it; to the friend with her, who has no such emotional association, it is only a blur. One of Lewis's former pupils wrote to the author's brother that his tutor "had a near-fanatical devotion to Charles Williams, but when Williams wrote a bad book Lewis readily described it as 'bloody awful.'"[2] Lewis liked *All Hallows' Eve* as much as he could any modern-day work. So was this thoroughly negative-toned story a homage to his friend—or a criticism?

The answer appears to be that Lewis was reacting not to a bad book, but to Williams's heroine, a superficial creature who personified his own opinion of half the population. Science fiction author Ursula Le Guin recognized this and wrote, after reading one of the Lewis fiction anthologies, "The spitefulness shown toward women in these tales is remarkable. 'The Shoddy Lands' is as startling in its cruelty as in its originality; it is, on several levels, a truly frightening story."[3] The dull and bovine Peggy is a variant of the "men without chests" Lewis deplored in *The Abolition of Man* (1943) and her world is equally one-dimensional. But the targets of the earlier work are well-educated people who rely on logic to the exclusion of human emotion, beauty, or poetry— that is, who use their brains and their gut instincts, but not the heart that should lie in between. Peggy, by contrast, lacks logic altogether. Aimless and self-absorbed, she is devoid of curiosity about the details of the world around her and, worse still, unaware of her ignorance. The narrator does not try to hide his contempt for her.

"Ministering Angels" (*F&SF,* January 1958) is no kinder to the female sex. In the near future, outlying planets have become long-term destinations for scientists and the occasional hermit. Daily existence on Mars is as lonely and bleak as the landscape itself. The more introverted of the planet's temporary residents are happy, but not the two young technicians from the latest mission (one of whom has already begun making tentative advances toward the other) nor their captain, a newlywed facing the prospect of three years away from a possibly unfaithful bride. Their situation begins to look brighter when a spaceship arrives bearing "comfort women" from the Woman's Higher Aphrodisio-Therapeutic Humane Organization. But the men soon discover that the only volunteers to have responded to WHAT-HO's recruiting pitch are a mannish, highly opinionated intellectual and a Cockney prostitute thirty years past her prime. Horrified by the prospect before them, one of the technicians and two of the new ship's crew sneak back to the spacecraft and blast off for Earth. The remaining men resign themselves moodily to months or years of what they consider to be unbearable company. The exception is the colony's lone contemplative, who thanks God for showing him his true purpose in life: to save the soul of the elderly tart.

As pointed out in its original and anthology introductions, "Ministering Angels" was written in belated response to Dr. Robert S. Richardson's article "The Day After We Land on Mars," published in *The Saturday Review* in late May of 1955. This nonfiction piece pondered what daily life would be like for Earth's first space colonists and surmised that occasional imports of attractive women would be necessary to preserve the sanity of what he presumed would be the all-male work crews. *The Magazine of Fantasy and Science Fiction* invited Dr. Richardson to expand on this notion and published a revised version of his article in December, just about the time Lewis was deciding where to submit "The Shoddy Lands."[4]

"Ministering Angels," like its predecessor, is decidedly misogynistic. As were so many male scholars of his time (and before, and since), Lewis was unconvinced of women's ability to reason. When he came across a woman who proved herself his intellectual equal he either—as in the case of Dorothy L. Sayers—accepted her as one of the boys, or, as with philosopher Elisabeth Anscombe, addressed her quietly and politely and steered their conversations away from subjects she was likely to dominate. Nor did Lewis treat intelligent women fairly in much of his fiction. His most vividly drawn woman characters, such as Orual from *Till We Have Faces* and Jane Studdock in *That Hideous Strength*, are emotion-driven and possessed of a certain naïveté. Characters with brains are more likely to be portrayed unsympathetically. The Thin Woman of "Ministering Angels" speaks in a continuous flow of pseudointellectual jargon and refuses to assume a subservient role in conversation. For all her brainpower, she lacks observation skills, never noticing that the young man she is trying hardest to seduce has no interest at all in women. For this reason, some of Lewis's fans have concluded that he wrote "Ministering Angels" with tongue in cheek. Ursula Le Guin disagreed, stating that as far as his treatment of the polytechnic lecturer was concerned, "However petty, this is hate."[5] Although the Monk's plan for the Fat Woman is admirable, she pointed out, it never occurs to him that her learned companion might also possess a soul.

Lewis's preferred method of delineating characters was to let information trickle out a bit at a time over the course of chapters. A short-story writer does not have this luxury. Most of the men in "Ministering Angels" are named or are at least given a paragraph or two of descriptive background. Lewis does not provide this touch to either of the newcomers: one of the pair is thin, the other very fat; one educated, the other ignorant; and one severely tailored, the other blowzy. Neither is a human being. Nor are they the only characters glossed over. Mars, whose varied environments Lewis described with such relish in *Out of the Silent Planet*, here resembles nothing so much as the Australian outback: flat, drab, arid, and home to vegetation that can be consumed by wildlife but is deadly to humans. After a dozen pages in this literary desert a reader longs for some of the sensual excesses of the book-length science fiction.

TWO "SUBSTANTIAL" FRAGMENTS

Literary and religious scholars have found C. S. Lewis a subject for study since the publication of *The Pilgrim's Regress* in 1933. Those whose interest extends beyond the finished works to the man and his creative process have access to a treasure trove of primary source material at two repositories: the Bodleian Library at Oxford University, Lewis's own choice to house his papers, and the Marion E. Wade Center at Wheaton College in Illinois, home to additional items donated by the author's brother Warnie. In recent years two Lewis scholars have revealed that hidden treasure exists in these archives: a pair of fragmentary works that the estate has yet to release in book form.

Like so many young men just out of school, seventeen-year-old Jack Lewis was intensely romantic, with the difference that his notions of adventure and love came not from Sunday matinees and popular novels, but Wagnerian operas and the great heroic works of literature. Having read and absorbed so many of these, Lewis was certain that he had it in him to create an epic of his own. The result is preserved in sixty-four manuscript pages at the Bodleian. "The Quest of Bleharis" was apparently written when young Lewis was just beginning his private studies under logician William T. Kirkpatrick. By way of introduction he wrote to his friend Arthur Greeves in May 1916 to describe his delight in *Sir Gawain and the Green Knight*, adding, "This letter brings you the first instalment of my romance . . ."[6] For the next five months Lewis provided Greeves with regular chapters of an allegorical epic he sometimes exulted over and at other times dismissed as "dull" or "stodgy." Because the story has yet to be reproduced in full, scholars wishing to learn more must rely on a published account by David C. Downing, whose essays on the science-fiction trilogy can be found elsewhere in the present volumes.

Lewis's first fictional hero is a young man in love with the notion of love, but not its practice. Bleharis is puzzled by his lack of joy at the prospect of marrying his beautiful but distant sweetheart, Alice, and decides to conduct a quest to prove himself worthy of her love. Fascinated by the news that the STRIVER, a miracle-working man—or creature, or spirit—has settled in the rough country far to the north, he decides to set out in search of him. On the first night, as is traditional in such tales, he encounters and must choose between three potential companions: Wan Jadis, a sad and beautiful youth who is on his own quest to find Yesterday; the tense and red-faced Gerce the Desirous, who is in search of Tomorrow; or Hyperites, a voice of calm reason and proponent of the STRIVER. He selects the first of these and sets out with him across a murky swamp. Their small boat founders within sight of their destination and, like the Romantic poet he so resembles, Wan Jadis drowns. Bleharis is saved from the same fate by a rose bush that comes to life in the form of a bound and naked young woman and draws him back to shore.

Downing writes that at this point Lewis seemed uncertain of what to do next. After introducing a character he may have intended to be the story's villain, he dispatched the three remaining men and a comic foil to a far-off city in pursuit of a runaway Alice. He planned eventually to reveal the rose-woman as Bleharis's true love, having written to Greeves with satisfaction that "when the heroine turns up she is in fairly sharp contrast to Alice the Saint."[7] But by October, bogged down in both the convoluted plot and his increasingly more difficult studies, the teenaged romantic gave up his own first quest and never returned to it.

While it is not possible to judge an entire heroic epic using only brief snippets of text, the quotes in Downing's article hint at the scope of Lewis's reading in and out of school. His affection for Thomas Malory's *Le Morte d'Arthur* is evident in his use of that classic work's narrative style; other settings and characters demonstrate his familiarity with Bunyan, Shelley, Samuel Johnson, Chaucer, Cervantes, and the Pearl Poet, among others—and, of course, world myths and Wagnerian opera. "The Quest of Bleharis" appears to demonstrate an insight, depth, and talent well beyond that of a typical seventeen-year-old and should be a valuable source for scholars when published in full.

A second work that "might have been" was incorporated into a multivolume family history begun by Warnie Lewis in the 1930s and donated by him to Wheaton College four decades later. As of 2001, when she paraphrased it for her study *Sleuthing C. S. Lewis*, literary scholar Kathryn Lindskoog was one of the few people outside the family circle to have read it. This 1927 novel in embryo—which she called "The Most Substantial People" after a repeated statement within the text—provides an intriguing glimpse into a single plot idea treated by its author in two very different ways.

The first fragmentary chapter introduces Dr. Easley, an Englishman of Irish parentage. He has worked his way up to a fine medical practice despite having been orphaned young and left to fend for himself by prosperous relations in Belfast. One of these, his cousin Scrabo, writes to him at intervals during their youth and reveals himself to the reader, if not the good-hearted doctor, as thoroughly selfish and insincere. One evening, en route to visit his cousin and aunt for the first time, Dr. Easley is forced into company with a scheming braggart of a businessman who looks and acts exactly as he pictures Scrabo, and who turns out to be one of his friends. For various reasons Lindskoog was unable to quote directly from the "Substantial" manuscript, but she revealed that this chapter is quite humorous and compared its tone to that of an American novel of five years before, *Babbitt*. To judge by her paraphrase, it resembles Sinclair Lewis's overt caricature less than it does a work by Barbara Pym or J. P. Marquand: that is, a skewering of social mores so subtle that a reader not expecting to find satire might overlook it.

All pretense of humor apparently disappears in the novel's second chapter, set some hours after the first. It is based in part on a terrible period in 1923 when Janie Moore's younger brother, a war veteran and physician whom Lewis admired, began suffering from bouts of dementia and eventually died. Arriving at his relatives' home, Dr. Easley finds that his elderly aunt is beginning to go mad, obsessing over thoughts of hell to the extent that she barely sleeps or eats. Her delusions are fostered by the family clergyman, the Reverend Bonner, who is convinced that meditation on the afterlife is the only way to save one's soul. An argument ensues between physician and clergyman over what is best for the old woman. This segues into a long debate on the role played by ethics within pure science or pure religion.

At this point Lewis set his narrative aside and never returned to it, at least not directly. Lindskoog notes a resemblance between Hughie McClinnichan, the sly businessman Dr. Easley meets on his way to Belfast, and the *Great Divorce* spirit whose determination to pocket a golden apple overcomes the seeming impossibility of his picking one up. As described, Dr. Easley's conversations with the Reverend Bonner—a man who believes that mental cruelty is justified, even proper, if it brings about spiritual salvation—clearly foreshadow Ransom's philosophical debates with the Un-Man in *Perelandra*. Given the wide spectrum of Lewis's reading, however, they may also echo Humphrey Van Weyden's talks with the logical madman Wolf Larsen in Jack London's *The Sea-Wolf* (1904).

These two fragments are apparently not the only unknown Lewis writings still to come. Warnie Lewis wrote in his introduction to a collection of his brother's letters that "in 1912, [Jack] had produced a complete novel, a creditable performance for a boy not yet thirteen; and the interesting thing to note is that this novel, like the sequel to it that followed soon after, revolved entirely around politics."[8] He was not speaking of the brothers' Boxen tales, which have since been collected. Rather, these book-length works were the result of the boy Lewis's conviction "that grown-up conversation and politics were one and the same thing; and that everything he wrote must therefore be given a political framework."[9] On the one hand, these sound very dry; on the other, an early twentieth-century Belfast boy's observations could shed new light on the turbulent politics of the day. The Lewis brothers squirreled away every scrap of their personal writings, so it seems safe to hope that these two juvenile novels will someday be located and published, perhaps accompanied by the fragmentary texts of "The Quest of Bleharis" and "The Most Substantial People."

APRÉS LEWIS . . .

Clive Staples Lewis died in November of 1963. A year and a half later, his literary executor, Walter Hooper, contributed an official bibliography of the author's works to the festschrift *Light on C. S. Lewis*. At that time, the only short stories listed were the two pulp science fiction tales described above. But less than a year after *Light*, the first U.K. edition of a Hooper-edited collection called *Of Other Worlds* introduced a new Lewis story, "Forms of Things Unknown," and fragments from a work of historical fiction, "After Ten Years." In 1977, amid much critical buzz, another collection, *The Dark Tower and Other Stories*, brought to light a third undocumented tale, "The Man Born Blind," as well as the collection's lead novella, *The Dark Tower*, which scandalized Lewis's fans with its scenes of sadism and sexuality.

It was at this point that controversy began to creep into the previously serene field of Lewis studies. Shortly after *The Dark Tower*'s publication, a teacher and literary scholar from Orange, California, the aforementioned Kathryn Lindskoog, noticed discrepancies between the historical record and claims laid out for the new works' existence. In particular she was skeptical of Hooper's statement that he had rescued a large cache of Lewis manuscripts only hours before they were to have been destroyed in a bonfire. She outlined her concerns in a methodical article for the journal *Christianity and Literature*. To her shock, there was an immediate backlash from readers and the Lewis estate, one of such vehemence that, rather than dissuading her, it made her more curious than ever. Lindskoog began to investigate not only the short fictional works she had originally questioned, but also the contents of every book of new Lewis material and, later, every posthumous reissue of the author's earlier works. For the next decade she contacted the dwindling number of people who had been close to Lewis in life and posed a series of pointed questions to each. Their written replies fueled her conviction that some of what had been published under C. S. Lewis's name since his death was, at best, misattributed work by fans, and at worst, the work of one or more literary forgers.

Although the product of a low-profile publishing house, Lindskoog's book *The C. S. Lewis Hoax* (1988) caused a sensation among scholars. A war of words began to rage in Lewis-themed publications and conferences, one that has lost none of its vitriol since spilling over onto the Internet. "If I attempted a detailed analysis of the Lewis feuds," biographer A. N. Wilson marveled in 1990, "I should probably fall into as many errors as if I were to attempt a discourse on the difference between Shiite and Sunni Muslims."[10] Readers taking part in this debate tend to fall into one of three categories. The first insist that Lewis is infallible and that the "bonfire manuscripts" are proof positive of his authorial genius. The second admit that the works are flawed but assert they are genuine Lewis productions. The third, like Lindskoog, are of the mind that at least some of the new writings are to the canon what cuckoos' eggs are to an aviary.

Of the controversial works, the earliest is said to be "The Man Born Blind" (undated but ca. 1926). Robin, the title character, has had his sight restored through surgery but after three weeks is still confused about the one thing he has always dreamed of seeing: light. His wife and friends have explained endlessly that light is all around him, but Robin cannot perceive it: he expects it to be an object, a tangible *something*. One morning the newly sighted man takes a solitary walk to an abandoned quarry. There he startles a landscape painter who claims to be in the process of capturing a light so real a person could bathe in it. Robin gladly rushes in the direction the man's finger is pointing—and plunges to his death in the water below.

A dozen years prior to the publication of "The Man Born Blind," Lewis's friend, Owen Barfield, wrote that the author had told him a story something like it in the late 1920s. (He added, "He told me afterwards he had been informed by an expert that the acquisition of sight by a blind adult was not in fact the shattering experience he had imagined for the purposes of his story."[11]) Nor did Barfield deny in later years that "The Man Born Blind" was the tale that had been related to him. This anecdotal evidence was not proof enough for Lindskoog, who declared the work nongenuine. As with all the other questioned items, her primary objection was that it was one of the manuscripts said to have been saved from burning. She scoffed at the notion that Lewis would have created the landscapist, a tremendously angry man who shouts all his dialogue, without giving an explanation for this odd behavior. Likewise she thought the author possessed enough scientific knowledge not to state that fog could part and then close back in on itself as a body passed through it. Access restrictions prevented her ever handling the original manuscript, but one of England's foremost librarians—a man who disagreed with her assertions—looked at it on her behalf and reported that the mid-1920s story was written in a shade of ink not manufactured until the 1950s. A second handwritten copy turned up in the United States in 1997 but at the time of Lindskoog's death had not yet been made available for public use. Few other critics have felt the need to comment on this story. Lewis's friend, Alastair Fowler, one of those who did, shrugged it off as "not very successful" and "reminiscent of the most minor [Walter] de la Mare."[12]

The more competent "Forms of Things Unknown" (undated, ca. 1958) traces the fourth attempt by scientists to send a man to the moon. Previous landings were successful but, in each case, the astronauts stopped communicating with the base after only a few minutes, once in mid-sentence. Blue over a failed romance and curious about his predecessors' fates, Lieutenant John Jenkin refuses a friend's offer of company and takes off alone into space. He exits his craft at the usual landing site and begins to explore. Within minutes, he senses that he is being followed—but by whom? Or what? His discomfort only grows when he comes across a group of detailed stone astronaut statues, each posed with head and upper body turned as if to look behind it. Jenkin pulls out a portable transmitter and begins radioing his find back to Earth. Then a shadow falls across him and he turns—to meet the eyes of the snake-haired goddess who makes the moon her home.

Once again, questions arose once this story reached print. A scholar named Richard Hodgens pointed out in a 1978 lecture to the New York C. S. Lewis Society that artist Virgil Finlay had used the concept of Medusa on the moon in a cover illustration for the U.S. science fiction magazine *Fantastic Universe* in late 1958, the year in which Lewis's story seemed to have been written. Hodgens was of the opinion that the author had seen the painting and written a story to fit it. A second scholar then pointed out that Finlay's painting had a predecessor of its own: "Island of Fear," a short story by William Sambrot published nine months previously in another U.S. periodical, *The Saturday Evening Post*. With the exception of the locale—an island near Greece—this tale's basic plot and that of "Forms of Things Unknown" are the same.

It is worth noting that in December 1959, only a year after Sambrot's story appeared, Lewis wrote to Alastair Fowler about an undergraduate who dropped out of Magdalen College after Lewis pointed out a "puerile trick" of plagiarism in one of his essays. The tutor stated scornfully that he had never discussed academic honesty with the young man because "I'd as soon think it my business to see that he washed behind his ears or wiped his bottom."[13] Whatever one's belief about the provenance of "Forms of Things Unknown," this letter does not state the opinions of a man who would deliberately copy the work of another writer.

A third fragmentary work written in around the same period as Lewis's pulp stories was first published in the collection *Of Other Worlds*. In five partially connected scenes, "After Ten Years" tells the familiar story of the Trojan War from an original point of view: that of cuckolded King Menelaus of Sparta. "Yellowhair" has spent a decade seething with rage over his wife Helen's abandonment—in truth an abduction—and dreaming of the torments he will inflict on her when he catches her. But when his troops exit the wooden horse inside the garrison walls and begin sacking Troy, he finds that the once indescribably beautiful Helen is now aging and sorrowful. He has her taken prisoner but not maltreated. The next morning Yellowhair's older brother, King Agamemnon of Mycenae, swaggers onto the scene and informs him with a laugh that the troops have already accepted Helen as their rightful queen. Menelaus begins to wonder if it is possible for a woman's appearance to change so very much in only ten years. His suspicions are fueled by an Egyptian who tells him he knows the location of the "real" Helen. At this suspenseful point the manuscript ends.

Critical reactions to "After Ten Years" focused mainly, once again, on its treatment of women. Ursula Le Guin discovered the story for the first time in its 1977 reprinting and rhapsodized in *The New Republic* that the opening sequence was "a torment of crowding, cramped muscles, sweat, fear, lust, daydream. . . . a superb beginning." She added that had its author finished it, this would have been a truly admirable work—then qualified her statement, "If Lewis had treated Helen as a human being. But would he have done so? The indications are that he was going to split her into two stereotypes, heartless beauty and soulless eidolon, the Witch and the Drudge, and would never have arrived at the woman, Helen."[14] Alastair Fowler, by contrast, thought the character was portrayed as altogether a queen and that Lewis had never dealt with the topic of the false image in such tender fashion.[15]

"After Ten Years" is undated, but the author's friend Roger Lancelyn Green wrote in one of the printed version's two "Afterwords" that Lewis had read portions to him in 1959 and 1960 as he composed them and revised one section to include facts Green had told him about the royal couple. Despite its being a "bonfire manuscript," Kathryn Lindskoog admitted that this was probably a genuine Lewis creation. Certainly it is the work of someone whose knowledge of classics extends beyond the titles taught in most U.S. schools. The second section reworks a scene from Euripides' *The Trojan Women*, with the major difference that, in the play, Helen escapes death through seduction, where in the story what saves her is a sad inquiry to Menelaus about the fate of their daughter. An amusing touch—typical of Lewis—is aimed at the select few of his readers who remember their classics. While for the hundredth time rubbing his brother's nose in his loss of Helen, Agamemnon boasts about the control he exerts over *his* wife and how proud she will be over his latest triumph. Readers of Aeschylus's *The Oresteia* know, however, that Clytemnestra and her lover murdered her husband as soon as he returned from Troy.

The greatest critical commotion to date has been in response to *The Dark Tower*, a fragmentary novel dated 1938. (The date and provenance of this unfinished work is still in dispute.) Said by Lewis's executor to be a bridge between *Out of the Silent Planet* (1938) and *Perelandra* (1943), the sixty-two-page manuscript follows a group of scholars—including Lewis himself—as they ponder for weeks over *camera obscura* scenes of a civilization that lies either in a parallel universe or their own in a future time. One of them surmises that it might be in hell. The setting is always in or near a tower room the scholars recognize as part of the university library in Cambridge. In this room sits a dark and sinister Something shaped like a man but with an oozing, thornlike sting growing from the center of its forehead. The residents of this "Othertime" are in thrall to the creature and present themselves in turn for sacrifice. Its venom apparently does away with their minds and spirits and they become hard-working automata.

The scientists soon notice that one of the Stingingman's victims bears a strong resemblance to Scudamour, assistant to the projection machine's inventor. Reacting as if the action on screen is happening to their friend, they watch as this Doppelgänger endures a night of agony, emerges as a second Stingingman, and takes the place of the first in the tower room. When the real Scudamour sees the double of the woman he plans to marry approaching for sacrifice, he leaps for the machine, damages it, and somehow changes places with the creature, which flees from the other scientists through the streets of Cambridge. In his new Stingingman persona, Scudamour confronts his "fiancée" and learns that Othertime is under threat of invasion by creatures who look as he does but have no barb. In hopes that it will save their nation, ordinary people allow themselves to be stung, an act that drains them of emotion but extends their lifespans and capacity for work. Scudamour begins to delve into the society's knowledge of science. But at this point, the manuscript ends in mid-sentence.

The Dark Tower is unlike any other work credited to C. S. Lewis, in the main because of its overt sexual content. Although Lewis sympathized with individual friends who struggled with issues of sexual identity, he was openly contemptuous of nonheterosexuals in general, once writing to a friend to complain about "the widespread freemasonry of the highbrow homos who dominate so much of the world of criticism . . ."[16] By contrast, *The Dark Tower* reads like an awkward attempt at pornography. Its victims are a series of handsome, muscular, nearly naked young men; and its villain, a phallocephalic monster that pierces each painfully through the lower spine. After his first day's sacrifices the Stingingman horrifies his audience by first seeming to gaze back at them through the projection device, then performing a series of solo sex acts for the "camera." Though the latter suggests *Gargantua and Pantagruel*, there is nothing Rabelaisian about it: it disgusts the reader as Lewis-the-narrator suggests it disgusted him. Yet he admits that he and the others were transfixed by the sight; significantly, none of them turned away. These supposed heroes, university scholars all, are in the end nothing but common voyeurs—as, if inadvertently so, is the reader.

Even for a draft, *The Dark Tower* lacks characterization to a surprising degree. Its protagonist would seem to be Scudamour, a bland young man who remains a background figure until the discovery of his Othertime double. Elwin Ransom, Lewis's usual science-fiction hero, here appears only as part of a group: this man whose personality was so sharply defined in three novels could change places with any of the others without its making a difference. Even Lewis himself is something of a cipher: the only real character trait given him is a kind of perpetual anxious irritation. Two of *The Dark Tower*'s players have genuine personalities. One, the cynical (or sensible) Scotsman MacPhee, also plays a prominent role in the final volume of the Space Trilogy. The other, Cyril Knellie,[17] is an author of suggestive scholarly works who wanders onto the scene of the experiment and reacts with delight to the artistic quality of what seems to him to be a sort of live erotic entertainment. These are interesting and fairly strong characters but their presence is not enough to carry the story.

Biographer A. N. Wilson dismissed this fragmentary novel as, variously, "depressing," "semi-obscene," and "one of Lewis's feebler posthumous works."[18] Fowler took the opposite view, pronouncing it a compulsively readable, even Spenserian story and writing in the *Times Literary Supplement* that had his friend finished it, "it might have been his best."[19] Le Guin noted that in general, "There's a good deal of hatred in Lewis, and it is a frightening hatred, because this gentle, brilliant, lovable, devout man never saw the need even to rationalize it, let alone apologize for it."[20] She recognized certain strengths in *The Dark Tower* that were common to the Space Trilogy volumes, but was of the opinion that the former was "weakened by embarrassingly naive sexual overtones" and that the author was "not in control of his material."[21] David Downing, whose 1992 study *Planets in Peril* provides the best explication of the Space Trilogy to date, devotes three pages at the end of that work to *The Dark Tower*. He points out that certain elements of character and setting were later carried out more fully in the third of the series, the dystopic *That Hideous Strength* (1945): both nightmare societies favor a beetle motif in decoration, for example, and the original Stingingman's description was reused as that of a decapitated master criminal in the later work. Downing suggests that one reason the author abandoned the project was that the successful works always balanced good and evil in equal portions, but in *The Dark Tower* he had little to offer "to counterbalance this miserific vision."[22]

Kathryn Lindskoog devoted large portions of *The C. S. Lewis Hoax* and its follow-ups to all that she found suspect about *The Dark Tower*. She noted multiple similarities between this unpublished ca. 1938 work, three Cold War–era science-fiction films, and Madeleine L'Engle's classic children's fantasy *A Wrinkle in Time* (1962), and described the findings of "literary detectives" who subjected the Lewis work to computer-based proximity and topical analyses. Lindskoog was particularly pleased to report in a later version of having examined the novella's original manuscript. On the back of the first page was an item seemingly in Lewis's handwriting: a variation on the first paragraph of *The Lion, the Witch and the Wardrobe* describing air raids on London and the evacuation of children to safer areas of the country. But, as she noted gleefully, *The Dark Tower* was dated 1938, two years before Germany began its aerial bombardments of England. On the reverse of the second page was the start of a second, autobiographical work. Its first sentence, in the same pale blue ink used to write "The Man Born Blind," stated that the author was born in 1946, a date that had been scratched out and replaced with "1898." Lindskoog triumphantly pointed out that even if this was an innocent mistake, "It seems unlikely that Lewis would have started an autobiography in 1946 on the second page of a manuscript he abandoned in 1938, using ink that did not exist until 1950."[23] Whether her conjectures about this work will prove true in time remains to be seen. The curious are invited to read both *The Dark Tower* and the scholarship that followed and decide for themselves.

The works of fiction are not the only posthumous publications to have come under scrutiny, nor has Lindskoog been their only critic. Scholars are beginning to focus on Lewis's letters and life-writings and the book introductions and notes written by others. In recent years the latter seem increasingly determined to portray the author as either a saint or, in his younger days at least, a would-be sadist. A. N. Wilson, whose 1990 biography of Lewis was based on interviews with surviving friends and colleagues, confirmed that in their eyes the author

was argumentative and bullying. His jolly, red, honest face was that of an intellectual bruiser. He was loud, and he could be coarse. He liked what he called "man's talk," and he was frequently contemptuous in his remarks about the opposite sex. He was a heavy smoker—sixty cigarettes a day between pipes—and he liked to drink deep, roaring out his unfashionable views in Oxford bars.[24]

Which is to say, Jack Lewis was a human being. But, Wilson reported with some puzzlement, it was hard to see that in the biographical introductions to some of the posthumous books, which embellished the writer's moral sense to an unusual degree. He noted that some of this was the work of U.S. publishers who were afraid that mentions of tobacco and liquor use would offend their hard-line Protestant readership (and added, "one has the strong feeling that this is not so much because they themselves disapprove of the activities as because they need a Lewis who was, against all evidence, a nonsmoker and a lemonade drinker."[25]) He found even more surprising the published statements by literary executor Walter Hooper that Lewis had lived with Janie Moore for three decades on a purely platonic basis, and that he never consummated his four-year marriage to U.S. divorcée Joy Davidman Gresham, and even that he had died a virgin. Hooper was at that time a recent convert to Catholicism and Wilson theorized that "for him Lewis has become a sort of Catholic saint, and one can hardly believe in a Catholic saint both of whose sexual relationships were with women who had husbands still living. Therefore, when Lewis wrote in *A Grief Observed* that he and his wife were lovers ... he was in fact writing a work of fiction."[26] The executor has since acknowledged Lewis's normalcy in this area but the earlier statements remain in print and in use as reference materials.

The allegations of sadism are curious in that they too originate with the estate. Brief hints in introductions and biographies built over time to the assertion that, under X-ray, shocking passages were visible under scribbles in the author's early correspondence with Arthur Greeves. These letters were published in 1979 as *They Stand Together*, with the controversial portions set off in triangular brackets. (In truth, these references are offhand and rather dull, making extensive use of Greek and the code word "That.") By the time the letters appeared, of course, *The Dark Tower* had revealed to the reading public that C. S. Lewis was capable of cruel fantasies seemingly fueled by a sublimated libido. After that it was anticlimactic to read that one night at Oxford a certain collegian, befuddled by alcohol, began offering his classmates money to submit to flogging.

And perhaps he did just that. Perhaps he did not.[27] In any case, the question is, should it matter? Lewis would hardly have been the first British writer to have thought deeply about giving or receiving pain: in fact, it is difficult to find the autobiography of a pre-1970 public school man who does not have something to say on the subject. The majority of these fixations take the negative view: Thackeray, for example, tossed sometimes-gratuitous beating references into his works to express loathing for the school that made his youth a misery. Frederick Marryat, whose novels were still popular schoolboy fare during Lewis's youth, took a more personal interest: he seemed to enjoy creating extended episodes from different perspectives, often several per book. The most extreme case was the poet Swinburne, whose obsession developed into active sadomasochism and some of whose recreational writings are unlikely ever to appear in a printed "Complete Works." Even if Lewis had similar unnatural desires in his youth, the point is that he matured beyond them, fully and naturally.[28] Stints on the battlefield and in a convalescent hospital opened his eyes to the senselessness of cruelty. University studies, late-night teaching sessions, and the long-term relationship with Janie Moore then filled his hours and kept his thoughts in their proper place. His decision in 1931 to rejoin the Episcopal Church sealed his future and he became the man and the writer we recognize today.

... LE DÉLUGE

The steady stream of print publications bearing Lewis's name has in recent years become a flood. In the first four decades after the author's death his estate released three new volumes of poetry, four of original Christian and philosophical essays, seven of letters (one of them already in type in 1963), five of literary essays, the all-fiction *Dark Tower* collection, a truncated edition of the author's 1920s diaries, and an illustrated compilation of Jack and Warnie Lewis's Boxen juvenilia, as well as countless repackagings of older material. More recently it has begun issuing slim volumes of thematic extracts from the earlier works, the majority on Christian themes. The simple Oxford don has in the twenty-first century become a one-man theological-literary industry.

California gadfly Kathryn Lindskoog had comments to make about many of the new releases. For details, the reader is referred to the third and final version of her book, published in 2001 under the new title *Sleuthing C. S. Lewis: More Light in the Shadowlands.* The second version had used footnotes to indicate newer information; by the time the third appeared these took up nearly as much space as the original text. The book's tone is shrill at times, an understandable fault given that to compile it, its author battled two handicaps: alleged denials of access to primary sources and a growing debilitation due to multiple sclerosis. By the turn of the millennium she was confined to a wheelchair and had to send other researchers to copy archival holdings, sometimes by hand, for her study at home. Lindskoog's ailment finally claimed her life in 2004. The controversy did not die with her: Lewis scholarship today remains firmly divided by what Wilson had earlier termed the Great Schism.

Readers who appreciate this thoughtful, dedicated, and talented author have a great deal to hope for in the coming years. They can hope that "The Quest of Bleharis," "The Most Substantial People," and—assuming they still exist—the two juvenile political novels finally make their way into print. They can hope for additional, less heavily edited diary volumes. They can hope that caches of previously unknown letters will be discovered in private attics and public archives. Best of all, they can hope that, when the time is right, the trustees of the Lewis estate will authorize an independent, unbiased research team to conduct tests that establish the validity of the posthumously published works once and for all. A sterling literary reputation is at stake and C. S. Lewis deserves nothing less.

NOTES

1. C. S. Lewis, "The Shoddy Lands," in *The Dark Tower and Other Stories*, ed. Walter Hooper (New York: Harcourt Brace Jovanovich, 1977), 109.

2. H. M. Blamires, undated post-1963 letter quoted in Warren H. Lewis, ed. *Letters of C. S. Lewis* (New York: Harcourt, Brace & World, 1966), 18–19.

3. Ursula K. Le Guin, Review, *The Dark Tower and Other Stories*. *The New Republic* 176 (April 16, 1977), 29.

4. True, the highbrow *Saturday Review* was more typical of Lewis's taste in periodicals, but he was more likely to have held onto his copy of the pulp for two years afterward, knowing the latter to be a potential story market.

5. Le Guin, Review, *The Dark Tower and Other Stories*, 30.

6. C. S. Lewis, *They Stand Together: The Letters of C. S. Lewis to Arthur Greeves*, ed. Walter Hooper (New York: Macmillan, 1979), 99. Undated letter from ca. May 16, 1916.

7. Ibid., 126. Letter dated July 25, 1916.

8. W. H. Lewis, *Letters of C. S. Lewis*, 6.

9. Ibid.

10. A. N. Wilson, *C. S. Lewis: A Biography* (London: Collins, 1990), xv.

11. Owen Barfield, Introduction to *Light on C. S. Lewis* (London: Geoffrey Bles, 1965), xviii.

12. Alastair Fowler, "The Aliens of Othertime," Review of *The Dark Tower and Other Stories*. *Times Literary Supplement* (July 1, 1977), 795.

13. W. H. Lewis, *Letters of C. S. Lewis*, 291.

14. Le Guin, Review, *The Dark Tower and Other Stories*, 29.

15. Fowler, "The Aliens of Othertime," Review. 795.

16. W. H. Lewis, *Letters of C. S. Lewis*, 292.

17. The use of this outdated epithet for an effeminate man is typical of *The Dark Tower*'s subtlety overall.

18. Wilson, *C. S. Lewis: A Biography*, xiv.

19. Fowler, "The Aliens of Othertime," Review, 795.

20. Le Guin, Review, *The Dark Tower and Other Stories*, 29.

21. Ibid., 30.

22. David C. Downing, *Planets in Peril: A Critical Study of C. S. Lewis's Ransom Trilogy* (Amherst, MA: University of Massachusetts Press, 1992), 161.

23. Kathryn Lindskoog, *Sleuthing C. S. Lewis: More Light in the Shadowlands* (Macon, GA: Mercer University Press, 2001), 109.

24. Wilson, *C. S. Lewis: A Biography*, xii.

25. Ibid., xvi.

26. Ibid., xvi.

27. The other students must have been just as drunk as he, for none of them ever recalled the event publicly.

28. A sinner in young manhood turned saintly in middle age following a journey-related epiphany—it all begins to sound very much like the story of Saul. It will be interesting to note whether some future biography takes exactly this approach, using as evidence the published record of Lewis's evil thoughts and spiritual reformation. How interesting it would be if the road to Tarsus led in fact to the Whipsnade Zoo!

BIBLIOGRAPHY

Barfield, Owen. "Introduction." In *Light on C. S. Lewis*. London: Geoffrey Bles, 1965, ix–xxi.

Downing, David C. "'The Dungeon of His Soul': Lewis's Unfinished 'Quest of Bleheris.'" *SEVEN* 17 (1998).

———. *Planets in Peril: A Critical Study of C. S. Lewis's Ransom Trilogy*. Amherst, MA: University of Massachusetts Press, 1992.

Fowler, Alastair. "The Aliens of Othertime." Review, *The Dark Tower and Other Stories. Times Literary Supplement* (July 1, 1977), 795.

Le Guin, Ursula K. Review, *The Dark Tower and Other Stories. The New Republic* (April 16, 1977), 29–30.

Lewis, C. S. *The Dark Tower and Other Stories*. Edited by Walter Hooper. New York: Harcourt Brace Jovanovich, 1977.

———. "The Most Substantial People." Typescript in Volume 9 of *Memoirs of the Lewis Family 1850–1930*. Marion E. Wade Center, Wheaton College, Norton, MA. Copies at the Bodleian Library, Oxford University, and the University of North Carolina, Chapel Hill, NC.

———. "The Quest of Bleheris." ca. 1916. Manuscript in the Bodleian Library, Oxford. MS Eng. Lett. c. 220/5 fols. 5–43). Copy at the Marion E. Wade Center, Wheaton College, Norton, MA.

———. *They Stand Together: The Letters of C. S. Lewis to Arthur Greeves*. Edited by Walter Hooper. New York: Macmillan, 1979.

Lewis, W. H., Editor. *Letters of C. S. Lewis*. New York: Harcourt, Brace & World, 1966.

Lindskoog, Kathryn. *The C. S. Lewis Hoax*. Portland, OR: Multnomah, 1988.

———. *The Linden Tree*. A Web site with previously published articles about the author's investigations into the provenance of various Lewis writings. Accessed April 2, 2006, at http://lindentree.org.

———. *Sleuthing C. S. Lewis: More Light in the Shadowlands*. Macon, GA: Mercer University Press, 2001.

London, Jack. *The Sea Wolf*. New York: Macmillan, 1904.

Wilson, A. N. *C. S. Lewis: A Biography*. London: Collins, 1990.

10

The Screwtape Letters: Telling the Truth Upside Down

Devin Brown

"My dear Wormwood."

So begins one of C. S. Lewis's most unusual and most successful works: *The Screwtape Letters.*

On May 2, 1941, British readers opened *The Guardian*, a weekly Anglican religious newspaper, to find the first in a series of thirty-one strange letters that would arrive in weekly installments, claiming to have been written by a senior devil named Screwtape to his nephew, a novice tempter named Wormwood. When the entire collection was published in Britain in 1942 and in the Untied States a year later, *The Screwtape Letters* became, as Alan Jacobs notes, Lewis's "first truly popular book."[1] It would propel Lewis to international fame and eventually put him on the cover of *Time* magazine (September 8, 1947), where he was pictured with a little devil standing on one shoulder. The cover story "Don versus Devil," a reference to Lewis's position as an Oxford don, noted that by 1947 all of Lewis's books added together had sold something over a million copies. Today the number of copies of *Screwtape* alone stands at several million.

The origins for the series of devilish epistles can be found in a letter that Lewis wrote to his brother Warnie, dated July 20, 1940. In it, Lewis tells how the idea came to him one Sunday at church:

Before the service was over—one could wish these things came more seasonably—I was stuck by an idea for a book which I think might be both useful and entertaining. It would be called *As One Devil to Another* and would consist of letters from an elderly retired devil to a young devil who has just started work on his first "patient." The idea would be to give all the psychology of temptation from the *other* point of view.[2]

Once starting on the project, it did not take Lewis long to finish and find a publisher, with the first installment in *The Guardian* appearing less than a year after the letter to Warnie.

This practice of taking the "other" point of view was a technique Lewis had used previously to great advantage in *Out of the Silent Planet*, the first book of his Space Trilogy, published in 1939 three years before *Screwtape*. In one instance, readers find a description of two strange creatures as they approach Ransom, the story's protagonist. Here Lewis allows readers, through Ransom, to see the two creatures from the point of view of an inhabitant of Mars (whom the natives call Malacandra):

They were much shorter than any animal he had yet seen on Malacandra, and he gathered that they were bipeds, though the lower limbs were so thick and sausage-like that he hesitated to call them legs. The bodies were a little narrower at the top than at the bottom so as to be very slightly pear-shaped. . . . Suddenly, with an indescribable change of feeling, he realized that he was looking at men . . . and he, for one privileged moment, had seen the human form with almost Malacandrian eyes.[3]

Lewis would again turn to this technique of presenting a story from the other point of view, nine years after *Screwtape*. In *Prince Caspian* (1951) he would place the four Pevensie children in the position of feeling what it is like to be the ones who are called by Susan's magic horn rather than being the ones calling for help.

In an essay on J. R. R. Tolkien's *The Lord of the Rings* titled, "The Dethronement of Power," Lewis points out the need humans have to penetrate what he calls "the veil of familiarity" so that we can see more clearly "all the things we know."[4] While the impact Lewis achieves by showing events from the other point of view is always striking, he did not invent this literary technique. It can be seen in works such as *Gulliver's Travels*, a book that Lewis labels as one of his favorites in his autobiography, *Surprised by Joy*.[5] In one memorable illustration of this practice, Swift allows readers see the contents of Gulliver's pockets through the eyes of the Lilliputians. Viktor Shklovsky, the Russian Formalist critic, coined the term *defamiliarization* to describe this technique of making the familiar strange in order to counter the deadening effect of habit and by doing so forcing a greater awareness. Certainly Lewis's choice to write from a devil's perspective in *Screwtape*, his decision to tell the truth upside down, adds poignancy and power to his depiction of the psychology of human temptation.

As in the fourth book of *Paradise Lost*, where Milton has Satan declare, "Evil, be thou my good," a similar reversal of perspective is throughout *Screwtape*. As Mark Deforrest has pointed out, an awareness of this other point of view used by Lewis is "crucial to understanding the content of the letters."[6] Thus "the Enemy" in the story is Screwtape's way of referring to God. What Screwtape calls "Our Father's House" is of course, Hell, not Heaven. Deforrest concludes, "Thus to really understand the book, it is necessary to keep in mind that what Screwtape sees as good is really negative, and what are setbacks for him are actually victories in the struggle against evil."[7] Or as Jocelyn Easton Gibb notes, "Screwtape's whites are our blacks and whatever he welcomes we should dread."[8]

One would think this point hardly needed mentioning. However in the preface to the 1961 edition of *Screwtape*, Lewis relates the story of the country clergyman who wrote a letter to the editor canceling his subscription to *The Guardian* complaining that "much of the advice given in these letters seemed to him not only erroneous but positively diabolical."[9]

In the original 1942 preface, found in most modern editions of *Screwtape*, Lewis warns, "Readers are advised to remember that the devil is a liar. Not everything that Screwtape says should be assumed to be true even from his own angle."[10] When Screwtape's potential dishonesty is compounded with the fact that his perspective is, for us, inverted, the exact point that Lewis wants to make in each passage may from time to time be obscured. Fortunately, many of the topics in *Screwtape* are explored from the more normal perspective and refined and elaborated on in other books which Lewis produced—in works written around the same time, such as the *Broadcast Talks* (1941–1942), which would eventually be published as *Mere Christianity* (1952), and in works that Lewis would pen much later, such as *Letters to Malcolm* (1964).

OF DEVILS AND INFLUENCES

When Lewis expressed his views on devils in his 1942 preface, he explained there are two equal and opposite errors that humans can make concerning devils: "One is to disbelieve in their existence. The other is to believe, and to feel an excessive and unhealthy interest in them. They themselves are equally pleased by both errors and hail a materialist or a magician with the same delight."[11] Interestingly, the villains from the first two Chronicles of Narnia can be seen as examples of the two types of evils mentioned here by Lewis. The White Witch from *The Lion, the Witch and the Wardrobe* could be described as an evil magician. King Miraz from *Prince Caspian* is equally bad as a materialist. Nineteen years later, in the preface to the 1961 edition, Lewis felt it worthwhile to answer some of the questions that *Screwtape* had raised in the minds of readers in the two decades since its publication. The most frequent question, Lewis reports, was whether or not he really believed in the Devil. Lewis's response is somewhat nuanced. First, he points out: "Now, if by 'the Devil' you mean a power opposite to God, self-existent from all eternity, the answer is certainly No. There is no uncreated being except God. God has no opposite. No being could attain a 'perfect badness' opposite to the perfect goodness of God."[12] Lewis goes on to explain that the proper question is whether he believes in *devils*. He elaborates, "I believe in angels, and I believe that some of these, by the abuse of their free will, have become enemies to God and, as a corollary, to us. These we may call devils."[13] He also distinguishes between his belief in angels, both good and evil, and his disbelief in demonic creatures with bird wings or bat wings, representations that he considered purely symbolic and not particularly helpful.

Lewis makes his own beliefs very clear in the 1961 preface, but he adds, "The question of my own opinion about devils, though proper to be answered when once it was raised, is really of very minor importance for a reader of *Screwtape*."[14]

He states that readers who share his beliefs will see the devils in *Screwtape* as symbols of a concrete reality. Readers who do not will see Wormwood and Screwtape as personifications of abstractions, and for these readers the book will be an allegory. Either way, Lewis claims it makes little difference, for the book was not written in order to speculate about devils but "to throw light from a new angle on the life of men."[15]

Lewis's extensive reading would have provided him with many insights into the Devil. Lewis's first epigram in *Screwtape* is the advice of Martin Luther: "The best way to drive out the devil, if he will not yield to texts of Scripture, is to jeer and flout him, for he cannot bear scorn." The second epigram, a line quoted from Thomas More, indicates the Devil's besetting sin is his "prowde spirite," a pride of self-importance that "cannot endure to be mocked." In Lewis's *A Preface to Paradise Lost*, which began as a series of lectures given in 1941, the same year Screwtape's letters began appearing in *The Guardian*, he points out that Satan suffered from "a sense of injur'd merit,"[16] a description taken directly from Milton. Lewis then expands on this point, noting, "In the midst of a world of light and love, of song and feast and dance, he could find nothing to think of more interesting than his own prestige."[17]

In choosing to open with the quotes from Luther and More, Lewis reveals his intention in writing *The Screwtape Letters* is to use satire and mocking to "drive out the devil." The best weapons against the deadly seriousness with which the devils view themselves, Lewis suggests, are humor and ridicule and reading the letters partly as exercises in humor is key to appreciating them. It is most likely that Lewis was influenced by the Catholic writer G. K. Chesterton, whom Lewis greatly admired, to use humor and laughter in *Screwtape*. In Lewis's 1961 preface, he refers to Chesterton's suggestion in *Orthodoxy* that Satan "fell by the force of gravity."[18] Lewis continues with the observation, "We must picture Hell as a state where everyone is perpetually concerned about his own dignity and advancement, where everyone has a grievance, and where everyone lives the deadly serious passions of envy, self-importance, and resentment."[19] By contrast, as Chesterton notes in *Orthodoxy*, "A characteristic of great saints is their power of levity. Angels can fly because they can take themselves lightly."[20] A related use of humor in another Lewis work is in "Rabadash the Ridiculous," the final chapter of *The Horse and His Boy* (1954), in which ridicule is used to deflate a Calormen Prince who has a similarly exaggerated sense of self-importance.

Lewis dedicated *The Screwtape Letters* (1942) to J. R. R. Tolkien, whom he first met at Oxford in 1926 and who persuaded Lewis to take the Christian story seriously, as fact and not mere myth. As Alan Jacobs has observed, there would come a point when Tolkien would dislike the tenor of Lewis's Christian works, a view that "stemmed from the insistence of Tolkien's Catholic tradition on the very different roles of clergy and laity."[21] However, there does not seem to be much indication that Tolkien had any problems with *Screwtape*. In fact, as Colin Duriez points out, "There was much that Tolkien liked of *The Screwtape Letters*. . . . His letters at the time often reflect concepts explored in *Screwtape*."[22] It is clear Tolkien never forgot *Screwtape* had been dedicated to him. In a letter written to his son Michael in November 1963, shortly after Lewis's death, Tolkien complained about the numerous inaccuracies in the published obituaries. Among the misrepresentations that Tolkien notes is the suggestion by the *Daily Telegraph* that Lewis was never that fond of *The Screwtape Letters*, a claim clearly untrue. Tolkien concludes ironically with the observation, "He dedicated it to me. I wondered why. Now I know—says they."[23]

Letters 1 to 3: Reason, the New Convert, and His Mother

Lewis's friend and biographer George Sayer rightly argues that *Screwtape* "brilliantly combines spiritual profundity and a remarkable psychological understanding."[24] A. N. Wilson claims that *The Screwtape Letters* brings into literary use qualities that Lewis had possessed to a highly developed degree since adolescence, among them Lewis's "ability to see through human failings," his "capacity to analyze other people's annoyingness," and his "rich sense of comedy and satire."[25] From the very first letter, evidence to support Sayer's and Wilson's favorable evaluations appears in abundance, making it clear why *Screwtape* is many readers' favorite work by C. S. Lewis.

The first letter begins with Screwtape admonishing Wormwood not to think that reading or argument is the way to keep his patient "out of the Enemy's clutches."[26] Lewis here is drawing from his own experience, for, in fact, he was moved closer to Christian beliefs by both of these activities as he relates in his autobiography, *Surprised by Joy*: "In reading Chesterton, as in reading MacDonald, I did not know what I was letting myself in for. A young man who wishes to remain a sound Atheist cannot be too careful of his reading."[27] When Lewis was thirty-two, it was argument, meaning a reasoned discussion, which played a pivotal role in changing his beliefs. On the night of September 19, 1931, Lewis had invited Tolkien and Hugo Dyson to dine with him at his college, and they talked well into the night about Christianity. Soon after that night, Lewis professed belief not in just God but in the claims of Jesus Christ, and it was that night of "argument" with Tolkien and Dyson that proved instrumental in guiding Lewis along his path toward becoming one of the world's greatest writers of Christian apologetics.

Screwtape also notes in the first letter that Wormwood's patient is not in the practice of evaluating a doctrine on the basis of whether it is true or false, but rather by whether it is academic or practical, outworn or contemporary, and the senior devil urges his nephew to keep the focus on this kind of jargon. As with the previous points about reading and argument, here again Lewis was drawing from his own experience. In *Surprised by Joy*, Lewis calls attention to a condition he calls "chronological snobbery," which he describes as "the uncritical acceptance of the intellectual climate common to our own age and the assumption that whatever has gone out of date is on that account discredited."[28] Later in *Screwtape*, in Letter 27, Screwtape will expand on the issue of chronological snobbery, calling it the Historical Point of View. As Screwtape explains to Wormwood:

Put briefly, [it] means that when a learned man is presented with any statement in an ancient author, the one question he never asks is whether it is true. He asks who influenced the ancient writer, and how far the statement is consistent with what he said in other books, and what phase in the writer's development, or in the general history of thought, it illustrates, and how it affected later writers. . . . To regard the ancient writer as a possible source of knowledge—to anticipate that what he said could possibly modify your thoughts or your behavior—this would be rejected as unutterably simple-minded.[29]

Lewis said he suffered from this malady until the helpful "counterattacks" from his friend Owen Barfield freed him from this view forever, and one can see how Lewis would want *The Screwtape Letters* to be of similar value for his readers.

In Screwtape's opening letter, Lewis makes his position clear: Christians are not to be afraid of reasoned discussions about the faith, for as Screwtape warns, argument "moves the whole struggle on to the Enemy's own ground."[30] Lewis uses the prominence of the opening sentence in the first letter to counter the fear some Christians have that argument or further reading leads to a loss of faith. He makes the same point in *Mere Christianity* where he asks, "If you examined a hundred people who had lost their faith in Christianity, I wonder how many of them would turn out to have been reasoned out of it by honest argument? Do not most people simply drift away?"[31] With this emphasis on the positive relationship between reading and argument and the Christian faith, Lewis also responds to the notion that one could or should become a Christian *despite* his reason. In *Mere Christianity* Lewis makes his position very clear, stating, "I am not asking anyone to accept Christianity if his best reasoning tells him that the weight of the evidence is against it."[32] Lewis would return to the vital role of reason and logical argument a decade later when writing *The Lion, the Witch and the Wardrobe*. When the Professor hears of Lucy's claim to have visited an imaginary world, he reminds Peter and Susan that they have no rational grounds for presuming Lucy's account is untrue. "Logic!" he complains, "Why don't they teach logic at these schools?"[33]

In Screwtape's second letter we learn that Wormwood's patient has become a Christian. Screwtape points out to his young charge this is no call to despair because hundreds of similar converts have been reclaimed after "a brief sojourn in the Enemy's camp."[34] According to Screwtape, one of the devils' greatest allies in leading these believers to abandon their newfound faith is the Church itself, by which he means the patient's local congregation, and not the church universal, which he describes as "spread out through all time and space and rooted in eternity," a spectacle that Screwtape admits "makes our boldest tempters uneasy."[35]

Lewis includes several penetrating insights in this second letter, one of which relates to a topic that he would later describe in *Surprised by Joy* as "the false identification which some people make of refinement with virtue."[36] Screwtape suggests that at his local church the newly Christian patient will encounter the very neighbors he has previously avoided; and provided that any of those neighbors "sing out of tune, or have boots that squeak, or double chins, or odd clothes," Wormwood's patient will quite easily, though erroneously, conclude that their religion "must therefore be somehow ridiculous."[37] Readers who know of Lewis's dislike for poor church singing—he typically attended the 8 A.M. service to avoid the 10:30 A.M. Sung Eucharist—may wonder if the first prejudice in the list had, at least for a time, been one of which Lewis himself was guilty.

Lewis's own admission of sins gives us good reason to look at his experience as the origins for many of Screwtape's ideas for temptations. In the 1961 preface, with a reference to Psalm 36:1, Lewis points out:

Some have paid me an undeserved compliment by supposing that my *Letters* were the ripe fruit of many years' study in moral and ascetic theology. They forget that there is an equally reliable, thought less creditable, way of learning how temptation works. "My heart"—I need no other's—"showeth me the wickedness of the ungodly."[38]

Screwtape moves on to the topic of how the patient's moods will certainly change, urging Wormwood to work hard on the disappointment or anticlimax that the elder devil assures will come to the patient during his first few weeks as a Christian. Screwtape will return to this topic in Letter 8, where he will call this pattern the Law of Undulation, a condition of continually changing "troughs and peaks," which for humans is the "nearest approach to constancy."[39] In *Mere Christianity*, Lewis explored the topic of peaks and troughs and defined faith as "the art of holding on to things your reason has once accepted, in spite of your changing moods."[40] Screwtape concludes with the warning that if Christians are able to get through this initial period of dryness successfully, they become much less dependent on their feelings and therefore become much harder to tempt.

In the final paragraph of the second letter, Lewis raises an issue that modern readers may puzzle over. Screwtape has instructed Wormwood to encourage his patient's belief that the religion of the people in the next pew is somehow dubious or ridiculous because of irrelevant external elements such as their appearance. Screwtape advises Wormwood that he must also exploit any valid grounds the patient may think he has for assuming a holier-than-thou attitude toward his commonplace neighbors; for example if it turns out that the churchgoer with the squeaky boots is also a miser or an extortioner. Then by way of another illustration, Screwtape proposes the possibility that "the woman with the absurd hat is a fanatical bridge player."[41]

Why Lewis places fanatical bridge playing alongside miserly behavior and extortion is not immediately clear. In an essay titled "An Approach to Teaching *The Screwtape Letters*," Marvin Hinten wonders about Lewis's choice of illustration: "Personally, I dislike the example; since when is excessive playing bridge on a par with illegal activities like extortion? But my students usually defend the example, bringing in Scriptures such as I Corinthians 10:23 about lawfulness vs. helpfulness. This year they meandered into how a person can actually tell if they are 'fanatical' about something."[42] Lewis mentions bridge playing and fanaticism again in the following passage from *Mere Christianity*, which may help to place Screwtape's comments in clearer context. In a chapter about the cardinal virtues, Lewis writes:

One great piece of mischief has been done by the modern restriction of the word Temperance to the question of drink. It helps people to forget that you can be just as intemperate about lots of other things. A man who makes his golf or his motor-bicycle the center of his life, or a woman who devotes all her thoughts to clothes or bridge or her dog, is being just as "intemperate" as someone who gets drunk every evening. Of course, it does not show on the outside so easily: bridge-mania or golf-mania do not make you fall down in the middle of the road. But God is not deceived by externals.[43]

Certainly most believers would agree that the commandment "Thou shalt have no other gods before me" was meant to include all activities, not just one's normally thought of sins. As Screwtape will point out near the close of Letter 12, "It does not matter how small the sins are provided that their cumulative effect is to edge the man away from the Light and out into the Nothing. Murder is no better than cards if cards can do the trick."[44]

In Letter 3, Screwtape urges Wormwood to encourage the minor annoyances between the patient and his mother, what he calls the "daily pinpricks." Readers who have been expecting the clash between good and evil—the battle against principalities and powers mentioned in Ephesians 6:12—to be somewhat more majestic may be surprised to find Screwtape's emphasis on aspects as mundane as the odd clothes and double chins mentioned in Letter 2 and the "tones of voice and expressions of face" discussed here. However, these elements are in keeping with Screwtape's counsel to keep the patient's mind off "the most elementary duties" and focused on only "the most advanced and spiritual ones." (It is worth noting that if commonplace, ordinary annoyances prove useful in keeping the patient from the Enemy, Lewis will later suggest that common pleasures also do the same work. In Letter 13, after a temporary turn away from the faith, the patient will experience a genuine repentance and renewal, which begins with the simple pleasures of taking a walk through some country that he really likes and reading a book that he really enjoys.) Screwtape's specific pieces of advice in Letter 3 about guiding the patient's relations with his mother—suggestions such as having the patient demand that his utterances must all be taken at face value, judged simply on his actual words, while at the same time he will judge his mother's utterance with the broadest and the most oversensitive interpretation possible[45]—are part of a general strategy of a double standard, or hypocrisy, one that the patient is to remain completely unaware of. As Lewis observes elsewhere, "Those who do not think about their own sins make up for it by thinking incessantly about the sins of others."[46] Vital to the double standard and hypocrisy encouraged in the patient will be a complete lack of capacity for self-criticism. Screwtape urges that he must be brought to the point where he can practice self-examination for an hour without discovering any of the flaws clear to anyone who has lived or worked with him for fifteen minutes.

For much of his adult life, Lewis lived with and cared for an older woman named Mrs. Moore, the mother of a wartime friend. Shortly after Lewis's conversion, we find this short comment about Mrs. Moore in Warnie's diary: "She nags Jack about having become a believer."[47] An echo of this situation appears in Screwtape's words in the final paragraph of Letter 3 where Screwtape says, "Tell me something about the old lady's religious position. Is she at all jealous of the new factor in her son's life?"[48] Green and Hooper, while acknowledging that Lewis would have been aware of "many instances where mothers resented their children becoming Christians," go on to point out that it is hard to reject the idea that Lewis had Mrs. Moore in mind in his portrait of the patient's mother.[49] Whether the mother in *Screwtape* comes from personal experience or not, Lewis would return to this topic of family jealousy again in *The Four Loves* (1960), observing, "Few things in the ordinary peacetime life of a civilized country are more nearly fiendish than the rancor with which a whole unbelieving family will turn on the one member of it who has become a Christian."[50]

Letters 4 to 6: Prayer, the Outbreak of War, and Maximum Uncertainty

Screwtape turns to the topic of prayer in his fourth letter. He tells Wormwood to remind the patient of the "parrot-like" prayers of his childhood, so that in reaction he will turn to prayers that are "entirely spontaneous, inward, informal, and unregularised."[51] Readers at this point might mistakenly conclude that Lewis is arguing for ready-made prayers and against using one's own words. However, Screwtape's purpose for advocating personal prayers here is to move the patient toward a focus on producing "a vaguely devotional *mood* in which real concentration of will and intelligence have no part," in which the patient is to estimate the value of each of his prayers by his "success in producing the desired feeling." [52] Another goal is for Wormwood's patient to think he can practice the prayer of silence that only those who are very far in the Enemy's service can achieve. In Lewis's *Letters to Malcolm, Chiefly on Prayer,* another one of Lewis's collection of fictional letters, published in 1964, the year after Lewis's death, he writes a similar passage of advice on prayer:

For many years after my conversion I never used any ready-made forms except the Lord's Prayer. In fact I tried to pray without words at all. . . . I still think the prayer without words is best—if one can really achieve it. But I now see that in trying to make it my daily bread I was counting on a greater mental and spiritual strength than I really have. To pray successfully without words one needs to be "at the top of one's form." Otherwise the mental acts become merely imaginative or emotional acts—and a fabricated emotion is a miserable affair.[53]

If the patient cannot be taken in with the suggestion that he can successfully practice the prayer of silence, Screwtape urges Wormwood to at least persuade him that "bodily position makes no difference."[54] In another letter to Malcolm, we find an elaboration on Screwtape's point:

On a day of traveling . . . I'd rather pray sitting in a crowded train than put it off till midnight when one reaches a hotel bedroom with aching head and dry throat and one's mind partly in a stupor and partly in a whirl. On other, and slightly less crowded, days a bench in a park, or a back street where one can pace up and down, will do. . . . When one prays in strange places and at strange times one can't kneel, to be sure. I won't say this doesn't matter. The body ought to pray as well as the soul. Body and soul are both the better for it. . . . The relevant point is that kneeling does matter, but other things matter even more. A concentrated mind and a sitting body make for better prayer than a kneeling body and a mind half asleep.[55]

In Letters 5 and 6 readers learn that "the European humans have started another of their wars,"[56] a fact that Screwtape warns Wormwood should not hope for too much from the patient because the war may also lead to thousands "turning in this tribulation to the Enemy" and even more turning to values and causes bigger than themselves. "How disastrous for us," Screwtape laments, "is the continual remembrance of death which war enforces."[57] Lewis, who had served and been wounded in the first World War, had small need himself to be reminded of his own mortality by another conflict. Near the start of the second Great War, he wrote in a letter to his friend Dom Bede Griffiths, "My memories of the last war haunted my dreams for years . . . I think death would be much better than to live through another war . . . I do not doubt that whatever misery He permits will be for our ultimate good unless, by rebellious will, we convert it to evil."[58] Screwtape suggests in Letter 6 that it is preferable to be "possible, but by no means certain" that the young man will be called up for service in the military, this way the patient will be in a position of maximum uncertainly and, according to Screwtape, so full of anxiety that his mind will be barricaded against the Enemy. The senior devil reminds Wormwood, "Our business is to keep them thinking about what will happen to them." [59]

In the last paragraph of Letter 6, Screwtape points out there will be benevolence as well as malice in the patient's soul and advises Wormwood to direct the malice to the patient's immediate neighbors and to focus the benevolence on people he does not know. This way, "the malice becomes wholly real and the benevolence largely imaginary."[60] Here Lewis provides an upside-down version of the famous statement that Jonathan Swift made in a letter to his friend Alexander Pope: "I hate and detest that animal called man, although

I heartily love John, Peter, Thomas, and so forth."[61] Here Wormwood is to encourage his patient to imagine that he loves mankind in general, but all the while loathing his actual neighbors.

Letters 7 to 9: Encouraging Factions, Peaks and Troughs, Pleasures and Phases

One of the advantages in writing a work of fictional epistles such as *The Screwtape Letters* is that it allows its author to wander from topic to topic at will, in the way that actual letters might. And so from time to time, Lewis addresses more than one subject in a single letter without a direct connection between the various topics.

Letter 7 begins with the question of whether Wormwood's patient should know of his tempter's existence. Screwtape declares, "Our policy, for the moment, is to conceal ourselves."[62] The problem with making their presence known, Screwtape notes, is that it does not allow the possibility of the humans staying materialists, at least not yet. The elder tempter goes on to outline the hope that a belief in and even a worship of devils can be cultivated under different names. Here, Screwtape suggests that the Life Force, the worship of sex, and certain aspects of Psychoanalysis may "prove useful."

While devils in *Screwtape* remain hidden until the patient's moment of death, Lewis presents fictional manifestations of the demons in the second and third volumes of his space trilogy, books that he began immediately after *Screwtape*. In *Perelandra* (1943), Ransom must battle Weston who has become possessed by the Devil or by devils, and becomes, as Ransom calls him, an Un-man. In *That Hideous Strength* (1945), devils are present in the form of what are called dark eldils.

In Screwtape's final comments on concealment, readers find one of Lewis's most powerful insights. Should any suspicion of Wormwood's existence arise in the patient's mind, Screwtape urges him to suggest to the patient "a picture of something in red tights" and to persuade him that "since he cannot believe in that . . . he therefore cannot believe in you."[63] In the preface to the 1961 edition Lewis makes much the same point about the misrepresentation of angels, citing the "chubby infantile nudes of Raphael" and the soft, girlish angels of later artists.[64] Lewis reminds us that in scripture an appearance by an angel is always terrifying and so is typically accompanied by the command, "Fear not." Presumably an appearance by a fallen angel would be even more terrifying, and would produce the very opposite effect than seeing a comic red-costumed character with a pitchfork would.

Screwtape's also notes in Letter 7 that he supports all causes, extremes, divisions, and factions as a means to promote division, pride, and hatred, and to distract the patient from the real purposes for which these things exist: "Provided that meetings, pamphlets, policies, movements, causes, and crusades, matter more to him than prayers and sacraments and charity, he is ours."[65] Lewis was not opposed to such things, but thought they should be kept in their proper place. This idea of ordinate loves was a concept Lewis got from St. Augustine and one that he explored in a number of works. In *Letters to Malcolm* Lewis observes, "Our deepest concern should be for the first things, and our next deepest for second things, and so on down to zero—to the total absence of concern for things that are not really good, nor means to good at all."[66] In a letter to Dom Bede Griffiths, Lewis argues, "Put first things first and we get second things thrown in: put second things first and we lose *both* first and second things."[67]

Letter 8 begins with Wormwood's hope that "the patient's religious phase is dying away", a mistaken conclusion that opens the door for Screwtape to elaborate on the law of Undulation, the topic of troughs and peaks first touched on in Letter 2. Here the senior devil explains that the spiritual dryness and dullness the patient has been experiencing is not the result of Wormwood's workmanship but is a natural phenomenon, similar to the undulation found in every department of human life. According to Screwtape, the danger of this period of spiritual dryness comes in the use the Enemy wants to make of it. Screwtape warns that it is during this kind of trough period, much more than during the peak times, that Wormwood's patient has the greatest opportunity to grow into "the sort of creature He wants it to be."[68] In the next letter, Screwtape will add four additional pieces of advice for using these periods of spiritual dryness to the devils' advantage. First, Wormwood is to encourage the patient to assume that his first feelings of excitement should have lasted forever, and second, that his present dryness is "an equally permanent condition."[69] Third, Wormwood is told to keep the patient away from experienced Christians, and finally is advised to get his patient working on recovering his old feelings by sheer will power.

Letter 9 also explores some specific activities Wormwood is to promote during the trough times. According to Screwtape, the times of dullness provide excellent opportunity for sensual temptations, and sex and drink are listed as specific examples. Because these actions relate to abusing proper pleasures, which are healthy, and normal, and satisfying, Screwtape's plan is to encourage humans "to take the pleasures that our Enemy has produced, at times, or in ways, or in degrees which He has forbidden." In *The Lion, the Witch and the Wardrobe*, readers can see the enjoyment of a proper pleasure in the scene where Lucy has tea with Mr. Tumnus and also later in the delicious meal the children have with the Beavers. However, a proper pleasure is taken to an excessive degree when Edmund devours an entire box of Turkish Delight.

Letter 9 concludes with the suggestion that since the patient's initial excitement is now gone, he must think of his faith as a phase rather than as something that is either true or false, and better yet if he thinks of it as an "adolescent" phase, part of his progress and development, but a stage that he is now too mature for.[70]

Letters 10 to 12: New Acquaintances, Kinds of Laughter, and A Gradual Falling Off

In Letter 9, Wormwood was urged to keep his patient out of the way of experienced Christians. Now in Letter 10, we find the reverse to this advice. Screwtape is delighted that Wormwood's man has made the acquaintance of a middle-aged married couple who are just the sort of people Screwtape wants him to know since they are wealthy, smart, superficially intellectual, and "brightly skeptical about everything," the kind who belittle "anything that concerns the great mass of their fellow men."[71] Particularly helpful will be fact that this couple, unlike the unsophisticated churchgoers the patient encountered in Letter 2, will easily appeal to his social, sexual, and intellectual vanity. Screwtape foresees that when the patient is with these new acquaintances, the patient will connive: he will be silent when he should speak, and laugh when he should be silent. Soon he will assume first by manner and then by words "all sorts of cynical and skeptical attitudes," which are not really his, at least not yet—if assumed long enough they will become his own—for, as Screwtape argues, "All mortals tend to turn into the thing they are pretending to be,"[72] a claim worth further reflecting upon. The critical point here seems to be Screwtape's exact use of the word *pretending*. In *Mere Christianity* Lewis clarifies this point and notes that by pretending, he does not mean acting hypocritically:

Do not waste time bothering whether you "love" your neighbor; act as if you did. As soon as we do this we find one of the great secrets. When you are behaving as if you loved someone, you will presently come to love him . . . There is, indeed, one exception. If you do him a good turn, not to please God and obey the law of charity, but to show him what a fine forgiving chap you are, and to put him in your debt, . . . you will probably be disappointed.[73]

In Letter 11 Screwtape announces that he is glad to hear that the patient is now associating with the two friends' whole set of acquaintances, a group of "consistent scoffers" who are not guilty of any "spectacular" crimes but instead are progressing "quietly and comfortably towards Our Father's house."[74] As Wormwood's patient is more and more influenced by this new group of unbelievers, Screwtape's strategy will be one of gradualness, a policy he will expand on in the next letter. For the remainder of Letter 11, Screwtape explores the causes of human laughter with joy being the least favorable to the devils' cause and flippancy the most helpful in building up "amour-plating against the Enemy" (p. 56). Screwtape does not understand joy and cannot really explain it: he can only note that it is present when friends or lovers get together on the eve of a holiday. Screwtape comprehends flippancy, laughter's lowest form, much better. With flippancy every serious subject is discussed as though it were ridiculous. Lewis's point in this epistle seems to be that human laughter and levity can have heavenly origins or origins that are quite the opposite.

In Letter 12, Screwtape is concerned that Wormwood's patient may become aware that he has taken real steps away from his faith. He warns that this change of spiritual direction must always be gradual and always appear revocable. To this end, Screwtape is glad that the man is still going to church, for as long as he retains the external habits of a Christian, he can still be made to erroneously think of himself as someone who has merely "adopted a few new friends and amusements but whose spiritual state is much the same as it was."[75] Screwtape points out that the patient will undoubtedly experience a feeling of "dim uneasiness" about his state, a sensation that, if Wormwood is not careful, may have opposite results. Should the feeling get too strong, it may waken the patient to his condition. However, if, as Screwtape advises, it remains in the background, it can actually lead to a "reluctance to think about the Enemy"[76] much in the same way that a person in financial trouble would be reluctant to think about his checking account, eventually causing the patient to dislike religious duties he formerly relished. If this condition of dim uneasiness can be more fully established, Screwtape describes how it can then lead to a condition of increasing misery, when the man's attention will then wander, and his prayers, work, and even his sleep will deteriorate. In one of Lewis's most perceptive observations about a life of sin, Screwtape concludes, "All the healthy and out-going activities which we want him to avoid can be inhibited and *nothing* given in return."[77] Letter 12 concludes with the patient started on the gradual road to Hell, which Screwtape describes as "the gentle slope, soft underfoot, without sudden turnings, without milestones, without signposts."[78]

Letters 13 to 15: A Return to Grace, Regarding Humility, and Staying Future-Focused

In Letter 13 Screwtape responds to the news that Wormwood has let the man experience repentance and a return to the faith, which for the devils is "a defeat of the first order."[79] There is a heightening of the conflict between the two, and Screwtape implies there will consequences for Wormwood's blunder. As a subplot to the patient's story, this conflict between Screwtape and Wormwood will slowly escalate over the remainder of the letters and will serve as an illustration of the dog-eat-dog, competitive mentality of Hell, which Screwtape will describe in Letter 18.

Notwithstanding Screwtape's previous claim that the man will be increasingly unable to enjoy normal pleasures, the patient has found delight in reading a book and taking a walk. This discrepancy with what Screwtape had predicted suggests an intervention, a counterattack, by the patient's good angels. Screwtape informs Wormwood that these two real pleasures killed by contrast "all the trumpery," which he had been teaching his patient to value, and brought him to a sense of recovery, of coming home again. Screwtape claims, "Of course I know that the Enemy also wants to detach men from themselves, but in a different way."[80] According to Screwtape, God values human distinctness and, unlike the devils, seeks to preserve it. God's idea of detachment means abandoning self-will, not their unique personalities and individual tastes.

Letter 13 concludes with Screwtape urging that the important thing for Wormwood is not to let the patient do anything, not to let him convert the recent repentance into action. Screwtape advises Wormwood to let him wallow in his repentance, even better, to write a book about it. The letter concludes with the probing assertion: "The more often he feels without acting, the less he will be able ever to act."[81]

Letter 14 begins with what may be a surprise for readers: Screwtape is disappointed that Wormwood's patient, now that he has returned to the faith, is *not* making promises of perpetual virtue, as he originally did at his conversion. Screwtape ruefully observes that the man is now humbly asking only for the "daily and hourly pittance to meet the daily and hourly temptation."[82] Screwtape's solution for the patient's genuine humility is to have Wormwood draw his attention to it and to encourage him to have pride at his own humbleness. Should this not work, Wormwood is encouraged to twist humility, a virtue, into its dark version, self-contempt—a misstep that then can be gradually extended into contempt for others.

This transformation of humility into self-contempt runs counter to the Enemy's goal. As Screwtape notes, "He wants each man, in the long run, to be able to recognize all creatures (even himself) as glorious and excellent things."[83] Lewis's healthy expression of self-worth here is one of his most timely statements, sounding as though it could have been written yesterday, rather than in 1940. In a letter dated June 20, 1952, Lewis echoes his position here, writing: "I would prefer to combat the 'I'm special' feeling not by the thought 'I'm no more special than anyone else,' but by the feeling 'Everyone is as special as me.'"[84]

Letter 15 opens with the news that there is a lull in the war, which has produced a similar calm in the patient's anxieties. Screwtape returns to and expands on his policy of keeping the patient focused on the future, which was seen earlier in Letter 6 in his strategy of maximum uncertainty. Screwtape points out that the Enemy wants humans to attend to eternity and the present. "Our business," he declares to Wormwood, "is to get them away the eternal, and from the Present."[85] Screwtape further notes that, of course, the Enemy *does* want humans to think of the future in order to plan for acts of justice or charity. But according to Screwtape, "This is now straw splitting. He does not want men to give the Future their hearts, to place their treasure in it. We do."[86]

Letters 16 to 18: Church Shopping, Gluttony, and Sexual Temptation

Screwtape is critical of the fact that the patient is still attending the same church as when he started attending church and declares, "If a man can't be cured of churchgoing, the next best thing is to send him all over the neighborhood looking for the church that 'suits' him" (p. 81). For all of his Christian life, Lewis, attended the same Anglican church in the Oxford suburb of Headington Quarry, a few blocks from his home. In this he was following the parochial principle, which Screwtape objects to here, since it "brings together people of different classes and psychology together in the kind of unity the Enemy desires" (p. 81). Much better, Screwtape suggests, is the congregational principle, which makes each church more like a club or faction. Lewis's point about critiquing churches is somewhat nuanced. On the one hand, the churchgoer may, and in fact should, be critical if what he is rejecting is "false or unhelpful," but at the same time he is to remain open to any nourishment available. Having made this point, Lewis, through Screwtape, appraises two churches: the first has a vicar whose unbelief astonishes his parishioners, rather than the reverse; the second has a pastor who preaches hatred-filled sermons intended "to shock, grieve, puzzle, or humiliate his parents and their friends."[87] Certainly Lewis is not advocating remaining at the local parish church if the doctrines preached there are false, but exactly which set of aspects could be included under Lewis's heading of "unhelpful" is not entirely clear. In *Letters to Malcolm* there is a partial elaboration. Lewis argues that "mere inadequacy" is not a valid excuse for church hopping and offers several examples of elements, which would be invalid reasons for leaving, including "an ugly church, a gawky server, or a badly turned-out celebrant."[88] But Screwtape mentions "candles and clothes and what not" as elements which, under his plan, could serve to send the patient looking for a church more suitable to his tastes.

In Letter 17 readers learn that the patient's mother suffers from an inordinate focus not on the *quantity* of food but on its *quality*, a condition

Screwtape calls the gluttony of Delicacy. Screwtape notes how gluttony, once one of the seven deadly sins, is now considered neither deadly nor even a sin by most Christians. The patient's mother is kept completely unaware of her selfishness: she "never recognizes as gluttony her determination to get what she wants, however troublesome it may be to others."[89] Just as the patient has Wormwood assigned to tempt him, the mother has a devil named Glubose who has led her into a condition of greed, which Screwtape labels the "All-I-want" state of mind.

Knowing that Christians, and humans in general, have a tendency to gravitate toward one extreme or the other, Lewis next charts a course away from both an ascetic renunciation of all pleasures, the view that enjoying the pleasures of life is somehow sinful in and of itself, and a gluttonous insistence that one's sensual desires always be satisfied. In *Mere Christianity* Lewis argues that the devil "always sends errors into the world in pairs—pairs of opposites," and that the solution is to "go straight through between both errors."[90] So how is one to know when proper enjoyment has crossed the line into unwarranted love or enslavement? The key can be found in Screwtape's suggestion to have the denial of any of the pleasures the patient likes be enough to "put him out." When an unmet physical desire results in a loss of charity, justice, or obedience, the enjoyment has gone beyond its proper bounds.

In Letter 18, as part of his discussion of sexual temptation, Screwtape contrasts "love" with "being in love" and the philosophies of Hell on this topic with the philosophies of Heaven. From the perspective of Hell, there can be no love; there can be no gain without someone else's loss, for "to be" means "to be in competition." Readers have already been given glimpses of this state of everpresent rivalry through the underlying antagonistic relationship between Screwtape and Wormwood. The senior devil explains that in order for a physical object to expand it must push aside or absorb whatever objects are in its way, and claims the same is true for beings. Screwtape is interested in "the sucking of will and freedom out of a weaker self into a stronger," but in Heaven, the opposite principle prevails: "The good of one self is to be the good of another,"[91] although Screwtape insists that this philosophy of the Enemy is merely an attempt to evade the obvious truth of the competitive nature of existence. Screwtape observes that the Enemy's plan involves contradiction: "Things are to be many, yet somehow one," and gives the example of how sexual desire and the family are results of what the Enemy calls love.

Letters 19 to 21: Love, Sexuality, and My Time Is My Own

The Devil's fundamental principle, as Screwtape explains in Letter 19, is "all selves are by their very nature in competition," which leads to the conclusion that all the Enemy's talk about love "must be a disguise for something else."[92] Screwtape's dilemma is he cannot comprehend anything beyond competition and greed as motivation, and yet at the same time his observations lead him to conclude, "He really loves the human vermin and really desires their freedom and continued existence,"[93] a conclusion he then attempts to back away from lest he be accused of heresy. Screwtape is at a loss to understand the Enemy's real motive but he recognizes that this lack of understanding is the very problem that caused the original break between Satan and God.

In Letter 20 readers learn that Wormwood's attacks on the patient's chastity have been thwarted by the Enemy, presumably with the help of the patient's guardian angels whose efforts are pointed out in the final letter. Screwtape immediately switches his focus. "If we can't use his sexuality to make him unchaste," he urges Wormwood, "we must try to use it for the promotion of a desirable marriage,"[94] and, of course, desirable here means undesirable from the patient's perspective. In Letter 21, when Screwtape turns to the topic of "My Time is My Own," it is significant that immediately following an attack on the patient's chastity comes an attack on the patient's "peevishness." The patient has committed, at least in theory, to "a total service of the Enemy" and yet if minor interruptions to what he falsely claims as "his" day are enough to "throw him out of gear" then the patient will be distracted from the Enemy. This is in keeping with Screwtape's point from Letter 12 that it does not matter how small the sin is, provided that the cumulative effect is to edge the man away from the Light. If not by a "great" sin of sexual immorality, then Screwtape would be equally happy if "lesser" sins did the job.

Letters 22 to 24: In Love, Corrupting Christian Influence, and Spiritual Pride

The patient has fallen in love with a girl, readers learn in Letter 22, in fact, with a Christian girl, who is not at all to Screwtape's liking, particularly since, while she appears to be timid and meek, she is in fact courageous and witty. Worst of all, Screwtape laments, is that she is "the sort of creature who'd find *ME* funny!"[95] a response in harmony with the Luther epigram declaring that the devil cannot bear scorn. Careful readers might conclude that this relationship has come about as a result of an equally intense effort by the patient's good angels to counter Wormwood's attempts to encourage a "desirable" marriage proscribed earlier in Letter 20. (In the final letter when the patient sees these guardian angels, he will realize how they have been instrumental in shaping his life.)

The disturbing thought of the sensual delights, which the patient and his girl will properly enjoy, leads Screwtape to return to the topic of the Enemy's use of pleasures, touched on previously in Letter 9. Here Screwtape rants against the fact that at the Enemy's right hand are "pleasures for evermore," a reference to Psalms 16:11, and that for the devils to make use of anything they have to twist it. To counter the non-Christian friends and their associates, the patient's guardian angels have brought him into contact not only with a Christian girl but also with her family, and, as seen in the next letter, with their entire circle of Christian friends as well. Screwtape complains of a deadly odor, which surrounds the house, giving it a resemblance of heaven and sending him into an even deeper rant. At the end of his outbursts, Screwtape suddenly turns on Wormwood with the words, "Meanwhile *you*, disgusting little,"[96] and then there is a break in the writing. Presumably Screwtape is about to lash out at his apprentice for his failures in keeping the patient from the Christian girl and her family, antagonism that will continue to increase. But when the narrative resumes, Screwtape does not finish his thoughts about Wormwood, but instead explains the reason for the break. Screwtape claims that he inadvertently allowed himself to assume the form of a centipede, but the implication is that this change in form has come as chastisement from God.

At the close of Letter 22, Screwtape mentions a modern writer "with a name like Pshaw" who has understood the real truth behind Screwtape's change; rather than punishment, Screwtape's transformation should be viewed as a manifestation of the Life Force. Here Lewis is referring to George Bernard Shaw, a modern philosopher he elaborates on in the chapter "What Lies Behind the Law" from *Mere Christianity*. There Lewis notes that so far he has discussed only the Materialist and the Religious views, and then further describes Shaw's beliefs:

But to be complete I ought to mention the In-between view called Life-Force philosophy, or Creative Evolution, or emergent Evolution. The wittiest expositions of it come in the works of Bernard Shaw.... People who hold this view say that the small variations by which life on this planet "evolved" from the lowest forms to Man were not due to chance but to the "striving" or "purposiveness" of a Life-Force.[97]

Screwtape has already mentioned the Life Force in Letter 7 as a way to encourage a belief in devils but under a different name. In *Perelandra*, Lewis provides us with a character who serves this Life Force, Professor Weston, who describes it as "blind, inarticulate purposiveness thrusting its way upward and ever upward in an endless unity of differentiated achievements."[98] Weston then cries out, "I call that Force into me completely,"[99] it becomes clear that the Life Force is, indeed, merely a disguise for a diabolical force.

Letter 23 begins with Screwtape's admission that since the patient is getting to know more Christians every day, and intelligent Christians at that, it will be "quite impossible to *remove* spirituality from his life."[100] So the question becomes, as with the other positive elements in the patient's life, how can Wormwood corrupt it? Screwtape says there has been a specific progression to his strategy. First they used the world to tempt the man, and failed. Then they turned to the temptations of the flesh, and failed again. Now Screwtape states that a third power remains, corrupted religion, and asserts this third kind of success to be "the most glorious of all," for in Hell a spoiled saint is even better sport than a tyrant. Lewis is likely not suggesting this three-step pattern is the general sequence of temptation for everyone, and merely that it is for this patient.

Screwtape's tactic for twisting the patient's spirituality will be to emphasize the social implications of the patient's faith, yet another good element with potential to be used for evil. Screwtape's plan to use social justice concerns in order to lead the man away from Christianity opens the door for a lengthy discussion of attempts by modern thinkers to distinguish a historical Jesus from the Jesus of the Gospels, a distinction Screwtape says should always be encouraged. He notes that there will be a different historical Jesus "every thirty years or so,"[101] and since the current version emphasizes a Marxian, revolutionary leader, this becomes the connection with warping the patient's concerns for social justice.

In Letter 24, Screwtape briefly turns to the possibility of corrupting the girl's spirituality by encouraging in her a feeling of superiority toward outsiders who do not share her beliefs. Screwtape has little hope that pride will be her downfall, but sees great potential for this seed to take root in the patient, a novice Christian. Wormwood is to make the patient feel that he and his new set of Christians are an exclusive group, better than the unbelievers around them, and even better than other believers. Screwtape tells Wormwood that the idea of belonging to an inner ring will be "very sweet" to the patient and that he should "play on that nerve."[102]

Lewis himself encountered a malevolent inner circle while a student at Malvern College and then again later at Oxford, so it is not surprising that he addresses the temptations and abuses of belonging to an inner ring in a number of his works. In *Surprised by Joy*, he describes the negative effects of the all-consuming desire to be included in an exclusionary group. From this impulse, Lewis argues, "all sorts of meanness flow; the sycophancy that courts those higher in the scale, the cultivation of those whom it is well to know, the speedy abandonment of friendships that will not help on the upward path, the readiness to join the cry against the unpopular, the secret motive in almost every action."[103] When he was invited in 1944 to give the Commemoration Oration to students at King's College in London, he delivered an address later published as "The Inner Ring," in which he observed that the longing to be part of an inside group takes "many forms which are not easily recognizable as ambition," and warns, "Of all passions the passion for the Inner Ring is most skillful in making a man who is not yet a very bad man do very bad things."[104]

Letters 25 to 27: "Christianity" and, Unselfishness versus Charity, and More on Prayer

Screwtape opens Letter 25 complaining about the fact that the patient's new friends are *merely* Christian, meaning that while they have their own unique interests, these personal interests are always subordinate to their Christianity. Lewis took the title of his book *Mere Christianity*, from the Puritan divine Richard Baxter (1615–1691), explaining there that he used this term to refer to beliefs that have been common to nearly all Christians at all times.[105] In contrast to mere Christianity, Screwtape encourages *Christianity and*, Christian beliefs inexorably woven with the latest trend or fashion, a coloring stimulated by humans' horror of "the same old thing." Screwtape's alternative to mere Christianity is mere preference, mere taste, and mere novelty. Here again in *Screwtape* we see a proper delight, specifically the natural pleasantness of change, twisted into a negative element, the demand for absolute novelty. This demand for novelty, by its very nature, fulfills Screwtape's formula from Letter 9 of "an ever increasing craving for an ever diminishing pleasure."[106]

In Letter 26, Lewis uses an implied comment made by Wormwood in the intervening correspondence to allow Screwtape to jump to the wholly different topic of unselfishness—how it contrasts with the virtue of charity, and how it may be used to create misunderstandings between the patient and his girl. Screwtape explains that while unselfishness for women means taking trouble for others, for men it means not giving trouble. Lewis through Screwtape suggests that in each trying to be unselfish, often a couple can often end up doing what neither person wants, leading to resentment, claims for preferential treatment in the future, and further disagreement.

As Alan Jacobs has noted, Lewis would often develop an idea "one way in a science fiction novel, another way in a scholarly book, yet another way in a work of Christian apologetics, and in even a different way in one of the Narnia tales."[107] Jacobs argues these echoes are not mere repetitions but rather "a set of powerful insights or concerns being refracted through different facets of experience."[108] In "The Weight of Glory," a sermon preached in the same year the *Guardian* letters appeared, Lewis opens with the very same contrast seen here in *Screwtape*: "If you asked twenty good men today what they thought the highest of the virtues, nineteen of them would reply, Unselfishness. But if you had asked almost any of the great Christians of old, he would have replied, Love. You see what has happened? A negative term has been substituted for a positive."[109] Lewis's point in both the sermon and in *Screwtape* is that the suppression of our natural desires, self-denial, has been raised to position it has not previously held. As Lewis makes clear in the sermon, while the New Testament often speaks about self-denial, it is never about self-denial as an end in itself.

To reinforce his idea of how Wormwood must use unselfishness to his advantage, Screwtape provides an ironic comment from an unnamed human: "She's the sort of woman who lives for others—you can always tell the others by their hunted expression" (p. 145). Nineteen years after *Screwtape* in *The Four Loves* (1960), Lewis would further develop this idea of an "unselfish" mother whose "Gift-love" has been twisted:

I am thinking of Mrs. Fidget, who died a few months ago. It is really astonishing how her family have brightened up. . . . There was always a hot lunch for anyone who was at home and always a hot meal at night (even in midsummer). They implored her not to provide this. They protested almost with tears in their eyes (and with truth) that they liked cold meals. It made no difference. She was living for her family.[110]

In the final paragraph of Letter 26, Screwtape notes that if people knew how much ill feeling this form of unselfishness generates, it would not be "so often recommended from the pulpit."[111]

Letter 27 opens with Screwtape chiding Wormwood for not using the patient's infatuation to distract him from the Enemy. Wormwood's efforts have been counterproductive because the patient has made his distraction the very subject of his prayers, causing Screwtape to state, "Anything, even a sin, which has the total effect of moving him close up to the Enemy, makes against us in the long run."[112] Since the patient's distraction has not proved useful, Wormwood is to try to corrupt the patient's prayer by sowing doubt in his mind about praying in a way that is purely petitionary. The patient is to be led to believe that an offering of praise and communion is more spiritual than a request for daily bread, and in addition, to believe that requests that then come about would have happened anyway and those not granted are proof this type of prayer does not work. Lewis would return to this point in 1959 in an essay titled "The Efficacy of Prayer," where he concludes:

Now even if all the things that people prayed for happened, which they do not, this would not prove what Christians mean by the efficacy of prayer. For prayer is request. The essence of request, as distinct from compulsion, is that it may or may not be granted. And if an infinitely wise Being listens to the requests of finite and foolish creatures, of course He will sometimes grant and sometimes refuse them.[113]

Lewis, through Screwtape, considers the problem of prayer and pre-destination—how is it possible that God knows what our prayers will be to-morrow but yet "leaves room" through our free will for us to decide whether to pray or not? Screwtape explains to Wormwood that this is no problem at all because "the Enemy does not *foresee* the humans making their free con-tributions in a future, but *sees* them doing so in His unbounded Now."[114] Screwtape concludes that to watch someone do something is not the same as making him do it.

Letters 28 to 30: The Uses of Middle Age, Danger, and Fatigue

Around the time Lewis was writing *Screwtape,* he would have had vivid reminders of the German air raids on England, not only through the news, but also in the fact that children evacuated from London stayed at the Kilns and also through his own service as a member of The Home Guard, a duty that involved weekly late-night patrols on the outskirts of Oxford. In Letter 28, Screwtape complains about Wormwood's glee about the heavy air raids on the patient's town, but in one of book's most startling reversals, Screwtape tells Wormwood that the patient's death is "precisely what we want to avoid" since if he were to be killed he would "almost certainly be lost to us."[115] Screwtape then lists Wormwood's defeats—which are, of course, victories from the patient's perspective—and here we find the same three-stage progression outlined in Letter 23. First the patient escaped the entanglement of the worldly friends Wormwood provided. Then through his relationship with the Christian girl, he escaped the attacks on his chastity. Finally, as we learn here in Letter 28, the attempts to corrupt his spiritual life—the temptations to subordinate his faith to social justice and the attacks on his prayer life—have also failed. Wormwood's patient, despite all the devils' efforts, remains more in the Enemy's camp than ever, and so his death at this point would be, for them, a disaster. Humans, thanks to the devils' instruction, have come to think of death as the greatest evil and of survival as the greatest good, but Screwtape warns Wormwood that he should not be taken in by this propaganda. Due to Wormwood's failures with his patient, failures at least partly due to the fact that "the Enemy has guarded him," Screwtape's negative tone is once again stepped up in this letter.

Screwtape claims that although the recent battles for the patient's soul have been lost, the war is not over; and in this, he claims, time is the devils' ally. Why exactly Lewis is not more balanced here about the possibilities that a long life will hold for good as well as for evil is not clear. Perhaps this is one of the occasions where Screwtape is not telling the entire truth. Certainly, middle age can be filled with temptations, but unlike other moments in *Screwtape* there is no double-edged sword here to suggest that living longer can cut against as well as for the devils' cause. Should the patient's middle age be one of adversity, Screwtape claims that it will try his ability to "persevere." If his middle age is prosperous, it will be easier to tempt him with worldly success.

Lewis was in his early forties when he wrote *Screwtape*, so the question arises, "To what extent might he have been drawing from his own experience in describing middle age as a fruitful time for temptations?" Certainly he was tempted with the comfortable aspects of middle age. In a letter written to his friend Arthur Greeves in 1939, Lewis claims that one positive aspect of the outbreak of the war was that it helped to break the spell of self-satisfaction he had fallen under. "I was just beginning to get too well settled in my profession," Lewis writes, "too successful, and probably self-complacent."[116] So it can be easily argued that Lewis—with the success of three recently published books, regular meetings of the Inklings, and status as one of Oxford's most popular lecturers—fit Screwtape's description of a man who was finding his place in the world. The senior devil observes: "His increasing reputation, his widening circle of acquaintances, his sense of importance, the growing pressure of absorbing and agreeable work, build up in him a sense of being really at home in earth, which is just what we want."[117]

But what about the other side, which Screwtape claims middle age can have, the "routine of adversity, the gradual decay of youthful loves and youthful hopes"?[118] What about the "quiet despair" of overcoming the same chronic temptations again and again? What about the "drabness" that Screwtape associates here with middle age? What evidence is there that these elements could also have come from Lewis's own life during this time? Later in life, Lewis would write a good deal on the trials and temptations of aging, but at this point in his life there is less to go on. We do have Lewis's own admission in the 1961 preface that his own heart provided a reliable source for the temptations in *Screwtape*. In addition, there is evidence from an address he gave around the time of *Screwtape* titled "*De Futilitate.*" In this essay, Lewis declares it hard to believe that anyone could have reached "the middle forties" without having doubts that there was any good reason for the world to continue, without feeling the monotony and futility of human existence.[119] And finally in the preface to *The Problem of Pain*, a work published the year before Screwtape's debut, Lewis confesses to be unqualified to teach anything about "fortitude and patience,"[120] a confession that suggests he himself struggled in these two areas at this time and that he himself was finding it hard to persevere.

Screwtape's musings on the good sense and maturity that the middle years *supposedly* produce allow him to bring Letter 28 to a conclusion by quoting "a great human philosopher" who, in speaking about virtue, claimed that "experience is the mother of illusion."[121] The quote comes from Kant's *Critique of Pure Reason*, a book that Screwtape claims the Historical Point of View has rendered innocuous.

The air raid bombings will surely keep the patient in peril, and Screwtape ponders what use can be made of this heightened, constant feeling of danger. Should Wormwood encourage cowardice, pride, hatred, fear, or despair in his patient? A bravery that results in pride would be a good choice, but Screwtape observes as he did with the pleasures, the virtues are something the devils are unable to produce on their own. Hatred, on the other hand, is easier for the devils to encourage, particularly since the noise, danger, and fatigue of the bombings make the humans prone to violent emotions. So all Wormwood need do is simply guide the patient's natural susceptibility into the proper channel, but in Letter 30 readers learn that Wormwood has been unsuccessful in using the air raids to tempt the patient into any of the negative emotional conditions suggested by Screwtape. Although the young man was afraid, he did his duty and more. Wormwood has complained that his attacks on the patient have been beset with difficulties that should be taken into account along with his intentions and his lack of opportunities when determining the punishment for his lack of success. Screwtape chides his young charge for adopting the Enemy's idea of justice, a stance that amounts to heresy since the justice of Hell looks only at results.

Screwtape then warns Wormwood to bring back food, meaning the patient, otherwise he will become food himself. In the 1961 preface, Lewis thought it worthwhile to expand on this point. Bad angels, Lewis argues, are entirely practical, having only two motives: their fear of being punished and a type of perpetual hunger. Lewis explains further:

I feign that devils can, in a spiritual sense, eat one another; and us. Even in human life we have seen the passion to dominate, almost to digest, one's fellow; to make his whole intellectual and emotional life merely an extension of one's one. . . . In Hell, I feign that they recognize [this desire] as hunger. . . . There, I suggest, the stronger spirit— there are perhaps no bodies to impede the operation—can really and irrevocably suck the weaker into itself and permanently gorge its own being on the weaker's outraged individuality.[122]

The air raids have left the patient exhausted and Screwtape urges that devilish use can be made of this, although he notes that fatigue can also lead to positive results—gentleness, quiet of mind, and even vision. The key will be to add unexpected demands on top of the patient's fatigue; for, as Screwtape says in one his most insightful observations: "Whatever men expect they soon come to think they have a right to,"[123] a continuation of the "My Time is My Own" policy seen earlier in Letter 21.

Screwtape closes his last regular correspondence by revisiting a topic addressed near the close of his first letter: the need to confuse what is real and what is not. In all the positive experiences the patient has, Wormwood is to suggest that the physical elements are real and the spiritual ones are subjective. For those experiences that can "discourage or corrupt," the opposite is to be encouraged. Thus blood and pain, the physical elements that accompany a birth, are what is real; the joy is not. In death, the terror and horror must be thought of as the main reality. Screwtape concludes with a second apt illustration of this policy: Any emotions produced by happy children or beautiful weather are to be dismissed as mere sentiment, while the patient's emotions at the sight of human entrails are to be taken as a valid revelation of what is real.

Letter 31: All Is Lost

Screwtape begins his final letter with a string of elaborate pet names for Wormwood, terms of diabolical endearment signaling, not his affection, but his craving to consume the younger devil. Readers have speculated on the unique names which Lewis assigns to his seven devils—not just Screwtape and Wormwood, but also *Glubose* who is responsible for the patient's mother; *Slumtrimpet* who is responsible for the young woman; *Slubgob* who heads up the tempter's college; *Toadpipe* who serves as Screwtape's scribe; and *Triptweeze* who has some relationship with the non-Christian acquaintances. In the 1961 preface, Lewis confesses to the fact that his devils' names had excited a great amount of curiosity leading to "many explanations, all wrong."[124] His intention, Lewis explains, was merely to make them nasty by their sound and by the associations with that sound. Thus, Lewis speculates that *Scrooge, screw, thumbscrew, tapeworm, and red tape* all went into creating Screwtape's name, and that *slob, slobber, slubber* (to perform in a slipshod manner), and *gob* played a role in Slubgob. *Wormwood*, besides having some negative sound associations, also is a word itself meaning *something bitter*.

We learn the patient has died and is lost to the devils forever when Screwtape accuses Wormwood of having "let a soul slip through your fingers."[125] Lewis's portrait of the moment of death is comforting and thrilling. One moment bombs are screaming and houses falling around the patient, the next moment all the horror is gone like a bad dream, left behind for good. His entrance into eternal life is all quite natural, "as if he'd been born for it."[126] Not only does the patient see Wormwood, but he also can finally see the angels who played key parts at vital times in the his life, spirits whom Wormwood can only cower before. In a phrase filled with beauty, Lewis states: "The dim consciousness of friends around him which had haunted his solitudes from infancy was now at last explained; that central music in every pure experience which had always just evaded memory was now at last recovered."[127] The patient sees "Him," a heavenly being described as one who "wears the form of a man," Screwtape's description of Christ, and the presence of this heavenly being is blinding, suffocating fire to Wormwood, but cool light and clarity to the patient. Screwtape implies there may be further purgation and pain for the patient, but it will be of a different nature than the pains of this life—and here Screwtape ends his discussion of the patient, claiming "Once more, the inexplicable meets us."[128] Screwtape concludes his final letter confessing that he is near despair. He takes comfort in that the fact that Wormwood, or a piece of him, will be given him as a dainty morsel to devour.

CONCLUSION

Lewis claimed that *Screwtape* was an unpleasant book to for him to write. After many requests for more correspondence from Screwtape, he finally wrote an additional piece called "Screwtape Proposes a Toast," which appeared in *The Saturday Evening Post* on December 19, 1959, and in later editions of the book. In the preface to the 1961 edition—the first to include this toast, which was more an address than an epistle—Lewis tells how for many years he felt no inclination to answer calls for another letter, declaring: "Though I had never written anything more easily, I never wrote with less enjoyment. . . . The work into which I had to project myself while I spoke through Screwtape was all dust, grit, thirst, and itch. Every trace of beauty, freshness, and geniality had to be excluded."[129]

According to Lewis, the work nearly smothered him to write it, but it remains a wonderfully uplifting book to read. As Mark DeForrest rightly points out, "Despite the impressive array of tactics used by the forces of darkness, Lewis's book also bespeaks of the optimism of faith. . . . Despite the snares of Satan, the young man's faith in Christ triumphs over the forces of evil and, in this triumph serves as an example of the ordinary Christian running an extraordinary race of faith."[130]

Perhaps because it was the first of his books with a large, international success, Lewis always seemed ready to poke fun at the notoriety that *The Screwtape Letters* enjoyed. In the 1961 preface, he refers to it as "the sort of book that gets given to godchildren" or that "gravitates towards spare bedrooms, there to live a life of undisturbed tranquility in company with *The Road Mender, John Inglesant,* and *The Life of the Bee.*"[131] Lewis also recounts the story of the hospital worker preparing for job interviews who chose *Screwtape* from a list of books to read because "it was the shortest."[132]

Among the reviews that followed the release of *Screwtape* in 1942, were the comments of C. E. M. Joad, who claimed "Mr. Lewis possesses the rare gift of being able to make righteousness readable."[133] A *Times Literary Supplement* critic claimed, "A reviewer's task is not to be a prophet, and time alone can show whether it is or is not an enduring piece of satirical writing."[134] With well over half a century gone since May 2, 1941, when the first of Screwtape's letters appeared in *The Guardian*, time has indeed shown Lewis's diabolical fiction to be truly enduring.

NOTES

1. Alan Jacobs, *The Narnian: The Life and Imagination of C. S. Lewis* (New York: HarperSanFrancisco, 2005), 161.

2. C. S. Lewis, *Letters of C. S. Lewis* (New York: Harcourt Brace & Company, 1993), 355.

3. C. S. Lewis, *Out of the Silent Planet* (New York: Scribner, 2003), 124.

4. C. S. Lewis, "The Dethronement of Power," in *On Stories and Other Essays on Literature* (New York: Harcourt Brace, 1966), 90.

5. C. S. Lewis, *Surprised by Joy: The Shape of My Early Life* (New York: Harcourt, 1955), 14.

6. Mark Edward Deforrest, "*The Screwtape Letters*," in *The C. S. Lewis Readers' Encyclopedia*, ed. Jeffrey D. Schultz and John G. West (Grand Rapids, MI: Zondervan, 1998), 367.

7. Ibid.

8. Jocelyn Easton Gibb, Preface to "*Screwtape Proposes a Toast*," in *The Screwtape Letters*, C. S. Lewis (New York: HarperCollins, 2001), 180.

9. C. S. Lewis, *The Screwtape Letters: Revised Edition* (New York: Collier, 1961), v.

10. C. S. Lewis, *The Screwtape Letters* (New York: HarperSanFrancisco, 2001), x.

11. Ibid., ix.

12. C. S. Lewis, *The Screwtape Letters: Revised Edition*, vii.

13. Ibid.

14. Ibid., xii.

15. Ibid.

16. C. S. Lewis, *A Preface to Paradise Lost* (New York: Oxford University Press, 1961), 95.

17. Ibid., 96.

18. G. K. Chesterton, *Orthodoxy* (Wheaton, IL: Harold Shaw, 1994), 129.

19. Lewis, *A Preface to Paradise Lost*, ix.

20. Chesterton, *Orthodoxy*, 128.

21. Jacobs, *The Narnian*, 199.

22. Colin Duriez, *Tolkien and C. S. Lewis: The Gift of Friendship* (Mahwah, NJ: HiddenSpring, 2003), 342.

23. J. R. R. Tolkien, *The Letters of J. R. R. Tolkien*, ed. Humphrey Carpenter (New York: Houghton Mifflin, 2000), 342.

24. George Sayer, *Jack: A Life of C. S. Lewis* (Wheaton, IL: Crossway Books, 1994), 275.

25. A. N. Wilson, *C. S. Lewis: A Biography* (London: Flamingo, 1991), 177.

26. Lewis, *The Screwtape Letters*, 1.

27. Lewis, *Surprised by Joy*, 191.

28. Ibid., 207.

29. Lewis, *The Screwtape Letters*, 150–151.

30. Ibid., 2.

31. C. S. Lewis, *Mere Christianity* (New York: HarperSanFrancisco, 2001), 141.

32. Ibid., 140.

33. C. S. Lewis, *The Lion, the Witch and the Wardrobe* (New York: HarperTrophy, 1994), 48.

34. Lewis, *The Screwtape Letters*, 5.

35. Ibid.

36. Lewis, *Surprised by Joy*, 5.

37. Lewis, *The Screwtape Letters*, 6.

38. Lewis, *The Screwtape Letters: Revised Edition*, xiii.

39. Lewis, *The Screwtape Letters*, 37.

40. C. S. Lewis, *Mere Christianity*, revised and enlarged (New York: Macmillan, 1952), 140.

41. Lewis, *The Screwtape Letters*, 8.

42. Marvin Hinten, "An Approach to Teaching *The Screwtape Letters*," in *The Lamp-Post*, 28(3) (Fall 2004), 4.

43. Lewis, *Mere Christianity*, 79.

44. Lewis, *The Screwtape Letters*, 60–61.

45. Ibid., 13–14.

46. Lewis, "Miserable Offenders" in *God in the Dock* (Grand Rapids, MI: Eerdmans, 1970), 124.

47. Warren Lewis, *Brothers & Friends: The Diaries of Major Warren Hamilton Lewis*, ed. Clyde S. Kilby and Marjorie Lamp Mead (New York: Ballantine Books, 1988), 146.

48. Lewis, *The Screwtape Letters*, 14.

49. Roger Lancelyn Green and Walter Hooper. *C. S. Lewis: A Biography* (New York: Harcourt Brace and Company, 1974), 234.

50. C. S. Lewis, *The Four Loves* (New York: Harcourt, 1988), 46.

51. Lewis, *The Screwtape Letters*, 15.

52. Ibid., 16, 17.

53. C. S. Lewis, *Letters to Malcolm: Chiefly on Prayer* (New York: Harcourt, 1992), 17.

54. Lewis, *The Screwtape Letters*, 16.

55. Lewis, *Letters to Malcolm,* 17–18.

56. Lewis, *The Screwtape Letters*, 21.

57. Ibid., 24.

58. Lewis, *Letters of C. S. Lewis*, 320.

59. Lewis, *The Screwtape Letters*, 25.

60. Ibid., 28.

61. Jonathan Swift, "Letter to Mr. Pope, September 29, 1725," in *Gulliver's Travels* (New York: Penguin), ix.

62. Lewis, *The Screwtape Letters*, 31.

63. Ibid., 32.

64. Lewis, *The Screwtape Letters: Revised Edition*, viii.

65. Lewis, *The Screwtape Letters*, 34–35.

66. Lewis, *Letters to Malcolm,* 22.

67. Lewis, *Letters of C. S. Lewis*, 408–409.

68. Lewis, *The Screwtape Letters*, 40.

69. Ibid., 45.

70. Ibid., 47.

71. Ibid., 49.

72. Ibid., 50.

73. C. S. Lewis, *Mere Christianity*, Revised and enlarged (New York: Macmillan, 1952), 131.

74. Lewis, *The Screwtape Letters*, 53.

75. Ibid., 58.

76. Ibid.

77. Ibid., 60.

78. Ibid., 61.

79. Ibid., 63.

80. Ibid., 65.

81. Ibid., 67.

82. Ibid., 69.

83. Ibid., 71.

84. Lewis, *Letters of C. S. Lewis*, 423.

85. Lewis, *The Screwtape Letters*, 76.

86. Ibid., 77.

87. Ibid., 83.

88. Lewis, *Letters to Malcolm*, 101.

89. Lewis, *The Screwtape Letters*, 88.

90. Lewis, *Mere Christianity*, 186.

91. Lewis, *The Screwtape Letters*, 94.

92. Ibid., 99, 100.

93. Ibid., 99.

94. Ibid., 105.

95. Ibid., 118.

96. Ibid., 120.

97. C. S. Lewis, *Mere Christianity*, 26.

98. Lewis, *Perelandra* (New York: Scribner, 2003), 78.

99. Ibid., 82.

100. Lewis, *The Screwtape Letters*, 123.

101. Ibid., 124.

102. Ibid., 132.

103. Lewis, *Surprised by Joy*, 108.

104. C. S. Lewis, "The Inner Ring" in *The Weight of Glory and Other Addresses* (New York: HarperSanFrancisco, 2001), 151, 154.

105. Lewis, *Mere Christianity*, viii.

106. Lewis, *The Screwtape Letters*, 44.

107. Jacobs, *The Narnian*, 162.

108. Ibid.

109. C. S. Lewis, "The Weight of Glory" in *The Weight of Glory and Other Addresses* (New York: HarperSanFrancisco, 2001), 25.

110. C. S. Lewis, *The Four Loves* (San Diego, CA: Harcourt, 1960), 48–49.

111. Lewis, *The Screwtape Letters*, 145.

112. Ibid., 147.

113. C. S. Lewis, "The Efficacy of Prayer" in *The World's Last Night and Other Essays* (New York: Harcourt, 1987), 4–5.

114. Lewis, *The Screwtape Letters*, 150.

115. Ibid., 153, 154.

116. C. S. Lewis, *The Collected Letters of C. S. Lewis: Books, Broadcasts, and the War 1931–1949*, ed. Walter Hooper (New York: HarperSanFrancisco, 2004), 274.

117. Lewis, *The Screwtape Letters*, 155.

118. Ibid.

119. C. S. Lewis, "*De Futilitate*," in *Christian Reflections* (Grand Rapids, MI: Eerdmans, 1995), 57.

120. C. S. Lewis, preface to *The Problem of Pain* (New York: Touchstone, 1996), 10.

121. Lewis, *The Screwtape Letters*, 156.

122. Lewis, Preface to *The Screwtape Letters: Revised Edition*, xi.

123. Lewis, *The Screwtape Letters*, 166.

124. Lewis, *The Screwtape Letters: Revised Edition,* viii.

125. Lewis, *The Screwtape Letters*, 171.

126. Ibid., 172.

127. Ibid., 174.

128. Ibid., 175.

129. Lewis, *The Screwtape Letters: Revised Edition*, xiii–xiv.

130. Deforrest, "The Screwtape Letters," in *The C. S. Lewis Readers' Encyclopedia*, 368.

131. Lewis, *The Screwtape Letters: Revised Edition*, vi.

132. Ibid.

133. C. S. Lewis, *The Collected Letters of C. S. Lewis, vol. 2: Books, Broadcasts, and the War, 1931–1949*, 276.

134. Ibid., 275–276.

BIBLIOGRAPHY

Carpenter, Humphrey, Editor. *The Letters of J. R. R. Tolkien.* New York: Houghton Mifflin, 2000.

Chesterton, G. K. *Orthodoxy.* Wheaton, IL: Harold Shaw, 1994, 129.

Deforrest, Mark Edward. *"The Screwtape Letters." The C. S. Lewis Readers' Encyclopedia.* Edited by Jeffrey D. Schultz and John G. West. Grand Rapids, MI: Zondervan, 1998, 367–368.

Duriez, Colin. *Tolkien and C. S. Lewis: The Gift of Friendship.* Mahwah, NJ: Hidden-Spring, 2003, 342.

Gibb, Jocelyn Easton. Preface to *"Screwtape Proposes a Toast."* In *The Screwtape Letters, C. S. Lewis.* New York: HarperCollins, 2001, 180–182

Green, Roger Lancelyn and Walter Hooper. *C. S. Lewis: A Biography,* New York: Harcourt Brace and Company, 1974, 234.

Hinten, Marvin. "An Approach to Teaching *The Screwtape Letters.*" In *The Lamp-Post,* 28(3) (Fall 2004): 4–8.

Hooper, Walter. *The Collected Letters of C. S. Lewis: Books, Broadcasts, and the War 1931–1949.* Edited by Walter Hooper. New York: HarperSanFrancisco, 2004, 274.

Jacobs, Alan. *The Narnian: The Life and Imagination of C. S. Lewis,* New York: HarperSanFrancisco, 2005, 161.

Lewis, C. S. *"De Futilitate," Christian Reflections.* Grand Rapids, MI: Eerdmans, 1995.

———. "The Dethronement of Power." In *On Stories and Other Essays on Literature.* New York: Harcourt Brace, 1966.

———. "The Efficacy of Prayer." In *The World's Last Night and Other Essays.* New York: Harcourt, 1987.

———. *The Four Loves.* New York: Harcourt, 1988.

———. "The Inner Ring." In *The Weight of Glory and Other Addresses.* New York: HarperSanFrancisco, 2001.

———. *Letters of C. S. Lewis.* Revised Edition. Edited by Walter Hooper and Warren H, Lewis. New York: Harcourt Brace & Company, 1993.

———. *Letters to Malcolm: Chiefly on Prayer.* New York: Harcourt, 1992.

———. *The Lion, the Witch and the Wardrobe.* New York: HarperTrophy, 1994.

———. *Mere Christianity.* New York: HarperSanFrancisco, 2001.

————. "Miserable Offenders." *In God in the Dock.* Grand Rapids, MI: Eerdmans, 1970,

————. *Out of the Silent Planet.* New York: Scribner, 2003.

————. *Perelandra.* New York: Scribner, 2003.

————. *A Preface to Paradise Lost.* New York: Oxford University Press, 1961.

————. *The Problem of Pain.* New York: Touchstone, 1996.

————. *The Screwtape Letters.* New York: HarperSanFrancisco, 2001.

————. *The Screwtape Letters: Revised Edition.* New York: Collier, 1961.

————. "The Weight of Glory," *The Weight of Glory and Other Addresses.* New York: HarperSanFrancisco, 2001.

Lewis, Warren. *Brothers & Friends: The Diaries of Major Warren Hamilton Lewis.* Edited by Clyde S. Kilby and Marjorie Lamp Mead. New York: Ballantine Books, 1988, 146.

Sayer, George. *Jack: A Life of C. S. Lewis.* Wheaton, IL: Crossway Books, 1994.

Swift, Jonathan. "Letter to Mr. Pope, September 29, 1725." In *Gulliver's Travels.* New York: Penguin, 1975.

Wilson, A. N. *C. S. Lewis: A Biography.* London: Flamingo, 1991.

11

Columns of Light: The Preconversion Narrative Poetry of C. S. Lewis

Don W. King

Although Lewis's first published book was a collection of lyrical poems, *Spirits in Bondage* (1919), for the first thirty-five years of C. S. Lewis's life he worked hard to write a great narrative poem. Many versions were attempted and later abandoned. Those that survive are notable primarily because they offer insight into two important matters: his desire to achieve literary acclaim as a great poet and his literary strivings before his conversion to Christianity. This essay will focus upon the two most important of these early narrative poems.[1]

The first, *Descend to Earth, Descend, Celestial Nine*, dated by Warren Lewis as having been written between summer 1912 and summer 1913, is a Valhalla poem based on summaries Lewis read in *The Soundbox* of Wagner's *The Ring of Nibelung*.[2] Its 794 lines of heroic couplets show unusual maturity. We know from *Surprised by Joy* that sometime early in 1911 after his move to Cherbourg House, Malvern, Lewis, one day musing in the library, came across the title of a new book listed in a literary periodical, *Siegfried and the Twilight of the Gods*. When he read the title he was suddenly transported into realms of pure "northernness,"[3] and he attempted his version of *The Rhinegold* (the "prelude" of the *Ring*) without having read a line-by-line translation or heard a score.[4] We also know Lewis was so enthralled by Wagner's *Ring of the*

Nibelung through his reading of synopsis of that opera in *The Soundbox* that he immediately began work on *Descend to Earth, Descend, Celestial Nine*.[5] Accordingly, *Descend to Earth* is an impressive accomplishment.[6]

Unlike Wagner's opera, Lewis's "Descend" is narrative rather than dramatic. Three complete books survive and a fragmentary fourth, suggesting that Lewis was structuring a work of twelve books imitating the Greek and Latin epics he so admired. Accordingly, we are not surprised when he begins with a six-line invocation to the Muses:

> Descend to earth, descend, celestial Nine
> And sing the ancient legend of the Rhine:
> What races first upon the world did dwell
> In earliest days, descend Oh Muse and tell.
> Who did the mighty hills inhabit, who
> The earth's deep clefts: narrate the story true.[7]

Recalling Milton's "Sing, Heavenly Muse" opening to Book I of *Paradise Lost*, Lewis follows by merging his love of classical narrative poetry in the next six lines with his new passion for Norse literature:

> Upon the mountain tops in happy light
> Abode the gods with majesty and might,
> Whom Wotan ruled as chief. The sluggish Rhine
> Rhine maidens sheltered, nymphs of form divine,
> Who for their sire a noted treasure held,
> The Rhinegold, and in watch of this they dwelled.[8]

It is not hard to imagine Lewis seeing himself in the tradition of great epic poets. Homer had his Odysseus, Virgil his Aeneas, Milton his Adam, Tennyson his Arthur, and Lewis his Wotan.

Book I introduces Alberich, the misshapen king of the Niblung, who while rising one day from the river's depth, sees the beautiful Rhine maidens swimming and is inflamed with lust. Once aware of him, the maidens mock and tease him: "'Does Alberich indulge in dreams of love / And steer his mind through thoughts of his state above?' /... They tantalize with dance the tiny king, / The waters wide with wanton laughter ring."[9] Alliteration, particularly effective here, is notable throughout the poem. While the opera then has the maidens one by one cruelly feign love for Alberich, effectively lacerating his emotions and humiliating him, in Lewis's version they collectively taunt him, all the while inflaming his lust. Tiring of the Niblung king's pursuits, Lewis's maidens decide to give him a vision of the Rhinegold, hoping this will deflect interest away from them. This fatal error is compounded when they foolishly reveal the awful power of the gold:

> Knows he not the key
> By which alone the hoard his own may be?
> Knows he not as he tries to grasp in vain
> The treasure, that who would the Rhinegold gain
> Must first curse love before his hands may hold
> The glistening and so much desired gold.
> And he, should he but gain the pile he wants
> (If there be truth in legendary vaunts)
> If to a RING he forge it by the art
> Of goldsmith, then to rule shall be his part;
> Whoe'er the treasure keeps and wears the RING
> Shall rule the world, an everlasting king.[10]

Having seen Alberich's lust, the maidens are confident he can never renounce love. However, the book ends with him seizing the gold, the maidens fleeing in disarray, and Alberich returning to the underworld in proud arrogance, this latter detail Lewis's addition.[11]

In Book II the scene shifts to Asgard where Lewis summarizes Wotan's agreement with the giants, Fasolt and Fafnir: if they build him a castle, he will give them his sister-in-law, Freia. Frika, Wotan's wife, is incensed by the agreement and blames Logie, god of fire and Wotan's favorite counselor, for advising him to accept the giants' conditions.[12] Before Wotan can respond, Fasolt and Fafnir appear, demanding payment. Wotan withdraws to retrieve Freia, in the mean time sending out Freia's brothers, Froh, god of joy, and Donner, god of thunder, advising them to buy time while Wotan waits for Logie to appear. Using "oily words and counsels fair," Freia's brothers for a time have limited success, but Fasolt's desire (his "blue eyes the fire flames fiercer still") will not be thwarted. As the four of them prepare to fight, Wotan returns with Logie, demanding that he discover a way to void the agreement with the giants. Logie says that in his journeys he has learned of the story of the Rhine maidens and Alberich. Fafnir, fascinated by Logie's story of the powerful gold, offers Wotan an unexpected deal:

> I had fondly hoped
> Freia to gain: But since you do not choose
> To give her up, I will not therefore lose
> My whole reward. Freia to thee I'll give,
> (So may she always in Valhalla live).
> Give me that treasure which the god of fire
> Hath told us of: for that I most desire.[13]

Wotan points out that the treasure is not his to give; after the giants lead Freia away, Logie urges Wotan to reconsider, reminding them that without Freia's harvest of golden apples, the gods of Walhalla will grow weak and lose power. The book ends with Wotan reluctantly agreeing to take on the quest and to descend to the Nibelheim.

Book III descends to the Nibelheim where we find Alberich lording his new power over his goldsmith Mime, who he has commissioned to forge a magic helmet. Mime, while cognizant the gold has power, does not know what the power is, so he is physically abused by Alberich for not having the helmet ready when he demands it. The helmet's power is substantial: "For the Tarnhelm—so the cap was named / This virtue for the golden helmet claim; / Whoe'er the headgear wore, at any time / What form he wished could take."[14] When Alberich puts it on for the first time, he becomes invisible and rewards Mime for his hard work by beating him senseless.

Into this dark, noxious atmosphere, Wotan and Logie suddenly appear. Pretending to care about Mime's mistreatment by Alberich, Logie offers to conspire with Mime against his cruel king. Before they can come to an agreement, Alberich appears, pitilessly driving a crew of Niblungs before him with a whip and holding a ring of gold above his head. Logie tries to flatter Alberich, but he sees through Logie and bitterly scorns Asgard:

> Do gods
> Descend the dark and unfrequented roads
> That lead to my dark realm, respects to pay
> To Alberich? Or leave the glowing day
> To seek the caverns of a king they hate?
> Or doth the eagle with the beetle mate?
> Am I a child that I should thus believe
> Ye come love-laden spirits to relieve
> With kindly words? Nay: never was there yet
> A god but did all misery beget
> With lofty schemes. The price of Asgard's good
> Is running rivulets of human blood.[15]

These lines, perhaps the best poetry in the poem, reveal Lewis writing almost effortlessly, using effective imagery, unforced rhymes, and pointed rhetoric.

Though Alberich scorns Wotan and Logie, he cannot resist demonstrating his newly acquired power, so he threatens to use his ring and helmet against them. Fate, he says, has permitted Asgard to rule until the present, but now "fate hath prepared its downfall and its shame: / The ring hath made me monarch of ye all."[16] Wotan, his pride offended, is enraged at this threat;

before Wotan lashes out, however, Logie intervenes and cleverly demands Alberich give a demonstration of his power; unless they see him change shape, they will not believe his words. Initially, Alberich rejects this demand, wisely seeing through Logie's scheme: "And think ye, friends, / I do not know your avaricious ends: / Shall I a small and feeble beast become, / That you may bear the treasure from my home?"[17] Logie, undeterred, presses Alberich, shaming his pride so that he forgets his own warning; Alberich transforms himself into a vicious fox.[18] Wotan is horrified when he witnesses this, but Logie seizes the chance to appeal to Alberich's vanity. Feigning awe, Logie flatters Alberich and asks for another demonstration. Alberich, his reason blind to the danger, foolishly does exactly what he said he would not: "And where the dwarf in form of fox had been / There writhed a slimy toad upon the floor."[19] At this Wotan rushes forward, pinning Alberich to the floor, and Logie seizes the helmet. The book concludes as the gods embrace, grab the toad, and ascend from Nibelheim.

Book IV is a fragment of forty-three lines and departs radically from Wagner. It begins with Wotan and Logie bringing the toad to Walhalla, while Valkryies, Brunhilda in particular, are seen riding in the distance. As Wotan is about to speak to Fricka, the manuscript breaks off. Lewis himself says the work breaks down here because he begins "to try to convey some of the intense excitement I was feeling, to look for expressions which would not merely state but suggest. Of course I failed, lost my prosaic clarity, spluttered, gasped, and presently fell silent."[20] That Lewis never returned to the poem, although he does deal with related characters and issues in *Loki Bound* several years later, is our loss, for he achieves much, especially in the three complete books. For example, we see him handling rather effectively the demands of narrative poetry, combining an effective meter and rhyme with a compelling story. Furthermore, his characterization suggests insights to human nature we might not expect from one so young and far exceed Wagner's flat, almost melodramatic characters. While Lewis can be criticized for lacking his own creative impulse and thus writing a derivative narrative, within the limits of the genre and his age, *Descend to Earth* is unusually powerful, containing sustained passages of very good poetry; in addition, in this poem we see him working through ideas and themes that later surface in works as dissimilar as *Dymer* and *Till We Have Faces*.

Lewis's second important narrative poem is *Dymer*, his primary verse pre-occupation from 1920 to 1926.[21] In his introduction to the 1950 edition of *Dymer*, Lewis summarizes what the poem means to him:

My hero was to be a man escaping from illusion. He begins by egregiously supposing the universe to be his friend and seems for a time to find confirmation of his belief.

Then he tries, as we all try, to repeat his moment of youthful rapture. It cannot be done; the old Matriarch sees to that. On top of his rebuff comes the discovery of the consequences which his rebellion against the City has produced. He sinks into despair and gives utterance to the pessimism which had, on the whole, been my own view about six years earlier [note this would mean anytime between 1917–1919, corresponding with Lewis's battlefield experiences]. Hunger and a shock of real danger bring him to his senses and he at last accepts reality. But just as he is setting out on the new and soberer life, the shabbiest of all bribes is offered him; the false promise that by magic or invited illusion there may be a short cut back to the one happiness he remembers. He relapses and swallows the bait, but he has grown too mature to be really deceived. He finds that the wish-fulfillment dream leads to the fear-fulfillment dream, recovers himself, defies the Magician who tempted him, and faces his destiny.[22]

However, an author's reading of his own poem is always suspect since rarely can he know all *that goes into it*; even less under his control is all *that comes out of the poem* as the text is engaged by various readers. Accordingly, I believe a better approach to *Dymer* is one informed by viewing Dymer as a haughty adolescent intent on living an autonomous life. As he faces the consequences of his selfish, cruel actions, however, he achieves humility and wisdom albeit at high personal cost. Moreover, in *Dymer* we hear a voice stripped of religious dogma, utterly unbound by conventional, orthodox Christianity. In addition, the impact of Lewis's World War I experiences and the influences of Norse mythology and literature are intrinsic to a fuller understanding of the poem.[23] The first hint that Lewis's love of Norse literature is at work in *Dymer* is found opposite the title page in the first edition published by Dent in 1926. There we find this epigram from *Havamal*, Odin's High Song from *The Poetic Edda*, essentially a code of laws and ethics his people are to use to govern their conduct: "Nine nights I hung upon the Tree, wounded with the spear as an offering to Odin, myself sacrificed to myself."[24] This epigram offers a key to understanding *Dymer*'s cryptic conclusion.

The first of nine cantos introduces us to Dymer, a nineteen-year-old student, living in a repressed, constrained, and totalitarian state.[25] Stimulated by Nature's fecundity, he rebels against his situation, murders his teacher in class, and escapes to Nature. There, he strips off his clothes and wanders about in a mad desire for desire. In a forest clearing he discovers and enters a castle. Dymer's emotional upheaval in this stanza is stimulated no doubt in part because he has been repressed for nineteen years, but also it is awakened by the longing for beauty that nature inspires in him. For instance, the narrator appears to excuse Dymer's inattention in a rigid classroom one April morning since "who ever learned to censor the spring day?"[26] Challenged by his teacher, Dymer murders him, echoing the actions of Siegfried against his teacher and foster parent, Mime, from Wagner's *Siegfried*.[27] Dymer turns to nature as a first resort; seeking to divorce himself from his previous life, he strips naked and wanders about a forest, crushing "wet, cool flowers against his face: / And once he cried aloud, 'O world, O day, / Let, let me,'—and then found no prayer to say" (p. 111). Dymer, is quickly overcome, like Shakespeare's Caliban, by powerfully evocative music coming from an unidentified source, and for the remainder of Canto I he follows "the music, unendurable / In stealing sweetness wind from tree to tree" until it leads him to a light coming through an arch in a forest glen (p. 112).

In Canto II Dymer boldly moves through the arch; inside he finds great beauty enclosed by a high dome, further exciting his desire. However, when he catches a glimpse of himself in the mirror, Narcissus-like, he becomes fascinated with his own physical beauty. Finding lavish clothing hanging near the mirror, he vainly dresses himself and "wondered that he had not known before / How fair a man he was" (p. 113). Dymer, in full flight from the totalitarian state that bred him, embraces total self-indulgence, even planning to return to the city as a self-proclaimed hero. Believing himself an autonomous man, Dymer thinks he can be the savior of the ignorant, deluded beings he left in the city. As the narrative continues his cocky man-child soon comes upon a rich banquet that attracts his palate: "When Dymer saw this sight, he leaped for mirth, / He clapped his hands, his eye lit like a lover's. / He had a hunger in him that was worth / Ten cities" (p. 113). The language of this passage is revealing. While on the one hand it literally refers to Dymer's physical hunger, so long unsated in the forest, on the other hand, it figuratively refers to his unrealized sexual desires. Accordingly, the eating binge at the table that follows foreshadows his sexual encounter at the end of the canto. Rejecting his past, he intends instead to push forward to unrestrained desire.

Dymer next sees a low door hidden by "dark curtains, sweepy fold, night-purple pall," and is mysteriously attracted to it: "Sudden desire for darkness overbore / His will, and drew him towards it. All was blind / Within. He passed. The curtains closed behind" (p. 114).[28] Within the place is richly evocative with a cool smell "that was holy and unholy," and a soft thicket of "broad leaves and wiry stems." Sensuous and sensual, this lush, dark place causes Dymer's body to thirst for sensual fulfillment: "With body intent he felt the foliage quiver / On breast and thighs. With groping arms he made / Wide passes in the air" (p. 115). In addition, as he senses consummation coming to his long burning desire, "a sacred shiver / Of joy from the heart's centre oddly strayed / To every nerve." Groping forward with excitement and fear, he finds "a knee-depth of warm pillows on the ground." He sinks down into the luxurious bedding feeling it a "sweet rapture to lie" there. Then, unexpectedly, out of the silent darkness "as if by stealth" a hand touches his and he hears "a low grave laugh and rounded like a pearl / Mysterious, filled with home" (p. 115). Dymer, now in a fever pitch of longing, does not wait to respond:

> He opened wide
> His arms. The breathing body of a girl
> Slid into them. From the world's end, with the stride
> Of seven-leagued boots came passion to his side.
> Then, meeting mouths, soft-falling hair, a cry,
> Heart-shaken flank, sudden cool-folded thigh. (p. 115)

The canto ends with one of the best passages of poetry in the entire poem:

> The same night swelled the mushroom in earth's lap
> And silvered the wet fields: it drew the bud
> From hiding and led on the rhythmic sap
> And sent the young wolves thirsting after blood,
> And, wheeling the big seas, made ebb and flood
> Along the shores of earth: and held these two
> In dead sleep till the time of morning dew. (p. 115)

These passages can easily be seen as autoerotic since initially the hand that touches him as well as the source of the laugh is not identified; even after the girl is introduced we do not know if she is the source of the initial touch and laugh. Regardless, in this creature Dymer realizes his inarticulate longing for desire as sexual passion, unimpeded, and all consuming. His heretofore unfocused longing finds outlet in this mysterious girl. The canto, therefore, begins with Dymer initially attracted by idealized beauty and moves him to the end where he experiences the intensity of raw sexual passion.

Canto III marks the peak of Dymer's emotional high in the poem, but it also begins his descent into despair. It starts the morning after his spent passion with the unidentified girl. Dymer awakens to a sanguine morning of still, lovely beauty, conscious of a warm, breathing body next to him. Curiously, however, he never looks at the girl; instead he arises to go out and to enjoy the forest beauty alone. He lingers here leisurely stretching, yawning, sighing, and laughing softly to himself, apparently completely satisfied. As an adolescent, he does not understand that the joy he revels in is cheaply purchased, unable to sustain him. This knowledge, however, is not long in coming, for as he suddenly remembers the girl, he longs to return to her. He sentimentalizes his affection for her when he reflects the forest would be a frightful place, "but now I have met my friend / Who loves me, [and] we can talk to the road's end" (p. 117).

He returns to the low door, but is unsure whether it is the same one he entered the night before. At the same moment, he realizes he does not even know the girl's name, so he hastens to find her. The path to his bower of bliss is blocked, however; Lewis describes a creature the opposite of what Dymer imagines he enjoyed the previous evening:

> And it had hands, pale hands of wrinkled flesh,
> Puckered and gnarled with vast antiquity,
> That moved. He eyed the sprawling thing afresh,
> And bit by bit (so faces come to be
> In the red coal) yet surely, he could see
> That the swathed hugeness was uncleanly human,
> A living thing, the likeness of a woman. (p. 117)

In addition, she is mantled in thick cloth that draped to the ground, giving the impression she is rooted to the earth. Ominously, her face is not visible. Dymer shrinks from her, turns, and runs to another entrance. To his horror, he finds the same enigmatic creature blocking his path; when he goes to other doors, she is always waiting. Sick with despair and anticipation, he calls out to his unidentified lover, again sentimentalizing their relationship. He tries yet another door, but the hag is there as well; he turns to swagger and bravado: "Out of my path, old woman. For this cause / I am new born, new freed, and here new wed, / That I might be the breaker of bad laws." He claims she will "not wrest / My love from me. I journey on a quest / You cannot understand, whose strength shall bear me / Through fire and earth. A bogy will not scare me" (p. 118).

Nevertheless, the assertion his lawlessness is stronger than old rules and his pompous, vain claims of autonomy are ineffectual. Seeing the hag intractable, he falters; his last desperate plea is for pity and shows him willing to recant and confess his sin if only she will let him pass. Still she remains silent. Driven wild by desire, Dymer attempts to force his way by the old hag, but is knocked senseless for his efforts. The canto ends with an image recalling the eviction of Adam and Eve from the garden of Eden; Dymer is seen coming away from the entrance "slowly, drunkenly reeling, / Blind, beaten, broken, past desire of healing, / Past knowledge of his misery, he goes on / Under the first dark trees and now is gone" (p. 119).

Who is this old woman?[29] She has strong connections to Erda of Wagner's *Siegfried* and the Norns of Norse literature. Erda, ancient prophetess of the underworld, is sought out by Wotan in the third act of the play when he comes and asks her how he can conquer his fear of the future, particularly his knowledge that the twilight of the gods is certain. While Erda does speak to him, unlike the old hag who remains silent, her words are evasive and without comfort. Interestingly, however, she defends Brunnhilde from Wotan's anger and attempts to reconcile him to her. The Norns, the three Northern goddesses of fate, are not subject to the other gods, and their main tasks are "to warn the gods of future evil, to bid them make good use of the present, and to teach them wholesome lessons from the past."[30] Daily they weave the web of fate, albeit it blindly and not according to their own wishes; instead they are subject to Orlog, the eternal law of the universe. Urd (wurd or weird), later portrayed by Wagner as Erda, is the Norn with the most affinities to Lewis's old hag. As a personification of time, she appears "very old and decrepit, continually looking backward, as if absorbed in contemplating past events and people."[31] If Lewis based his old hag upon Urd, her silence indicates Dymer's spent passion is just that: spent, finished, over, with no hope of repeating itself in spite of his eagerness to consummate it again. He can no longer hope to return to the past, either to his unidentified lover or to the totalitarian state; he is alone, without comfort, finally realizing in full the awful loneliness of attempting to live as an autonomous man. The old hag, therefore, is the first concrete evidence in his experience giving the lie to Dymer's quest for autonomy.

Cantos IV and V function together, first portraying Dymer's descent into morose emotional despair; and then, after he realizes his nadir, his mood lightens as Canto V ends. Canto IV begins with Dymer, who is now devastated and wandering about the forest, suffering the deluge of a fierce rainstorm, symbolic of the terrible tempest in his mind.[32] Dymer longs for the storm to punish him for his folly. Eventually the storm lessens but not Dymer's morose despair; in fact, "then came the worst hour for flesh and blood" (p. 120). Dymer is in his worst hour because he now knows he is totally alone, and his dream of autonomy carries the bitter price of isolation, estrangement, and alienation. He no longer hopes to find the fulfillment of his dreams in an inarticulate longing, since the everyday, humdrum world is all about him.

Even yet he has not experienced the worst, for at the moment he thinks he is most alone in his misery, he hears someone nearby breathe out in pain. He discovers a horribly wounded soldier. When Dymer beckons him to reach out his hands for help, the soldier curses him and says: "They've done for me. / I've no hands. Don't come near me. No, but stay, / Don't leave me . . . O my God! Is it near day?" (p. 121).[33] Dymer, stunned by this man's condition, has yet not reached the depth of his own despair, for as the wounded soldier tells his story, Dymer learns the ironic truth: he is responsible for not only this man's injuries but for the slaughter of many. The wounded soldier recounts how the story of Dymer's rebellion and longing for personal fulfillment had infected many, spreading like disease through the society: As many of the young in the society joined the rebellion, exulting in their own newly discovered autonomy, the leaders of the totalitarian state cracked down. Still, led on by a charismatic leader, Bran, the rebellion proceeded, ostensibly inspired by Dymer.

In describing the fighting, Lewis draws upon his own World War I battlefield memories. As the rebels press forward amid "charge and cheer and bubbling sobs of death, / We hovered on their front. Like swarming bees / Their spraying bullets came—no time for breath" (p. 122). Instead of men, they become brutes: "I saw men's stomachs fall out on their knees; / And shouting faces, while they shouted, freeze / Into black, bony masks. Before we knew / We're into them . . . "Swine!"—"Die, then!"—"That's for you!" The wounded soldier recalls seeing "an old . . . man / Lying before my feet with shattered skull" while Bran moves to commit atrocities against prisoners; he wants "to burn them, wedge their nails up, crucify them" (p. 122). When this unbridled revenge occurs, the "noble rebellion" becomes simply a blood bath. As the rebels win victory after victory, they torch the city and become ever more bloodthirsty: "We had them in our power! / Then was the time to mock them and to strike, / To flay men and spit women on the pike, / Bidding them to dance." To Dymer's horror, he hears the wounded soldier say "wherever the most shame / Was done the doer called on Dymer's name" (p. 122). After the rebels claim bloody victory, however, Bran's paranoia causes him to solidify his power by making an example of a few in order to intimidate all the rest. So it is, says the soldier, he is randomly selected and "they cut away my two hands and my feet / And laughed and left me for the birds to eat." He dies cursing Dymer, who "sat like one that neither hears nor sees. / And the cold East whitened beyond the trees" (p. 122).

Canto V begins with Dymer having wandered aimlessly away from the corpse until he comes to a deep valley; when he gazes down into the valley, he experiences deep despair. Overcome by weariness, he falls asleep. But this is no peaceful sleep; rather, he has a nightmare filled with battlefield horror. When he awakens, he indulges in self-pity, regretting his loss of fulfilled longing with the unknown girl and his actions that have caused the slaughter of so many. Tormented by the thought of the latter, he tries to comfort himself with sentimental thoughts of his beloved. Unfortunately, he has no solid memory of her to comfort him, and so is left pathetically alone. Still, Dymer has much to learn, for instead of admitting his own responsibility in both disasters, he blames a cruel, malicious God. He blames this God for his joy denied, and attempts to move back into his position as an autonomous man. He rejects the dead soldier's implication that he is responsible for the rebellion, claiming he acted only for himself. Though he thinks about killing himself, instead he falls to the ground, reverting to a fetal position: "he crouched and clasped his hands about his knees / And hugged his own limbs for the pitiful sense / Of homeliness they had" (p. 124). Except for the impulsive murder of his teacher and his almost accidental liaison with the unknown girl, Dymer is no man of action.

Moreover, once his desire is spent, he wanders purposelessly. As a matter of fact, the rest of the canto describes his descent into the deep valley, gradual at first, but then, when he slips on a steep slope, he clutches desperately to the hillside. In this moment of crisis, he finds impetus to go on, hugging the earth to himself, feeling "it was the big, round world beneath his breast, / The mother planet" who saved him at the moment of his greatest need. Humility finally follows: "The shame of glad surrender stood confessed, / He cared not for his boasts. This, this was best, / This giving up of all. He need not strive; / He panted, he lay still, he was alive" (p. 124). After this and for the first time since he murdered his teacher, Dymer sleeps a deep, restful slumber, marked only by a comforting dream where he hears a lark sing the promise of the world never ending.

After this dream, Dymer awakens cleansed, reconciled with himself, and prepared to face the consequences of his previous actions. Moreover, he no longer seeks to live autonomously. Cantos I–V take Dymer through emotional extremes beginning with haughty spiritual and personal pride, moving through profound depression and despair, then finishing with calm acceptance. Reminiscent of the emotional roller coaster Coleridge's Ancient Mariner endured, Dymer's story might best be finished at the conclusion of Canto V. However, Dymer has more to learn about himself and the consequence of his rebellious, self-willed actions earlier in the poem.

Cantos VI and VII illustrate through the appearance of a great Magician that Dymer is not yet free from destructive dreams. Indeed, in this Magician Dymer sees the frightening image of what he will become if he continues such dreams. In brief, Canto VI finds Dymer following the song of the lark in a search for food. His peaceful search has a shadow fall across it when he hears in the distance a gun fired, and a short time later he comes to the house of a Magician. This Magician "was a mighty man whose beardless face / Beneath gray hair shone out so large and mild / It made a sort of moonlight in the place. / A dreamy desperation, wistful-wild, / Showed in his glance and gait."[34] Furthermore, "over him there hung the witching air" (p. 126). In this Magician Dymer encounters the image of what he can become: an autonomous man completely divorced from the concerns of the world and other human beings, selfishly indulging his egoistic appetites. The Magician lives only for himself and the constant pursuit of realizing in full the dreams he seeks.

In his first words to Dymer, the Magician reveals the extent of his self-focus. He asks how Dymer discovered him, wondering if he heard the gunshot. Dymer is horrified when the Magician casually explains he had killed the lark. The Magician's action is capricious and selfish; he excuses the shooting by saying the lark sang too long and disturbs his dreams in sleep. His self-focus is further exposed when he takes Dymer to his garden and explains his plantings are intended to enclosed the house from the outside world. Interestingly, he confesses that nothing he plants in the garden grows; this detail suggests that his attempt to live an autonomous life is sterile. One who lives only for himself and his dreams in the end atrophies and withers. Dymer, even though offended by the execution of the lark, never passes moral judgment upon the Magician. He accepts the invitation to eat supper there. He also listens to the Magician's tales of magic words until he begins to nod off.

So powerful are the Magician's words that Dymer forgets his earlier resolution to forswear his dreams, quickly telling the Magician about this girl he loved but never saw. As he listens, the Magician, perhaps to lure Dymer ever deeper into his dreams, claims the girl of his dreams is not imaginary but heavenly. When Dymer tries to discuss Bran and the rebellion, the Magician loses interest. Why? Because Bran and the rebellion have to do with the real world, not the realm of dreams. For the Magician and his desire to live an autonomous life, the real world has little interest. Lewis's Magician falls prey to his own art and rejects human fellowship. Isolation is the substance of his enclosed, restricted life. Consequently, he offers Dymer the chance to learn the technique of living constantly in dreams. Based on his most recent experiences, however, Dymer initially resists the Magician's suggestion. Dymer wants to live in the world with other human beings, not autonomously in a world of dreams.

In fact, Dymer exposes a flaw in the Magician's thinking because he claims his beloved was not a dream; she was a real woman in the forest grot. Still, the Magician presses his point and makes powerful arguments, even ascribing to dreams biblical merit: "There the stain / Of oldest sins—how do the good words go?— / Though they were scarlet, shall be white as snow" (p. 127).[35] The Magician's philosophy, that morality is narrow and limiting, recalls Dymer's youthful pride and rebellion. Furthermore, when Dymer, still struggling against the Magician's rhetoric, insists he must undo his sins and repent, the Magician scorns such resolutions: "Throw down your human pity; cast your awe / Behind you; put repentance all away" (p. 127). The amorality of the Magician is transparent to Dymer, who claims he would happily serve as a slave on earth for anyone, if, at the end of the year, he could see his beloved's face just for a moment and hear her urge him to live with courage for another year. Such virtues the Magician mocks, for they are false promises of future reward that restrain autonomous living.

The canto ends conspiratorially, as the Magician finally reveals he is not human; as a consequence, when the Magician offers Dymer a drink from his cup that will take him to the valley of dreams, he is tempted. Moreover, the Magician's final argument convinces Dymer to succumb: "Earth is a sinking ship, a house whose wall / Is tottering while you sweep; the roof will fall / Before the work is done. You cannot mend it. / Patch as you will, at last the rot must end it" (p. 128). Although he does so reluctantly, even admitting suspicions, Dymer decides to accept the Magician's claim that dreams can make a heaven of hell and a hell of heaven.

In Canto VII the Magician joins Dymer in drinking. While Dymer's dreams are somewhat unsettling, the Magician's dreams are fantastic, and he teeters on the edge of madness. In passages anticipating Weston's demonic possession in *Perelandra* and the mad, chaotic, dissolution of Belbury at the conclusion of *That Hideous Strength*, Lewis describes the Magician's descent into a personal hell. As the drug from the cup begins to take affect, the Magician staggers about, eyes bulging, catching sight, apparently of his personal hell The Magician's reliance on the occult to bolster his dream of autonomy finally catches up to him, and in the middle of the Magician's nightmarish dream sequence, Dymer, groggy with the drug and unaware of his master's descent into madness, affirms the dream world of the Magician is a lie.

Accordingly, when his own dream shows him his beloved, he knows she is "the mirror of my heart, / Such things as boyhood feigns beneath the smart / Of solitude and spring. I was deceived / Almost. In that first moment I believed" (p. 129). He describes how her beauty momentarily caused him to listen to her invitation to live forever in the dream world. Like the *femme fatale* of Keats' "La Belle Dame Sans Merci," she has a powerful affect upon him:

> She told me I had journeyed home at last
> Into the golden age and the good countrie
> That had been always there. She bade me cast
> My cares behind forever:—on her knee
> Worshipped me, lord and love—oh, I can see
> Her red lips even now! Is it not wrong
> That men's delusions should be made so strong? (p. 129)

The adolescent Dymer could never have reasoned thus, clearly indicating his maturation in the poem. Indeed, in spite of his being "besotted" with this dream of his beloved, he manages to see through the scheme: "She went too fast. Soft to my arms she came. / The robe slipped from her shoulder. The smooth breast / Was bare against my own." The eroticism of this passage, much more explicit than anything we saw earlier in the autoerotic sequence at the end of Canto II, ironically does not serve to stimulate Dymer. In point of fact, he sees his dream of her is simply love of self: "She shone like flame / Before me in the dusk, all love, all shame— / Faugh!—and it was myself" (p. 129). Dymer realizes the great deception in attempting to live an autonomous life is that he is in love with himself; he finally comes to see himself as a self-indulgent narcissist.

This realization, however, is followed by a fierce temptation to return to autoeroticism. An unbridled orgy of sexual temptation and revelry is then described, a passage George Sayer calls "perhaps one of the most powerful in the whole range of English poetry."[36] Like the brown girls of *The Pilgrim's Regress*, various figures accost Dymer, singing "we are the lust / That was before the world and still shall be /. . . We are the mother swamp, the primal sea /. . . Old, old are we. / It is but a return . . . it's nothing new, / Easy as slipping on a well-worn shoe" (p. 130). The most offensive of these is a parody of his dream beloved, who baldly offers: "I am not beautiful as she, / But I'm the older love; you shall love me / Far more than Beauty's self. You have been ours / Always. We are the world's most ancient powers" (p. 130). Although we cannot be sure, Lewis intimates Dymer resists these autoerotic temptations since he scorns the Magician, and turns to leave. However, the Magician, hopelessly mad in the deception of his own dreams, pulls out his gun; as with the lark who disturbed his dreams and had to be eliminated, so with Dymer. Besides, he cannot afford to have someone leave his autonomous world since he may become an agent to help pull it down. Dymer tries to avoid the shot, but he is wounded and swoons as the canto ends. In Cantos VI and VII Lewis strips Dymer to yet another layer of understanding; that is, any who attempt to live autonomously, be it literally or via dreams, are certain to be frustrated. Dymer finds himself now unable to rely upon either his physical or imaginative faculties. He is now ready to learn his final lesson and in the process become greater than he might have ever imagined; he has to be humbled before he can be exalted.

Cantos VIII and IX portray the redemption of Dymer (recalling that Lewis titled an early version of this story *The Redemption of Ask*). Canto VIII portrays Dymer coming to a full knowledge of himself and his failings, while undergoing a final stripping away of the layers of self-will. Canto IX illustrates how such knowledge equips him for a final denial of self, something he is incapable of in his youthful pride and rebellion. In short, the autonomous man rejects self and dies a sacrificial death for others. Canto VIII opens when Dymer regains consciousness; he has managed to drag himself away from the Magician's house and garden, lying by a country lane. Immediately he feels the sharp, terrible pain in his side from the Magician's gunshot, perhaps a battlefield detail and certainly one Lewis knew firsthand via his shrapnel wound. Initially he feels the cold air and earth about him and believes he is alone. Turning on his side, however, he sees a woman standing nearby, "and while he looked the knowledge grew / She was not of the old life but the new" (p. 131). What follows is a fascinating dialogue between them, and whether Dymer dreams it, has a vision, or actually experiences it is less important than what he learns about himself. By the ends of their conversation he is a "new" man.

In answer to many questions, she tells Dymer she is "the loved one, the long lost." To his complaint that she should never have permitted him to suffer the pangs of longing and the mental agony of not having her, she shocks him by saying he should have asked her name, in effect telling him he was deceived from the very beginning about who she was. Bitterly, though still not sure who she is, he tells her to leave him since she neither loves him nor understands human tears and pain. Again she stuns him when she says she actually know them all. She then goes on to reveal she is one of the gods, "the eternal forms," who lives "in realms beyond the reach of cloud, and skies / Nearest the ends of air . . . / [Who has] looked into their eyes / Peaceful and filled with pain beyond surmise" (p. 131). She understands human pain, she implies, because she has watched humans love the beauty of the world rather than the beauty behind the world—the "real beauty" that serves to infuse the beauty men see on earth. Scales fall off Dymer's eyes as he realizes his early love for nature was misdirected; in effect he loved the creature rather than the creator.

Yet Dymer still questions her. Why, he asks, do the gods lure spirits like himself, "the weak, the passionate, and the fool of dreams," when stronger men who "never pine / with whisperings at the heart, soul-sickening gleams / Of infinite desire, and joy that seems / The promise of full power" are left alone? Why, he presses, has he suffered for mistaking earthly beauty for real beauty? How can this have been sin? Do the gods have no voice to direct men? Must creatures of dust "guess their own way in the dark?" Tersely, she replies, "They must." Dymer's anger grows as he recounts how she came to him in "sweet disguise / Wooing me, lurking for me in my path, / Hid your eternal cold with woman's eyes, / Snared me with shows of love—and all was lies." Her surprising response is "our kind must come to all / If bidden, but in the shape for which they call," and she goes on to add the gods are not at fault if humans shape and mold eternal beauty into earthly forms (p. 131). Her implication is transparent: we fashion our idols according to our own desires. Dymer is momentarily appeased as he considers this and realizes his error.

However, his anger flares when he cries out that had he loved a beast it would have at least responded warmly. Is there no comfort, no human love left for him? She warns him against asking such questions and instead tells him he is learning the great truth that life is a process of learning how to die. His own process begins now as he sees the death of his dream of beauty: "Your eyes / First see her dead: and more, the more she dies" (p. 132). More importantly, she finishes her conversation by pointing Dymer toward the truth he must eventually know for himself:

You are still dreaming, dreams you shall forget
When you have cast your fetters, far from here.
Go forth; the journey is not ended yet.
You have seen Dymer dead and on the bier
More often than you dream and dropped no tear,
You have slain him every hour. Think not at all
Of death lest into death by thought you fall. (p. 132)

Dymer learns his has been a life of dreams, and that he is to go on from this point, even though terribly wounded, to live. His story is not over, as he has himself to blame for his wounds. He has been his own worst enemy. His death wish, she warns, will be self-fulfilling. After she vanishes, Dymer thinks deeply about her words, leading to the first obvious signs of his renewal: "Link by link the chain / That bound him to the flesh was loosening fast / And the new life breathed in unmoved and vast" (p. 132). He remembers the wounded soldier, identifying with him and wondering if he had the same realizations Dymer is just now having; he even blesses him for having revealed the truth of Dymer's deceived nature then.

In doing so, Dymer finally rejects his selfish life and the desire to live as an autonomous being:

How long have I been moved at heart in vain
About this Dymer, thinking this was I . . .
Why did I follow close his joy and pain
More than another man's? For he will die,
The little cloud will vanish and the sky
Reign as before. The stars remain and earth
And Man, as in the years before my birth. (pp. 132–133)

This passage is very significant since we see Dymer for the first time thinking of others rather than himself. In addition, this self-abnegation is followed by the very mature reflection that the universe is not all about Dymer. Indeed, his passing will have little impact upon the great scheme of things. This moment of self-knowledge is the climax of the poem, for now Dymer can move out of himself and his selfish egoism to engage fully in the lives of others. He can turn away from his conceited introspections, autoerotic compulsions, and autonomous yearnings to a new life yet to be discovered:

> There was a Dymer once who worked and played
> About the City; I sloughed him off and ran.
> There was a Dymer in the forest glade
> Ranting alone, skulking the fates of man.
> I cast him also, and a third began
> And he too died. But I am none of those.
> Is there another still to die . . . Who knows? (p. 133)

With these resolutions made, the canto ends and Dymer struggles to reach a tower he sees nearby. When he reaches it, he sinks down in the grass surrounding it to rest.

Canto IX provides Dymer the opportunity to complete his redemption through a total giving of himself. As Dymer is lying in the grass, a great wind begins to blow—perhaps a metaphor for his coming renewal. Echoing the words of Christ on the cross, he cries out "Why hast Thou forsaken me?" though it appears his question is addressed not to the gods but to earthly beauty. Before he receives an answer, he becomes aware of a sentry, an angelic guardian in his vision. Reminiscent of Gabriel from Book IV of *Paradise Lost*, the sentry explains he watches for a beast who walks at night bent on destroying whoever it meets. Dymer offers to assist the sentry, but he is initially rebuffed since he is of weak human flesh. Dymer admits that while he is flesh and weak from his wound, he is eager to do some good deed. In fact, Dymer claims his past wrongs equip him the more to assist: "I am come out of great folly and shame, / The sack of cities, wrongs I must undo" (p. 133).

Dymer begs to know more of this beast, and the sentry tells him of a fabulous monster and his parentage. As he listens to the story, Dymer realizes that the monster is the offspring of his sexual encounter with the unknown girl in the forest. Dymer sees now that his earlier actions have far-reaching consequences, and that it is incumbent upon him to bear the responsibility of resolving the problem he literally begat. With newly found authority, he tells the sentry he must fight the beast, "for either I must slay / This beast or else be slain before the day" (p. 134). The sentry, sensing Dymer's words are true, agrees to his request, even offering Dymer his armor and playing the role of squire in helping Dymer put on the gear. Dymer also has the sentry agree not to intervene in the fight, regardless of the apparent outcome.

The end of the canto is filled with battlefield imagery. The earth, where the fight is to occur, is stripped and sterile, a vivid evocation of World War I, no-man's land. In the moments before battle and certain death, Dymer bids farewell to earthly beauty and asks to be made part of its greater whole. Like Birhtnoth, the brave but foolhardy Anglo-Saxon warrior-king of *The Battle of Maldon,* and the old Beowulf in his doomed fight with the dragon, Dymer is ready to face an overwhelming foe. Indeed, almost instinctively he springs forward, his armor rattling for action, when the "ashen brute wheeled slowly round / Nosing, and set its ears towards the sound, / The pale and heavy brute, rough-ridged behind, / And full of eyes, clinking in scaly rind." Dymer throws his spear ineffectually, and his end comes quickly with little elaboration: "A leap—a cry—flurry of steel and claw, / Then silence." All that can be seen beneath the beast are "the ruined limbs of Dymer, killed outright / All in a moment, all his story done" (p. 135).

However, the poem builds to an unexpected climax. Immediately upon Dymer's death the sun rises, the sky and landscape are flooded with rich, colorful light, and the earth bursts forth "with dancing flowers / Where flower had never grown; and one by one / The splintered woods, as if from April showers, / Were softening into green." Additionally, songbirds trill happily as Dymer's body is surrounded by "crocus and bluebell, primrose, [and] daffodil / Shivering with moisture." The air itself grows sweet. All this imagery is furthered enhanced by the astonishing transformation of the beast who becomes "a wing'd and sworded shape, whose foam-like hair / Lay white about its shoulders, and the air / That came from it was burning hot. The whole / Pure body brimmed with life, as a full bowl." Dymer's giving of himself, his dying to destroy the monster his efforts to live autonomously created, transforms that hideous distortion into something beautiful. This explains why Lewis includes in the first edition the reference to Odin's High Song from the *Havamal:* "Nine nights I hung myself upon the Tree, wounded with the spear as an offering to Odin, myself sacrificed to myself." Dymer has not *merely died*, a meaningless, insignificant waste. Instead his death has transfused nature, bringing new life to the scorched, barren wasteland, a fact made clear by the final lines of the poem:

And from the distant corner of day's birth
He [the sentry] heard clear trumpets blowing and bells ring,
A noise of great good coming into earth
And such a music as the dumb would sing
If Balder had led back the blameless spring
With victory, with the voice of charging spears,
And in white lands long-lost Saturnian years. (p. 135)

The allusion to Balder who was "worshipped as the pure and radiant god of innocence and light"[37] is a fitting conclusion to *Dymer*, a narrative poem rich in Norse imagery and influence.

Without question *Dymer* is a difficult poem, requiring careful reading and reflection. As a narrative it is coherent, but Lewis's tendency to shift from one scene to the next without adequate transition is problematic. Given the reluctance of modern readers to read poetry in general, much less complex narrative poetry, it is not surprising *Dymer* has few admirers. Yet, it is the highest expression of Lewis's earliest literary aspirations as both the many years he spent working on it and the various versions it went through clearly illustrate. Owen Barfield recalled, for instance, that the myth of Dymer had long haunted Lewis.[38] Accordingly, *Dymer* is worth a careful reading, particularly since it shows how his strong affection for poetry consumed his earliest literary efforts. In addition, it is instructive to see how much Lewis improved his narrative technique in subsequent years when he turned to prose fiction. While *Dymer* was not Lewis's final effort to write narrative poetry, it was his longest, most consciously realized effort in the genre. Although flawed, it is a workmanlike poem in which we see him exercise poetic sensibilities that mature in his prose fiction.

Descend to Earth and *Dymer*, written during critical periods of Lewis's poetic maturation, are columns of light throwing into relief the passion with which he aspired to achieve acclaim as a poet; moreover, both suggest the nature of his literary preoccupations before his conversion to Christianity. In short, along with *Spirits in Bondage*, these poems reveal a "pre-Christian" voice in Lewis that most readers have not encountered before. Lewis's jaundiced views of God in these poems make his later apologetics all that more appealing; that is, these early poems illustrate Lewis's theological dilemma—on the one hand he wants to deny God, while on the other he is angry with God for permitting human suffering. The fact that he later becomes the most effective Christian apologist in the twentieth century is all that more ironic. At the same time Lewis's arguments against God revealed in these poems also suggests why he became such an effective apologist later—he knew the arguments against Christianity from the other side and this well-equipped him to offer compelling counter arguments.

NOTES

1. Other surviving narrative poems (some are fragments) are: *Loki Bound* (1914), "On Cupid and Psyche" (1923), "The Silence of the Night" (1923), "The Nameless Isle" (August, 1930), "Launcelot" (early 1930s), and "The Queen of Drum" (1933–1934). See *C. S. Lewis, Poet: The Legacy of His Poetic Impulse* (Kent, OH: Kent State University Press, 2001) for a comprehensive discussion of all these narrative poems.

The complete texts of *Loki Bound,* "On Cupid and Psyche," and "The Silence of the Night" appear in *C. S. Lewis, Poet,* 265–275. The complete texts of "The Nameless Isle," "Launcelot," and "The Queen of Drum" appear in *Narrative Poems* (1969).

2. For a complete discussion of this poem, see *C. S. Lewis, Poet: The Legacy of His Poetic Impulse,* 28–35; to see the entire text, see 245–265.

3. *Surprised by Joy: The Shape of My Early Life* (New York: Harcourt, Brace & World, 1955), 72–73. The book title Lewis saw was *Siegfried & The Twilight of the Gods.* Translated by Margaret Armour. Illustrations by Arthur Rackham (London: Heinemann, 1911). This is the second volume of two, the first being *The Rhinegold & The Valkryie.* Eventually a one-volume edition is published, *The Ring of Nibelung: A Trilogy with a Prelude by Richard Wagner.*

4. Furthermore, Warren Lewis reproduced a lengthy essay on Richard Wagner his brother wrote while at Cherbourg House. As a piece of writing for someone this young, the essay is remarkable although it adds little to our critical understanding of Wagner. In the essay Lewis surveyed Wagner's important work, made general comments upon opera, and finished by priggishly dismissing those incapable of appreciating opera. About the *Ring* he says: "His next, and perhaps his greatest work, was his immortal 'Nibelung Ring,' a trilogy whose three parts, the 'Walkyrie,' 'Siegfried,' and the 'Twilight of the Gods' are preceded by a prelude, 'The Rhinegold.' It is based on the great Scandinavian epic, the *Nibelungen Lied or Lot,* and is a beautiful piece of work." Cited in *C. S. Lewis, Poet,* 28.

5. C. S. Lewis, *Surprised by Joy,* 74–75.

6. Warren Lewis thought so, noting it was written "between the summers of 1912 and of 1913. Its absolute merit and its astonishing maturity make it . . . a remarkable production for a boy of between 14 and 15." Cited in *C. S. Lewis, Poet,* 28.

7. *C. S. Lewis, Poet,* 28.

8. Ibid., 29. Though Lewis does not name the Rhine maidens, in Wagner they are Woglinde, Wellgunde, and Flosshilde.

9. Ibid., 29.

10. Ibid.

11. Wagner's Alberich is shown cursing love; we do not see Lewis's Alberich curse love, but the implication is he does.

12. Lewis's Wotan and Frika are more sympathetically drawn than Wagner's arrogant husband and shrewish wife; indeed, all Lewis's characterizations are more human and less one-dimensional than Wagner's.

13. *C. S. Lewis, Poet,* 31.

14. Ibid., 32.

15. Ibid., 32–33.

16. Ibid., 33.

17. Ibid., 33.

18. This scene is reminiscent both of Canto XXV of the *Inferno* where thieves are transfigured into loathsome giant serpents and Book X of *Paradise Lost* where Satan

and the fallen angels unwillingly become huge snakes driven to consume ash and cider as a part of God's judgment upon them for having perverted Adam and Eve. Wagner's version also makes Alberich a serpent; why Lewis does not is puzzling. Later, of course, in Letter XXII of his *Screwtape Letters* he uses a serpent transformation episode, even referring to the *Paradise Lost* story.

19. *C. S. Lewis, Poet*, 34. This follows Wagner's version.

20 C. S. Lewis, *Surprised by Joy*, 74.

21. The complete text of *Dymer* is available in *Narrative Poems*. I offer a comprehensive discussion of the poem in *C. S. Lewis, Poet*, 108–136.

22. From "Preface by the Author to the 1950 Edition," Reprinted in *Narrative Poems* (New York: Harvest Books, 1969), 5–6.

23. Indeed, *Dymer* is profoundly influenced by the poetry of Lewis's first published book, *Spirits in Bondage: A Cycle of Lyrics* (London: Heinemann, 1919. Reprint, with an introduction by Walter Hooper. New York: Harcourt Brace Jovanovich, 1984); this is clearly evident in the emotional undulations of Dymer himself, reflected by his alternating sanguine highs and morose lows. Furthermore, there are battlefield descriptions surpassing those Lewis includes in *Spirits in Bondage* and rivaling those written by other World War I poets.

24. The complete reference is:

> I ween that I hung on the windy tree
> Hung there for nights full nine:
> With the spear I was wounded, and offered I was
> To Othin, myself to myself,
> On the tree that none may ever know
> What root beneath it runs.

From *The Poetic Edda*. Trans. Henry Adams Bellows (New York: The American-Scandinavian Foundation, 1923), 60. The windy tree refers to the "ash Yggdrasil (literally 'the Horse of Othin,' so-called because of this story), on which Othin, in order to win the magic runes, hanged himself as an offering to himself, and wounded himself with his own spear."

25. Canto I begins by echoing several qualities of Byron's *Don Juan*. First, the narrator, whose appearance gradually fades into the background, attempts to create a friendly, conspiratorial relationship between himself and his readers: "This moment, if you join me, we begin/A partnership where both must toil to hold/The clue that I caught first. We lose or win/Together; if you read, you are enrolled" (I, 2, 1–4). Given the struggles many have understanding the poem, "toil" is not hyperbole. Furthermore, readers unaccustomed to reading narrative poetry welcome the narrator's promise of assistance. Unfortunately, however, unlike the intrusive narrator of *Don Juan*, the narrator in *Dymer* rarely intrudes after this introduction; even when he breaks into the narrative to offer commentary, our understanding of the poem is not appreciably enhanced. Second, the rhyme schemes of the two poems, while not

identical, are similar; both the rhyme royal of *Dymer* (*ababbcc*) and the ottava rima of *Don Juan* (*abababcc*) rely primarily on end rhyme and effectively portray the alternating morose and sanguine moods. In effect both poems contain passages fluctuating between violent agitation and sublime longing. Finally, both poems employ satire though that of *Don Juan* is more fully and consistently realized, while in *Dymer* it is limited primarily to the first few cantos.

26. *C. S. Lewis, Poet*, 111. From this point forward reference to *C. S. Lewis, Poet* will be given parenthetically.

27. For more on these parallels, *C. S. Lewis, Poet*, 111–112.

28. *C. S. Lewis, Poet*, 114. This passage will be variously interpreted and no doubt those informed by Freud have much grist for the mill here. At the least this can be seen as Dymer's descent into hell, albeit it is one he fails to recognize, for the realm he enters is a void.

29. Her physical description clearly has affinities to Sin in Book II of *Paradise Lost* though Lewis's hag lacks the serpentine qualities of Milton's portress to hell.

30. H. A. Guerber, *Myths of the Norsemen*. (London: Harrap & Co., 1908), 166.

31. Ibid., 167.

32. The connection here between Dymer's state and that of King Lear as he wanders on the heath is clear.

33. Lewis' own war time experiences certainly inform this passage and illustrate that while *Spirits in Bondage* avoids explicit battlefield scenes, in *Dymer* he draws upon his vivid memories of the trenches to create this compelling episode.

34. Lewis says in his introduction to the 1950 edition of the poem the physical description of the Magician is based on his undergraduate memories of having twice met W. B. Yeats in Oxford.

35. *C. S. Lewis, Poet*, 127. Isaiah 1:18: "Come now, let us reason together," says the Lord. "Though your sins be as scarlet, they shall be as white as snow; though they are red as crimson, they shall be like wool."

36. "C. S. Lewis's *Dymer*." *SEVEN: An Anglo-American Literary Review* 1 (1980), 109.

37. Guerber, *Myths of the Norsemen*, 197.

38. "C. S. Lewis." An address given at Wheaton College, Wheaton, IL: October 16, 1964. The Wade Center.

BIBLIOGRAPHY

Christopher, Joe. "Comments on *Dymer*." *The Lamp-Post of the Southern California C. S. Lewis Society* 20 (Autumn 1996): 17–22.

———. "'From the Master's Lips': W. B. Yeats as C. S. Lewis Saw Him." *Bulletin of the New York C. S. Lewis Society* 6 (November 1974): 14–19.

————. "A Study of C. S. Lewis's *Dymer*." *Orcrist* 6 (Winter 1971–1972): 17–19. This is a revision of "Chapter Two: *Dymer*" from his Ph. D. Dissertation *The Romances of Clive Staples Lewis*, University of Oklahoma, 1969.

Guerber, H. A. *Myths of the Norsemen*. London: Harrap & Co., 1908.

Hodgens, Richard. "Notes on *Narrative Poems*." *Bulletin of the New York C. S. Lewis Society* 7 (April 1976): 1–14.

Hooper, Walter. "Preface." *Narrative Poems*. New York: Harcourt Brace Jovanovich, 1969, vii-xiv.

King, Don W. *C. S. Lewis, Poet: The Legacy of His Poetic Impulse*. Kent, OH: Kent State University Press, 2001.

————. "*Dymer*" and "*Narrative Poems*." In *The C. S. Lewis Readers' Encyclopedia*. Edited by Jeffrey D. Schultz and John G. West. Grand Rapids, MI: Zondervan, 1998.

Milne, Marjorie. "*Dymer*: Myth or Poem?" *The Month* 194 (September 1952): 170–173.

Murphy, Patrick. "C. S. Lewis's *Dymer*: Once More with Hesitation." *Bulletin of the New York C. S. Lewis Society* 17 (June 1986): 1–8. Reprinted in *The Poetic Fantastic: Studies in an Evolving Genre*. Edited by Patrick Murphy and Vernon Hyles. Westport, CT: Greenwood Press, 1989, 63–78.

Purcell, James. "*Narrative Poems*." *Bulletin of the New York C. S. Lewis Society* 2 (November 1972): 2–3.

Sayer, George. "C. S. Lewis's *Dymer*." In *SEVEN: An Anglo-American Literary Review* (1980): 94–116.

Slack, Michael. "Sehnsucht and the Platonic Eros in *Dymer*." *Bulletin of the New York C. S. Lewis Society* 11 (August 1980): 3–7.

12

Early Lyric Poetry: *Spirits in Bondage* (1919) and "Joy" (1924)

Don W. King

Although C. S. Lewis is best known as a prose writer for his clear, lucid, literary criticism, Christian apologetics, and imaginative Ransom and Narnia stories, he actually began his publishing career as a poet. His first two published works, *Spirits in Bondage* (1919) and *Dymer* (1926), were volumes of poetry published under the pseudonym of Clive Hamilton. In addition, he wrote many other poems that were later collected by Walter Hooper and published as *Poems* (1964). Hooper also published *Narrative Poems* in 1969, a volume that reprints *Dymer* as well as three other narrative poems. In addition, Hooper has published *The Collected Poems of C. S. Lewis* (1994), a work that reprints *Spirits in Bondage* and *Poems*, but includes for the first time "A Miscellany of Additional Poems," a supplement of seventeen other short poems.[1] Despite this body of work, Lewis has not achieved acclaim as a poet. While Thomas Howard calls *Poems* "the best—the glorious best—of Lewis,"[2] other critics view his poetry less favorably. Chad Walsh refers to Lewis as "the almost poet,"[3] and Dabney Hart believes that Lewis "will never have a major place in the canon of . . . poets."[4] Charles Huttar says that given the current of critical taste, Lewis as a poet is viewed as a "minor figure" and "barring a revolution in taste, he will never be accorded a higher position."[5] On the other hand, George Sayer's brilliant study of *Dymer* argues, "the time may come when it will be ranked higher than much of Lewis's prose work."[6] W. W. Robson, a Lewis colleague and friend, has published an article, "The Poetry of C. S. Lewis," in which he reevaluates his own earlier negative view of Lewis's poetry, arguing that in some of Lewis's poems he "touches greatness."[7] Luci Shaw has celebrated Lewis's poetic "ability to see and probe reality and express it in vivid and illuminating metaphors."[8]

While critics debate the quality of Lewis' poetry, anyone interested in Lewis as a writer should become aware of the important role his early poetry has in shaping his literary life, particularly his aspirations to achieve acclaim as a poet and the literary influences that shaped him. Owen Barfield remembers Lewis when he first met him as one "whose ruling ambition was to become a great poet. At that time if you thought of Lewis you automatically thought of poetry."[9] Tracing these aspirations and influences as he moved from boyhood to mature adult is fascinating and sheds significant light upon the prose for which he later became best known. His autobiography, *Surprised by Joy*, letters, particularly to Arthur Greeves, diaries, and journal entries provide ample chronological evidence of his early enthusiasm for poetry, the writers most influencing him, and his sustained desire to achieve acclaim as a poet.[10] Furthermore, throughout we see his attempt to establish his own theory of poetry, something he pursued throughout his life via a number of different forums culminating in his published debate with E. M. W. Tillyard, *The Personal Heresy*.[11] What all these sources make clear is how integral poetry was to Lewis's life. He did not sip or taste poetry in a casual, off-handed manner; rather it was for him a stream intricately weaving through his life becoming a literary well—a nourishing reservoir almost without bottom— one from which he drank deeply and passionately.

Lewis's earliest efforts at writing poetry led to the publication of *Spirits in Bondage*, a watershed in his literary life.[12] While limited in its scope and technique, *Spirits in Bondage* reveals much about Lewis the youthful poet and prepares the way for *Dymer* seven years later. Above all else, *Spirits in Bondage*, written under the shadow of his service in World War I, shows Lewis living as a frustrated dualist. On the one hand, in a number of *morose* poems he rails against man's inhumanity to man and against a God he denies yet blames for man's painful condition; as a whole these poems see life as demeaning, futile, and empty, primarily as a result of wartime brutalities. Other morose poems comment upon a God who is hateful, cruel, and red; Lewis intimates that this God "kills us for His sport."[13] On the other hand, many *sanguine* poems in *Spirits in Bondage* show his delight in Nature's beauty and mystery, while others expose his longing to know more intimately a reality that transcends the merely physical, often characterized by the world of 'faery'; overall these poems view Nature as kindly and benevolent in the lyrical and romantic tradition of Wordsworth, Shelley, Keats, and Yeats. Moreover, the sanguine poems intimate beauty is the evidence there is "something" beyond the material world, often connected to faery, and experiencing such beauty is the only way to transcend life's bleak reality.

The "Prologue" conveniently establishes the thematic bifurcation of *Spirits in Bondage*. Lewis identifies himself with ancient Phoenician sailors, who, after setting out for England to recover "Brethon treasure" (tin), sing of their homeland and gods as well as their looked for adventures and eventual success. They sing "above the storm and the strange sea's wailing" in order to forget "their burden" and the hardship of a long sea journey. Like them he will use the poems of *Spirits in Bondage*, his "coracle of verses," to sail "in mighty deeps alone on the chainless breezes" where he "will sing of lands unknown." Lewis lessens his task by referring to a coracle, a diminutive water-craft-for-one that barely displaces enough water to keep from sinking, but his is a worthy effort since he strives to flee "from the scarlet city where a Lord that knows no pity / Mocks the broken people praying round his iron throne, / [and to]—Sing about the Hidden Country fresh and full of quiet green. / Sailing over seas uncharted to a port that none has seen."[14] These lines clearly illustrate Lewis's intention to use the poetry of *Spirits in Bondage* in order to transcend an ugly reality characterized by a cruel god and impoverished people. In seeking the hidden country, he alludes to the world of faery where he can experience a redemptive beauty far from the flux and flow of a mean, diminished present. Though the "Prologue" lacks the grandeur of the opening lines of *Paradise Lost* (and Lewis is not so vain as to consider himself Milton's equal), his desire to "sing of lands unknown" and to sail "over seas uncharted to a port that none has seen" are transparent echoes to the prologue of *Paradise Lost*. In effect Lewis pays homage to Milton and his invocation to the "Heavenly Muse" [(the Holy Spirit)] where he similarly requests assistance in his "adventurous song" to "pursue things unattempted yet in prose or rhyme."[15]

"French Nocturne (Monchy-Le-Preux)" may be the first poem Lewis wrote directly focusing upon his trench experiences and, thus it becomes the natural place to begin considering Lewis's morose poems focusing upon war.[16] It opens with a portrayal of what an "independent contemplator" sees; trenches stretch out in either direction in an apparently endless fashion. Nearby "the jaws of a sacked village, stark and grim, / Out on the ridge have swallowed up the sun, / And in one angry streak his blood has run / To left and right along the horizon dim." Lewis's image of the sunset is characteristic of World War I poetry, according to Paul Fussell: "When a participant in the war wants an ironic effect, a conventional way to achieve one is simply to juxtapose a sunrise or sunset with the unlovely physical details of the war. . . . These sunrises and sunsets . . . move to the very center of English poetry of the Great War."[17] "French Nocturne" continues with the persona following a plane that appears to fly straight into the moon; this leads him to associate the plane's upward movement with the world of dreams he once held dear. However, it is only a brief reprieve since the reality of the battlefield quickly recalls itself:

> False, mocking fancy! Once I too could dream,
> Who now can only see with vulgar eye
> That he's no nearer to the moon than I
> And she's a stone that catches the sun's beam.
>
> What call have I to dream of anything?
> I am a wolf. Back to the world again,
> And speech of fellow-brutes that once were men
> Our throats can bark for slaughter: cannot sing.

War reduces everything to the merely physical. For instance, there is nothing enchanting about the moon; it is simply a cold, reflective rock. Furthermore, soldiers cannot dream, a distinguishing human quality, since now they are vicious animals, brute predators intent on blood and destruction. Even their capacity to sing, to make harmonious music, has been reduced to the rasping, grating snapping of wolves.

"Victory" continues this theme by noting how war has stripped life of its magic, mystery, and wonder. Lewis illustrates this loss of the numinous by noting the death of two mythic warrior heroes: Roland, hero of Charlemagne's army and *The Song of Roland*, and Cuchulain, ancient Irish hero noted in *The Cattle Raid of Cooley* for single-handedly defending Ulster from the forces of Medb, queen of Connaught. In addition, he laments the passing of the mythic beauty of Helen of Troy and Iseult (from Malory's *Morte d'Arthur*), the absence of faery-inhabited woodlands, dryads (tree spirits), Triton from the sea, and King Arthur. All the poetry written to celebrate these figures has been useless; even Shakespeare is deprecated: "All poets have been fools who thought to mould / A monument more durable than brass."[18] While decay marks such human efforts, what does endure is the "yearning, high, rebellious spirit of man." Lewis may be recalling Prometheus from Shelley's *Prometheus Unbound*, a figure representing the indomitable, unbroken will of man. It is this spirit that strives mightily in the midst of war with "red Nature and her ways," a phrase intentionally echoing Tennyson's "Lyric 56" from *In Memoriam*. "Victory" is Lewis's answer to this lyric. Tennyson suggests the human spirit will not endure against "Nature, red in tooth and claw." Lewis, while admitting "in the filth of war, the baresark shout / Of battle, [the spirit of man] is vexed,"[19] affirms that the human spirit will not be crushed, a theme he returns later in "De Profundis." In fact, the poem ends with an affirmation negating much of the poem's earlier morose tone: "Though often bruised, oft broken by the rod, / Yet, like the phoenix, from each fiery bed / Higher the stricken spirit lifts its head/And higher—till the beast become a god."

Another morose war poem that can be glossed to *In Memoriam* is "Spooks." Tennyson's "Lyric 7" imagines him standing at the door to Hallam's home looking to grasp "a hand that can be clasped no more." Similarly, Lewis's poem is set outside the home of a beloved: "Last night I dreamed that I was come again/Unto the house where my beloved dwells / After long years of wandering and pain."[20] However, the lover cannot enter the "warmth and light" of his true love's house, at first believing some "secret sin" or "old, unhappy anger" keeps him outside. However, his alienation is explained when it "suddenly came into my head / That I was killed long since and lying dead." No doubt influenced by the many corpses Lewis saw in the trenches and on the battlefield, "Spooks" ends with the dead lover still standing outside his beloved's home "unseen amid the winter night / And the lamp burned within, a rosy light, / And the wet street was shining in the rain." Though moving, Lewis's poem lacks the poignant power of Tennyson's ending: "He is not here; but far away / The noise of life begins again, / And ghastly through the drizzling rain / On the bald street breaks the blank day." The loss of a loved one, painful regardless the context, is heightened during war since battlefields are places where death is manufactured, leading to alienation, estrangement, and isolation. Consequently, this poem demonstrates that the longing to see loved ones causes some to seek them in places once shared; in effect, both the dead and the living become spooks.

"Apology" is Lewis's most bitter and ironic war poem, giving an explanation for why he will not write verse celebrating the glory of war. He begins by addressing Despoina, another name for Persephone, Queen of Hades,[21] telling her he has a reason for speaking "of nothing glad nor noble in my verse / To lighten hearts beneath this present curse / And build a heaven of dreams in real hell."[22] The poem may work on two levels. On the one hand, he directs Despoina to tell the dead why his verse is morose and cannot bring them comfort, while on the other hand, he, in the role of Despoina, explains why he will not give the lie about the glory of war to soldiers in nightmarish battlefield conditions (their "real hell"). Just as it is a cruelty to remind the dead "down in the rotting grave where the lithe worms crawl, / [Of] green fields above that smiled so sweet," so it is to remind soldiers, living in vile trenches where rats gorge on human flesh, of green fields back home.[23] Neither the dead nor soldiers want to be told how wonderful and vital life is for those not experiencing their hell. To emphasize this, Lewis asks what good is it "to tell old tales of Troynovant / Or praises of dead heroes, tried and sage," a slight variation on same point he makes in "Victory." The old stories of war's valor, heroism, and honor ring hollow: "Can it be good / To think of glory now, when all is done, / And all our labour underneath the sun / Has brought us this—and not the thing we would." "This" is their "present curse": for the dead, hell, and for the soldier, the trenches. It is as futile for them to build a case for the glory of their deeds as it was for Mammon in Book III of *Paradise Lost* to argue the fallen angels can build a literal Heaven in Hell: "As he [God] our darkness, cannot we his light / Imitate when we please? . . . / What can Heaven show more?"[24] Though Lewis's final comments are not as sarcastic as Beelzebub's who mocks Mammon for "hatching vain empires," he does reject the idea of using the old myths of glory: "All these were rosy visions of the night, / That loveliness and wisdom feigned of old. / But now we wake. The East is pale and cold, / No hope is in the dawn, and no delight." Because of its nihilistic ending, this is Lewis's most morose battlefield poem.

Other morose poems illustrate Lewis's attempt to come to grips with a God he does not want to exist, yet blames for human misery. Two poems with the same title offer us the chance to see how Lewis's thoughts about his malicious God developed. "Satan Speaks" (I) begins by recalling Lewis's comments to Greeves when he writes "I have formulated my equation Matter=Nature=Satan."[25] Later he adds *Spirits in Bondage* "is mainly strung round the idea that I mentioned to you before—that nature is wholly diabolical & malevolent and that God, if he exists, is outside of and in opposition to the cosmic arrangements."[26] The poem opens with Lewis emphasizing a God of rules, laws, and universal force: "I am Nature, the Mighty Mother, / I am the law: ye have no other." After clearly establishing there is no grace, no charity, no empathy in this Darwinian God of Nature, he follows with couplet stanzas underscoring this God's mechanistic nature, making frequent use of war imagery: "I am the battle's filth and strain, / I am the widow's empty pain. / I am the sea to smother your breath, / I am the bomb, the falling death." This God is brutish, oppressive, insatiable, unapproachable, and destructive.

However the later "Satan Speaks" (XIII) presents a slightly different God, revealing Lewis's evolving thoughts about his "diabolical & malevolent" deity. The God here is also connected to nature—"I am the Lord your God: even he that made / Material things"—but Lewis's blasphemous parody goes on to demonstrate this God is more "personal," being malicious, proud, and condescending. He harangues his creatures, reminding them he uses pain and suffering to remind them he, and only he, is God, and that there is no softer, gentler deity as they would like to believe. He mocks their "dreams of some other gods," by giving them a miserable existence, calls them vermin, and then appears surprised "they hate my world!" As if to prove his ultimate authority, he sardonically challenges "that other God" to come from his realm of glory to "steal forth my own thought's children into light." Then he claims the softer, gentler God (if He exists) is detached, unconcerned for man as "he walks the airy fields of endless day." The poem ends with the malicious God reasserting his supremacy: "My order still is strong / And like to me nor second none I know. / Whither the mammoth went this creature too shall go." Whether "this creature" refers to man or the softer, gentler, God, the malicious God countenances no competitors.[27] He prophesies man or the other God will follow the mammoth into extinction.[28]

The speaker in "De Profundis" frankly challenges the authority of such a malicious deity, almost certainly reflecting Lewis's reading of Shelley's *Prometheus Unbound*.[29] In effect, he damns this God: "Come let us curse our Master ere we die, / For all our hopes in endless ruin lie. / The good is dead. Let us curse God most High."[30] The shocking tone of this opening explains Warren Lewis' reaction to his first reading of *Spirits in Bondage* when he writes to his father:

While I am in complete agreement with you as to the excellence of part of IT's book, I am of the opinion it would have been better if it had never been published. Even at 23 [Warren's age when writing this letter] one realizes that the opinions of 20 are transient things. Jack's Atheism is I am sure purely academic, but, even so, no useful purpose is served by endeavouring to advertise oneself as an Atheist. Setting aside the higher problems involved, it is obvious that a profession of a Christian belief is as necessary a part of a man's mental make-up as a belief in the King, the Regular Army, and the Public Schools (January 28, 1919).[31]

When Lewis learned of Warren's "misreading," he attempted to mollify his father: "You know who the God I blaspheme is and that it is not the God that you or I worship, or any other Christian" (March 5, 1919).[32] This is, of course, only a partial truth, since Lewis was not worshipping the "Christian" God at this time.

Lewis's reassurances aside, the tone of "De Profundis" reflects an angry adolescent, shaking his fist at a malicious God he denies, rejects, hates, yet fears. In a patent slap at meliorism, the popular pre-war notion the world was gradually getting better and could be improved further by human effort, Lewis says: "Four thousand years of toil and hope and thought / Wherein men laboured upward and still wrought / New worlds and better, Thou hast made as naught." All human effort to build beautiful cities and to acquire knowledge and wisdom are nothing but offal to the malicious God, for "the earth grew black with wrong, / Our hope was crushed and silenced was our song." The speaker momentarily entertains the thought that perhaps somewhere there is "a just God that cares for earthly pain," but this, too, is rejected, since, even if true, "yet far away beyond our labouring night, / He wanders in the depths of endless light, / Singing alone his musics of delight." What is left man against this malicious God, this "universal strength"? Though admitting "it is but froth of folly to rebel," this is precisely what he advocates. The indomitable spirit of man will resist forever the interfering, capricious hand of a cruel, malicious God:

> Yet I will not bow down to thee nor love thee,
> For looking in my own heart I can prove thee,
> And know this frail, bruised being is above thee.
>
> Our love, our hope, our thirsting for the right,
> Our mercy and long seeking of the light,
> Shall we change these for thy relentless might?
>
> Laugh then and slay. Shatter all things of worth,
> Heap torment still on torment for thy mirth—
> Thou art not Lord while there are Men on earth.

Though foolhardy, man's best shall not be traded for the malicious God's might. He may kill man, even delighting in the carnage, but he will not conquer man's will. Indeed, although it is false bravado, the speaker claims the malicious God will never truly be Lord as long as men live. The malicious deity of *Spirits in Bondage* is like Moloch of Milton's *Paradise Lost*—angry, bloodthirsty, and vindictive.[33]

The last two morose poems are short meditations on the futility of life and the fear of death. "In Prison" concerns one who cries out "for the pain of man" that leads "from death to death." One evening he imagines he transcends the earth and views in "endless depths of nothing" the earth falling as "a lonely pin-prick spark of light" through the "wide, enfolding night." Although light is associated with it, the earth's isolation and insignificance among the stars is emphasized:

> And if some tears be shed,
> Some evil God have power,
> Some crown of sorrows sit
> Upon a little world for a little hour—
> Who shall remember? Who shall care for it?[34]

With the angry passion of the speaker from "De Profundis" spent, all that remains "In Prison" is ennui. Instead of Christ, the world is crowned with thorns the malicious God intends for it, and what remains is for man to accept this judgment. "Alexandrines" relates the fears of the speaker about "a house that most of all on earth I hate."[35] Though he has known pain and anguish "in bloody fields, sad seas, and countries desolate," clear allusions to wartime experiences, "yet most I fear that empty house where the grasses green / Grow in the silent court the gaping flags between, / And down the moss-grown paths and terrace no man treads / Where the old, old weeds rise deep on the waste garden beds." This description takes us to a cemetery, and we realize the house he fears is his own grave. However, his is not fear of annihilation. Instead, it is his inevitable confrontation in death with the malicious God: "For in that house I know a little, silent room / Where Someone's always waiting, waiting in the gloom / To draw me with an evil eye, and hold me fast— / Yet thither doom will drive me and He will win at last."[36] The broken, almost docile tone of the speaker here is a far cry from the defiant one of "De Profundis." Taken together, however, they reveal the range of Lewis's attitude toward the malicious God he confronted in his morose poems.

Lewis's war poems and those dealing with a malicious God reveal the extent to which he was living as a frustrated dualist. Without question Lewis's atheism was profoundly influenced by W. T. Kirkpatrick's, his great tutor, as well as the philosophical ideas he encountered elsewhere. Yet the battlefield horrors he witnessed informs these poems even more deeply, exposing a young man grappling to understand his place in a world that appeared to be teetering on the brink of collapse. Although his angry, defiant responses in some of the poems were immature and adolescent, they are a measure of the passion with which he imbued his poetry. It was poetry, not prose, he used to work through the crises he was experiencing, giving outward expression to his deeply internalized feelings. What saves *Spirits in Bondage* from turning into teenage angst, however, is the sanguine poetry representing the other dimension of Lewis's dualism. Here, too, we find immaturity, but even greater maturity as Lewis focused upon his love of nature and beauty. Indeed, Lewis's sanguine poems are among his first poetic attempts to put in writing his longing for joy he later recounted in *Surprised by Joy*; as such these poems reveal his yearning to experience transcendent truth. Ironically, in these poems, we see the genesis of Lewis the theist.

The first group of sanguine poems are primarily lyrical and celebrate land-scapes, rest, literature, music, nature (Wordsworthian instead of Darwinian), stars, and human love. For instance, "Irish Nocturne" celebrates Lewis's homeland. It begins with a description of an eerie landscape with mist filling a valley like "evil drink in a wizard's hand," and then alludes to ghosts, demons, Grendel (the *Beowulf* monster), and other ominous supernatural creatures. Lewis then uses the mist as a metaphor to indicate Ireland's obscured understanding of itself:

Bitter and bitter it is for thee, O my heart,
Looking upon this land, where poets sang,
Thus with the dreary shroud

Unwholesome, over it spread,
And knowing the fog and the cloud
In her people's heart and head
Even as it lies for ever upon her coasts
Making them dim and dreamy lest her sons should ever arise
And remember all their boasts.[37]

The poem ends with Lewis lamenting this mist since it breeds "lonely desire and many words and brooding and never a deed." Lewis's complaint against his countrymen for being dreamers and talkers rather than doers is stereotypical; however, because Lewis does not connect this poem to a specific incident, it is difficult to know how seriously we should take his lament. Another landscape poem, "The Roads," returns us to Lewis's favorite spot near Belfast: "I stand on the windy uplands among the hills of Down / With all the world spread out beneath, meadow and sea and town, / And ploughlands on the far-off hills that glow with friendly brown."[38] From this vantage point, Lewis looks out upon roads extending to the horizon in several directions. As his eye follows them, he feels a strong pull: "And the call of the roads is upon me, a desire in my spirit has grown / To wander forth in the highways, 'twixt earth and sky alone, / And seek for the lands no foot has trod and the seas no sail has known." The urge to explore, to find adventure, to discover, suggests this is an early poem, perhaps written in 1915, and marks it as well as one where he articulated early his yearning to find deep satisfaction in unknown external experiences.[39] If related to "Irish Nocturne" it also intimates that travel down these roads can be the escape from the homeland he loves yet laments.

Moving from an affection for the landscape, Lewis's "Night" (IX) and "To Sleep," a pair he intends to be read together, are sanguine pieces on rest. In "Night" (IX) he pictures night as a necessary comforter: "After the fret and failure of this day, / And weariness of thought, O Mother Night, / Come with soft kiss to soothe our care away / And all our little tumults set to right."[40] Like Shakespeare and Keats before him, Lewis finds sleep a simile for death when he calls sleep "most pitiful of all death's kindred fair." Imitating Keats' lyricism in particular, Lewis envisions Night as a goddess who drives a pair of magic steeds:

Thou from the fronting rim
Bending to urge them, whilst thy sea-dark hair
Fall in ambrosial ripples o'er each limb,
With beautiful pale arms, untrammeled, bare
For horsemanship, to those twin chargers fleet
Dost give full rein across the fires that glow

In the wide floor of heaven, from off their feet
Scattering the powdery star-dust as they go.

The poem ends as it begins as Lewis underlines night as a solace to man's weary life: "thou still art used to bind / With tenderest love of careful leeches' art / The bruised and weary heart / In slumber blind." Though derivative, this poem gives evidence of Lewis's working hard at the craft of poetry as well as its own dualism: the peace of night contrasts with the busyness of day. "To Sleep" continues this focus upon rest and is influenced by Keats' "Sonnet to Sleep" and "Ode to Psyche." Here Lewis seeks to retreat to "a hidden wood among the hill-tops green, / Full of soft streams and little winds that creep / The murmuring boughs between" where "in the fragrant twilight I will raise / A secret altar of the rich sea sod, / Whereat to offer sacrifice and praise / Unto my lonely god."[41] His earnest devotion to build such an altar, covering it with poppies,[42] is not altruistic, for he hopes such worship will be rewarded by "dreams of dear delight / And draughts of cool oblivion, quenching pain, / And sweet, half-wakeful moments in the night / To hear the falling rain." Although not directly a war poem, Lewis's desire for "draughts of cool oblivion, quenching pain" could mark this as more than a poem about his wanting sleep to refresh him from a particularly stressful day of academic study. The poem's concluding lines are a request that sleep silence the day's pain, extending perhaps to a similar desire at his death: "And when he meets me at the dusk of day / To call me home for ever, this I ask— / That he may lead me friendly on that way / And wear no frightful mask." "Sonnet," is still another Keatsian poem about sleep, and while sanguine, its tone is darker and may contain a veiled death wish. In the poem, set in a "dreaming garden still and sweet," the speaker longs "for a chamber dim, a pillow meet / For slumbers deep as death, a faultless sheet, / Cool, white and smooth." This time the poppies of sleep are like a "magic sponge" and can wipe away the hours or even the years: "Why not a year, / Why could a man not loiter in that bower / Until a thousand painless cycles wore, / And then—what if it held him evermore?" While "Night" (IX) and "To Sleep" portray rest as a necessary antidote to life's tumult, "Sonnet" suggests there is a more permanent way to achieve rest, one that is lasting.

This sequence of sanguine poems urging rest and retreat lead to two lyrics whose themes are withdrawal. "Milton Read Again (in Surrey)" is in the tradition of Keats's "On First Looking into Chapman's Homer" or Wordsworth's "London, 1802" (another panegyric to Milton); that is, it is a poem praising an author who influenced the writer.[43] Lewis's delight at being sent to study with Kirkpatrick and his withdrawal from Malvern and all he detested there created the context for this poem. Since we have already seen how highly Lewis regarded Milton, the poem is no surprise. In particular, Lewis appears to be celebrating his recent rereading of *Paradise Lost*: "Three golden months while summer on us stole / I have read your joyful tale another time, / Breathing more freely in that larger clime / And learning wiselier to deserve the whole."[44] Of course here Lewis's debt to Milton is primarily poetic not theological, though given Lewis's eventual turn to faith in Christ and his *A Preface to Paradise Lost*, we may see in "Milton Read Again" the dormant seeds of his later conversion. Regardless, Lewis credits Milton with guiding him to the treasures of poetry, opening his eyes to a rich imagination where before his has been barren. He compares his reading of Milton to one who returns to walk a familiar wood, suddenly overcome with "the weird spirit of unexplained delight, / New mystery in every shady place, / In every whispering tree a nameless grace, / New rapture on the windy seaward height." "Lullaby," another poem of withdrawal, focuses not upon literature but instead upon the power of music.[45] Recalling Tennyson's "Lady of Shalott," the poem describes three maidens who inhabit the upper chamber of a tower, who "spin both night and day," though in the evening they are transformed into swans.[46] They fly to the woods nearby "singing in swans' voices high / A lonely, lovely lullaby." More lyrical than "Milton Read Again," "Lullaby" has affinities with "The Ocean Strand" and "Noon" for both its language and use of female figures.

Moving from sanguine poems emphasizing rest or retreat, we see in "Hymn (For Boys' Voices)" a poem where Lewis says the wonders of nature's beauty are ever before us and accessible to us if only we will open our eyes and see. The things magicians do, the games faeries play, nature's power, immortality, even God's perspective—all these and more—can be ours: "If we could but understand! / We could revel day and night / In all power and all delight / If we learned to think aright."[47] Affirming this, however, does not make it happen, and the poem gives us no way to do what he recommends other than the poem's circular argument. Directly related to "Hymn" and following it in *Spirits in Bondage* is "Our Daily Bread," beginning: "We need no barbarous words nor solemn spell / To raise the unknown. It lies before our feet."[48] This poem also does not give us a coherent means to see what Lewis does. However it surpasses "Hymn" in its personal view as Lewis explains his visits to favorite spots in nature create the context where "the Living voices call" him, and he catches "a sight of lands beyond the wall, / I see a strange god's face." Furthermore, he intimates the allure of such visions will one day pull him out of the work-a-day world:

And some day this will work upon me so
I shall arise and leave both friends and home

And over many lands a pilgrim go
Through alien woods and foam,

Seeking the last steep edges of the earth
Whence I may leap into that gulf of light
Wherein, before my narrowing Self had birth,
Part of me lived aright.

Lewis returns to the idea of being a pilgrim looking for beauty below in "Song of the Pilgrims." Also of note is Lewis's clear debt to Wordsworth's "Ode: Intimations of Immortality":

Though inland far we be,
Our Souls have sight of that immortal sea
Which brought us hither,
Can in a moment travel thither,
And see the Children sport upon the shore,
And hear the mighty water rolling evermore.

Lewis's longing to become a part of the mysterious beauty of nature he sees is given expression more effectively in later poems where he directly connects nature to faery.

Sanguine poems unified by a focus upon faery, including specific faery creatures, general observations about faery, and the longing for faery have a central place in *Spirits in Bondage*. Lewis's affection for faery culminates in a series of poems illustrating his idea that the faery world proves transcendent beauty exists.[49] "The Satyr" describes the mythological creature normally thought of as a personification of Nature, appearing in literature under various names, Pan chief among them.[50] In the poem a satyr is pictured as heralding the arrival of spring by dancing through forest, meadow, and valley "carolling" and "making music evermore" as a means of rallying his "faerie kin." Lewis's physical description of the satyr gives the traditional view of him as half man/half goat, combining both native beauty with the darker suggestion ("his dreadful feet are cloven") of veiled power and mystery:

Though his brow be clear and white
And beneath it fancies bright,
Wisdom and high thoughts are woven
And the musics of delight,

Though his temples too be fair
Yet two horns are growing there
Bursting forth to part asunder
All the riches of his hair.[51]

The cloven feet and horns interrupt the reverie, not necessarily suggesting the demonic but hinting at danger. This is heightened when the poem concludes by emphasizing another traditional attribute of the satyr, sexual licentiousness: "Faerie maidens he may meet / Fly the horns and cloven feet, / But, his sad brown eyes with wonder / Seeing—stay from their retreat." The power of the satyr to lure maidens with "his sad brown eyes" is the first instance in *Spirits in Bondage* ("The Satyr" is the third poem in the volume) of a concept Lewis repeatedly underscores: the power of faery to draw us out of this world and into one of beauty, mystery, and danger.

In one of the few sanguine poems in *Spirits in Bondage* linked to dreams, "L'Apprenti Sorcier" concerns the power of faery to tempt the dreamer from bitter, dark, dreams to ones suggesting harmony. A dreamer hears the sound of mighty ocean breakers crashing on the distant shore of a realm inhabited by "frightful seraphim" and a fierce, cold, God whose eyes promise "hate and misery / And wars and famines yet to be." As he stands before the deafening breakers, he catches a vision of faery: "Out of the toiling sea arose / Many a face and form of those / Thin, elemental people dear / Who live beyond our heavy sphere."[52] They speak, inviting him to join them:

> "Leap in! Leap in, and take thy fill
> Of all the cosmic good and ill,
> Be as the Living ones that know
> Enormous joy, enormous woe,
> Pain beyond thought and fiery bliss:
> For all thy study hunted this,
> On wings of magic to arise,
> And wash from off thy filmed eyes
> The clouds of cold mortality."

Their invitation to submerge with them—to learn of good and evil, to know ultimate happiness and sorrow, to experience ecstatic sensory realities—is extremely attractive, for the dreamer has been searching for this all his life. Their call, therefore, to discover with them "real life" and their scorn if he slinks "again / Back to the narrow ways of men" pull strongly at him. With them he can enter faery and realize the opportunity to experience final truth. However, the poem ends much as dreams do: "So all these mocked me as I stood / Striving to wake because I feared the flood." His desire to awaken before he has to decide leaves the ending inconclusive, but again we see in the poem Lewis's fascination with faery's pull on him.

"Song of the Pilgrims" continues this theme of the longing for faery; indeed, it is Lewis's fullest expression of this yearning. The poem portrays a group of pilgrims who have been journeying endlessly trying to discover faery peoples and their land, here personified as "dwellers at the back of the North Wind."[53] The pilgrims have been told by some that there is no realm of faery, "but, ah God! we know / That somewhere, somewhere past the Northern snow / Waiting for us the red-rose gardens blow." Because of this conviction, the pilgrims

> Have forsaken all things sweet and fair,
> We have found nothing worth a moment's care
> Because the real flowers are blowing there.
>
> Land of the Lotus fallen from the sun,
> Land of the Lake from whence all rivers run,
> Land where the hope of all our dreams is won!

The promise of real life, the fulfillment of all desires, the living out of dreams are more than enough to stimulate the pilgrims in their quest. Like Odysseus' sailors enchanted by the island of the Lotus eaters, so these pilgrims do not want to be deflected in their search for faery. While they go on to admit that day-to-day life deadens them to perceiving faery and that even as they approach faery it causes them to tremble, they long to "wake again in gardens bright / Of green and gold for infinite delight, / Sleeping beneath the solemn mountains white." In faery they imagine a realm untouched by time where songbirds never cease singing, where queens rule without break, and where poets write forever and "whisper a wild, sweet song" revealing the deepest truths of the universe. It is their longing to merge with the eternal that drives the pilgrims. In their review of why they keep missing faery, they note having journeyed near places associated in the past with faery, wondering if they miss it because they have sinned. Or, they consider, "is it all a folly of the wise, / Bidding us walk these ways with blinded eyes / While all around us real flowers arise?" Perhaps *this* world is where they find "real flowers." Such self-doubt is only momentary and the poem ends with their powerful affirmation: "But, by the very God, we know, we know / That somewhere still, beyond the Northern snow / Waiting for us the red-rose gardens blow." The pilgrim's search for a real, eternal, nonchanging world indicates Lewis's own deeply felt Platonism, but their desire is not for a Platonic realm of forms; instead, they seek the richly imagined world of faery, one in a sense beyond both the earthly and Platonic. Though the pilgrims never answer the question of whether or not it is their sin that keeps them from entering faery, we should remember that traditionally pilgrims move from a state of sin to one of grace *through* the act of pilgrimage itself. It could be these pilgrims are nearer faery than they know.

In the only poem of *Spirits in Bondage* dealing with romantic love, Lewis imagines in "World's Desire" a kind of Valhalla of love; that is, the poem concerns a castle "built" in a desolate country, the whole scene strongly reminiscent of Wagner's influence upon Lewis:

Where the trees are grim and great,
Blasted with the lightning sharp—giant boulders strewn between,
And the mountains rise above, and the cold ravine
Echoes to the crushing roar and thunder of a mighty river
Raging down a cataract.[54]

In the midst of this rugged, wild, land, a castle rises, its towers strong, its gates "made of ivory, the roofs of copper red." Guarded by warders and "wakeful dragons," nothing can assail it, for it is "a resting-place, dear heart, for you and me." Faery touches the poem when a wild faery maiden who, homeless and torn by the forests, wanders beneath the castle: "Often to the castle gate up she looks with vain endeavour, / For her soulless loveliness to the castle winneth never." The castle is an escape, a retreat for the speaker and his beloved: "Within the sacred court, hidden high upon the mountain, / Wandering in the castle gardens lovely folk enough there be, / Breathing in another air, drinking of a purer fountain / And among that folk, beloved, there's a place for you and me." In this pinnacle of love, this fortress of passion, the speaker and his beloved will find the best place to dwell. Human love signals beauty, Lewis suggests, and in the midst of daily routine, love is its own castle of desire. If this is a battlefield poem, Lewis's longing to escape his terrible present for a palace of love is surely understandable.

Three poems include details about both war and beauty; as a result, they may be efforts by Lewis to bridge the bifurcation of *Spirits in Bondage*. "Oxford" itself shows bifurcation in that its first, fourth, and fifth stanzas concern how an enclave like Oxford serves as a citadel for beauty, while the second and third stanzas present war as a threat to such beauty. Lewis begins by saying it is good there are "palaces of peace / And discipline and dreaming and desire, / Lest we forget our heritage and cease / The Spirit's work—to hunger and aspire."[55] His use of "Spirit" is that of the "something" we have seen previously, and links his aspirations not with Christian faith but instead with transcendent beauty. In the second stanza he notes places like Oxford remind us beauty lives on in spite of the fact we now are "tangled in red battle's animal net, / Murder the work and lust the anodyne." The third stanza continues this thought, noting that unlike the battlefield where men are reduced to surviving on animal instincts, Oxford "has nothing of the beast, / That was not built for gross, material gains, / Sharp, wolfish power or empire's glutted feast." The final two stanzas leave the battlefield entirely ("we are not wholly brute"), focusing rather upon Oxford's function as a lighthouse of dreams, visions, aspirations, and beauty; if it is a kind of fortress in the midst of war, it is "a refuge of the elect." Oxford becomes an emblem of beauty's survival regardless the swirl of war: "She was not built out of common stone / But out of all men's yearning and all prayer / That she might live, eternally our own, / The Spirit's stronghold—barred against despair." This is not Lewis's attempt "to build a heaven out of hell" so much as it is his effort to remind himself and others that wartime brutality is not the only reality. It may be the most immediate one for soldiers, even one not easily put aside, but in "Oxford" he recalls there is another reality, a place where men aspire for beauty rather than gunshot, and one that gives motivation to him to live beyond the brute.

"Dungeon Grates" is Lewis's most comprehensive attempt to illustrate how faery is the evidence of transcendent beauty and how such beauty contradicts the sense produced by war that human existence is meaningless. Man's essential condition, heightened by war, the opening lines suggest, is one of loneliness, grief, burdens, and pain; these beat him down toward his death except for those moments when he captures "a sudden glimpse of spirit faces."[56] That is, though his life may appear to be lived in a cell behind dungeon bars, the apprehension of beauty, "the fragrant breath" of "flowery places," the longing "for which the hearts of men are always sore," reminds man of another reality beyond time. Anticipating what he comes to hammer home consistently in *Surprised by Joy*, however, Lewis says this reality is not one to seek actively:

It lies beyond endeavour; neither prayer
Nor fasting, nor much wisdom winneth there,
Seeing how many prophets and wise men
Have sought for it and still returned again
With hope undone.

In fact, beauty comes unlooked for, serendipitously: "But only the strange power / Of unsought Beauty in some casual hour / Can build a bridge of light or sound or form / To lead you out of all this strife and storm." For the first time he attempts to explain how beauty leads us, claiming that when we mesh with beauty, when "we are grown a part" of it until "from its very glory's midmost heart / Out leaps a sudden beam of larger light / Into our souls," then we will see all things as they really are, "seven times more true than what for truth we hold / In vulgar hours." This Wordsworthian ethos culminates in lines reminiscent of "Tintern Abbey":

The miracle is done
And for one little moment we are one
With the eternal stream of loveliness
That flows so calm, aloof from all distress
Yet leaps and lives around us as a fire
Making us faint with overstrong desire
To sport and swim for ever in its deep.

Though such epiphanies are momentary and rare, we feed off them for a long time, sustained by them because through them "we know we are not made of mortal stuff." Indeed, such momentary visitations of beauty help us survive our otherwise burdensome human condition: "And we can bear all trials that come after, / The hate of men and the fool's loud bestial laughter / And Nature's rule and cruelties unclean, / For we have seen the Glory—we have seen." As we shall see below, Lewis's poem "Joy" (1924) reexamines this same notion with a rather different and unexpected resolution. Here, however, Lewis honors the visitations of beauty as a harbinger whereby man can endure an otherwise dark, meaningless world.

"Death in Battle" we know is a war poem, because it was for that very reason first published by John Galsworthy in *Reveille*.[57] From the beginning the poem is escapist, with a particular longing to transcend the battlefield for "the peaceful castle, rosy in the West, / In the sweet dim Isle of Apples over the wide sea's breast." This desire is a direct result of battlefield experiences that have pressed "and driven and hurt" him almost beyond bearing; he has been blindly fighting "among men cursing in fight and toiling." As a consequence, he longs to escape, to be alone, "to be ever alone," above and beyond the turmoil of the fray, "in flowery valleys among the mountains and silent wastes untrod, / In the dewy upland places, in the garden of God." In such a retreat he no longer will have to see "the brutal, crowded faces around me, that in their toil have grown / Into the faces of devils—yea, even as my own." This realm of transcendent peace blots out war's tumult: "O Country of Dreams! / Beyond the tide of the ocean, hidden and sunk away, / Out of the sound of battles, near to the end of day, / Full of dim woods and streams." As he does in "Oxford" and "Dungeon Grates," Lewis resolves his frustrated dualism in "Death in Battle" via beauty. Only beauty can atone for war's hell.

One other early poem must be mentioned here. "Joy," published in 1924, is a critically important poem because in it Lewis renames the longing for transcendent beauty he wrote about so passionately in the sanguine poems of *Spirits in Bondage*; indeed, this poem was Lewis's earliest published attempt to describe the essence of joy.[58] While *Surprised by Joy* is an almost exhaustive attempt by Lewis late in his life to chronicle his determined pursuit for joy, in this early poem he sketches a sleeper's awakening to unexpected joy and beauty.[59] Alluding to the myth of Leda and the swan, where Zeus in the form of a gigantic bird ravishes a beautiful girl, Lewis compares the sleeper's wakening to this event: "As I woke, / Like a huge bird, Joy with the feathery stroke / Of strange wings brushed me over."[60] As Leda is overcome and overwhelmed by the swan, so the sleeper is by Joy, which then touches "the lair / Of each wild thing and woke the wet flowers everywhere." Drunk with such joy, the speaker believes he will have this powerfully vital sense of joy so constantly "that this mood could never die." Indeed, at least briefly he glories in the belief the joy he is experiencing makes him master of all he sees, even liberating him to see clearly and understand fully all that life holds for him: "Like Christian [from John Bunyan's *The Pilgrim's Progress*] when his burden dropt behind, / I was set free. Pure colour purified my mind." Yet he pauses after this and realizes:

> We do not know the language Beauty speaks,
> She has no answer to our questioning,
> And ease to pain and truth to one who seeks
> I know she never brought and cannot bring.
> But, if she wakes a moment, we must fling
> Doubt at her feet, not answered, yet allayed.
> She beats down wisdom suddenly. We cling
> Fast to her flying skirts and she will fade
> Even at the kiss of welcome, into deepest shade.[61]

This passage recalls Shelley's "Hymn to Intellectual Beauty" in several ways. On the one hand, Lewis takes issue with Shelley's claim that only Beauty can give "grace and truth to life's unquiet dream" since for him beauty "has no answer to our questioning." On the other hand, he supports Shelley's vow to "dedicate my powers / To thee and thine" so that when Beauty comes, one can find in her an "awful LOVELINESS, / [That] wouldst give whate'er these words cannot express." For Lewis Beauty is the swan beating wisdom down on the passive receiver; for Shelley Beauty is "the awful shadow of some unseen Power . . . Which like the truth / Of nature on my passive youth / Descended, to my onward life supply / Its calm."

As Lewis's poem continues, the speaker's sober realization that Beauty "will not stay" echoes Shelley's lament: "Spirit of BEAUTY, that dost consecrate / With thine own hues all thou dost shine upon / Of human thought or form,—where art thou gone?" However, at this point the two poems diverge radically. Shelley, while admitting Beauty is imperceptible, inconstant, and shadowy, still affirms it is ever-present although we may not realize this since it "floats ... unseen amongst us." Lewis's speaker disagrees:

> And then I knew that this was all gone over.
> I shall not live like this another day.
> To-morrow I'll go wandering, a poor lover
> Of earth, rejected, outcast every way,
> And see not, hear not. Rapture will not stay
> Longer than this, lest mortals grow divine
> And old laws change too much. The sensitive ray
> Of Beauty, her creative vision fine,
> Pass. I am hers, but she will not again be mine.[62]

For Lewis the breath of joy Beauty brings carries with it the melancholic realization it cannot last. Joy, full of aching beauty, is fleeting. The sense the speaker will never again experience Beauty contrasts sharply with Lewis's views in *Surprised by Joy* and elsewhere. This is not surprising when we recall this poem is written before Lewis connects his lifelong pursuit of joy with realizing in Christ the joy he desires: "But what, in conclusion, of Joy? for that after all, is what the story has mainly been about. To tell you truth, the subject has lost nearly all interest for me since I became a Christian ... It was valuable only as a pointer to something other and outer."[63] As a young man in his twenties, still struggling to achieve both academic success and literary acclaim and laboring under a genetic and philosophic moroseness exacerbated by the recent horrors of World War I, Lewis's misgivings about joy's capacity to offer him solace is to be expected.

An overall evaluation of Lewis's early poems suggests several things. First, the title of his first published work, *Spirits in Bondage*, underscores the bifurcation discussed above; that is, the book is about how the spirit of man—variously portrayed in the poems as either proud and indomitable or longing for beauty—is shackled by an earthly existence marked by suffering and theological uncertainty. *Spirits in Bondage* shows Lewis clearly disturbed by his sense that human life was directed by a malicious God, yet the many poems focusing upon faery provided him evidence of a mitigating, transcendental beauty. Second, his use of the lyric leads to many poems where we glimpse his deeply felt emotional life, but it also limits his range of poetic sensibilities. For instance, though he grappled with theological and aesthetic conundrums, the short nature of the lyric prevented him from anywhere working out a resolution to the tensions he was experiencing. Third, his early poetry gives

Lewis hope he might some day achieve acclaim as a poet. The rigor of academic study at Oxford after the war, while not a death knell to his muse, certainly muted his poetic efforts; quite properly he invested most of his time into high-level academic achievement as an undergraduate. Still, we know he continued to write poetry as letters and diaries indicate, and he actively sought to see his poetry published. Fourth, the fourteen poems in *Spirits in Bondage* influenced by his wartime experiences are deeply felt and communicate more immediately the reality of his experiences in France than his memories of the war later recorded in *Surprised by Joy*. Finally, his experience in writing *Spirits in Bondage*, particularly the war poems, served him well, though he largely abandoned lyric poetry from 1922–1926 to devote himself to a long narrative poem, *Dymer*, where he attempted to consider again the tensions he first explored in *Spirits in Bondage*.

NOTES

1. For a comprehensive discussion of Lewis' early poetry, see my *C. S. Lewis, Poet: The Legacy of His Poetic Impulse* (Kent, OH: Kent State University Press, 2001), chapters 1–3. One line of discussion I follow there is the relationship between Lewis's war poetry and that of Wilfred Owen and Siegfried Sassoon.

2. Thomas Howard, "*Poems*: A Review," *Christianity Today* 9 (June 18, 1965), 30.

3. Chad Walsh, *The Literary Legacy of C. S. Lewis* (New York: Harcourt Brace Jovanovich, 1979), 35.

4. Dabney Hart, "Editor's Comment," *Studies in the Literary Imagination* 22 (Fall 1989), 128.

5. Charles Huttar, "A Lifelong Love Affair with Language: C. S. Lewis's Poetry," in *Word and Story in C. S. Lewis* (Columbia, MO: University of Missouri Press, 1991), 86.

6. George Sayer, "C. S. Lewis's *Dymer*," in *Seven: An Anglo-American Literary Review*, 1 (1980), 113.

7. W. W. Robson, "The Poetry of C. S. Lewis," *The Chesterton Review* 17(iii–iv) (August–November, 1991), 437.

8. Luci Shaw, "Looking Back to Eden: The Poetry of C. S. Lewis," *Bulletin of the New York C. S. Lewis Society* 23 (February 1992), 3.

9. Barfield, address at Wheaton College, October 16, 1974.

10. C. S. Lewis, *Surprised by Joy: The Shape of My Early Life* (New York: Harcourt, Brace & World, 1955).

11. With E. M. W. Tillyard, *The Personal Heresy* (London: Oxford University Press, 1939).

12. C. S. Lewis, *Spirits in Bondage: A Cycle of Lyrics* (London: Heinemann, 1919). Reprinted, with an introduction by Walter Hooper (New York: Harcourt Brace Jovanovich, 1984); subsequent references are to this edition.

13. Peter Schakel in his *Reason and Imagination in C. S. Lewis: A Study of Till We Have Faces* (Grand Rapids, MI: Eerdmans, 1984) devotes a thoughtful chapter to Lewis's poetry in *Spirits in Bondage* and *Dymer*. Arguing the poetry demonstrates "a bifurcation and tension between the rationalism and the romantic"(p. 93) aspects of Lewis's personality, Schakel says "in [*Spirits in Bondage*] its 'enlightened' rationalism on the one hand and deep sense of longing for a world of the spirit on the other, the collection provides an early and immature version of themes which would be treated much more satisfactorily in *Till We Have Faces*" (p. 94). He then offers cogent though brief comments upon "De Profundis" (where he says these opposing themes are united), "The Philosopher," "The Escape," "Dungeon Grates," and "How He Saw Angus the God." Schakel says the volume as a whole "is uneven as a collection of poetry: there are a few gems, usually brief passages rather than entire poems. Its strength is expression of youthful emotions rather than handling of poetic skills. Its best quality as poetry is its visual imagery" (p. 98).

14. Lewis, *Spirits in Bondage*, xli.

15. Furthermore, the "Prologue" returns us to Lewis's penchant toward heavy allusion noted in his early poetry. Actually, *Spirits in Bondage* includes allusions to Greek, Latin, Celtic, Norse, Irish, English, and biblical sources. There are also numerous references to singing and music.

16. Walter Hooper in the "Preface" to *Spirits in Bondage* suggests this poem dates somewhere around December 1917, within a month of Lewis reaching the trenches; see p. xxx.

17. Paul Fussell, *The Great War and Modern Memory* (London: Oxford University Press, 1975), 55. In *Surprised by Joy* Lewis also notes that even before he went to the trenches, "I attended almost entirely to what I thought awe-inspiring, or wild, or eerie, and above all to distance. Hence mountains and clouds were my especial delight; the sky was, and still is, to me one of the principal elements in any landscape" (p. 152).

18. Lewis, *Spirits in Bondage*, 7. Lewis has in mind Shakespeare's "Sonnet 55" that begins: "Not marble, nor the gilded monuments/Of princes, shall outlive this powerful rhyme." Hooper speculates this poem dates from Christmas 1916. See his "Preface" to *Spirits in Bondage*, xxv–xxvi.

19. In the legends associated with Cuchulain, when he becomes enraged he is transformed into a hideous monster akin to a Scandinavian berserker.

20. Lewis, *Spirits in Bondage*, 11.

21. Two essays address the identity of Despoina: Joe R. Christopher's, "Is 'D' for Despoina?" *The Canadian C. S. Lewis Journal* 85 (Spring 1994): 48–59, and John Bremer's "From Despoina to Diotima: The Mistress of C. S. Lewis" *The Lewis Legacy* 61 (Summer 1994), 6–18.

22. Lewis, *Spirits in Bondage*, 12. Lewis shows his indebtedness to Milton as the last line here recalls Satan in *Paradise Lost* who claims: "The mind is its own place, and in itself/Can make a Heaven of Hell, a Hell of Heaven" (I, 254–255).

23. Lewis's allusion to the *Inferno* in these lines support the argument Despoina is being directed to speak to the dead.

24. Milton, *Paradise Lost*, II, 269–270, 273.

25. *They Stand Together: The Letters of C. S. Lewis to Arthur Greeves (1914–1963)*, ed. Walter Hooper (New York: Macmillan, 1979), 214.

26. Ibid., 230.

27. The Tennysonian allusion to lyrics 55–57 of *In Memoriam* suggests "this creature" is man.

28. The implications of Lewis's theological dualism is beyond the scope of this study. While a poem like this clearly suggests Lewis may have embraced such dualism for a brief time, it is not a position he holds very long. Much later in *Mere Christianity* he writes convincingly against holding this position, since logically it assumes even if there are two gods, a "good" one and a "bad" one, there must be another god behind these two that created them.

29. The title literally means "from the abyss," and is both an ironic allusion to Psalm 130: 1–2 ("Out of the depths I cry to you, O Lord; O Lord, hear my voice. Let your ears be attentive to my cry for mercy") and a gloss to Oscar Wilde's *De Profundis* (1905). About the latter Lewis writes to Greeves on September 18, 1919:

> "De Profundis" is hardly more than a memory to me. I seem to remember that it had considerable beauties, but of course in his serious work one always wonder how much is real and how much is artistic convention. He must have suffered terribly in prison, more perhaps than many a better man. I believe "The Ballad of Reading Goal" [1898] was written just after he came out, and before he had had time to smelt down his experiences into artificiality, and that *it* [Lewis's emphasis] rather than "De Profundis" represents the real effect on his mind. In other words the grim bitterness is true: the resignation not quite so true. Of course one gets very real bitterness in D. P. too. (*They Stand Together*, p. 260)

Wilde, a fellow Irishman, rebel, and poet, clearly interested Lewis at this time in his life.

30. Lewis, *Spirits in Bondage*, 20–21.

31. W. H. Lewis, *Letters and Papers: Memoirs of the Lewis Family, 1850–1930*, VI, 84.

32. Ibid., 96.

33. Lewis's view of God in *Spirits in Bondage* is similar to George Meredith, A. E. Housman, and Thomas Hardy, late nineteenth-century British poets. In particular this recalls Housman's lines from "The Chestnut Casts His Flambeaux": "We for certainty are not the first/Have sat in taverns while the tempest hurled/Their hopeful plans to emptiness, and cursed/Whatever brute and blackguard made the world."

34. Lewis, *Spirits in Bondage*, 19.

35. Ibid., 41.

36. For another interesting comparison to *In Memoriam*, see "Lyric 22."

37. Lewis, *Spirits in Bondage*, 9–10.

38. Ibid., 63–64.

39. This dating would place the poem before the Easter 1916 Irish uprising and Yeats's subsequent poem with the same title.

40. Lewis, *Spirits in Bondage*, 16.

41. Ibid., 18.

42. Interestingly, poppies came to be the flower symbolic of World War I, representing both heroic sacrifice and unimaginable bloodshed.

43. Though it is impossible to date this poem precisely, it certainly was written while Lewis studied with Kirkpatrick.

44. Lewis, *Spirits in Bondage*, 32.

45. This poem is first mentioned in a letter to Greeves on June 3, 1918, after he returns from France to recover from his wounds. See *They Stand Together*, p. 220. Since Lewis refers in the poem to Oxford, it is possible he writes the earliest version of the poem after he matriculates at University College, April 1917.

46. The three maidens may also be linked to the Norns of Norse mythology.

47. Lewis, *Spirits in Bondage*, 59.

48. Ibid., 60.

49. Joe R. Christopher's "C. S. Lewis Dances among the Elves: A Dull and Scholarly Survey of *Spirits in Bondage* and 'The Queen of Drum'" quickly surveys eleven poems in the volume with "poetic references to fairies and elves" (p. 11). In most of these poems ("*Te Ne Quaesieris*," "The Autumn Morning," "Victory," "Our Daily Bread," "In Praise of Solid People," "Ballade Mystique," "Night," "Song of the Pilgrims," "World's Desire," "Song," "Hymn [for Boys' Voices]," and "The Satyr") Christopher focuses upon how Lewis uses supernatural creatures "as a symbol of the mysterious, the Romantic, the dream of escape. In short, they are psychological symbols" (p. 12). He concludes his comments on these poems by noting Lewis has established "the land of faerie as an ideal of Romantic escape and the faeries, with one or two clear exceptions, as the attractive inhabitants of this golden realm" (p. 14). Christopher also sees the "The Satyr" as a depiction of the Victorian man—half human and half bestial.

50. This poem may later influence Lewis's portrayal of Mr. Tumnus in *The Lion, the Witch and the Wardrobe*.

51. Lewis, *Spirits in Bondage*, 5.

52. Ibid., 39.

53. Ibid., 47. Many readers will catch Lewis's possible allusion here to George MacDonald's *At the Back of the North Wind*.

54. Ibid., 72.

55. Ibid., 57.

56. Ibid., 25.

57. "Death in Battle." *Reveille* 3 (February 1919), 508. Under the pseudonym Clive Hamilton. In *Spirits in Bondage*, 74.

58. We know Lewis was working on this poem before April 18, 1922: "In the evening I copied out 'Joy' and worked a new ending: it is ready to be typed" (*All My Road Before Me: The Diary of C. S. Lewis*, ed. Walter Hooper, New York: Harcourt, Brace, Jovanovich, 1991, 22.) Interestingly, the editor who accepts if for publication in *The Beacon* is Owen Barfield: "A letter from Barfield accepting 'Joy' for the *Beacon* and saying nice things" (*All My Road Before Me: The Diary of C. S. Lewis*, May 2, 1922, 28). However, it is two years before the poem is actually published in *The Beacon* 3(31) (May 1924), 444–445 (Clive Hamilton). Reprinted in *Collected Poems*, 243–244.

59. Lewis, *Surprised by Joy* has numerous passages where Lewis discusses joy; see in particular pp. 16–18 and pp. 165–170. In addition, see Lewis's "Preface" to *The Pilgrim's Regress* where he offers an extended definition of what he means by joy and how it works in his experience.

60. Lewis, "Joy," 444. It is interesting to note that Lewis and Yeats use Leda in a poem at about the same time; see Yeats' "Leda and the Swan" (1923).

61. Ibid., 444–445.

62. Ibid., 445.

63. Lewis, *Surprised by Joy*, 238.

BIBLIOGRAPHY

Barfield, Owen. "C. S. Lewis." An address given at Wheaton College (Wheaton, IL), October 16, 1964. The Wade Center.

Bremer, John. "From Despoina to Diotima: The Mistress of C. S. Lewis." *The Lewis Legacy* 61 (Summer 1994), 6–18.

Christopher, Joe R. "Is 'D' for Despoina?" *The Canadian C. S Lewis Journal: The Inklings, Their Friends, and Their Predecessors* 85 (Spring 1994), 48–59.

Fussell, Paul. *The Great War and Modern Memory.* London: Oxford University Press, 1975.

Gilchrist, K. James. "2nd Lieutenant Lewis." In *SEVEN: An Anglo-American Literary Review* 17 (2000), 61–78.

Hart, Dabney. "Editor's Comment." *Studies in the Literary Imagination* 22 (Fall 1989): 125–128.

Hooper, Walter. ed. *All My Road Before Me: The Diary of C. S. Lewis.* New York: Harcourt, Brace, Jovanovich, 1991

———. *The Collected Poems of C. S. Lewis.* London: Fount, 1994.

———."Preface." In C. S. Lewis. *Spirits in Bondage: A Cycle of Lyrics.* New York: Harcourt Brace Jovanovich, 1984, xi–xl.

———. "Introduction" and "Introductory Letter." In C. S. Lewis. *The Collected Poems of C. S. Lewis*. London: Fount, 1994, ix–xxi.

Howard, Tom. "*Poems*: A Review." *Christianity Today* 9 (June 18, 1965), 30.

Kawano, Roland. "C. S. Lewis's Early Poems." *The Living Church* 186 (February 13, 1983), 9–10.

King, Don W. *C. S. Lewis, Poet: The Legacy of His Poetic Impulse*. Kent, OH: Kent State University Press, 2001.

———. "C. S. Lewis's *Spirits in Bondage*: World I Poet as Frustrated Dualist." *Christian Scholar's Review* 27 (Summer 1998), 454–474.

———. "Lost but Found: The 'Missing' Poems of C. S. Lewis's *Spirits in Bondage*." *Christianity and Literature* 53 (Winter 2004), 163–201.

———. "*Spirits in Bondage*." In *The C. S. Lewis Readers' Encyclopedia*. Edited by Jeffrey D. Schultz and John G. West. Grand Rapids, MI: Zondervan, 1998.

Lewis, C. S. *The Pilgrim's Regress*. London: Geoffrey Bles, 1933.

———. *Spirits in Bondage: A Cycle of Lyrics*. London: Heinemann, 1919. Reprint, with an Introduction by Walter Hooper, New York: Harcourt Brace Jovanovich, 1984.

———. *Surprised by Joy*. New York: Harcourt, 1955

Lewis, W. H. *Letters and Papers: Memoirs of the Lewis Family, 1850–1930*. Unpublished manuscript, 11 volumes. Wade Center, Wheaton College, Wheaton, IL.

Robson, W. W. "The Poetry of C. S. Lewis." *The Chesterton Review* 17(iii–iv) (August–November, 1991), 437–443. Also see his essay "The Romanticism of C. S Lewis." *Cambridge Quarterly* 1 (Summer 1966), 252–272. Reprinted in W. W. Robson. *Critical Essays*. London: Routledge & Kegan Paul, 1966.

Sayer, George. "C. S. Lewis's *Dymer*." In *SEVEN: An Anglo-American Literary Review* 1 (1980), 94–116.

Shaw, Luci. "Looking Back to Eden: The Poetry of C. S. Lewis." *Bulletin of the New York C. S. Lewis Society*. 23 (February, 1992), 1–7. Reprinted in *Radix* 21(iii) (1993), 12–15, 30.

Walsh, Chad. *The Literary Legacy of C. S. Lewis*. New York: Harcourt Brace Jovanovich, 1979.

13

Topical Poems: C. S. Lewis's Postconversion Poetry

Don W. King

Notwithstanding the narrative poems discussed in a previous essay, Lewis largely gave up writing narrative poetry after the disappointing reception of *Dymer*. However, he did not give up on poetry. Indeed, he continued to write and to publish poems from 1932 to 1963, and they appeared in journals, periodicals, and anthologies. Fortunately, they are readily accessible since many were later collected by Walter Hooper and published as *Poems* (1964) and *Collected Poems* (1994).[1] They are literally *topical* poems—ones in which he deals with social, literary, philosophical, personal, or religious topics.[2] If we consider the sheer number of topical poems Lewis published after *Dymer*—over one hundred and twenty—we see a writer consciously exercising his poetic muse. Obviously Lewis's determined efforts at publishing poetry throughout this period does not indicate someone who had given up on achieving acclaim as a poet, in spite of the fact many of these were published under "N. W." Lewis's Anglo-Saxon shorthand for *nat whilk*, "[I know] not whom." One approach to studying these topical poems would be chronological with an eye toward noting Lewis's continuing maturation as a poet. While there is much to commend this approach, in the end it would be a fragmented, digressive effort. A better approach is thematic since the topical poems largely fall into three major categories: comic and satiric poems, contemplative poems, and religious poems.[3]

Lewis's comic poems mix light-hearted musings with thoughtful reflections. For instance, "Abecedarium Philosophicum," is nonsense verse and a *tour de force*. Lewis and Owen Barfield collaborated to write a comic poem in heroic couplets where each line was dedicated to each letter of the alphabet and famous philosophers or philosophical ideas served as the butts of jokes.[4] Representative lines include "H is for Hume who awoke Kant from nappin.' / He said: 'There's no causes for things. They just happen'" and "Z? For poor Zeno who often felt faint, / When he heard you deny that Nonentity ain't." This gentle parody of philosophy is good fun.

   "Awake, My Lute" is good-natured playfulness along the lines of "Abecedarium Philosophicum."[5] Utilizing internal rhyme in each odd line and final rhyme in each even line, it appears to be incoherent revelries focusing at first upon a boring lecturer: "I stood in the gloom of a spacious room / Where I listened for hours (on and off) / To a terrible bore with a beard like a snore / And heavy rectangular cough." Unlike Dymer, who murders his boring lecturer, the speaker here finds he has a kinship with the lecturer. Indeed, they are shipmates on the Ark: "For the flood had begun and we both had to run / For our place in the queue to the Ark. / Then, I hardly knew how (we were swimming by now), / The seas got all covered with scum." The poem's thematic dissonance continues as the speaker imagines himself giving insufficient answers on an Oxford examination: "My answer was Yes. But they marked it N.[on] S.[atis], / And a truffle-fish grabbed at my toe, / And dragged me deep down to a bombulous town / Where the traffic was silent and slow." The key to this mishmash of ideas is that they are the disconnected fragments of a dream: "Then a voice out of heaven observed, 'Quarter past seven!' / And I threw all the waves off my head, / For that voice beyond doubt was the voice of my scout, / And the bed of that sea was my bed."[6] The comedy of the poem is heightened by humorous internal and final rhymes such as *off:cough, croup:soup, baboon:the moon, puns:Donne's, with scum:in -um,* and *blurbs:verbs.*

   Both "Abecedarium Philosophicum" and "Awake, My Lute" show the influence of Edward Lear and Lewis Carroll, the most famous practitioners of nonsense verse. For instance, Carroll's "Examination Statute," like "Abecedarium Philosophicum," is a comic poem with lines dedicated to each letter of the alphabet; however, instead of dedicating lines to famous philosophers, Carroll dedicated his to well-known Oxford examiners: "A is for [Acland], who'd physic the Masses, B is for [Brodie], who swears by the gases. / C is for [Conington], constant for Horace. / D is for [Donkin], who integrates for us."[7] In addition, Carroll's "Ode to Damon" uses internal rhyme and a similar meter of "Awake, My Lute": "Oh, do not forget the day when we met / At the fruiterer's shop in the city: / When you *said* I was plain and *excessively* vain, / "But I knew that *meant* I was pretty" (emphasis Carroll's).[8] It is not hard to imagine Lewis was influenced in nonsense poems by the work of Carroll.

Moving from the nonsensical, we turn to "March for Drum, Trumpet, and Twenty-one Giants," a poem where Lewis tries to create an apt rhythm for a procession of giants.[9] The poem opens with giants stomping along in a parade of pride and pomp: "With stumping stride in pomp and pride / We come to bump and floor ye. / We'll tramp your ramparts down like hay / And crumple castles into clay." Throughout the poem Lewis uses internal rhyme, alliteration, monosyllabic words, onomatopoeia, and an iambic meter in order to help us hear this comic procession. Furthermore, this emphasis on sound is reinforced by the progressive refrain at the end of each stanza. Indeed, each refrain (from trumpet, to thunder, to rumble) is accompanied by a musical direction. The trumpet refrain is to employ crescendo (cresc.), indicating a gradual increase in volume; the thunder refrain is to use fortissimo (ff), indicating it should be the loudest part of the poem; and the rumble refrain is diminuendo (dim.), indicating a softening of the sound. Lewis's use of these musical notations suggests the poem works like a shaped phrase in music, so that the rise and fall of the sound of music indicates a corresponding rise, climax, and fall in the tension of the poem. This is a comic poem clearly more about sound than meaning. The cumulative effect of these literary and musical devices is percussive, a characteristic shared by many his satiric poems.[10]

Another percussive comic poem is "The Small Man Orders his Wedding," given from the perspective of a bridegroom on the occasion of arranging details for his wedding."[11] His is to be an elaborate ceremony primarily characterized by a wide variety of sounds. For instance, he plans to have a nuptial parade of dancing maidens playing tambourines, smartly dressed soldiers, and powerful horses drawing the lovers' chariot; in addition, bells will be ringing from the belfries and trumpets will be blaring to announce their joy. At the wedding feast itself the boisterous noise of the outer parade will cease, while quieter, gentler sounds of flutes and lutes will serenade his beloved until all withdraw, leaving the two lovers alone, blessed by "Aphrodite's saffron light, / And Jove's monarchal presence bright / And Genius burning through the night / The torch of man's futurity." The poem ends with the happy couple sinking into "dreaming weariness" while the gods appear to bless their union. Written in the tradition of the epithalamium, this piece joyously celebrates wedded love.

Lewis's satiric poems often confront ideas he found destructive to traditional values and civilized life or they address specific individuals with whom he wishes to cross swords. Occasionally his satire is Horatian—gentle, smiling, and urbane—as in "Coronation March."[12] The coronation of George VI

(May 12, 1937) is the subject of this slightly irreverent commentary where he suggests the glory and heraldry associated with this event is all that is left of England's once proud stand on the international stage. Pomposity and pretension mark such elaborate ceremonies now:

> Bray the trumpet, rumble tragic
> Drum-beat's magic, sway the logic
> Of legs that march a thousand in a uniform,
> Flags and arches, the lion and the unicorn
> Romp it, rampant, pompous tramping...
> Some there are that talk of Alexander
> With a tow-row-row-row-row-row.

The poem's percussive elements place it in the tradition of "March for Drum, Trumpet, and Twenty-One Giants." A similar Horatian satire is the light-hearted "Impenitence," a mock defiance of those who are "too sophisticated" to find in animal stories, including clear references to Homer, E. Nesbit, and Kenneth Grahame, both delightful entertainment and fables of human foibles.[13] The opening stanza takes up arms: "All the world's wiseacres in arms against them / Shan't detach my heart for a single moment / From the man-like beasts of the earthy stories— / Badger or Moly." Lewis confesses he is "not so craz'd as to think the creatures" behave as portrayed in such fictions, yet he argues they "all cry out to be used as symbols, / Masks for Man, cartoons, parodies by Nature / Formed to reveal us / Each to each, not fiercely but in her gentlest / Vein of household laughter."[14] Lacking a rhyme scheme, the poem achieves its poetic effect through its stanza pattern—each quatrain has three lines with eleven syllables and a final line with five syllables.

"An Expostulation (against too many writers of science fiction)," written in tetrameter couplets, is gentle rebuke of science fiction writers who take us to other worlds only to tell the same tired old stories we have on Earth: criminals on the run, conspirators and their schemes, or lovers' triangles.[15] Instead, what Lewis wants is stories that focus on the "otherness" of these other worlds. Why, he asks, should he leave this world for stories unless

> outside its guarded gates,
> Long, long desired, the Unearthly waits,
> Strangeness that moves us more than fear,
> Beauty that stabs with tingling spear,
> Or Wonder, laying on one's heart
> That finger-tip at which we start
> As if some thought too swift and shy
> For reason's grasp had just gone by?

In the essay, "On Science Fiction," he makes the same point:

I will now try to divide this species [science fiction] into its sub-species. I shall begin with that sub-species which I think radically bad, in order to get it out of our way. In this sub-species the author leaps forward into an imagined future when planetary, sidereal, or even galactic travel has become common. Against this huge backcloth he then proceeds to develop an ordinary love-story, spy-story, wreck-story, or crime-story. This seems to me tasteless . . . I am . . . condemning not all books which suppose a future widely different from the present, but those which do so without a good reason, which leap a thousand years to find plots and passions which they could have found at home.[16]

For Lewis a major charm of science fiction was the creation of enchanting other worlds where we can imagine experiencing life differently.

"Evolutionary Hymn" is perhaps the funniest of Lewis's Horatian satires.[17] Tongue-in-cheek, this hymn of praise blithely adopts a Darwinian view of the world and assumes the inevitability of human progress:

Lead us, Evolution, lead us
Up the future's endless stair:
Chop us, change us, prod us, weed us.
For stagnation is despair:
Groping, guessing, yet progressing,
Lead us nobody knows where.

Old static norms of good and evil are to be rejected since new ways and ideas are inherently superior; this notion, what Lewis calls chronological snobbery, is the peculiarly modern notion that the present has more to tell us about the human condition than the past. Thus, "far too long have sages vainly / Glossed great Nature's simple text; / He who runs can read it plainly, / 'Goodness = what comes next.'" Darwinian utilitarianism is also celebrated: "By evolving, Life is solving / All the questions we perplexed." This bit of gentle satire is worth a sing.

If Lewis's Horatian satire is good-natured criticism, his Juvenalian satire is acidic and scathing. For instance, "A Cliché Came Out of its Cage" is a sharp attack upon moderns who believe they are heralds of a return to the "golden age" of paganism.[18] In particular, he mentions F. R. Leavis, whose ideas on literary criticism he disliked, and Bertrand Russell, whose ideas on society, morality, and philosophy he directly opposed: "I saw . . . Leavis with Lord Russell wreathed in flowers, heralded with flutes, / leading white bulls to the cathedral of the solemn Muses / to pay where due the glory of their latest theorem." In fact, Lewis suggests their "scientific" approaches to literature and social mores show they know little about classical paganism, and that they mistake their pale, insipid, godless modern version for the healthy, robust, theistic paganism of old. Lewis's disregard for these ugly ideas is mirrored in the ugly unrhymed heptameter of the poem.

Even more bitter is "*Odora Canum Vis* (A defence of certain modern biographers and critics)."[19] The title comes from Virgil's *Aeneid* 4.132 and means "With keen-scented hunting dogs."[20] Biting and barbed, this scathing, ironic defense of writers who churn out works that titillate, glorifying and headlining smut, is an example of what it was like to fall under the wrath of Lewis's unsheathed critical sword:

> Come now, don't be too eager to condemn
> Our little smut-hounds if they wag their tails
> (Or shake like jellies as the tails wag them)
> The moment the least whiff of sex assails
> Their quivering snouts. Such conduct after all,
> Though comic, is in them quite natural.

These writers, Lewis continues, who are culturally atrophied, know "neither God, hunger, thought, nor battle, [so] must / Of course hold disproportionate views on lust." In effect, he gives them over to themselves: "So! Cock your ears, my pretties! Play your part! / The dead are all before you, take your pick. / Fetch! Paid for! Slaver, snuff, defile and lick." The virulent tone of this poem shows Lewis the public gladiator, eager to slay the dragons of character assassination.

"Prelude to Space: An Epithalamium" presents the idea that human exploration of space will be characterized by pride, arrogance, and imperialism; themes Lewis explored as well in the Ransom trilogy. The first stanza is a jingoistic parody:

> So Man, grown vigorous now,
> Holds himself ripe to breed,
> Daily devises how
> To ejaculate his seed
> And boldly fertilize
> The black womb of the unconsenting skies.

Lewis's frank use of sexual imagery throughout the poem—he refers to a space ship on the launching pad as "the large, / Steel member grow[n] erect"—is intended to communicate his disgust with human imperialism and its "lust to stamp / Our likeness on the abyss." All humanity can promise space, he says, are "bombs, gallows, Belsen camp, / Pox, polio, Thais' kiss / Or Judas'" and similar catastrophes. The last stanza asks the rhetorical question should humanity celebrate when the first space ships head off to explore space: "Shall we, when the grim shape / Roars upward, dance and sing? / Yes: if we honour rape, / If we take pride to fling / So bountiful on space / The sperm of our long woes, our large disgrace." This no tender bridal poem celebrating man's fathering of himself across the universe; instead, it an acrid warning of man's probable rape of the cosmos. Such bitter irony marks much of Lewis's writings about space exploration—from the Ransom trilogy to essays like "Religion and Rocketry"—but Lewis is not against progress; instead, he fears the first space explorers will be space exploiters as portrayed so devastatingly in Weston from *Perelandra*.[21] His poem is a caustic caution against space exploration, but it is not a reactionary prohibition.

Lewis's sober cautions about human pillage through space travel was related to his deep distrust of modern life. For instance, "On a Vulgar Error" is a Juvenalian satire on chronological snobbery.[22] Lewis begins by admitting that new ideas are not always bad: "Was the first pointed arch esteemed a blot / Upon the church? Did anybody say / How modern and how ugly? They did not." That said, he poses the question: "If, then, our present arts, laws, houses, food / All set us hankering after yesterday, / Need this be only an archaising mood?" In reply, he says the answer to this is found in the examples of the man who finds his money drained away by swindlers (he "must compare how he stands with how he stood") and the man who loses a leg: "If a quack doctor's breezy ineptitude / Has cost me a leg, must I forget straightway / All that I can't do now, all that I could?" In other words, newness—ideas, fashions, technology, and so on—are not in themselves bad; again, Lewis is no reactionary. The questions that have to be asked, however, are: "How does modernity impact the human condition? Does its manifestations enhance our understanding of who we are, our place in the universe, and our notions of beauty, honor, and virtue? Or does it simply drain away our resources and cut us off at the knees, reducing us to cogs in a mechanistic, naturalistic, meaningless world?" He uses interconnected rhymes in the tercets (*aba aba aba cbc cbc cbc*) to lead up to his ironic concluding couplet (*dd*): "So, when our guides unanimously decry / The backward glance, I think we can guess why."

"*Spartan Nactus*" is Lewis's sharpest attack on modern misuse of language, especially modern poetry.[23] He feigns being a dunce who cannot understand the subtle nuances of contemporary poetic metaphor and imagery, condemned instead only to have stock responses to the figurative language of the past. Tongue in cheek, Lewis uses couplets, traditional poetic form, and begins with: "I am so coarse, the things the poets see / Are obstinately invisible to me." This opening serves as his platform from which he attacks modern poetry, particularly T. S. Eliot, and its absurd metaphors: "For twenty years

I've stared my level best / To see if evening—any evening—would suggest / A patient etherized upon a table; / In vain. I simply wasn't able." He ends the poem, still tongue in cheek, taking the pose of a foolish, uneducated person ("I am like that odd man Wordsworth knew, to whom / A primrose was a yellow primrose") who can only appreciate stock responses, those emotional reactions to ideas, objects, and notions intrinsically connected with the past:

[I am] one whose doom
Retains him always in the class of dunces,
Compelled to offer Stock Responses,
Making the poor best that I can
Of dull things . . . peacocks, honey, the Great Wall, Aldebaran,
Silver streams, cowslip wine, wave on the beach, bright gem,
The shape of trees and women, thunder, Troy, Jerusalem.

While not a poetic manifesto, Lewis was clearly throwing down the gauntlet against modern poetry.

"Epitaph" is a scathing English sonnet attacking democracy. Lewis suggests democracy's greatest weakness is the incessant noise its endless discussions and debates cause.[24] Using the constant drone of a wireless (radio) as a symbol for democratic clamoring, the speaker would prefer one quiet spot in Hell for a Heaven filled with such "music." Thus his epitaph: "And therefore, stranger, tiptoe by this grave, / And let posterity record of me, / 'He died both for, and of, democracy.'"[25] "Consolation" is another Juvenalian satire with a political focus. While it ostensibly begins as if celebrating the end of World War II, it concludes with a sharply satirical bite, suggesting postwar England is once again setting on a course of appeasement. This time, however, it is the Soviet Union, not Germany, that is the focus of England's appeasement.[26] The persona is ironically happy, even if "beer is worse and dearer / And milk has got the blues, / Though cash is short and rations / Much shorter than the queues." In spite of the increase in strikes, crime, and business failures, he says "yet sing like mad that England / Is back to peacetime ways." What, he says, of "butter, eggs, or mutton, / Freedom or spacious days. / All those were non-essentials." The surest test of peace is this: "If we thus caress the Muscovite, / England has turned to rest." The last stanza of the poem uses a historical allusion to further its satire:

To ease my doubts Appeasement
Returns. Peace must be here!
The tune of glorious Munich
Once more salutes my ear;

An ancient British melody—
We heard it first begin
At the court of shifty Vortigern
Who let the Heathen in.

Lewis mocks those concessions made to the Soviet Union at the end of World War II as Europe was divided among the Allied forces. To him they sound like the same tune played when the British Prime Minister, Neville Chamberlain, went to Munich and acquiesced to Hitler in 1939, believing such appeasement would prevent large-scale conflict. In fact, such appeasement, he says, is "an ancient British melody," first evident in the actions of Vortigern whose commitment to compromise led to the destruction of his empire by the Saxon invaders he thought he could appease.[27]

Lewis's comic and satiric verse is not Lewis's best poetry. While his exuberant playfulness with meter and sound in the comic pieces is engaging, the nonsense verse is second-rate. On the other hand, when he turns to satire he is querulous, pedantic, and brittle. The percussive characteristics of the comic and satiric poetry, while sometimes effective in creating rhythm and cadence, more often than not lead to poor, "creaky" verse. It is hard to take these poems seriously because they are either inane or venomous; in neither instance do we find the subtle beauty and powerful nuance of language illustrated in his more effective poems. Lewis achieved greater success when he turned contemplative verse.

Lewis's contemplative poems are reflective pieces denoting personal and public concerns he felt compelled to consider in verse. In general, Lewis wrote contemplative poems that fall into two broad categories. The first group consists of poems that deal with the shallowness of modern life. By and large these poems muse upon the vacuity of life in large cities, the destructive encroachment of civilization on the English countryside, and the deconstruction of language, meaning, and objective truth. The second group consists of poems that reflect upon the human condition and focus upon both the positive and negative realities of existence. Accordingly, he wrote poems on the one hand dealing with joy and on the other hand dealing with uncertainty, obsessive love, despair, loss, and death. If the poems dealing with the shallowness of modern life may be thought of as public analysis and social criticism, those dealing with the human condition may be thought of as personal reflections and private ruminations.

In "Finchley Avenue," Lewis reflects at length upon the quiet unease he connects with those who live in large English cities like London.[28] Although the poem, written in alexandrine couplets, begins "we are proud of Finchley Avenue" and goes on to chronicle its attributes—its quietness, good views of London, copper beeches, beautiful stands of laurel and rhododendron, banks of lush grass, finely manicured driveways, and stately homes—we sense a hollowness and emptiness in such streets. The Tudor homes, once a symbol of bourgeois success, are now ironic commentaries on the vacuity of modern life. The only laudatory aspects of the homes are the gardens: "That garden lawn / Is the primordial fountain out of which was drawn / All you have since imagined of the lawn where stood / Eve's apple tree, or of the lands before the flood." Nostalgia is also captured:

> In that suburban attic with its gurgling sound
> Of water pipes, in such a quiet house, you found
> In early days the relics of still earlier days,
> Forgotten trumpery worn to act forgotten plays,
> Old books, then first remembered, calling up the past
> Which then, as now, was infinitely sweet and vast.
> There first you felt the wonder of deep time, the joy
> And dread of Schliemann standing on the grave of Troy.[29]

Human activity on the avenue is limited to the rush of the owners of the houses to get to work and tradesmen making their daily rounds; by one o'clock in the afternoon the street sinks "to the dead silence of the afternoon." Lewis emphasizes the loneliness of such streets:

> No countryside can offer so much solitude.
> I have known the world less lonely in a winter wood,
> For there you hear the striking of a village clock
> Each hour, or the faint crowing of a distant cock.
> But here is nothing. Nobody goes past. No feet
> But mine. I doubt if anyone has used this seat,
> Here in the shade, save only me. And here I sit
> And drink the unbroken silence and reflect on it.

The poem concludes with the speaker wondering about the families living in these homes. He assumes most of the children are grown and gone, leaving for the most part only the wives of the men who own the homes: "The whole long avenue exhales the sense / Of absent husbands, housework done, uncharted hours."[30] He wonders if this gives the wives "painful emptiness" or "a blessed state / Of truancy wherein they darkly celebrate / Rites of some *Bona Dea* which no man may see?" Regardless, while he affirms the wives of this street may be virtuous, he feels it is "an eerie rashness to possess a wife / And house that go on living with their different life, / For ever inaccessible to us, all day." The last lines reflect a final musing: "For as we knew in childhood, if the fathers stay / At home by chance, that whole day takes a different tone, / Better, or worse, it may be; but unlike its own." The poem suggests suburban life serves to drive apart a husband and a wife—he to a life of work and activity outside the home and she to a dull if settled life of housework. For neither is there vital, meaningful living. This sober meditation on the shallowness of modern life may not be his best poetry, but it reveals his concern with the social constructs of his day that he found disturbing.

"The Future of Forestry" extended his social critique of contemporary life beyond the limits of the modern city; the concern in this is the encroachment of the modern world upon the English countryside.[31] The poem, written in blank verse, asks, when all the trees are gone, sacrificed to roads and shops, who will tell the children what trees were: "'What was a chestnut? / Say what it means to climb a Beanstalk? / Tell me, grandfather, what an elm is. / What was Autumn? They never taught us.'" He insists some remnants of the existence of trees will be passed down, of "creatures of lower nature / Able to live and die, though neither / Beast nor man." Actually he extends the poem beyond the natural world to include questionings about the "future" of faery, returning to central themes of *Spirits in Bondage* (hereafter *SB*) and "The Queen of Drum." For instance, rumors of "trees as men walking," goblins, and the pale faces of birch girls will never cease: "So shall a homeless time, though dimly / Catch from afar (for soul is watchful) / A sight of tree-delighted Eden."[32] For Lewis there is always more to reality than just the natural world; faery is always there, hidden only by the veil of our own blindness.

"The Country of the Blind" shifts Lewis's concern about the shallowness of modernity to the disconnect between language and meaning.[33] He pictures a race of people who think they can see, but who are actually blind: "Hard light bathed them—a whole nation of eyeless men, / Dark bipeds not aware how they were maimed." While the disconnect between language and meaning has occurred gradually, moderns are now blind to what words really mean: "Whose blind mouths would abuse words that belonged to their / Great grandsires, unabashed, talking of *light* [Lewis's emphasis] in some / Eunuch'd, etiolated, / Fungoid sense, as a symbol of / Abstract thoughts." As a result of this, no objective truth can be conveyed through words:

If a man, one that had eyes, a poor
Misfit, spoke of the grey dawn or the stars or green-
Sloped sea waves, or admired how
Warm tints change in a lady's cheek,

None complained he had used words from an alien tongue,
None question'd. It was worse. All would agree. "Of course,"
Came their answer. "We've all felt
Just like that."

Such mawkish woolly headedness, has resulted in jargon: "The words— / Sold, raped, flung to the dogs—now could avail no more; / Hence silence. But the mould warps, / With glib confidence, easily / Showed how tricks of the phrase, sheer metaphors could set / Fools concocting a myth, taking words for things." To prove his point, he invites readers to speak with others about the old, vital truths: "Attempt speech on the truths that once, / Opaque, carved in divine forms, irremovable, / Dread but dear as a mountain- / Mass, stood plain to the inward eye." Sadly, Lewis intimates, all one will receive in response is the blank stare of the blind. Philosophically, this is one of Lewis's most profound poems, a thoughtful antidote to attempts to strip meaning from language.[34]

"Re-Adjustment" amplifies Lewis's concern that modern man has lost the ability to connect words with meaning.[35] The poem, an unrhymed "sonnet," begins with the speaker confessing he had hoped old age would bring comfort: "I thought there would be a grave beauty, a sunset splendour / In being the last of one's kind: a topmost moment as one watched / The huge wave curving over Atlantis, the shrouded barge / Turning away with wounded Arthur, or Ilium burning." This persona is an example of what Lewis terms Old Western Man in his inaugural address *De Descriptione Temporum* delivered upon his assuming the chair of Medieval and Renaissance English literature at Cambridge in 1954, and this poem has obvious affinities with the address.[36] The speaker says he had assumed the next generation would look on the cultural accomplishments of the past with gratitude, gentleness, and understanding. However, he realizes this will not be, since language and meaning are under attack: "Between the new *Hominidae* and us who are dying, already / There rises a barrier across which no voice can ever carry, / For devils are unmaking language." The next generation has cut itself off from the old core values of civilized life, desiring instead to find purpose and direction in modernity: "Uproot your loves, one by one, with care, from the future, / And trusting to no future, receive the massive thrust / And surge of the many-dimensional timeless rays converging / On this small, significant dew drop, the present that mirrors all."[37] This ironic conclusion suggests not only his own "re-adjustment" but also one many will have to make because of the future that will result from the current modernity. Although Lewis never lived to encounter deconstruction as a literary theory, his poem anticipates its approach to language and the possibility (or impossibility) of meaning.

Lewis's contemplative poems musing on the human condition are among his best. "Sweet Desire" is about joy from the perspective of one who has been so often disappointed in experiencing joy that he is tentative, even fearful, about giving himself over completely to the pursuit of joy.[38] In alliterative half-lines recalling Anglo-Saxon verse, a the speaker addresses God and says he is being haunted by faint hints of "*s*weet *s*tabbing" joy "*c*oming from your country" reminding him of past experiences.[39] This disturbs him, and he compares himself to a man in a dungeon who has heard in past "the *h*inge on the *h*ook turning / *O*ften. *A*lways that *o*pened door / Let new tormentors in." As the door to joy appears to be opening again, he, like a jaded prisoner, retreats into a corner of his cell rather than risk a disappointing attempt at escape: "So, fearing, I / *T*aste not but with *t*rembling. I was *t*ricked before."[40] In his past disappointments with joy, he has mistaken imitations of joy for the real thing, and so he is wary of yet another cheat. But he cannot resist:

> But what's the *u*se? For *y*ield I must
> Though *l*ong de*l*ayed, at *l*ast must dare
> To give *o*ver, to be *e*ased of my *i*ron casing,
> *M*olten at thy *m*elody, as *m*en of snow
> In the *s*olar *s*mile. *S*low-paced I come,
> *Y*ielding by inches. And *y*et, oh *L*ord, and *y*et,
> —Oh *L*ord, *l*et not *l*ikeness fool me again.

This alliterative admission exposes the speaker's passion for joy and reflects Lewis's own persistent pursuit of joy.[41]

"The Day with the White Mark" suggests how joy comes unexpected, unexplained, and unsolicited.[42] In a boisterous opening, we find that joy invades every action of the speaker's day: "All day I have been tossed and whirled in a preposterous happiness." Oddly, however, the speaker's reality shouts that all is bleak and grim: "Reason kept telling me all day my mood was out of season. / It was too; all ahead is dark or splashed with hideous light. / My garden's spoiled; my holidays are cancelled; the omens harden; / The plann'd and the unplann'd miseries deepen; the knots draw tight." But joy sweeps reason aside so that he "could have kissed the very scullery taps." He says "the colour of / My day was like a peacock's chest." Joy washes reason away:

> In at each sense there stole
> Ripplings and dewy sprinkles of delight that with them drew
> Fine threads of memory through the vibrant thickness of the soul.
>
> As though there were transparent earths and luminous trees should grow there,
> And glimmering roots were visibly at work below one's feet,
> So everything, the tick of the clock, the cock crowing in the yard,
> Probing my soil, woke diverse buried hearts of mine to beat,
>
> Recalling either adolescent heights and the inaccessible
> Longings, the ice-keen joys that shook my body and turned me pale.

The unpredictability of joy leads him to wonder "who knows if ever it will come again, now the day closes?"[43] He ends by noting joy is never predictable: "I question if the angel himself / Has power to choose when sudden heaven for me begins or ends." Lewis's "sudden heaven" recalls his affirmation in *Surprised by Joy* (hereafter *SJ*) that joy cannot be actively sought:

Only when your whole attention and desire are fixed on something else—whether a distant mountain, or the past, or the gods of Asgard—does the "thrill" arise. It is a by-product. Its very existence presupposes that you desire not it but something other and outer. . . . Often I frightened it away by my greedy impatience to snare it, and, even when it came, instantly destroyed it by introspection, and at all times vulgarized it by my false assumption about its nature.[44]

"The Day with the White Mark," published six years before *Surprised by Joy*, affirms how it is that joy comes as a surprise in the human experience.

While Lewis's contemplative poems on joy are primarily positive, his reflections upon other sobering issues that confront humanity tend to be introspective, often communicating an uncertain, tentative perspective about the human condition. For instance, "Essence" initially published anonymously from the anthology *Fear No More: A Book of Poems for the Present Time by Living English Poets* is very introspective.[45] It is an internal musing on thought and will and their relationship to the essence of self.[46] While the speaker frankly admits his reluctance to speak about the inner world ("Thoughts that go through my mind, / I dare not tell them"), he rejects the bifurcation of *SB*. Instead, he seeks an integration of thought and will in defining the essence of self: "That essence must have been / Which still I call / My self, since— thus unclean— / It dies not at all." "Pilgrim's Problem" continues this kind of introspection, and its conclusions are tentative as well since it challenges the notion age brings wisdom and settled peace.[47] A walker, late in the day, relies on his map and assumes he is nearing a restful end to his journey. The poem becomes symbolic when we read of how he looks forward to charity, humility, contemplation, fortitude, temperance, and chastity. In fact, he realizes none of these: "I can see nothing like all this." He wonders rhetorically is it the map or him that is flawed: "Maps can be wrong. But the experienced walker knows / That the other explanation is more often true."[48] Ironically, he implies it must be him rather than the map that is flawed.

Perhaps the most disturbing poem questioning the significance of the human condition is "The Salamander."[49] Sitting before a fire, the speaker gazes mindlessly into burning coals where "blue waves / Of shuddering heat . . . r[i]se and f[a]ll, / And blazing ships and blinding caves, / Canyons and streets and hills of hell." However, this familiar atmosphere is suddenly changed, when "amidst it all / I saw a living creature crawl." From this point on the fiery salamander gives a soliloquy about what he "sees" outside the fire; his melancholic reflections are compared to ones men make since he looks with "sad eyes...as men [look] out upon the skies." Gazing into the dark room, the salamander says, "this is the end," the place "where all life dies," the universe of "blank silence, distances untold / Of unimaginable cold." The lights from the room he can see only dimly, since they "are but reflections cast from here, / There is no other fire but this. / This speck of life, this fading spark / Existed amid the boundless dark." The creature intimates, therefore, that the real world, the world of meaning is found only within the fire; outside there is isolation, estrangement, and alienation.[50] Because he can only see what is physically in front of him, the only world he is willing to accept is the tangible one. That there could be an invisible or spiritual realm beyond his fiery world is unthinkable. And, of course, by implication mankind has a similar mindset; rather than face boldly the prospect of another dimension, we, like the salamander, deny anything we cannot perceive as a part of the material world about us. He ends with a nihilistic credo, one suggesting even values are hollow:

> Blind Nature's measureless rebuke
> To all we value, I received
> Long since (though wishes bait the hook
> With tales our ancestors believed)
> And now can face with fearless eye
> Negation's final sovereignty.

Yet, he confronts such nihilism courageously "with fearless eye, / Negation's final sovereignty." The salamander's affirmation of nihilism implies, if we make the invited comparison between the salamander and the human condition, that men often make a similar discovery and affirmation about their own existence. Life may be without meaning, yet man's task is to face that reality courageously. This is a very different voice of Lewis, a distant voice, contrasting dramatically with the confident, buoyant voice of so much of his prose.[51]

A variation on this distant voice occurs in "Infatuation," unique for Lewis since it considers the obsessive nature of romantic love.[52] One of Lewis's longest poems, it is a poignant internal monologue a man has concerning both the character of the woman he loves and his inability to control his thoughts about her. His dilemma is expressed succinctly in the opening lines: "Body and soul most fit for love can best / Withstand it. I am ill, and cannot rest, / Therefore I'm caught." Echoing themes from Shakespeare's sonnets, Lewis expands the analogy between sickness and love[53]: "Disease is amorous, health / At love's door has the pass both in and out." Most frustrating to the persona is his complete incapacity to block her out of his mind. When he strains with every fiber to keep her out, "then in she comes by stealth." This is compounded by the fact she is not worth his obsession: "Her brain's a bubble, / Her soul, a traveller's tale." Yet time and again she "comes between / My thoughts and me." He tries to force himself to read a book, but this does not help. In fact, it drives him to delve ever deeper into his soul in an effort to understand his obsession. He confesses, "I do not love her, like her, wish her well," yet he says he is not driven by lust either. As he reflects back over their relationship, he realizes he has fallen in love with the idea of love:

> She stood, an image lost as soon as seen,
> Like beauty in a vision half-caught between
> Two aimless and long-lumbering dreams of night.
> The thing I seek for was not anywhere
> At any time on earth.

Sadly, when he finds she cannot live up to his idea of love, he finds himself still driven to want her; the visceral rules the cerebral. Consequently, he considers trying to teach her love through an exercise of charity toward her, but he knows this will not work: "She can never learn; / And what am I, whose voice should wake the dead?" Such honest self-revelation on his part saves the poem from being self-righteous invective.

As he analyzes her character more, he notes she is really a product of what she thinks men want, and she is ever ready to play "the rapt disciple," to flatter whichever man she happens to be with at the moment. She is beautiful on the outside, but empty on the inside:

> Her holiest moods are gaudy desecrations
> Of poor half holy things: her exaltations
> Are frothed from music, moonlight, wine and dances;
> Love is to her a dream of bridal dresses,
> Friendship, a tittering hour of girl's caresses,
> Virtue, a steady purpose to advance,
> Honoured, and safe, by the well-proven roads,
> No loophole left to passion or to chance.

Recalling a party they attended together the previous evening, he remembers how he longed to tell her the truth about herself. But she, enjoying her triumph as men buzzed about her and other women envied her, would never have listened. Even he was momentarily deflected from his purpose: "Could she have looked so noble, and no seed / Of spirit in her at all?" Eventually, however, he knows "Venus infernal taught such voice and eyes / To bear themselves abroad for merchandise."[54] The poem ends with him, in spite of his obsession with her, being relieved that "she'd never have me," for he imagines how awful a life with her would be. Yet in his obsession he believes he learns something about the human condition: "For each one of us, down below / The caldron brews in the dark. We do not know / By whom, or on what fields, we are reined and ridden. / There are not acts; spectators of ourselves / We wait and watch the event, the cause hidden." Whatever confidence we might have in ourselves, our good name, our native abilities, and so on is vanity. The truth is darker: "The motion / That moves us is not ours, but in the ocean / Of hunger and bleak fear, like buoys we ride, / And seem to move ourselves, and in the waves / Lifting and falling take our shame and pride." The speaker ends by affirming the essential impotence of human intention. Even if we think we have some ability to control our fortunes, the truth is we ride upon the waves of time and providence, and like buoys we ride rather than direct our destinies. "Infatuation" is among Lewis's most mature pieces of writing as he dealt frankly and openly with the subtleties of the human obsession. Indeed, Lewis managed a poem that well illustrates the eternal war between the mind and the will, the spirit and the flesh, reason and passion. Avoiding "pat" answers about the human experience, Lewis demonstrated here a mind fully awake to the danger of human choice and will.

"Reason" continues Lewis's focus upon the human condition and the inner conflicts noted above in "Infatuation."[55] This time, however, the conflict is between reason and the imagination.[56] He personifies reason as "a virgin, arm'd, commercing with celestial light" and claims the absolute necessity of joining with her. Yet he equally argues the necessity of uniting with imagination, "warm, dark, obscure and infinite, daughter of Night." The poem turns upon discovering some way to reconcile these two and "make imagination's dim exploring touch / Ever report the same as intellectual sight." If he can ever discover a way to bring these two together, "then could I truly say, and not deceive, / Then wholly say, that I BELIEVE" (Lewis's emphasis). The poem itself never achieves such reconciliation, but instead reveals how important these two concepts are to Lewis's creative and intellectual process. Perhaps the most impressive work where Lewis achieves such reconciliation is *Perelandra*. There we see both his rich and powerfully evocative imagination illustrated in his lush physical descriptions of that world as well as the dialectic of reason in the lengthy, closely argued debate between the Green Lady, Weston, and Ransom.

Not surprisingly, among the most moving of Lewis's poems dealing with the human condition are those considering loss and death. For instance, one of Lewis's most poignant treatments of death appears in "On the Death of Charles Williams." This poem records the shock of losing a friend and how it throws one's mistaken view of the human condition into a tailspin: "I can't see the old contours; the slant alters. It's a bolder world / Than I once thought. I wince, caught in the shrill winds that dance on this ridge. / Is it the first sting of a world's waning, the great Winter? Or the cold of Spring?"[57] The old comfortable thought that human life had meaning is challenged by death. Indeed, the knowledge that life is fragile causes him to "wince" and question whether or not such a loss is just the tip of the iceberg. Although he allows that he may be overreacting, he never answers the question, and we are left with the impression that the loss of a friend challenges wellworn assurances about life having ultimate meaning and purpose. Ironically, Lewis notes that it would only be with Williams that he could hope to talk through and make sense of this death: "I have lost now the one only friend wise enough to advise, / To touch deftly such problems. I am left asking. Concerning your death / With what friend now would it help much to spend words, unless it were you?" Like other poems Lewis wrote lamenting the loss of friends, this poignant piece indicates the presence of the distant voice of dissonance and disorientation.

While "Lines Written in a Copy of Milton's Works" hints subtly at Lewis's literary indebtedness to both Marvell and Milton, the poem concerns the personal isolation one feels as the result of lost friendship.[58] It begins with a persona noting how natural creatures blithely carry on in harmony with one another: "Alas, the happy beasts at pasture play / All, all alike; all of one mind are they." Not only are the animals in harmony, but also they easily change companions and are blessed with disinterested friendship: "None loves a special friend beyond the rest." Indeed, even if a sparrow loses a friend to a bird of prey or to a hunter's arrow, "with a new friend next day, content, he wings his flight." The persona then contrasts this Wordsworthian ethos with the dissonant relationships between human beings. Man, the persona suggests, cannot unthinkingly and casually find the easy friend since he "in his fellows finds / (Hard fate) discordant souls and alien minds!" Actually, in the effort to find even one close friend, "one heart amidst a thousand like his own," he will encounter a good deal of difficulty. And, ironically, even if he does eventually find such a friend, it will only be temporary:

> Or if, at last relenting, fate shall send
> In answer to his prayer, the authentic friend,
> Him in some unsuspected hour, some day
> He never dreaded, Death will snatch away
> And leave behind a loss that time can ne'er allay.

Once bereft of that friend, he is left without a companion to "charm to rest each eating care," to share "the secrets of my bosom," or to "while away with delight / Of his discourse the livelong winter night." The last stanza begins with an emphasis upon the persona's sense of isolation: "Alone I walk the fields and plains, alone / The dark vales with dense branches overgrown." In his solitude he feels confined and aimless. In addition, the imagery of the last two lines of the poem indicate an overwhelming sense of estrangement: "Here, as day fades, I wait, and all around / I hear the rain that falls with sullen sound." The cold dampness of the fading day suggests a pathetic fallacy, especially as the rain falls with "sullen sound." The melancholy tone of this poem links it with "To G. M." and "On the Death of Charles Williams."

The final three poems are deeply emotional sonnets concentrating upon loss.[59] "Joys that Sting" is almost certainly a melancholic reverie about a terminated romantic friendship.[60] The persona is saddened "to take the old walks alone, or not at all, / To order one pint where I ordered two, / To think of, and then not to make, the small / Time-honoured joke (senseless to all but you)." That he now only orders "one pint where I ordered two," indicates an erotic if not marital connection since two male friends would probably have ordered separately; on the other hand, a husband would normally order for his wife.[61] He goes on to underscore his estrangement and comments that his life is now little more than show:

> To laugh (oh, one'll laugh), to talk upon
> Themes that we talked upon when you were there,
> To make some poor pretence of going on,
> Be kind to one's old friends, and seem to care,
> While no one (O God) through the years will say
> The simplest, common word in just your way.

The grief this poem expresses over the loss of the beloved is both simple and profound: "it is the joys once shared that have the stings."

"Old Poets Remembered" is more about suffering than lost friendship, although the speaker clearly senses impending loss.[62] As he watches his friend suffer with dignity, he is initially buoyed, yet when he sees his friend's pain, "down through a waste world of slag and sewers / And hammering and loud wheels once more I go." The only hint the friend might be a woman occurs in the third stanza: "Thus, what old poets told me about love / (Tristram's obedience, Isoud's sovereignty . . .) / Turns true in a dread mode I dreamed not of, / What once I studied, now I learn to be." Lewis, the scholar who writes *The Allegory of Love*, a scholastic treatise on medieval courtly love, communicates in this poem something of the emptiness of academic knowledge about romantic love when compared to the actual experience of love, especially when the beloved is suffering painfully.

The third poem, "As the Ruin Falls" is actually about the anticipated loss of Eros.[63] In the poem the persona rebukes himself with bitter honesty: "All this is flashy rhetoric about loving you. / I never had a selfless thought since I was born. / I am mercenary and selfseeking through and through: / I want God, you, all friends, merely to serve my turn." His confession about his egocentricity continues as he admits that he "cannot crawl one inch outside my proper skin"; he has spoken of love in the past, but he recognizes that his has not been a giving love: "self-imprisoned, [I] always end where I begin." The beloved, however, has taught the persona by example both what loving means (giving) and how his has been self-centered: "Only that now you have taught me (but how late) my lack." But there is an added dimension; the beloved appears to be leaving him, whether because of circumstance or death we cannot be sure: "I see the chasm. And everything you are making / My heart into a bridge by which I might get back / From exile, and grow man. And now the bridge is breaking." To the beloved he credits his own faltering steps toward a love that is giving; indeed, the beloved has given him the capacity to be less selfish—she has made his heart a bridge—and less isolated— she has helped to end his "exile, and grow man." His comment that the bridge is now breaking almost certainly refers to his anticipated loss of her. And so he blesses her: "For this I bless you as the ruin falls. The pains / You give me are more precious than all other gains." Given the intensely emotional nature of these last three poems, it is not surprising that some critics have assumed they deal explicitly with Lewis's relationship with Joy Davidman.[64] Because all three poems exist only in holographs and are not dated, there is no way to establish definitively this connection. Regardless, they are powerful witnesses of Lewis's ability to mine the depths of the human condition.

Lewis's contemplative poems illustrate deep and seasoned reflection. While the ones concerned with the shallowness of modern life tend to be public, perhaps even being offered as social criticism, they lack the biting, acerbic tone of his satirical poems; instead they are measured soundings illustrating a profoundly nostalgic sensibility. In most cases they lament the erosion of core values important to civilized life. Tracing these values back to the Greek and Roman writers he so admired—Homer, Virgil, and Ovid—as well as the towering figures of western literature—Dante, Chaucer, Shakespeare, Milton, Wordsworth, Shelley, Keats, and Yeats—Lewis's contemplative poems are framed by his conviction that honor, courage, bravery, honesty, charity, respect, and related values infuse human existence with purpose and meaning. At the same time, his contemplative poems considering the commonalties of human existence—doubt, obsession, loss, death, and grief—offer compelling evidence that he was fully human. While the tone of these poems may disturb some who believe Lewis was always the confident, buoyant Christian apologist, they actually make his corpus complete. That Lewis endured the same shifting sand of life, not glibly dismissing it, makes his work "ring" true. His contemplative poems lead naturally to his religious verse, perhaps the finest body of poetry he produced.

Lewis's religious poems focus upon the character of God; biblical themes, events, or motifs; and the Christian life, including prayer, the nature of love, joy in Christ, spiritual pride, the incarnation, the resurrection, angels, thanksgiving, grief, doubt, heaven, hell, and temptation.[65] A thematic survey of Lewis's religious verse first notes his youthful, jaundiced perception of God as found in *Spirits in Bondage* where he portrays God as cruel and malicious. However, a radical shift in his understanding of God is revealed in the poetry of *The Pilgrim's Regress*; these poems reflect Lewis's conversion to Christ and his initial growth as a believer.[66] Later religious poems offer mature ruminations on life in Christ. In total, Lewis's religious verse provides us valuable insights into his efficacy as a communicator of Christian truth while powerfully supplementing his work as a prose apologist.

By the time Lewis published *The Pilgrim's Regress* (hereafter *PR*) in 1933, fourteen years after *SB* and two years after his conversion to Christ, his view of God had undergone profound changes. He no longer viewed God as malicious, arbitrary, and cruel, and many passages in *SJ* chronicle this change. The culmination of Lewis's evolving view of God is revealed where he writes of his conversion from atheism to theism, perhaps the most quoted portion of *SJ*:

You must picture me alone in that room in Magdalen, night after night, feeling, whenever my mind lifted even for a second from my work, the steady, unrelenting approach of Him whom I so earnestly desired not to meet. That which I greatly feared had at last come upon me. In the Trinity Term of 1929 I gave in, and admitted that God was God, and knelt and prayed: perhaps, that night, the most dejected and reluctant convert in all England. I did not then see what is now the most shining and obvious thing; the Divine humility which will accept a convert even on such terms. The Prodigal Son at least walked home on his own feet. But who can duly adore that Love which will open the high gates to a prodigal who is brought in kicking, struggling, resentful, and darting his eyes in every direction for a chance of escape? The words *compelle intrare*, compel them to come in, have been so abused by wicked men that we shudder at them; but, properly understood, they plumb the depth of the Divine mercy. The hardness of God is kinder than the softness of men, and His compulsion is our liberation.[67]

Not surprisingly, his religious verse reflects these views. *PR* contains sixteen poems that focus primarily upon the spiritual life; as a group they rank among the best of Lewis's poems, perhaps in part because they so intimately and immediately reflect aspects of Lewis's new life in Christ.[68]

The first poem, "He Whom I Bow To" (pp. 144–145),[69] sonnet-like although written in alexandrine couplets, does not appear until three-quarters of the way through *PR*. This late appearance suggests that as John, the hero of *PR*, awakens to the beauty of poetry, he correspondingly awakens to the truth of his broken spiritual condition and need for God's grace.[70] The speaker confesses that language used to address God is so inadequate "prayers always, taken at their word, blaspheme" and "all men are idolaters, crying unheard / To senseless idols, if thou take them at their word." Accordingly, anticipating the later "Legion," the poem ends with the prayer "take not, oh Lord, our literal sense, but in thy great, / Unbroken speech our halting metaphor translate."

Among the most powerful poems in *PR* is "You Rest Upon Me All My Days" (pp. 147–148),[71] reflecting a tone similar to poems in *SB*, which confront the cruel, malicious God; the difference here is that God, while demanding and jealous, loves rather than hates the speaker. The speaker grapples with a fierce omnipotence, much as a dog strains at the leash of an unyielding master. He feels like a person trapped in a burning desert bathed by unrelenting, suffocating, light and heat. God, like the sun, is the "inevitable Eye" that confines a desert traveler in smothering tents and "hammers the rocks with light." He is an unyielding, unrelenting, and uncompromising force. In desperation the speaker longs for "one cool breath in seven / One air from northern climes / The changing and the castleclouded heaven / Of my old Pagan times." It is difficult not to slip into the "personal heresy" and to read these lines as recalling Lewis's affection for Norse myth and literature in terms of both its religious and metaphorical influences on his youth and young adulthood. Regardless, these lines suggest a powerful longing for freedom from the "heat" of God's eye; he is ready to retreat from the demands of an unyielding God toward the comfortable fastness of his pagan days. Such an option, however, is denied him: "But you have seized all in your rage / Of Oneness. Round about / Beating my wings, all ways, within your cage, / I flutter, but not out." Here a God is pictured as possessive, jealous, and demanding, and the speaker pictures himself as a bird trapped in a cage, straining earnestly though vainly to wing his way out.

The poem leaves two distinct impressions. The first is of a "convert" who yearns for his preconversion days where, rightly or wrongly, he believes life held more freedom, more satisfaction. Indeed, the tone is similar to George Herbert's "The Collar" where the speaker advises himself to "leave thy cold dispute / Of what is fit and not. Forsake thy cage, / Thy ropes of sands, / Which petty thoughts have made." As in Herbert's poem, Lewis's speaker is frustrated ("beating my wings") yet thwarted ("I flutter, but not out"). The second is that God is an all encompassing, smothering, demanding deity, uncompromising in His jealous possession of a follower. Such a God seizes "all in [His] rage / Of

Oneness." These impressions combine to highlight the speaker in "You Rest Upon Me All My Days" as one who regards with nostalgia his preconversion lifestyle, yet he also has grudging appreciation for this jealous God. He senses it is now Yahweh, not Odin that he serves.

Since "You Rest Upon Me All My Days" largely resolves the question of God's real character, Lewis's religious verse in *PR* turns to consider what it means to live as a Christian. For example, "My Heart Is Empty" (p. 162),[72] with its alternating alexandrines and trimeters examines the contradiction between living the expected "abundant life" and the cold reality of spiritual torpor. It is a candid admission the speaker's spiritual life is a dry, arid waste-land: "All the fountains that should run / With longing, are in me / Dried up. In all my countryside there is not one / That drips to find the sea." What is worse, he has no desire to experience God's love, except as it serves to lessen his own pain. Yet the speaker avoids despair by calling out to the one "who didst take / All care for Lazarus in the careless tomb." The vigor of his faith in Christ is seen in his belief that if God will intervene in his own Lazarus-like life, he may survive for later rebirth, much as a seed "which grows / Through winter ripe for birth." Just as the dormant seed avoids the chilling winter wind, so he will endure this winter of his life: "Because, while it forgets, the heaven remembering throws / Sweet influence still on earth, / —Because the heaven, moved moth-like by thy beauty, goes / Still turning round the earth." The pleading tone of Lewis's poem is similar to many of Herbert's. For instance, "Dullness" from *The Temple* begins "Why do I languish thus, drooping and dull, / As if I were all earth? / O give me quickness, that I may with mirth / Praise the brim-full!"[73]

The next three poems in *PR* anticipate material Lewis returns to *The Screwtape Letters* and *The Great Divorce*. The rhyming alexandrines of "Thou Only Art Alternative to God" (p. 177)[74] baldly posit we either serve God or Satan; there is no other choice: "God is: thou art: / The rest illusion." The speaker notes he can either serve the pure "white light without flame" of God or the "infernal starving in the strength of fire" of Satan. It ends with the speaker noting fearfully: "Lord, open not too often my weak eyes to this!" The poem's portrayal of a malicious Satan borrows heavily from "Satan Speaks" (I) and "Satan Speaks" (XIII) of *Spirits in Bondage*. In addition, this poem contains the kernel of Screwtape's counsel to Wormword about keeping his patient from engaging in dialectic thinking, encouraging him instead to promote muddle-headedness and hazy logic. The focus upon Hell continues in Lewis's triolet "God in His Mercy" (p. 180),[75] a terse, pithy, epigrammatic observation about why God created Hell. Framed around the refrain "God in his mercy made / The fixed pains of Hell," the poem says God actually limits misery by creating Hell as a fixed area for the suffering of those within. That is, God's creation of Hell is not cruel, but merciful, since God limits the place and thus the extent of suffering for those who reject him. He could have just as easily permitted Hell to be boundless, limitless, and formless. By carving out a limited sphere for those who choose Hell, God is being kind, echoing the line from *SJ*, "the hardness of God is kinder than the softness of man."[76]

In the third poem about Hell, "Nearly They Stood Who Fall" (pp. 181–182),[77] Lewis, reflecting the pervasive influence of Milton, considers both the angels who fell and those who did not. He imagines those who fell, looking back and seeing "the one false step" they took and realizing the "lightest swerve / Of foot not yet enslaved" could have meant they "might have been saved." However, such insight is not limited to the fallen angels, since Lewis notes the unfallen angels know similarly how easily they could have fallen, "and with cold after fear / Look back to mark how near / They grazed the Sirens' land / . . . The choice of ways so small, the event so great." The poem ends by forcing men to consider how angelic examples speak to us, warning us of "the road that seems so clear" and reminding us "which, being once crossed forever unawares, / Denies return." Almost certainly Lewis had in mind Satan's speech at the beginning of Book IV of *PL* where he says:

> Oh had his powerful Destiny ordain'd
> Me some inferior Angel, I had stood
> Then happy; no unbounded hope had rais'd
> Ambition. Yet why not? some other Power
> As great might have aspir'd, and me though mean
> Drawn to his part; but other Powers as great
> Fell not, but stand unshak'n, from within
> Or from without, to all temptations arm'd.
> Hadst thou the same free Will and Power to stand?
> Thou hadst.[78]

Playing off Satan's realization that he could have chosen not to fall, Lewis affirms in "Nearly They Stood Who Fall" that human choices and their consequences are critically important; they are deadly serious and connect us to a spiritual reality that exists whether we recognize it or not. The three poems on hell in *PR* are sober reflections on the nature of man's spiritual adversary, the extent of God's mercy, and the spiritual significance of human responsibility.

The next two poems concern spiritual pride, what Lewis calls the "great" sin in *Mere Christianity*, and already noted as something he struggled with throughout his life.[79] The first poem, "I Have Scraped Clean the Plateau" (p. 183),[80] centers its alexandrines on the ugliness of self-righteous pride. The female persona, echoing the autonomy of Dymer, rejects both the earth—it is filthy, unchaste, a "sluttish helot"—and man—"filthy flesh," embracing instead a hard, flinty, asceticism: "I have made my soul (once filthy) a hard, pure, bright / Mirror of steel . . . / I have a mineral soul." Her rejection and isolation are attempts to live only for self, unsullied by aspects of human life that might shake her belief in her own superiority: "So I, borrowing nothing and repaying / Nothing, neither growing nor decaying, / Myself am to myself, a mortal God, a self-contained / Unwindowed monad, unindebted and unstained." These lines anticipate Orual's self-righteousness and self-sufficiency through Part I of *Till We Have Faces* and the initial self-absorbed pride of Jane Studdock in *That Hideous Strength*.

"Because of Endless Pride" (pp. 184–185),[81] treats spiritual pride from an opposite perspective as the persona recognizes that in every hour of his life he looks "upon my secret mirror / Trying all postures there / To make my image fair."[82] Instead of delighting in the luscious, rich grapes God gives him for nourishment, he admires the "white hand" holding them. Though he catches himself admiring himself in the mirror of his soul, he is sensitive enough to know "who made the glass, whose light makes dark, whose fair / Makes foul, my shadowy form reflected there / That Self-Love, brought to bed of Love may die and bear / Her sweet son in despair." The answer to spiritual pride, therefore, is humility, and recognizing it is God, not self, who rules human life and the natural world. Lewis may have been influenced in part by Herbert's "The Bunch of Grapes" that ends:

But can he want the grape, who hath the wine?
I have their fruit and more.
Blessed be God, who prosper'd Noah's vine,
And made it bring forth grapes good store.
But much more him I must adore,
Who of the laws sowre juice sweet wine did make,
Ev'n God himself, being pressed for my sake.[83]

Moving from poems focusing upon spiritual pride, "Iron Will Eat the World's Old Beauty Up" (p. 187)[84] is a direct commentary on the modern world as Lewis sees it, employing themes from *SB* and echoing his distrust of human progress when it occurs at the expense of beauty and truth. He imagines the industrial revolution, particularly the new machines of his own day, involved in the destruction of nature; as the new cities and buildings emerge (the "iron forests"), they will block out nature so there will be "no green or growth." In addition, the growing popularity of sensational journalism—"the printing presses with their clapping wings"—shall drown out the wisdom of the past: "Harpy wings, / Filling your minds all day with foolish things, / Will tame the eagle Thought: till she sings / Parrot-like in her cage to please dark kings."[85] The poem also reflects Lewis's disgust with chronological snobbery by parodying it in the last stanza: "The new age, the new art, the new ethic and thought, / And fools crying, Because it has begun / It will continue as it has begun!" Indeed the inevitably of human progress is undercut throughout the poem since each stanza ends with a parenthetical portion noting God's continued presence and rule in the world, regardless of human pride and arrogance. The last parenthesis is an apt way to finish the poem: "(Though they [man] lay flat the mountains and dry up the sea, / Wilt thou yet change, as though God were a god?)."

Lewis follows this up with two poems emphasizing the relationship between the spiritual life and sexual temptation.[86] In both he is frank without being prurient. The three sonnet-like quatrains of "Quick!" (p. 189),[87] recalling portions of *Dymer*, almost certainly deals with autoeroticism, particularly as the speaker emphasizes his struggles when "old festering fire begins to play / Once more within" and he wrenches his "hands the other way." To his credit, the speaker, with the passion of John Donne in his "Holy Sonnet: Batter My Heart," appeals to God to overpower his perverse desire and to replace it with a heavenly one: "Quick, Lord! Before new scorpions bring / New venom—ere fiends blow the fire / A second time—quick, show me that sweet thing / Which, 'spite of all, more deeply I desire."[88] Donne puts it this way: "Batter my heart, three person'd God; for, you / As yet but knocke, breathe, shine, and seeke to mend; / That I may rise, and stand, o'erthrow mee, and bend / Your force, to breake, blowe, burn and make me new.[89] The heat of unbridled lust is continued in "When Lilith Means to Draw Me" (pp. 190–191),[90] a poem that suggests there is something ultimately unfulfilling, even emptying, when one reaches the end of repeated sexual gratification. The persona freely confesses Lilith, symbolizing sexual temptation, "does not overawe me / With beauty's pomp and power." As a matter of fact, he sees the cup (sexual gratification) she offers as unable to satisfy: "Her cup, whereof who taste, / (She promises no better) thirst far more." In spite of this, he ponders why he returns again and again to her cup. His realization is that her offerings, while insipid and sterile, *appear* more satisfying than the dry, arid reality in which he moves and lives: "The witch's wine, / Though promising nothing, seems / In that land of no streams, / To promise best—the unrelished anodyne." These two poems, as well as the sexually explicit portions of *Dymer*, reveal that like most human beings Lewis knew the powerful pull of sexual temptation.

"Once the Worm-laid Egg Broke in the Wood" (pp. 192–193)[91] is an almost humorous poem in blank verse given from the point of view of an old, lonely dragon; full of self-pity over his isolation, he cannot bring himself to give up his golden hoard in exchange for fellowship with others. Actually, he has even eaten his mate since "worm grows not to dragon till he eat worm." In particular he fears men who plot "in the towns to steal my gold," whispering of him, "laying plans, / Merciless men." He prays that God will give him peace, yet it is a hollow request since he wants such peace on his terms: "But ask not that I should give up the gold, / Nor move, nor die; others would get the gold. / Kill, rather, Lord, the men and the other dragons / That I may sleep, go when I will to drink." "Soul's ease," serving God on our terms, praying, like King Claudius in *Hamlet* without truly repenting for the murder of his brother—"My words fly up, my thoughts remain below: / Words without thoughts never to heaven go" (III. iii. pp. 69–70)—these sophisticated spiritual dodges are specious, revealing the bankruptcy of our souls.[92] In addition, the poem implies many human beings are like the dragon—preferring material things over vital engagement with others. The second dragon poem focuses upon a dragon-slayer rather than a dragon.[93] In "I Have Come Back with Victory Got" (pp. 195–196),[94] the tercets reveal a warrior returning from killing a dragon. The warrior is filled with joy for having defeated his greatest foe and prepared to fight even greater battles. After describing the details of his victory, he claims that when he bit into the heart of his vanquished enemy, "I felt a pulse within me start / As though my breast would break apart." Flushed with victory, he feels invincible: "Behemoth is my serving man! / Before the conquered hosts of Pan / Riding tamed Leviathan."[95] Still in celebration, he sings: "RESVRGAM and IO PAEAN, / IO, IO, IO, PAEAN!!"[96] He realizes his conquest of the dragon has been a rite of passage, signifying his bravery, courage, and honor: "Now I know the stake I played for, / Now I know what a worm's made for!" Avoiding pride, the warrior delights in experiencing his victory.[97]

The last three poems of *PR* concern God's authority, man's dignity, and angel's wonder. In "I Am Not One That Easily Flits Past in Thought" (p. 197),[98] the speaker considers the authority of God, especially over death and time. The rhyming alexandrines express the paradox that God both makes and unmakes: "Therefore among the riddles that no man has read / I put thy paradox, Who liveth and was dead. / As Thou hast made substantially, thou wilt unmake / In earnest and for everlasting." While we might wish to recall those who have died, such musings are really futile:

Whom Thy great *Exit* banishes, no after age
Of epilogue leads back upon the lighted stage.
Where is Prince Hamlet when the curtain's down?
Where fled
Dreams at the dawn, or colours when the light is sped?
We are thy colours, fugitive, never restored,

Never repeated again. Thou only art the Lord,
Thou only art holy.

In this, the most theocentric poem in the *PR*, Lewis affirms God's sovereign rule over time as well and ends by recalling lines from Psalm 139: "Thou art Lord of the unbreathable transmortal air / Where mortal thinking fails: night's nuptial darkness, where / All lost embraces intermingle and are bless'd, / And all die, but all are, while Thou continuest."[99] This paradoxical ending, that although all die they nonetheless "live" under the eternal authority of God, also echoes lines from the *Te Deum*: "When Thou hadst overcome the sharpness of death, / Thou didst open the Kingdom of Heaven to all believers."

"Passing To-day by a Cottage, I Shed Tears" (p. 198)[100] shifts the focus to how God lends us the dignity of being created in His image, replete with both the positive and negative this encompasses. For instance, as humans we can know the pain of loss: "Passing to-day by a cottage, I shed tears / When I remembered how once I had dwelled there / With my mortal friends who are dead." Nor does time heal such losses: "I, fool, believed / I had outgrown the local, unique sting, / I had transmuted away (I was deceived) / Into love universal the lov'd thing." That is, God created us, unlike angels, with "the tether and pang of the particular"; because we are created in His image, we can know experientially the heights of pleasure but also the depths of pain. This profound dignity means that while we share His nature, we also enter into His knowledge, one involving responsibility and consequence. Accordingly, though we are small compared to Him, we "quiver with fire's same / Substantial form as Thou—nor reflect merely, / As lunar angel, back to thee, cold flame. / Gods we are, Thou hast said: and we pay dearly." Entering into the divine image means entering into divine suffering, but such price is worth the anguish it necessarily involves. The last poem in *PR*, "I Know Not, I" (pp. 198–199),[101] plays off the previous poem as it presents an angel pondering over what it must be like to be a man: "I know not, I, / What the men together say, / How lovers, lovers die / And youth pass away." He has no understanding of romantic love, aging, love of country, and especially human grief: "Why at grave [do] they grieve / For one voice and face, / And not, and not receive / Another in its place." Yet, while the angel has in the past appeared satisfied with his even, emotionally balanced existence, the poem's conclusion belies this: "Sorrow it is they call / This cup: whence my lip, / Woe's me, never in all / My endless days must sip." Paradoxically, the angel's sorrow is his regret that he cannot experience the pang of the particular reserved only for human beings.[102]

The sixteen poems in *PR* are Lewis's most moving, unified, and deliberate attempt at sustained religious verse. Although the poems appear within the text of this prose allegory, and thus rightly must be read as commentary on the story of John, the poems also exist outside the text,[103] offering us insight into Lewis's own spiritual and poetic maturation.[104] In them we see him striving to come to grips with what his new faith in Christ means to his intellectual, sexual, and spiritual life. Lewis never again clusters this many poems around such a unified theme, and so the poems of *PR* testify to the artistic and spiritual progress of his poetic pilgrimage.

As Lewis matured in Christ, he continued to write religious verse from pieces on the incarnation and the resurrection to ones on the seven deadly sins and the life of the soul. A favorite topic was prayer. He discussed it in disparate prose works such as *The Screwtape Letters* and *Letters to Malcolm*, while petitionary prayer was the subject of the essay "The Efficacy of Prayer" where he pondered over the following questions: If God is sovereign and omniscient, of what value is prayer? That is, if He knows already what is going to happen, why bother to ask Him to change His mind? Can our petitions to God *really* change His will?[105] In the poems on prayer, Lewis does not offer a systematic theology of prayer, but rather snapshots of his thinking about prayer. For instance, in "Sonnet" Lewis connects the defeat of the cruel Assyrian conqueror, Sennacherib, recorded in *2 Kings* 19 and by the historian Herodotus to the relationship between prayer and divine action.[106] The biblical account suggests angels intervene to save Israel, while Herodotus ascribes the reason for Sennacherib's defeat to mice "innumerably nibbling all one night . . . to eat his bowstrings piecemeal as warm wind eats ice." This English sonnet in alexandrines melds the two accounts, suggesting the defeat occurred when angels worked through mice. Lewis does not find this odd, but instead sees in it a glimpse of God working through human prayer: "No stranger that omnipotence should choose to need / Small helps than great— no stranger if His action lingers / Till men have prayed, and suffers their weak prayers indeed / To move as very muscles His delaying fingers." Lewis suggests, the divine enfeebles itself in order to work through the weak, thus lending the latter a dignity not its own: "Who, in His longanimity and love for our / Small dignities, enfeebles, for a time, His power."

More often than not, however, Lewis's poems dealing with prayer do not focus upon the nature of prayer; instead, they *are* prayers. Sometimes they are powerful pleas for God's intercession. The Italian sonnet "Legion" is such a poem. Akin to "Quick" from *PR* and Donne's "Batter My Heart," "Legion" implores God to see the *real* character of the speaker. The real man is the one who desperately turns to Him at the very moment of the poem's composition: "Lord, hear my voice; this present voice, I mean, / Not that which may be speaking an hour hence / When pride or pity of self or craving sense / Blunt the mind's edge, now momentarily clear."[107] He implores God not to consider the myriad of other selves within him that in only a few minutes will feign to be the real him. While he knows God will not override his free will, he beseeches Him to see his real will in this moment; if not, his warring selves may cancel God's work in him: "Hold me to this. Oh strain / A point; use legal fictions. For, if all / My quarreling selves must bear an equal voice, / Farewell— thou hast created me in vain." The desperate tone suggests the state of the soul familiar to many Christians who struggle with the internal war between the flesh and the spirit. Like Lewis, many have despaired of self and longed for Christ to overrule their wills. This is a poignant prayer for God's grace.

Rather than being an intercession for grace, "They Tell Me, Lord" is a poem where a speaker comes to a surprising conclusion about the dialogue of prayer.[108] He notes some think prayer a futile exercise, "since but one voice is heard, it's all dream, / One talker aping two." He admits there is but one voice, but with this twist: the voice is not his, but God's: "Seeing me empty, you forsake / The listener's role and through / My dumb lips breathe and into utterance wake / The thoughts I never knew." Since, therefore, it is God speaking to him through prayer, God has no need to reply to Himself: "While we seem / Two talkers, thou are One forever, and I / No dreamer, but thy dream."[109] Lewis's deeply penetrating spiritual insight about prayer—that when we are empty, then God can speak through and to us—rivals similar ones in *The Problem of Pain* and *Mere Christianity*.

Other poems are prayerful meditations. For instance, Lewis's "No Beauty We Could Desire" is about how one who seeks joy eventually finds it in Christ.[110] The poem begins almost with a sigh as the speaker admits, "Yes, you are everywhere," but then goes on to say he "could never bring the noble Hart to bay." When he tried to track what he longed for, he was thwarted by confusing scents: "Nowhere sometimes, then again everywhere. / Other scents, too, seemed to them almost the same." As a result, he stopped the search for joy through things (including poetry), and made himself available instead to be found by the source of the joy: "Not in Nature, not even in Man, but in one / Particular Man, with a date, so tall, weighing / So much, talking Aramaic, having learned a trade." This realization was the fulcrum leveraging his understanding that in Christ there is a beauty beyond any earthly one: "Not in all food, not in all bread and wine / (Not, I mean, as my littleness requires) / But this wine, this bread . . . no beauty we could desire." In the person of Christ there was no greater beauty for him to desire, and the Eucharist became a visible symbol of this beauty. The joy he found in Christ surpassed all earthly joys, and this poem becomes the measure of Lewis's personal devotion to His Lord.

Another prayerful meditation is "Epitaph," a poem that finds the dead person it commemorates both a microcosm of the universe and a promise of future life in Lenten lands.[111] Its opening lines effectively suggest the vastness of the universe summed up in this person's life: "Here lies the whole world after one / Peculiar mode; a buried sun, / Stars and immensities of sky / And cities here discarded lie."[112] "Epitaph for Helen Joy Davidman" is a later powerful reworking of this epitaph. Lewis concentrates his imagery more intensely in the opening lines of the revision: "Here the whole world (stars, water, air, / And field, and forest, as they were / Reflected in a single mind)." In addition, the revision contains Christian motifs, culminating in the promise of resurrection: "Like cast off clothes was left behind / In ashes yet with hope that she, / Re-born from holy poverty, / In lenten lands, hereafter may / Resume them on her Easter Day."[113]

In addition to prayers of intercession and meditation, several of Lewis's religious poems are confessions. For example, a confessional prayer with a tone similar to "Legion" is "The Apologist's Evening Prayer," written in heroic couplets.[114] The speaker, famous for his brilliant defenses of the faith, his "cleverness shot forth on Thy behalf / At which, while angels weep, the audience laugh," pauses and asks to be delivered from his own high opinion of himself: "Let me not trust, instead / Of Thee, their thin-worn image of Thy head." As he approaches sleep, he prays to be delivered from all thoughts, even his thoughts of God, and especially from his thoughts of self: "Lord of the narrow gate and the needle's eye, / Take from me all my trumpery lest I die." This frank admission of the danger of spiritual pride in the life of one who defends God is consistent with Lewis's other writings on spiritual pride. He knows well that regardless of his best intentions, an outwardly successful apologist can seek self-glory rather than God's. This prayer is a sober reminder against self-promotion.

Lewis rarely wrote poems directly connected to a biblical narrative, perhaps in part because he saw little need to plow well-tilled ground. However in the instances where he plays off biblical narratives, the results are engaging. For example, "The Sailing of the Ark" is loosely based on the Old Testament story of Noah and the flood.[115] In one of his most rhythmic and speculative poems, he imagines Ham, the youngest son of Noah, denying entry to one last animal as the rains begin.[116] Ham is shown to be a shirker when one last animal is heard knocking at the door of the Ark. He warns his brothers not to answer because it will awaken their father: "Once he comes to see / What's at the door it's sure to mean more work for you and me."[117] Awakening finally to the pounding on the ark's door, Noah is horrified to discover the forsaken animal is the unicorn. When it turns away, Noah curses his son: "Now all the world, O Ham, may curse the hour that you were born— / Because of you the Ark must sail without the Unicorn." Despite this somewhat somber theme, the lively musical rhythm of the iambic heptameter lines makes this seriocomic poem very enjoyable to read aloud.

"Stephen to Lazarus" melds two biblical narratives as the poem imagines St. Stephen, the first Christian martyr as described in Acts 6: 8–7:60, reflecting upon the resurrection of Lazarus found in John 11.[118] In an interesting twist, Stephen wonders if Lazarus was not in fact the first martyr; he reasons this way by noting that while Stephen "gave up no more than life," Lazarus gave up death and its peace. That is, while Stephen left this life and its vale of tears for the peace of death in Christ, Lazarus had to give up the peace of death and "put out a second time to sea / Well knowing that [his] death (in vain / Died once) must be all died again?" Stephen implies, therefore, that Lazarus' resurrection to the pain of life is a more noble martyrdom than his to the peace of death.

While poems linked to a biblical narrative are rare, those connected to biblical themes appear frequently. For example, in addition to "Sonnet" mentioned above where angels and mice work together to accomplish the defeat of Sennacherib, several poems focus upon angels. In "On Being Human" Lewis notes that while angels have some real advantages over mankind, they are also limited.[119] Although the poem admits angels have direct knowledge of spiritual and philosophical truth denied to mankind, it subtly underscores that they lack the five senses God shares with mankind. Lewis uses humor to show that while angels understand the Platonic eternal forms of earthly realities, they lack rich, sensuous understanding of earthly experience:

> The lavish pinks, the new-mown field, the ravishing
> Sea-smell, the wood-fire smoke that whispers *Rest*;
> The tremor on the rippled pool of memory
> Which from each scent in widening circle goes,
> The pleasure and the pang—can angels measure it?
> An angel has no nose.[120]

Lewis's point, therefore, is that in some ways it is better to be human than angelic. The playfulness of the poem is characteristic of many others, and its theme is an insightful gloss to the angelic *eldila* of the Ransom space trilogy. There Lewis describes them as "white and semi-transparent—rather like ice" with "inorganic" voices speaking syllables sounding "more as if they were played on an instrument than as if they were spoken . . . as if rock or crystal or light had spoken."[121]

Two religious poems deal with the biblical theme of Christ's nativity. "The Turn of the Tide" is finely crafted; for instance, Lewis uses internal rhyme in each odd line and final rhyme in each even line. In the poem Lewis focuses upon the very moment of Christ's birth and how this marks a universal turn of the tide: from the certitude of death for all to the promise of new life for all.[122] Profoundly influenced by Milton's "On the Morning of Christ's Nativity,"

Lewis, in a slow and deliberate fashion, chronicles how the spiritual impact of Christ's birth quietly yet inexorably sweeps over the world invigorating and bringing to life a dead, silent planet.[123] For instance, at the moment just before Christ's birth, Lewis pictures a world on the verge of its dying moment: "Breathless was the air over Bethlehem; black and bare / The fields; hard as granite were the clods; Hedges stiff with ice; the sedge, in the vice / Of the ponds, like little iron rods. / The deathly stillness spread from Bethlehem." By comparing the frozen, dead landscape to the adamantine spiritual torpor of mankind before Christ's birth, Lewis effectively highlights the world's inevitable spiritual ebb tide. He vividly portrays this deadly pallor by noting various notions connected with Christ's nativity, beginning with Caesar and the Palatine and culminating in great Galactic lords asking:

> "Is this perhaps the last
> Of our story and the glories of our crown?—
> The entropy worked out?—the central redoubt
> Abandoned?—The world-spring running down?"
> Then they could speak no more. Weakness overbore
> Even them; they were as flies in a web,
> In lethargy stone-dumb. The death had almost come,
> And the tide lay motionless at ebb.

Yet at this critical juncture in the history of the universe, Lewis likens Christ's birth to a stabbing "shock / Of returning life, the start, the burning pang at heart, / Setting galaxies to tingle and rock." This event promises "rumor and noise of resuming joys / Along the nerves of the universe."

Symbolic of this renewal is "a music infinitely small," yet clear, loud, and deep: "Such a note as neither Throne nor Potentate had known / Since the Word created the abyss." At this universal sound "Heaven danced" and "revel, mirth and shout / Descended to" earth and the frozen universe began to thaw: "Saturn laughed and lost his latter age's frost / And his beard, Niagara-like, unfroze." The reviving universe reaches its fever pitch of rebirth in the reigniting of the Phoenix, which functions as a metaphor for Christ:[124]

> A shiver of re-birth and deliverance round the Earth
> Went gliding; her bonds were released;
> Into broken light the breeze once more awoke the seas,
> In the forest it wakened every beast;
> Capripods fell to dance from Taproban to France,
> Leprechauns from Down to Labrador;
> In his green Asian dell the Phoenix from his shell
> Burst forth and was the Phoenix once more.

In spite of the universal significance and magnitude of this paradoxical rebirth—the condemned cosmos revived by God's incarnation—Lewis manages to treat it with great tenderness and poignancy: "So Death lay in arrest. But at Bethlehem the bless'd / Nothing greater could be heard / Than sighing wind in the thorn, the cry of One new-born, / And cattle in stable as they stirred." Omnipotent God—Author, Creator, and Sustainer of all that was, is, and will be—contracted into a little child lying seemingly unnoticed in this humble of birth places. Furthermore, in these last lines Lewis alludes to Christ's later crown of thorns and crucifixion by noting the ominous thorns through which the wind sighs. In his deft handling of the theme, images, and language in "The Turn of the Tide" we experience one of Lewis's most powerful poems.

"The Nativity" continues Lewis's interest in God's physical incarnation, but here he focuses instead upon the animals present at the nativity and links them to human parallels.[125] Specifically, Lewis personifies three animals and attributes we associate with them to the state of the speaker's spiritual condition. First, he says he is slow like an ox, but he sees "glory in the stable grow" so that "with the ox's dullness" he eventually might gain "an ox's strength." Second, he says he is stubborn as an ass, but he sees "my Saviour where I looked for hay" so that through his ass-like folly he may learn "the patience of a beast." Finally, he is like a straying sheep watching "the manger where my Lord is laid" so that his "baa-ing nature" (repentance) would someday win "some woolly innocence!" The spiritual condition of the speaker—from being as slow and dull as an ox to as stubborn and hard as an ass to as broken and contrite as an erring sheep—is nicely encapsulated in this brief reflection.

Still other religious poems concern God's glory, as does the Italian sonnet "Noon's Intensity."[126] Utilizing the light of the sun as a metaphor for God's glory, the octet identifies God's "alchemic beams [that] turn all to gold." The speaker then describes how sunlight, and by extension God's glory, is spread over all the earth: "From the night / You will not yet withdraw her silver light, / And often with Saturnian tints the cold / Atlantic swells at morning shall enfold / The Cornish cliffs burnished with copper bright." The poem goes on to suggest our sight may one day be "trained by slow degrees" until "we have such sight / As dares the pure projection to behold." Biblical allusions come into focus in the sestet. For instance the lines "When Sol comes ascendant, it may be / More perfectly in him our eyes shall see / All baser virtues" recall Moses' encounter with God in Exodus 33: 18-19a: "Then Moses said, 'I pray Thee, show me Thy glory!' And He said, 'I Myself will make all My goodness pass before you, and will proclaim the name of the Lord before you" (NAS).[127] The speaker delights in the fact that now he can "hear you [God] talking / And yet not die." He adds that until he is given the opportunity "the pure projection to behold," God has "left free, / Unscorched by your own noon's intensity / One cool and evening hour for garden walking." The final line alludes to a prelapsarian state and the immediate fellowship the speaker has with God when they would walk together in "the cool of the day" (Genesis 3:8). This ending also echoes the descent of Perelandra-Venus, a reflection of God's glory and love, at the conclusion of *That Hideous Strength*:

And now it came. It was fiery, sharp, bright and ruthless, ready to kill, ready to die, outspeeding light: it was Charity, not as mortals imagine it, not even as it has been humanised for them since the Incarnation of the Word, but the translunary virtue, fallen upon them direct from the Third Heaven, unmitigated. They were blinded, scorched, deafened. They thought it would burn their bones. They could not bear that it should continue. They could not bear that it should cease. So Perelandra, triumphant among planets, whom men call Venus, came and was with them in the room.[128]

"Noon's Intensity" similarly celebrates God's glory and his compelling love for man.

A different kind of spiritual insight occurs in "Deadly Sins" where Lewis reflects upon the all-pervasive nature of the seven deadly sins in human life."[129] The history of the seven deadly sins in the church, especially the development of a list of seven, is somewhat problematic. Early church fathers, including Hermas, Tertullian, and Augustine, while never actually listing specific "deadly" sins, did suggest some sins were worse than others, perhaps with 1 John 5:16–17 in mind: "If anyone sees his brother committing a sin not leading to death, he shall ask and God will for him give life to those who commit sin not leading to death. There is a sin leading to death; I do not say that he should make request for this. All unrighteousness is sin, and there is a sin not leading to death." What eventually resulted, therefore, were numerous lists of especially harmful sins. However, the list that came to be most influential in the church was the one developed by Gregory the Great (pp. 540–605) characterized by its Latin acronym, *saligia*: *superbia* (pride), *avaritia* (greed), *luxuria* (luxury, later lust), *invidia* (envy), *gula* (gluttony), *ira* (anger), and *acedia* (sloth).[130]

Lewis was no stranger to the literary life of these sins since they appear in works he knew well including William Langland's *Piers Plowman*, Dante's *Divine Comedia*, Chaucer's "The Parson's Tale," and Spenser's *Faerie Queene*. Furthermore, Lewis writes about them himself in *The Allegory of Love*. For example, while commenting on Langland, Lewis says that his "excellent satiric comedy, as displayed in the behavior of the seven Deadly Sins belongs to a tradition as old as the *Ancren Riwle*."[131] In addition, in other works he refers to specific sins on the list. For instance, in *Mere Christianity* he saves an entire chapter for pride ("the great sin"); in *Screwtape Letters* he devotes letters to lust (IX, XVII), and pride (XXIV); and in *The Great Divorce* he pictures sinners unable to choose heaven because of greed, sloth, and envy. Accordingly, it is no surprise that he writes a poem centered on the seven deadly sins.[132]

He begins by noting how all of them "through our lives [their] meshes run / Deft as spiders' catenation, / Crossed and crossed again and spun / Finer than the fiend's temptation." He then devotes a four-line stanza to each. Sloth, "deadly" according to the church fathers because it deadened one to vigorous spiritual life, Lewis portrays in like manner: "Sloth that would find out a bed / Blind to morning, deaf to waking, / Shuffling shall at last be led / To the peace that know no breaking." In *Piers Plowman* Langland shows Sloth similarly:

I've never visited the sick, or prisoners in their cells. And I'd much rather hear a filthy story or watch a shoemakers' farce in summer, or laugh at a lot of lying scandal about my neighbours, than listen to all that Gospel stuff—Matthew and Mark and Luke and John. As for vigils and fast-days, I give all that a miss; and in Lent I lie in bed with my girl in my arms till mass and matins are well and truly over. I then make off for the friars' church, and if I get to the place before the priest's "go, mass is finished," I feel I've done my bit. Sometimes I never get to confession even once in a year, unless a bout of sickness scares me into it; and then I produce some confused mishmash or other.[133]

About greed, Lewis writes: "Avarice, while she finds an end, / Counts but small the largest treasure. / Whimperingly at last she'll bend / To take free what has no measure." Lewis uses a clever sexual pun to illustrate the pull of lust: "Lechery, that feels sharp lust / Sharper from each promised staying, / Goes at long last—go she must— / Where alone is sure allaying." In each case, the particular sin leads eventually to God because the sin simply repeated does not ultimately satisfy: "So inexorably thou / On thy shattered foes pursuing / Never a respite dost allow / Save what works their own undoing." Ironically, deadly sins both consume and feed our fractured experience.

In spite of sin's very real presence in our lives, Lewis's most powerful religious poem, "Love's as Warm as Tears," is not about sin; instead it is about love.[134] In four brief stanzas Lewis helps us see that love exists in at least four forms reminiscent of his *The Four Loves*. The loves are often in striking contrast to one another. For instance, the first stanza focuses upon affectional love, or what he calls *storge* in *The Four Loves*: "Love's as warm as tears, / Love is tears: / Pressure within the brain / Tension at the throat." This is familiar, weeping, tender, emotional love common to those who know each other well. Yet in the second stanza, he considers bold, passionate, burning love: "Love's as fierce as fire, / Love is fire: / All sorts—infernal heat / Clinkered with greed and pride." This is what he calls eros in *The Four Loves*; it is the consuming, painful, possessive, sexual love known best to lovers. In the third stanza he writes of love that is anticipated: "Love's as fresh as spring, / Love is spring: / Bird-song hung in the air, / Cool smell in a wood." Such love is expectant, exciting, and encouraging.

The final stanza tells us of sacrificial, selfless, unconditional love; it is a hard love born of total giving, what he calls *agape* in *The Four Loves*:

> Love's as hard as nails,
> Love is nails:
> Blunt, thick, hammered through
> The medial nerves of One
> Who, having made us, knew
> The thing He had done,
> Seeing (with all that is)
> Our cross, and His.

The tone of this stanza is unexpected, and the abrupt shift to the cross and Christ's suffering catches us by surprise; we can feel the pounding of the hammer and the nails piercing flesh. At the same time, this refocus is entirely appropriate and raises the poem from being just another poem about human love to a moving testimony about the depth and breath of divine love. In order to secure man for Himself, God, who spans the universe with his outstretched hands, contracts Himself onto the cross and willingly takes our place of suffering. This is certain, costly, and compassionate love. "Love's as Warm as Tears" is without doubt Lewis's finest religious poem.

This survey of Lewis's religious verse shows him moving from the cruel, malicious deity of *SB* to the possessive, jealous Yahweh of *PR* to the sacrificial savior of "Love's as Warm as Tears."[135] In addition, the religious poems reveal Lewis as using poetry to reflect deeply about life in Christ, while avoiding self-conscious navel-gazing or self-righteous posturing. Perhaps most noticeable is the absence of mawkish, maudlin emotion, too often a detrimental characteristic of religious verse. While Lewis's religious poems as a whole are not as effective as those of George Herbert and John Donne—the two poets who combined most winsomely their faith in Christ with their craft as lyric poets—Lewis's religious poetry offers powerful testimony to the role faith and verse played in his imaginative life.

In reviewing Lewis's comical, satirical, contemplative, and religious poems, several points should be noted. First, the poems of the 1930s are split between the theologically introspective pieces of *The Pilgrim's Regress* and eleven others, the majority with literary or environmental themes. Second, Lewis's production of these poems peaked in the 1940s, suggesting this was the decade where he reached his imaginative pinnacle. This is supported when we note this was also the decade when he wrote *The Problem of Pain*, *The Screwtape Letters*,

The Abolition of Man, Perelandra, The Great Divorce, That Hideous Strength, Miracles, and *The Lion, the Witch and the Wardrobe*. Moreover, during this same time period he delivered the BBC radio broadcasts that later resulted in *Mere Christianity*. It is tempting, therefore, to think of Lewis during the 1940s as a literary dynamo. Third, the number of poems he published in the 1950s dropped significantly, ranging from pointed satires, to dark prophecies, to mature musings. While there is no way to determine why he published fewer poems, given the passing of Mrs. Janie Moore and his evergrowing responsibilities, including the start of his friendship with Joy and his shift from Oxford to Cambridge, the simple demands upon his time may have precluded opportunities to work on poems. Fourth, Lewis sometimes used topical poems to retreat into himself in order to counterbalance his much more public appearances in prose, since these were the decades of his prolific production of combative Christian apologetics. Having essentially abandoned narrative verse, Lewis employed these short topical poems to give voice to his muted but never forgotten poetic sensibilities. Finally, Lewis's "public" poetry—poems that are primarily comic and satiric—is often witty, combative, percussive, shrill, and/or rhetorical. When he turns to social commentary, he is critical of the contemporary, favoring traditional core values and "stock responses." On the other hand, his "private" poetry—poems that are contemplative and religious—is personal, subjective, reflective, and vulnerable. As he considers issues central to the human condition, he engages in analysis and frequently is tentative, open-ended, searching, and questioning. Throughout all, Lewis employed the topical poems to give voice to his muted but never abandoned poetic sensibilities.

NOTES

1. *Poems*, ed. Walter Hooper (New York: Harcourt Brace Jovanovich, 1964); *The Collected Poems of C. S. Lewis*, ed. Walter Hooper (London: Fount, 1994); hereafter *Collected Poems*.

2. For a complete discussion of Lewis's topical poems, see *C. S. Lewis, Poet: The Legacy of His Poetic Impulse* (Kent, OH: Kent State University Press, 2001), chapters 6–8, 169–223.

3. Lewis often linked comic and satiric poems. For example, in his *English Literature in the Sixteenth Century* (Oxford: Oxford University Press, 1944) he writes that "a third group of [William Dunbar's] poems is comic; if you will, satiric, though 'abusive' would be a better word" (p. 93).

4. *The Oxford Magazine* 52 (November 30, 1933), 298 (with Owen Barfield).

5. *The Atlantic Monthly* 172 (November 1943), 113, 115. Reprinted in *Collected Poems*.

6. Lewis may be imitating songs of W. S. Gilbert in his poem. For instance, his use of internal rhyme and meter (loosely) is akin to Little Buttercup's opening aria in *H. M. S. Pinafore or The Lass that Loved a Sailor*: "I've snuff and tobaccy and excellent jacky, / I've scissors, and watches, and knives; / I've ribbons and laces to set off the faces / Of pretty young sweethearts and wives." Compare to the opening of "Awake, My Lute": "I stood in the gloom of a spacious room / Where I listened for hours (on and off) / To a terrible bore with a beard like a snore / And a heavy rectangular cough."

7. See *The Complete Works of Lewis Carroll* (New York: The Modern Library, n. d.), 920–921.

8. Ibid., 901.

9. *Punch* 225 (November 4, 1953), 553 (Nat Whilk). Revised and reprinted in *Poems* and *Collected Poems* as Part 2 of "Narnian Suite." No less than four different versions of this poem exist in holograph indicating either Lewis's enjoyment of the sounds he fashions for the poem or his frustrations in trying to get the right combination of sounds.

10. However, in the satiric poems the percussive tone that comes across is brittle, pedantic, querulous, combative, or acidic. I am indebted to James Prothero for the term percussive.

11. *Poems*, 31; reprinted in *Collected Poems*. A holograph of this poem is available in the Bodleian Library. Interestingly, another holograph, "A Wedding Has Been Arranged," is a slightly different version of "The Small Man Orders His Wedding." Still another version is in the Bodleian, MS. Eng. C. 2724, fol. 55; it has the title "An Epithalamium for John Wain feigned to be spoken in his person giving orders for his wedding" signed C. S. L., June 1947. There also appear to be fragments of early drafts of this version of the poem.

12. *The Oxford Magazine* 55 (May 6, 1937), 565 (N. W.). Reprinted in *Poems* and *Collected Poems*.

13. *Punch* 225 (July 15, 1953), 91 (N. W.). He uses the Sapphic stanza here. Reprinted in *Poems* and *Collected Poems*. In the essay "On Three Ways of Writing for Children," reprinted in *Of Other Worlds: Essays & Stories* (New York: Harcourt Brace Jovanovich, 1966), Lewis defends his "Peter Pantheism" from similarly scornful critics (see below).

14. Lewis takes up the same issue in his essay "On Three Ways of Writing for Children" where he defends his love of fairy tale:

> Now the modern critical world uses "adult" as a term of approval. It is hostile to what it calls "nostalgia" and contemptuous of what it calls "Peter Pantheism." Hence a man who admits that dwarfs and giants and talking beasts and witches are still dear to him in his fifty-third year is now less likely to be praised for his perennial youth than scorned and pitied for arrested development. If I spend some little time defending myself against these charges, this is not so much because it matters greatly whether I am scorned and pitied as because

the defence is germane to my whole view of the fairy tale and even of literature in general. (In *Of Other Worlds*, p. 25)

15. *The Magazine of Fantasy and Science Fiction* 16(6) (June 1959), 47. Reprinted in *Poems* and *Collected Poems*.

16. *Of Other Worlds*, 61–62. For more on this, see in the same volume "On Stories" as well as the complete text of "On Science Fiction."

17. *The Cambridge Review* 79 (November 30, 1957), 227 (N. W.). Reprinted in *Poems* and *Collected Poems*. Some have suggested Joy Davidman assisted Lewis in composing this poem and that they sang it as a parody of *Joyful, Joyful We Adore Thee* or *Lead Us, Heavenly Father, Lead Us*.

18. *Nine: A Magazine of Poetry and Criticism* 2 (May 1950), 114. Revised (a second stanza is added) and reprinted in *Poems* and *Collected Poems*.

19. *The Month* 11 (May 1954), 272. Revised and reprinted in *Poems* and *Collected Poems*.

20. Lewis himself fell under the gaze of such tabloids when a woman claimed Lewis was going to marry her. See Walter Hooper, *C. S. Lewis: A Companion and Guide* (London: HarperCollins, 1996), 55–65.

21. In the essay "Religion and Rocketry" Lewis puts it this way:

We know what our race does to strangers. Man destroys or enslaves every species he can. Civilized man murders, enslaves, cheats, and corrupts savage man. Even inanimate nature he turns into dust bowls and slag-heaps. There are individuals who don't. But they are not the sort who are likely to be our pioneers in space. Our ambassador to new worlds will be the needy and greedy adventurer or the ruthless technical expert. They will do as their kind has always done. What that will be if they meet things weaker than themselves, the black man and the red man can tell. (From *The World's Last Night and Other Essays* [New York: Harcourt Brace Jovanovich, 1952], 89)

22. *Poems*, 60; reprinted in *Collected Poems*.

23. *Punch* 227 (December 1, 1954), 685 (N. W.). The title means "Spartan having obtained." Revised and retitled "A Confession" in *Poems* and *Collected Poems*.

24. *The Spectator* 181 (July 30, 1948), 142. Revised and retitled "Epigrams and Epitaphs, No. 14" in *Poems* and *Collected Poems*.

25. Of course a literal reading gives it that democracy is the tyranny of majority rule that will not permit the radio to be turned off.

26. *Collected Poems*, 249.

27. Vortigen, also spelled Wyrtgeorn (fl. 425–450), was king of the Britons at the time of the arrival of the Saxons. "He accepted the assistance of the Saxons in order to protect his kingdom against the Picts and Scots, granting them land as compensation. Later the Britons made war on the Saxons in their Kentish strongholds. After the death in battle of Vortemir, Vortigern's son, against the Saxons, the *Historia Brittonum*

records the massacre of the British nobles, and Vortigern's subsequent grant of Essex and Sussex to the invaders." Except for this poem, Lewis does not write much poetry about World War II. In part this is because he was neither in active service nor on the battlefield; in part because he was older, more mature, and no longer angry with God; and in part because he used prose primarily to deal with the war, especially *The Screwtape Letters* and his essay "Learning In War-time."

28. *Collected Poems*, 250–252. A holograph of this poem exists and may be viewed in the Bodleian Library. London has a Finchley Lane, Finchley Court, Finchley Park, Finchley Place, Finchley Road, and a Finchley Way, but it does not have a Finchley Avenue. Kathryn Lindskoog has questioned the legitimacy of "Finchley Avenue," first published in *Occasional Poets: An Anthology* (1986) and subsequently published in *Collected Poems*; see her *The Lewis Legacy* 65 (Summer 1995).

29. This recalls a passage from C. S. Lewis's *Surprised by Joy: The Shape of My Early Life* (New York: Harcourt, 1955): "The New House [Little Lea] is almost a major character in my story. I am a product of long corridors, empty sunlit rooms, upstairs indoor silences, attics explored in solitude, distant noises of gurgling cisterns and pipes, and the noise of wind under the tiles" (p. 10).

30. In *Surprised by Joy* Lewis writes: "One dominant factor in our life [Lewis and Warren] at home was the daily absence of our father from about nine in the morning till six at night. . . . From the very first we built up for ourselves a life that excluded him" (pp. 40, 119).

31. *The Oxford Magazine* 56 (February 10, 1938), 383 (N. W.). Reprinted in *Poems* and *Collected Poems*.

32. Besides the inverted biblical allusion seen in "trees as men walking," this phrase may anticipate Tolkien's Ents.

33. *Punch* 221 (September 12, 1951), 303 (N. W.). Reprinted in *Poems* and *Collected Poems*. He uses the Asclepiadean stanza here.

34. In this regard the poem links to *The Abolition of Man* (London: Oxford University Press, 1943) since it is not just the loss of the meaning of language that concerns Lewis; he is as concerned with the loss of objective truth that follows the destruction of language: "You can hardly open a periodical without coming across the statement that what our civilization needs is more 'drive,' or dynamism, or self-sacrifice, or 'creativity.' In a sort of ghastly simplicity we remove the organ and demand the function. We make men without chests and expect of them virtue and enterprise. We laugh at honour and are shocked to find traitors in our midst. We castrate and bid the geldings to be fruitful" (p. 35).

35. *Fifty-Two: A Journal of Books and Authors* 14 (Autumn 1964), 4. Reprinted in *Poems* and *Collected Poems*.

36. "*De Descriptione Temporum*" is reprinted in *Selected Literary Essays* (Cambridge: Cambridge University Press, 1969).

37. Lewis's "timeless rays" may be thought of as objective truths reflected in the "dew drop" of the present moment.

38. *Poems*, 114–115; reprinted in *Collected Poems*.

39. The poem recalls passages from *Spirits in Bondage*.

40. The language in the poem anticipates the more belligerent attitude of the dwarves in *The Last Battle* (London: Bodley Head, 1956) who refuse to believe they are enjoying a feast in the stable in celebration of Aslan's return. Refusing to "be taken in," they taste hay, turnips, old cabbage leaves, and trough water instead of pies, pigeons, ices, and rich wine. They insist at the end: "We haven't let anyone take us in. The Dwarfs are for the Dwarfs." Aslan notes, "they have chosen cunning instead of belief. Their prison is only in their own minds, yet they are in that prison; and so afraid of being taken in that they cannot be taken out" (p. 148). At least initially the persona in the poem has the same reluctance to enter into joy; he does not want to be "taken in" yet again.

41. Also helpful regarding the theme and language of this poem is Stephen Metcalf, "Language and Self-Consciousness: The Making and Breaking of C. S. Lewis's Personae," in *Word and Story in C. S. Lewis*, ed. Peter J. Schakel and Charles A. Huttar (Columbia, MO: University of Missouri Press, 1991), 109–144.

42. *Punch* 217 (August 17, 1949), 170 (Nat Whilk). Revised and reprinted in *Poems* and *Collected Poems*.

43. The sentiment expressed here links the poem to Lewis's earlier "Joy." See "Early Lyric Poetry: *Spirits in Bondage* (1919) and 'Joy' (1924)."

44. Lewis, *Surprised by Joy*, 168–169.

45. All the poems in this volume are published anonymously; however, six copies contain an additional leaf giving the names of the authors of the poems; one of these is in the Bodleian Library, Oxford.

46. *Fear No More: A Book of Poems for the Present Time by Living English Poets* (Cambridge: Cambridge University Press, 1940), 4. Reprinted in *Collected Poems*.

47. *The Month* 7 (May 1952), 275. Reprinted in *Poems* and *Collected Poems*.

48. What does the map represent? His settled way of seeing the world, one characterized by "stock responses" and tradition? His spiritual convictions? Biblical texts? While we cannot be certain what the map represents, the significant point is that he momentarily questioned its validity. Such contemplation may be seen by some as disturbing; nonetheless, the poem reveals one who was always thinking, reflecting, and musing.

49. *The Spectator* 174 (June 8, 1945), 521. See erratum: "Poet and Printer," ibid. (June 15, 1945), 550. Reprinted in *Poems* and *Collected Poems*.

50. Of course the salamander could be the butt of Lewis' satire if Lewis is subtly glossing the poem to Plato's myth of the cave from Book VII of *The Republic*.

51. His genetic propensity toward pessimism and the general gloom and darkness of the world because of the competing philosophies of World War II—nazism, communism, socialism, totalitarianism, capitalism, and so on—may have had a grip upon Lewis at this time.

52. *Poems*, 73–76; reprinted in *Collected Poems*. In *DSCL* Walter Hooper says: "The first version of this sonnet sequence survives in the same notebook as the last portion of the Diary. A revised version of it, entitled 'Infatuation,' is found in Lewis's *Poems*" (p. 403). If accurate, this means Lewis first worked on the poem in 1926.

53. See Shakespeare's sonnets "129," "138," and "147."

54. Lewis also uses the idea of Venus infernal in Letter XX of *The Screwtape Letters*.

55. *Poems*, 81; reprinted in *Collected Poems*.

56. Kathryn Lindskoog's fascination with this poem turns on her seeing in Lewis's use of reason and imagination in the poem a confirmation the right brain/left brain polarity. She brings in references to *Till We Have Faces* and *The Pilgrim's Regress* as well as allusions to right brain/left brain authorities to bolster her contention. See her "Getting It Together: Lewis and the Two Hemispheres of Knowing." *Journal of Psychology and Theology* 3 (Fall 1975), 290–293. Reprinted in *Mythlore* 6 (Winter 1979), 43–45. Also revised and published as "Appendix Two" in *Finding the Landlord* (Chicago, IL: Cornerstone Press, 1995*)*. A very fine discussion of the poem may be found in Peter Schakel, *Reason and Imagination in C. S. Lewis: A Study of Till We Have Faces* (Grand Rapids, MI: Eerdmans, 1984), ix and 179–188.

57. *Britain Today* 112 (August 1945), 14. Revised and retitled "To Charles Williams" in *Poems* and *Collected Poems*. Williams died May 15, 1945.

58. *Poems*, 83; reprinted in *Collected Poems*.

59. Joe Christopher offers criticism of these poems assuming Lewis was writing about Joy Davidman. See his "C. S. Lewis, Love Poet." *Studies in the Literary Imagination* 22 (Fall 1989), 161–173, and "C. S. Lewis's Poems to Joy Davidman." *The Canadian C. S. Lewis Journal* 94 (Autumn 1998), 20–37.

60. *Poems*, 108; reprinted in *Collected Poems*.

61. I am indebted to Dabney Hart for her helpful insight on this point.

62. *Poems*, 109; reprinted in *Collected Poems*.

63. *Poems*, 109–110; reprinted in *Collected Poems*.

64. Joe Christopher argues similarly in his essay "C. S. Lewis, Love Poet." He says "Joys That Sting," "Old Poets Remembered," and "As the Ruin Falls" are sonnets probably written to Joy Davidman: "In all of them the woman addressed is dying: they could have been written during Davidman's first bout with cancer, but—since Lewis only began to know he loved her during that time—the probability is stronger for the second and final bout with cancer" (pp. 167–168). His analyses of these poems are more prosaic than enlightening, though he is right when he says these are among "Lewis's best verse, clever, polished, and . . . highly successful" (p. 173).

65. Given the popularity of *The Problem of Pain*, *Miracles*, and *Mere Christianity*, attention should be given to his religious verse since many offer commentary on his prose apologetics as well as powerful insights into his maturation in Christ.

66. Lewis, *The Pilgrim's Regress* (London: Geoffrey Bles, 1933).

67. Lewis, *Surprised by Joy*, 228–229.

68. In the "Introduction" to *Collected Poems* Hooper notes a number of these poems may have existed in early variants: "Fourteen of [his] religious lyrics were sent to Owen Barfield during the summer of 1930 under the general title 'Half Hours with Hamilton,' and they are some of the most beautiful poems Lewis wrote. Most of these same poems were to appear a couple of years later in his semiautobiographical *The Pilgrim's Regress* (1933). They were always Lewis's favourites of his own poems" (p. xv). "Half Hours with Hamilton" in holograph is available at the Wade Center.

69. In *Poems* Hooper titles this "Footnote to All Prayers" (p. 129).

70. Must reading in connection with *Pilgrim's Regress* is Kathryn Lindskoog's *Finding the Landlord*. Because my focus is upon the poetry of *Pilgrim's Regress*, I will discuss the poems in isolation from the prose text of *Pilgrim's Regress*. However, I will offer commentary about the context of the poem's placement in *Pilgrim's Regress* in the accompanying notes.

71. In *Poems* this is "Caught" (pp. 115–116). The poem is found in *Pilgrim's Regress*, Book 8, chapter 6 entitled "Caught."

> John, having thought he had escaped from the Landlord, suddenly awakened to the fact that there was nowhere to escape him: "In one night the Landlord—call him by what name you would—had come back to the world, and filled the world, quite full without a cranny. His eyes stared and His hand pointed and His voice commanded in everything that could be heard or seen . . . All things said one word: CAUGHT—caught into slavery again, to walk warily and on sufferance all his days, never to be alone; never the master of his own soul, to have no privacy, no corner whereof you could say to the whole universe: This is my own, here I can do as I please." (p. 147)

72. In *Poems* this is "The Naked Seed" (p. 117). The poem is found in *Pilgrim's Regress*, Book 8, chapter 10, entitled "Archetype and Ectype." John and the hermit (History) discuss John's fear that "the things the Landlord really intends for me may be utterly unlike the things he has taught me to desire." The hermit assures him that the Landlord is the author of desire and that only He can fulfill John's desire. Furthermore, the hermit affirms that John's loss of his initial desire is normal: "First comes delight: then pain: then fruit. And then there is joy of the fruit, but that is different again from the first delight. And mortal lovers must not try to remain at the first step: for lasting passion is the dream of a harlot and from it we wake in despair. You must not try to keep the raptures: they have done their work. Manna kept, is worms" (p. 162). The hermit sings the poem and is overheard by John.

73. From *The English Poems of George Herbert*, ed. C. A. Patrides (London: Dent, 1974), 127.

74. In *Poems* this is "Wormwood" (p. 87). The poem is found in *Pilgrim's Regress*, Book 10, chapter 1 entitled "The Same Yet Different." John and Vertue are off on their regress, for John the start of his life in Christ. John complains that "Mother Kirk [the church] treats us very ill. Since we have followed her and eaten her food the way

seems twice as narrow and twice as dangerous as it did before" (p. 177). Vertue sings the poem as John and he start their journey.

75. In *Poems* this is "Divine Justice" (p. 98). The poem is found in *Pilgrim's Regress*, Book 10, chapter 3 entitled "Limbo." John learns from his Guide (Slikistein-sauga) that human wisdom is not adequate to know the Landlord. Sadly, those who rely upon wisdom cut themselves off from hope and God's mercy: "The Landlord does not condemn them to lack of hope: they have done that themselves. The Landlord's interference is all on the other side. Left to itself, the desire without the hope would soon fall back to spurious satisfactions, and these souls would follow it of their own free will into far darker regions at the very bottom of the black hole [hell]. What the Landlord has done is to fix it forever: and by his art, though unfulfilled, it is uncorrupted" (pp. 179–180). The Guide then sings the poem to John. For more on the triolet, see Joe R. Christopher, "A Theological Triolet," *Bulletin of the New York C. S. Lewis Society* 2 (September 1971), 4–5.

76. In *The Great Divorce* (New York: Macmillan, 1946) George MacDonald puts it differently: "There are only two kinds of people in the end: those who say to God, 'Thy will be done,' and those to whom God says, in the end, '*Thy* will be done.' All that are in Hell, choose it. Without that self-choice there could be no Hell" (p. 72).

77. In *Poems* this is "Nearly They Stood" (102–103). The poem is found in *Pilgrim's Regress*, Book 10, chapter 4 entitled "The Black Hole." John questions the goodness of the Landlord for having created the black hole. The Guide counters with the argument that the Landlord created humans with a free will able to make free choices. If they end up in the black hole, it is because that is where they want to be. Returning to his argument of the previous chapter, the Guide underscores that the black hole is actually merciful since it limits the sufferings of those who choose to be there: "A black hole is blackness enclosed, limited . . . But evil of itself would never reach a worst: for evil is fissiparous and could never in a thousand eternities find any way to arrest its own reproduction . . . The walls of the black hole are the tourniquet on the wound through which the lost soul else would bleed to a death she never reached. It is the Landlord's last service to those who will let him do nothing better for them" (p. 181). The Guide then sings the poem to John. Lewis's three eight-line stanzas follow a set pattern of six lines of trimeter, one line of pentameter, and one line of dimeter with a rhyme scheme of *ababcdcd*.

78. John Milton, *Paradise Lost*, 4:58–67.

79. Spiritual pride is also a central theme in his fiction.

80. In *Poems* this is "Virtue's Independence" (p. 88). The poem is found in *Pilgrim's Regress*, Book 10, chapter 5 entitled "Superbia." As John and Vertue continue their regress, they come upon a gaunt woman who was "scrabbling and puddering to and fro on what appeared to be a mirror; but it was only the rock itself scraped clean of every speck of dust and fibre of lichen and polished by the continued activity of this famished creature" (p. 182). The Guide tells them she is one of the Enemy's [Satan's] daughters. As they pass she "croaks out" the poem.

81. In *Poems* this is "Posturing" (p. 89). Also in "Superbia" Vertue sings this song after the Guide warns him and John about the dangers of self-sufficiency. Lewis's *ababcc* rhyme scheme (the last stanza adds *cc*) recalls the rhyme scheme of Wordsworth's "I Wandered Lonely as a Cloud."

82. This recalls an incident Lewis recounts in a letter to Greeves:

> What worreys [sic] me much more is *Pride* [Lewis's emphasis]—my besetting sin . . . During my afternoon "meditations" . . . I have found out ludicrous and terrible things about my own character. Sitting by, watching the rising thoughts to break their necks as they pop up, one learns to know the sort of thoughts that do come. And, will you believe it, one out of every three is a thought of self-admiration: when everything else fails, having had its neck broken, up comes the thought "What an admirable fellow I am to have broken their necks!" I catch myself posturing before the mirror, so to speak, all day long. (*They Stand Together: The Letters of C. S. Lewis to Arthur Greeves [1914–1963]*, ed. Walter Hooper [New York: Macmillan, 1979], 339 [hereafter *TST*]; January 30, 1930)

83. *The English Poems of George Herbert*, 140.

84. In *Poems* this is "Deception" (p. 90). The poem is found in *Pilgrim's Regress*, Book 10, chapter 6 entitled "Ignorantia." The Guide tells John and Vertue that the shift to a machine age is cutting people off from a knowledge of the truth: "Their labour-saving devices multiply drudgery; their aphrodisiacs make them impotent: their amusements bore them: their rapid production of food leaves half of them starving, and their devices for saving time have banished leisure from their country (p. 187). He then sings this poem. Lewis experiments with the unusual rhyme scheme of *abbbbbcd* in the three stanzas.

85. One wonders what Lewis would have said about the popular TV "talk-shows" of today. Also see his "*Odora Canum Vis*: A Defence of Certain Modern Biographers and Critics" discussed later in this chapter.

86. Appropriately both poems appear in the chapter entitled "Luxuria."

87. In *Poems* this is "Forbidden Pleasure" (p. 116). The poem is found in *Pilgrim's Regress*, Book 10, chapter 7 entitled "Luxuria." John notices on the side of the road men who "seemed to be suffering from some disease of a crumbling and disintegrating kind" (p. 188). As he looks closer, he sees tumors detach themselves from the bodies and turn into writhing reptiles. In a passage that merges elements of Cantos XXV and XXIX of Dante's *Inferno*, Lewis takes John through Luxuria, "a very dangerous place." He sees a witch (sexual indulgence) holding out a cup to the sufferers. In particular he sees a young man, who though like the others is diseased, "he was still a well-looking person. And as the witch came to him the hands shot out to the cup, and the man drew them back again: and the hands went crawling out for the cup a second time, and again the man wrenched them back, and turned his face away" (p. 189). The young man then cries out the poem.

88. The request here that God break in to override human will is similar to that of "He Whom I Bow To" and "Legion."

89. *The Complete Poetry of John Donne*, ed. John T. Shawcross (Garden City, NY: Anchor, 1967), 344.

90. In *Poems* this is "Lilith" (p. 95). An earlier version of this poem appears in *TST*, 353–354 (letter of April 29, 1930). This poem is also in "Luxuria." After John sees the young man sink into a horrible swamp, the witch approaches him with this temptation: "I will not deceive you . . . You see there is no pretence. I am not trying to make you believe that this cup will take you to your Island [the good that John has always desired—heaven]. I am not saying it will quench your thirst for long. But taste it, none the less, for you are very thirsty" (pp. 189–190). John continues his walk without acknowledging her. She tries two more times to tempt him, appealing primarily to the immediate satisfaction he will receive by succumbing to her offer, but he continues on, never even speaking to her. The temptation she offers him is very real, but he uses the poem he speaks to help put her temptation out of his mind. Lewis uses a variation on rhyme royal; instead of the traditional *ababbcc*, he uses *ababccb*.

91. In *Poems* this is "The Dragon Speaks" (pp. 92–93). The poem is found in *Pilgrim's Regress*, Book. 10, chapter 8 entitled "The Northern Dragon." John journeys to face the northern dragon (avarice, hardness, and coldness), but before he confronts him, John hears the dragon sing this poem. After hearing the poem, John almost feels pity for the dragon, but he recovers his senses and manages to slay the dragon after he is attacked.

92. Lewis explores this again in *The Voyage of the Dawn Treader* in the person of Eustace Clarence Scrubb.

93. The dragon (a symbol of evil here) is overcome by the warrior (the faithful believer) who exercises his prowess (God's blessing).

94. In *Poems* this is "Dragon-Slayer" (p. 94). The poem is found in *Pilgrim's Regress*, Book 10, chapter 9 entitled "The Southern Dragon." Vertue returns from his victory with the southern dragon (unrestrained emotion) and appears dazzling: "At first they thought that is was the sun upon his arms that made Vertue flash like flame as he came leaping, running, and dancing towards them. But as he drew nearer they saw that he was veritably on fire. Smoke came from him, and where his feet slipped into the bog holes there were little puffs of steam. Hurtless flames ran up and down his sword and licked over his hand. His breast heaved and he reeled like a drunk man" (p. 195). Delighting in his newfound passion, Vertue shouts out this poem as John and the Guide draw near to him.

95. Leviathan and Behemoth allude to legendary creatures of enormous size as found in Job 3:8 and 40:15.

96. RESVRGAM is "I shall rise again" and IO PAEAN is the cry of praise a Greek warrior would have made celebrating his victory over a foe.

97. Although there is always the temptation to reserve for self some of the glory that should rightly go to God, this poem intimates the warrior here

manages to delight in a job well done without subsuming to the pull of vainglory.

98. In *Poems* this is "When the Curtain's Down" (p. 97). The poem is found in *Pilgrim's Regress*, Book 10, chapter 10 entitled "The Brook." John and Vertue are now back in Puritania approaching the final stream (death). Vertue speaks this poem as evidence of his newly acquired passion, and he reflects that death is no longer a thing to fear.

99. Consider: "Where can I go from your Spirit? Where can I flee from your presence? If I go up to the heavens, you are there; if I make my bed in the depths, you are there. If I rise on the wings of the dawn, if I settle on the far side of the sea, even there your hand will guide me, your right hand will hold me fast. If I say, 'Surely the darkness will hide me and the light become night around me,' even the darkness will not be dark to you; the night will shine like the day, for darkness is as light to you" (Ps 139: 7–12).

100. In *Poems* this is "Scazons" (p. 118). The melancholic theme of this poem links it to both "Angel's Song" and "Lines Written in a Copy of Milton's Works." The poem is also in "The Brook." John reflects briefly on the Landlord's wisdom in creating humans with the capacities to love people and places before speaking this poem.

101. In *Poems* this is "Angel's Song" (p. 107). The poem is also in "The Brook" and ends *Pilgrim's Regress*. John and Vertue pass over the brook and the voice of the Guide is heard singing this poem.

102. Lewis's debt to Milton is evident in this poem as it recalls Adam's speech to Raphael in Book VIII of *Paradise Lost* where he thanks the angel for counseling him to be "lowly wise" regarding the ways of God:

> How fully hast thou satisfi'd me, pure
> Intelligence of Heav'n, Angel serene,
> And freed from intricacies, taught to live
> The easiest way, nor with perplexing thoughts
> To interrupt the sweet of Life, from which
> God hath bid dwell far off all anxious cares,
> And not molest us, unless we ourselves
> Seek them with wand'ring thoughts, and notions vain (pp. 180–187).

103. The independent "life" of the poems is clearly established by many having originally been a part of Lewis's "Half Hours with Hamilton" written in 1930, three years before the publication of *Pilgrim's Regress*.

104. For more on the relationship between the poems and the text of *Pilgrim's Regress* see Kathryn Lindskoog's *Finding the Landlord*.

105. See *The Atlantic Monthly* 203 (January 1959): 59–61. Reprinted in *The World's Last Night* (New York: Harcourt, Brace & Co., 1960).

106. *The Oxford Magazine* 54 (May 14, 1936), 575 (N. W.). Reprinted in *Poems*.

107. *The Month* 13 (April 1955): 210. Revised and reprinted in *Poems*. The desperate tone of the speaker in this sonnet recalls many of Donne's "Holy Sonnets."

108. First published in *Letters to Malcolm: Chiefly on Prayer*. (London: Geoffrey Bles, 1964), 67–68. Revised and retitled "Prayer" in *Poems*.

109. In *Letters to Malcolm* offers the following: "*Dream* makes it too like Pantheism and was perhaps dragged in for the rhyme. But is he not right in thinking that prayer in its most perfect state is a soliloquy? If the Holy Spirit speaks in the man, then in prayer God speaks to God" (p. 68).

110. For this reason it is an interesting gloss on *Surprised by Joy*. It is in *Poems*, 124–125.

111. *The Month* 2 (July 1949): 8. Retitled "Epigrams and Epitaphs, No. 17" in *Poems* and *Collected Poems*. Lewis later reworked this epitaph at Joy's request and used the revision as the epitaph marking her memorial at the Oxford Crematorium in "Epitaph for Helen Joy Davidman." Hooper publishes this in *Collected Poems*, 252. In the "Introduction" to *Collected Poems* Hooper explains how these variations came about:

> Sometimes [sic] before his marriage Lewis wrote two versions of an "Epitaph." The one he planned to use in *Young King Cole* appears as Epitaph 17 . . . When Joy read this poem she knew she was dying and she asked that it be used as her epitaph. In July 1963 Lewis revised the epitaph with her in mind and arranged for it to be cut into marble and placed in the Oxford Crematorium. (p. xviii)

112. This opening may owe something to the microcosm/macrocosm we find in Donne's "A Valediction: Of Weeping": "Let me pour forth / My tears before thy face whilst I stay here, / For thy face coins them, and thy stamp they bear, / And by this mintage they are something worth, / For thus they be / Pregnant of thee."

113. For more on this see Joe R. Christopher's "C. S. Lewis, Love Poet."

114. *Poems*, 129. Joe R. Christopher in "An Analysis of 'The Apologist's Evening Prayer.'" *Bulletin of the New York C. S. Lewis Society* 5 (October 1974), 2–4, looks at how the tone of this poem "is much like Donne" (p. 2). He notes similarities in the use of pronouns (for example, "Thou"), parallelism of the "From all" phrase, and the balanced, antithetical phrasing. Christopher sidesteps the question of whose poetry is best and ends with "we are left with a simpler-than-Donne poem in Donne's tradition" (p. 4).

115. The biblical narrative is found in Genesis 6–9.

116. *Punch* 215 (August 11, 1948): 124 (N. W.). Revised and retitled "The Late Passenger" in *Poems* and *Collected Poems*.

117. Lewis's portrayal of Ham supports the biblical narrative. For instance, in Genesis 9:20–27, Ham brings shame upon his father by viewing the nakedness of his drunken father and then telling his brothers about it. After Shem and Japheth take discreet measures to cover their father's nakedness and Noah awakens to discover

what has happened, he blesses the older two but curses Ham: "Cursed by Canaan [Ham]; / A servant of servants / He shall be to his brothers."

118. *Poems*, 125; reprinted in *Collected Poems*. For an account of Stephen's martyrdom, see Acts 6: 8–8: 1. Lewis treats the same subject in *A Grief Observed*, 34.

119. *Punch* 210 (May 8, 1946), 402 (N. W.). Revised and reprinted in *Poems* and *Collected Poems*.

120. Lewis writes to Ruth Pitter about this humor: "The bathos about angels having no nose etc. was intended: I wanted a serio-comic effect" (*Collected Letters of C. S. Lewis, volume 2*, ed. Walter Hooper. [London: Harper Collins, 2004], 736, August 10, 1946).

121. *Perelandra* (New York: Macmillan, 1944), 17, 18.

122. *Punch* (Almack) 215 (November 1, 1948), n.p. (N. W.). Revised and reprinted in *Poems* and *Collected Poems*.

123. Among the many similarities the two poems share include beginning with a frozen landscape, use of pagan and Christian imagery, the reviving power of music, the symbolic rebirth of the world at Christ's birth, similar lines (Milton's "The Oracles are dumb" becomes Lewis's "That oracle was dumb"), and ending focusing upon the poignancy of Christ in the manger.

124. This is akin to Father Christmas's influence on the winter of Narnia in *The Lion, the Witch and the Wardrobe*.

125. *Poems*, 122; reprinted in *Collected Poems*.

126. Ibid., 114.

127. The passage continues: "'And I will be gracious to whom I will be gracious, and will show compassion on whom I will show compassion.' But He said, 'You cannot see My face, for no man can see Me and live!' Then the Lord said, 'Behold, there is a place by Me, and you shall stand there on the rock; and it will come about, while My glory is passing by, that I will put you in the cleft of the rock and cover you with My hand until I have passed by. Then I will take My hand away and you shall see My back, but My face shall not be seen'" (Ex. 33:19b-23, NAS).

128. Lewis, *That Hideous Strength*. 323

129. *Poems*, 91–92; reprinted in *Collected Poems*.

130. The best study of the seven deadly sins is found in Morton W. Bloomfield's *The Seven Deadly Sins: An Introduction to the History of a Religious Concept, with Special Reference to Medieval English Literature* Ann Arbor, MI: Michigan State University, 1952, reprint, 1967).

131. C. S. Lewis, *The Allegory of Love: A Study in Medieval Tradition* (London: Oxford University Press, 1936), 159–160.

132. There has also been work on the possible relationship between Lewis's seven Narnia tales and the seven deadly sins. See my "Narnia and the Seven Deadly Sins," *Mythlore* 10 (Spring 1984), 14–19.

133. William Langland, *Piers Plowman: A New Translation of the B-Text*. Trans. A. V. C. Schmidt (Oxford: Oxford University Press, 1992).

134. *Poems*, 122–123.

135. Lewis apparently invested more time in refining his religious poems than others. In a letter to Greeves dated August 28, 1930, less than a year before his conversion to Christianity, he wrote: "It is a very remarkable thing that in the few religious lyrics which I have written during the last year, in which I had no idea of publication & at first very little idea even of showing them to friends, I have found myself impelled to take infinitely more pains, less ready to be contented with the fairly good and more determined to reach the best attainable, than ever I was in the days when I never wrote without the ardent hope of successful publication" (*TST,* 385). In the "Introduction" to *Collected Poems* Hooper adds Lewis did not revise his prose very much, but his poems "went through endless revisions, the best examples of which are the religious lyrics of 1930, which he was still revising up to the time he died" (p. xvi).

BIBLIOGRAPHY

Christopher, Joe R. "An Analysis of 'The Apologist's Evening Prayer.'" *Bulletin of the New York C. S. Lewis Society* 5 (October 1974): 2–4.

———. "An Analysis of 'Old Poets Remembered.'" *The Lamp-Post of the Southern California C. S. Lewis Society* 19 (Fall 1995): 16–18.

———. "C. S. Lewis' Lingusitic [sic] Myth." *Mythlore* 21 (Summer 1995): 41–50.

———. "C. S. Lewis, Love Poet." *Studies in the Literary Imagination* 22 (Fall 1989): 161–173.

———. "C. S. Lewis's Poems to Joy Davidman." *The Canadian C. S. Lewis Journal* 94 (Autumn 1998): 20–37.

———. "A Theological Triolet." *Bulletin of the New York C. S. Lewis Society* 2 (September 1971): 4–5.

Fear No More: A Book of Poems for the Present Time by Living English Poets. Cambridge: Cambridge University Press, 1940.

Hardie, A. M. and K. C. Douglas. *Augury: An Oxford Miscellany of Verse and Poetry*. Oxford: Blackwell, 1940.

Howard, Tom. "*Poems*: A Review." *Christianity Today* 9 (June 18, 1965): 30.

Huttar, Charles. "A Lifelong Love Affair with Language: C. S. Lewis's Poetry." In *Word and Story in C. S. Lewis*. Edited by Peter Schakel and Charles Huttar. Columbia, MO: University of Missouri Press, 1991, 86–108.

Kawano, Roland. "C. S. Lewis's Early Poems." *The Living Church* 186 (February 13, 1983): 9–10.

———. "C. S. Lewis: Public Poet." *Mythlore* 9 (Autumn 1982): 20–21.

King, Don W. "A Bibliographic Review of C. S. Lewis as Poet: 1952–1995, Part One." *The Canadian C. S. Lewis Journal* 91 (Spring 1997): 9–23.

———. "A Bibliographic Review of C. S. Lewis as Poet: 1952–1995, Part Two." *The Canadian C. S. Lewis Journal* 91 (Autumn 1997): 34–56.

————. *C. S. Lewis, Poet: The Legacy of His Poetic Impulse.* Kent, OH: Kent State University Press, 2001.

————. "C. S. Lewis's *Spirits in Bondage*: World I Poet as Frustrated Dualist." *The Christian Scholar's Review* 27 (Summer 1998): 454–474.

————. "C. S. Lewis' 'The Quest of Bleheris' as Prose Poetry." *The Lamp-Post of the Southern California C. S. Lewis Society* 23(1) (Spring 1999): 3–15.

————. "*The Collected Poems of C. S. Lewis*" and "*Poems*." In *The C. S. Lewis Readers' Encyclopedia.* Edited by Jeffrey D. Schultz and John G. West. Grand Rapids, MI: Zondervan, 1998.

————. "The Distant Voice in C. S. Lewis's *Poems*." *Studies in the Literary Imagination* 22 (Fall 1989): 175–184.

————. "Glints of Light: The Unpublished Short Poetry of C. S. Lewis." *SEVEN: An Anglo-American Literary Review* 15 (1998): 73–96.

————. "*A Grief Observed* as Free Verse." *Bulletin of the New York C. S. Lewis Society* 32 (March 2001): 1–7.

————. "The Poetry of Prose: C. S. Lewis, Ruth Pitter, and *Perelandra*." *Christianity and Literature* 49 (Spring 2000): 331–356.

————. "The Religious Verse of C. S. Lewis: Part One." *The Canadian C. S. Lewis Journal* 97 (Spring 2000): 12–27; "Part Two." *The Canadian C. S. Lewis Journal* 98 (Fall 2000): 41–54.

————. "Making the Poor Best of Dull Things: C. S. Lewis as Poet." *SEVEN: An Anglo-American Literary Review* 12 (1995): 79–92.

Kirkpatrick, John. "Fresh Views of Humankind in Lewis's Poems." *Bulletin of the New York C. S. Lewis Society* 10 (September 1979): 1–7.

Landrum, David. "Pindar, Prodigality, and Paganism: Natural Law Ethics in the Poetry of C. S. Lewis." *The Lamp-Post of the Southern California C. S. Lewis Society* 19 (Summer 1995): 4–13.

Lewis, C. S. *The Collected Poems of C. S. Lewis.* Edited by Walter Hooper. London: Fount, 1994.

————. *The Pilgrim's Regress.* London: Geoffrey Bles, 1933.

————. *Poems.* Edited by Walter Hooper. New York: Harcourt Brace Jovanovich, 1964.

————. *Surprised by Joy: The Shape of My Early Life.* New York: Harcourt, 1955.

Lindskoog, Kathryn. *Finding the Landlord: A Guidebook to C. S. Lewis's Pilgrim's Regress.* Chicago, IL: Cornerstone Press, 1995.

————. "Getting It Together: Lewis and the Two Hemispheres of Knowing." *Journal of Psychology and Theology* 3 (Fall 1975): 290–293. Reprinted in *Mythlore* 6 (Winter 1979): 43–45. Also revised and published as "Appendix Two" in *Finding the Landlord.*

Prothero, James. "Lewis's Poetry: A Preliminary Exploration." *Bulletin of the New York C. S. Lewis Society* 25 (March-April 1994): 1–6.

Robson, W. W. "The Poetry of C. S. Lewis." *The Chesterton Review* 17(iii–iv) (August–November, 1991): 437–443. Also see his essay "The Romanticism of C. S Lewis." *Cambridge Quarterly* 1 (Summer 1966): 252–272. Reprinted in W. W. Robson. *Critical Essays*. London: Routledge & Kegan Paul, 1966.

Shaw, Luci. "Looking Back to Eden: The Poetry of C. S. Lewis." *Bulletin of the New York C. S. Lewis Society*. 23 (February 1992): 1–7. Reprinted in *Radix* 21(iii) (1993): 12–15, 30.

Index

About the Editor and Contributors

THE EDITOR

BRUCE L. EDWARDS is Professor of English and Associate Dean for Distance Education and International Programs at Bowling Green State University in Bowling Green, Ohio, where he has been a faculty member and administrator since 1981. He has published several books on Lewis, most recently, *Not a Tame Lion: The Spiritual World of Narnia* (Tyndale, 2005) and *Further Up and Further in: Understanding C. S. Lewis's The Lion, the Witch and the Wardrobe* (Broadman and Holman, 2005). These are volumes in addition to two scholarly works, *A Rhetoric of Reading: C. S. Lewis's Defense of Western Literacy* and *The Taste of the Pineapple: Essays on C. S. Lewis as Reader, Critic, and Imaginative Writer*. For many years he has maintained a popular Web site on the life and works of C. S. Lewis (http://www.pseudobook.com/cslewis). During his academic career he has served as Fulbright Fellow in Nairobi, Kenya (1999–2000), a Bradley Research Fellow at the Heritage Foundation in Washington, DC (1989–1990), and as the S. W. Brooks Memorial Professor of Literature at The University of Queensland, Brisbane, Australia (1988). Edwards is also a Fulbright-Hays Grant Recipient to Tanzania (2005). Bruce and his wife, Joan, live in Bowling Green, Ohio. Edwards is General Editor of this four-volume reference set on C. S. Lewis.

THE CONTRIBUTORS

DEVIN BROWN is Professor of English at Asbury College. He earned his Master's Degree from the University of Florida's creative writing program and his Ph.D. from the University of South Carolina. As a Lilly Scholar, he has presented papers on Lewis and Tolkien at scholarly conferences in the United States as well as in London and Oxford, and has written numerous articles on these two writers for professional journals. His books include *Inside Narnia: A Guide to Exploring The Lion, the Witch and the Wardrobe* (Baker Books, 2005) and *Not Exactly Normal* (Eerdmans Books for Young Readers, 2005). *Not Exactly Normal* was recently put on Bank Street College's list of Best Children's Books of the Year (2006). In 2005, Devin was given the Francis White Ewbank Award for Teaching Excellence, Asbury College's highest honor.

MARGARITA CARRETERO-GONZÁLEZ is Senior Lecturer in English Literature at the English and German Department of the University of Granada (Spain). In 1996, she completed her doctoral thesis on J. R. R. Tolkien's *The Lord of the Rings*. Her current research interests include fantasy, utopia, children's literature, women's fiction, and ecocriticism as a tool for literary analysis, which combine two of her great passions: literature and environmentalism. In 1998 she and her colleague Encarnación Hidalgo-Tenorio, organized an international conference to commemorate the birth centenary of C. S. Lewis. Celebrated in Granada, the conference had Walter Hooper and Colin Duriez as experts on Lewis. A commemorative book anthologizing selected presentations from that conference was published by Peter Lang in January 2001, under the title *Behind the Veil of Familiarity: C. S. Lewis (1898–1998).*

DAVID C. DOWNING is R. W. Schlosser Professor of English at Elizabethtown College in Lancaster County, Pennsylvania. He has written numerous articles on C. S. Lewis, and his *Planets in Peril: A Critical Study of C. S. Lewis's Ransom Trilogy* (University of Massachusetts Press) was named as one of the five best books yet published on Lewis by the "C. S. Lewis and the Inklings Homepage." His *The Most Reluctant Convert: C. S. Lewis's Journey to Faith* was named one of Booklist's Best Religion Books for 2002 and was a 2003 ECPA Gold Medallion finalist. Downing was also awarded the Clyde S. Kilby Research Grant for 2000 by the Marion E. Wade Center in support of his research. His book, *Into the Region of Awe* (Inter Varsity Press) was listed by *Christianity Today* as one of the top ten best new books on C. S. Lewis.

KATHERINE HARPER is a writer and literary scholar based in northeast Ohio. She is a graduate of the College of Wooster and Bowling Green State University and has contributed to seven reference books to date. Her current project is a full-length critical biography of once-prominent American humor writer, Ellis Parker Butler.

MARVIN D. HINTEN is Professor of English at Friends University in Wichita, Kansas. Like C. S. Lewis, his specialization is British Renaissance literature. He earned his Ph.D. from Bowling Green State University (Ohio) in 1993. Hinten is the author of six books and also a contributing editor to *The Lamp-Post*, a C. S. Lewis journal.

DON W. KING has served on the faculty of Montreat College since 1974 in various capacities, including Professor of English, Dean of Arts and Science, and Interim President. He serves as Editor of the *Christian Scholar's Review*, and has published articles in *Books & Culture, The Canadian C. S. Lewis Journal, Christianity and Literature, CSL: The Bulletin of the New York C. S. Lewis Society, Christian Scholar's Review, The Lamp-Post of the Southern California C. S. Lewis Society, Mythlore, SEVEN: An Anglo-American Literary Review*, and *Studies in the Literary Imagination*, and has contributed articles on Lewis's poetry to *The C. S. Lewis Readers' Encyclopedia*. King is also author of *C. S. Lewis, Poet: The Legacy of His Poetic Impulse* (Kent State University Press, 2001). His book-length manuscript on British poet Ruth Pitter, *Hunting the Unicorn: A Critical Biography of Ruth Pitter*, will be published by Kent State University Press in Spring 2008. He is currently researching and writing a manuscript on the life, poetry, fiction, and nonfiction of the wife of C. S. Lewis, Joy Davidman, tentatively entitled *Yet One More Spring: A Critical Study of Joy Davidman Gresham*.

MARTA GARCÍA DE LA PUERTA is Professor of English at the University of Vigo (Spain). She earned her doctorate in English Philology with a thesis on C. S. Lewis titled "C. S. Lewis: un autor de literatura fantástica. Análisis de sus mundos secundarios" (2000), published under the title: *La literatura fantástica de C. S. Lewis* (2005). She has also published and contributed several chapters and essays on C. S. Lewis, J. R. R. Tolkien, and children's fantasy literature to various monographs, journals, and magazines.

KAREN ROWE is professor of English at Bob Jones University where she has taught undergraduate composition and literature classes for almost twenty years. She has a B.A. in English and a M.Ed. in Teaching English from Bob Jones University and a Ph.D. in English with a specialization in Rhetoric and Writing from Bowling Green State University in Bowling Green, Ohio. Her dissertation identified the inscriptions on the frames of Pre-Raphaelite artist William Holman Hunt's paintings as explanatory rhetoric.